COLONIALISM AND SOCIAL TRANSFORMATION IN INDIA

COLONIALISM AND SOCIAL TRANSFORMATION IN INDIA

MANISH SINGH

KALPAZ

First Published, 2019

Published by

Kalpaz Publications
C-30, Satyawati Nagar,
Delhi – 110052
Ph.: 011-47034999, 9811692060
www.kalpazpublications.com
E-mail: kalpaz@hotmail.com

Printed at: G. Print Process, Delhi

Cataloging in Publication Data—DK
Courtesy: D.K. Agencies (P) Ltd. <docinfo@dkagencies.com>

Singh, Manish *(Writer on history)*, **author.**
Colonialism and social transformation in India / by Manish Singh.
pages cm
Includes bibliographical references.
ISBN 9789353240226

1. India—History—British occupation, 1765-1947. 2. India—Politics and government—1765-1947. 3. India—Social conditions. I. Title.

LCC DS463.S56 2018 | DDC 954.03 23

Contents

Preface and Acknowledgements

At the outset I must make my position clear as a researcher employing interdisciplinary perspective in the present research work. In traditional universities like those of Bihar there have always been watertight compartments among different subjects and hence works done with an interdisciplinary perspective are quite rare or uncommon. Yet I have ventured to combine two diverse disciplines like Sociology and History here. It has been a really very demanding work for me because of differing orientation of the subjects. The difficulty has been also because sociology commonly uses micro level empirical data from primary sources, while the history uses macro level historical data from secondary sources which might have been used by other scholars before in some other contexts. The nature of subject is such that history and empiricism are usually incompatible. Despite such a serious limitation I have tried to combine two diverse disciplines as far as possible with the support and generous help of my guide J. P. Singh, a Professor of Sociology. Furthermore, a work of this kind possibly would not have been possible in the Department of History either, as an area of specialization like Social History is not so developed or rich in this country.

It also needs to be made clear that since I have been a student of history all through, the work is obviously heavier on the side of history rather than on the side of sociology. Herein I owe a deep sense of gratitude to my supervisor for helping me to produce a work of this order with an interdisciplinary perspective. I am also thankful to my supervisor for reading the whole thesis word by word and giving masterly treatment to presentation particularly with respect to style and language. Every possible effort has been made to strike a balance between the two subjects. Nevertheless I feel that some more sociological ideas should have been explored in the available historical facts or evidence to strike a better balance between the two disciplines. I, however, feel satisfied with the work because this is not the end of it rather a beginning of my research work. As knowledge is very vast and a fast expanding domain of human endeavour, I know it for sure that I have to go a long way as a researcher in the field of social science.

Here a word of caution is essential with regard to the use of spelling of certain words. I have retained the original spelling of a lot of words as they were spelled by different scholars in their writing those days. It is not proper to correct or modify the spelling of any proper or even common nouns and Hindi words used by other scholars. In fact, proper nouns do not always have a uniform system of spelling. For instance, words like Banerjee, Chatterjee, Kanpur, Maratha, Hindu, Pundits, Brahmin, Madarsa, Moghul, Mohamedans, labour, etc. have been often spelled differently by different scholars at different places in their books. In fact, the spelling of words under quotations or the inverted commas must not be modified by others for the sake of correctness.

It is also to be noted that a work of this kind based on the latest information would not have been possible in Patna or Bihar where research journals or latest books are rarely available in the university library. Thanks to the website and e-books and e-journals which are readily available for the users of computers. In fact, so much information is available on different websites that it is quite difficult, if not impossible, for a person to read the whole of literature and complete the work within the given timeframe. I am no less thankful to my younger brother, Avnish Singh, for familiarising me with different websites. Lastly, I am grateful to my Mom who shared the typing work with me despite being awfully busy with her own household chores. Special thanks are due to Deepak Kumar for making the manuscript ready for printing in a book form.

I cannot forget to thank Providence without whose help it would not have been possible for me to complete such an arduous work within a period of two and half years.

Manish Singh

Chapter - 1

Introduction

India is known for quite a long history of colonial rule with full of exciting events. It was nothing but the poor system of governance, lack of monolithic socio-cultural system and foresightedness on the part of governing elites and poor development of science and technology during the medieval period which paved the way for foreign rule in the country. The Europeans or the British succeeded to colonize India because India was a divided house in terms of socio-cultural and linguistic diversities and possessed a poor level of development in the use of technology of warfare. Anyway, what was done cannot be undone. The colonial masters indirectly gave us enough lessons to learn from our eventful history. The lessons society learnt, however, were quite high-priced both in terms of life and property. Such has been the course of India's history. A careful perusal of India's long history suggests that destiny has not been always kind to India that was Bharat. We do not know for sure who learnt and benefited more—the coloniser or the colonised or it was an equally gainful experience for both of them. While addressing this question one must keep in mind that India has been surviving and developing as a democratic republic since the middle of the 20th century despite considerable socio-cultural, ethnic and linguistic diversities and all sorts of odds both inside and outside the country, covering a population of over one billion spread over a vast expanse of geographical areas stretching from Jammu and Kashmir in the North and Andaman & Nicobar Islands in the Indian Ocean and Lakshadweep in the Arabian sea in the south. Despite all these it is believed that India is going to be a global power to reckon with much before the turn of this century.

The first European colonists had started visiting the shores of India from the 15th century onwards. In the early 16th century, Portuguese rule was established on the West coast of India at Goa. The Portuguese did not succeed in moving deep into the country. Their domination remained confined to the coastal periphery. The British dominions in India took shape gradually. In the very early years of the 17th century, British merchants of the East India Company set out to trade with the Mughal Empire. As that empire declined, the British took political and military control of the Indian territory, defeating the French and various Indian rulers to become the dominant power in South Asia. Initially the Britain ruled India through the East India Company and after the mutiny of 1857-58 India came to be ruled directly by the British crown. Though the Mughal Empire did survive till 1857, its heyday can be considered to have come to an end in 1707, with the death of Aurangzeb. The Marathas could not rise to the status of being the central authority for the entire country though at one time their armies had marched upto Attock beyond Peshawar near today's Afghanistan-Pakistan border.

The British ascendancy, which began with the battle of Plassey in 1757, did mark the beginning of the end of feudalism in India. The century from 1757 to 1857 was the transitory stage from feudalism to the modern era. Thus the decline of feudalism did not entirely come about due to its internal decay; rather, it was largely mediated through the intervention of European colonialism. But the decline of feudalism was facilitated by the general confusion that prevailed in the country after the eclipse of the Mughal Empire as the executive authority of the country.

As the British presence in India grew, Britons increasingly went to India to run businesses and as administrators, soldiers, and missionaries. By the 19th century and into the 20th a life in India became a regular existence for many English men and women. Their personal motives were various: to make money, to find excitement, to improve their status, to maintain family tradition, and— as a grand ideal of imperial service formed in Victorian times— to serve their own nation and India itself. In many ways, their personal motives were a microcosm of the reasons European nations and their societies sought imperial expansion.

Sometimes generations of the same family went to India. Some were born there, others recruited out of university or public school to join the police or the civil or the education or forest service. Whatever their backgrounds, those who went found themselves on a journey to a world very different from what they knew in the British Isles. Their literal passage on a steamship— from cool England, through Gibraltar and across the increasingly foreign Mediterranean, through the Suez Canal (symbolic divider of West from East), into the sun-scorched Red Sea and steamy Indian Ocean to a land full of new sounds, sights, and smells— was more than a mere trip but a rite of transition which often made a powerful impression.

Numerous studies have been carried out on the effects of colonialism in India. All most all the studies, particularly done by Indian scholars, have tried to harp on the same note that the British colonialism was merely a tool of economic exploitation of India. In fact, the studies on colonialism in India have given rise to two diverse kinds of perspectives in historical writings: nationalist and Marxist. Though both are two divergent schools of thought in history, both have contended vociferously that the British colonial masters were merely interested in economic exploitation of India (Marx and Engels, 1965; Dutt, 1949; Chand, 1961; Majumdar, 1963; Gopal, 1965; Hutchins, 1967; Seal, 1968; Chandra, 1972; Desai, 1976; Dutt, 1976; Chandra; 1989). They have merely depicted the Indian's point of view on British colonialism. The present study intends to do a different kind of exercise. This is an exercise in the study of impact of British rule on Indian society in general in an objective manner. Herein no effort is made to make a value judgement about any impact whether that change was good or bad in the interests of the country.

Historiography— The historiography of the British Empire refers to the studies, sources, critical methods and interpretations used by scholars to study the history of the British Empire. Scholars have long studied the Empire, looking at the causes for its formation, its relations to the French and other empires, and the kinds of people and their ideas who became imperialists or anti-imperialists. The history of the breakdown of the Empire has attracted the attention of scholars of the United States (which broke away in 1776), as well as India (1947) and the African colonies (1960s). In recent years scholars have paid special attention to its impact on the native peoples of Asia and Africa who became part of its domain, with respect to the impact on their economy, social structure, demography, politics and world view. The present work is a very small step in that direction.

Armitage (2000) traces the emergence of a British imperial ideology from the time of Henry VIII to that of Robert Walpole in the 1720s and 1730s. Using a close reading of English, Scottish and Irish authors from Sir Thomas Smith (1513-77) to David Hume (1711-1776), Armitage argues that the imperial ideology was both as a critical agent in the formation of a British state from three kingdoms and an essential bond between the state and the transatlantic colonies. Armitage thus links the concerns of the 'New British History' with that of the Atlantic history. Before 1700 Armitage finds that contested English and Scottish versions of state and empire delayed the emergence of a unitary imperial ideology. Furthermore the notions of republicanism produced in the writers a tension between "empire and liberty" and "imperium and dominium." However political economists Nicholas Barbon and Charles Davenant in the late 17th century emphasized the significance of commerce to the success of the state, arguing that "trade depended on liberty, and that liberty could therefore be the foundation of empire" (Armitage, 2000: 143). To overcome competing versions of 'empires of the seas' within Britain, Parliament undertook the regulation of the Irish economy, the Act of Union (1707) and the formation of a unitary and organic 'British' empire of the sea. Walpole's opponents in the 1730s in the "country party" and in the American colonies developed an alternative vision of empire that would be "Protestant, commercial, maritime and free" (Armitage, 2000: 173). Walpole's did not ensure the promised "liberty" to the colonists' colonies because he was intent on subordinating all colonial economic activity to the mercantilist advantages of the metropolis. Anti-imperial critiques emerged from Francis Hutcheson and David Hume, presaging the republicanism that swept the American colonies in the 1770s and led to the creation of a rival empire.

One of the most controversial aspects of the Empire is its role in first promoting and then ending slavery. In the 18th century British merchant ships were the largest element in the "Middle Passage" which transported millions of slaves to the Western Hemisphere. Most of those who survived the journey wound up in the Caribbean, where the Empire had highly profitable sugar colonies, and the living conditions were bad (The plantation owners lived in Britain). Parliament ended the international transportation of slaves in 1807, and used the Royal navy to enforce that ban. In 1833 it bought out the plantation owners and banned slavery. Historians before the 1940s argued that moralistic reformers such as William Wilberforce were primarily responsible for the abolition of slavery.

Historical revisionism arrived with West Indian historian Eric Williams in *Capitalism and Slavery* (1944), rejected this moral explanation and substituted a Marxist interpretation. He argued that abolition was now more profitable, for a century of sugar cane raising had exhausted the soil of the islands, and the plantations had become unprofitable. It was more profitable to sell the slaves to the government than to keep up operations. The 1807 prohibition of the international trade, Williams argued, prevented French expansion on other islands. Meanwhile British investors turned to Asia, where labour was so plentiful that slavery was unnecessary. Williams went on to argue that slavery played a major role in making Britain prosperous. The high profits from the slave trade, he said, helped finance the Industrial Revolution. Britain enjoyed prosperity because of the capital thieved from the unpaid work of slaves. This explanation is heavily biased in favour of Marxist perspective.

More recently historians have challenged Williams. They have shown that slavery remained profitable in the 1830s because of innovations in agriculture so the profit motive was not central to abolition (Ward, 1998: 415-39). Richardson (1998) finds Williams's claims regarding the Industrial Revolution are highly exaggerated, for profits from the slave trade amounted to less than 1% of domestic investment in Britain. Richardson further challenges claims that the slave trade caused widespread depopulation and economic distress in Africa—indeed that it caused the "underdevelopment" of Africa. Admitting the horrible suffering of slaves, he notes that many Africans benefited directly, because the first stage of the trade was always firmly in the hands of Africans. European slave ships waited at ports to purchase cargoes of people who were captured in the hinterland by African dealers and tribal leaders. Richardson finds that the "terms of trade" moved heavily in favour of the Africans after about 1750. That is, indigenous elites inside West and Central Africa made large and growing profits from slavery, thus increasing their wealth and power (Richardson, 1998: 440-64).

Debate continues about the economic impact of British imperialism on India. The issue was actually raised by conservative British politician Edmund Burke who in the 1780s vehemently attacked the East India Company, claiming that Warren Hastings and other top officials had ruined the Indian economy and society. Indian historian Rajat Kanta Ray (1998) continues this line of attack, saying the new economy brought by the British in the 18th century was a form of "plunder" and a catastrophe for the traditional economy of Mughal India. Ray accuses the British of depleting the food and money stocks and imposing high taxes that helped cause the terrible famine of 1770, which killed a third of the people of Bengal (Ray, 1998: 508-29).

P. J. Marshall (1998) shows that recent scholarship has reinterpreted the view that the prosperity of the formerly benign Mughal rule gave way to poverty and anarchy. Marshall argues the British takeover did not make any sharp break with the past. British control was delegated largely through regional Mughal rulers and was sustained by a generally prosperous economy for the rest of the eighteenth century. Marshall notes that the British went into partnership with Indian bankers and raised revenue through local tax administrators and kept the old Mughal rates of taxation. Instead of the Indian nationalist account of the British as alien aggressors, seizing power by brute force and impoverishing all of India, Marshall presents the interpretation, supported by many scholars in India and the West, in which the British were not in full control but instead were players in what was primarily an Indian play and in which their rise to power depended upon excellent cooperation with Indian elites. Marshall admits that much of his interpretation is still rejected by many historians working in India, who prefer to 'bash the British' (Marshall 1998: 487-507).

Objectives and Methodology

The fact that the British rule brought enormous changes in social, political and economic systems of the country through their system of governance has always remained overshadowed or has been underplayed by the scholars. While the Great Britain felt that they were being very generous to the Indian people in colonizing and modernizing the nation, the Indians do not always agree with this. Undoubtedly under the British rule, many new roads, railways and harbours were built, post and telegraph system was introduced. Numerous schools, colleges, universities and hospitals were opened to provided education and health services to the people. The positive effects of nineteenth and twentieth century colonialism can still be felt today. These effects can be felt on many different levels of life and culture in India. When Britain colonized India, the English language quickly spread and diverse indigenous languages of the natives began to become unimportant. In addition, the traditional culture of India was altered, taking on a more European style. With such changes to its culture, language, and way of life, the newly independent country was forced to rediscover itself in a fast-paced world. Willingly or unwillingly, the British ushered in a new era of rationality in India. The country slowly and steadily moved from tradition to modernity. For long the Indian society was highly imbued with traditional Hindu and Islamic values system. Because of prominently agrarian economy and massive illiteracy, the country was not prepared to experience rapid change in pre-British India. The British system of governance provided not only an impetus to change but also acted as catalytic agent of change.

This research work has to be based on purely secondary sources of data. As this is a sociological analysis of historical facts, it may be called an inter-disciplinary research. The work is, however, heavily tilted in favour of history because of my academic orientation as a student of history. A work of this kind is likely to fall within the rubric of social history. Not much work has been done in history following sociological perspective and similarly not much work has been done in sociology following historical perspective either. Hence, an effort is made to combine Sociology with History. It may be pointed out that no effort is made to counter or falsify the facts and arguments put forward either by Marxist and or the nationalist historians with regard to adverse or dysfunctional impacts of colonialism on India society and culture; rather, the main concern of the research is to focus upon changes which were encountered and experienced by the country during the period of about 150 years of *Pax Britannica* in India. A word of caution may be moved here. As this study has sought to offer a macro level analysis of historical facts, generalizations made can hold in broad terms only.

Defining Concepts

Concepts are the building blocks of any scientific knowledge. They are also the basic tools of encapsulating and communicating knowledge. Colonialism and social change are two main concepts used in this work. In fact, entire work centres round these two concepts. Both of them carry very specific connotation in social science. Hence, they are defined and elaborated here. Along with these two, we have also incorporated some other related concepts like imperialism, neo-colonialism, post neo-colonialism, slave trade, westernization, sanskritization and secularization.

Colonialism— It is the ideology relating to development and maintenance of colonies in one territory by people from another territory. Sovereignty over the colony is claimed by the metropole. Social structure, government and economics within the territory of the colony are changed by the colonists. Colonialism normally refers to a period of history from the 15th to the 20th century when people from Europe built colonies on other continents. Some colonists felt they were helping the indigenous population by bringing them Christianity and civilization. However, the reality was often subjugation, displacement or death.[1] A colony is part of an empire and so colonialism is closely related to imperialism.

Historians often distinguish between two forms of colonialism, chiefly based on the number of people from the colonising country who settle in the colony:

Settler colonialism involved a large number of colonists, typically seeking fertile land for farming.

Exploitation colonialism involved fewer colonists, typically interested in extracting resources to export to the metropole. This category includes trading posts but it also includes much larger colonies where the colonists would provide much of the administration and own much of the land and other capital but rely on indigenous people for labour.

There is a certain amount of overlap between these models of colonialism. In both cases people moved to the colony and goods were exported to the metropole. A plantation colony is normally considered to fit the model of exploitation colonialism. However, in this case there may be other immigrants to the colony- slaves to grow the cash crop for export. In some cases, settler colonialism took place in substantially pre-populated areas and the result was either an ethnically mixed population, or a racially divided population, such as in French Algeria or Southern Rhodesia. A League of Nations mandate was legally very different from a colony. However, there was some similarity with exploitation colonialism in the mandate system.

Historical view of colonialism— Colonialism is not a modern phenomenon (Osterhammel, 1997). A variety of ancient and more recent examples whereby ethnically distinct groups settle in areas other than their original settlement that are either adjacent or across land or sea. From about 750 BC the Greeks began 250 years of expansion, settling colonies in all directions. Phoenician civilization was an enterprising maritime trading culture that spread across the Mediterranean during the period 1550 BC to 300 BC. Other examples range from large empire like the Roman Empire, the Arab Empire, the Mongol Empire, the Ottoman Empire or small movements like ancient Scots moving from Hibernia to Caledonia and Magyars into Pannonia (modern-day Hungary). Turkic peoples spread across most of Central Asia into Europe and the Middle East between the 6th and 11th centuries. Recent research suggests that Madagascar was uninhabited until Malay seafarers from Indonesia arrived during the 5th and 6th centuries A.D. Subsequent migrations from both the Pacific and Africa further consolidated this original mixture, and Malagasy people emerged.

The historical phenomenon of colonization is one that stretches around the globe and across time, including such disparate peoples as the Hittites, the Incas and the British, although the term *colonialism* is normally used with reference to discontiguous European overseas empires rather than contiguous land-based empires, European or otherwise. Land-based empires are conventionally described by the term *imperialism*, such as Age of Imperialism which includes colonialism as a sub-topic, but in the main refers to conquest and domination of nearby lesser geographic powers. Examples of land-based empires include the Mongol Empire, Chinese Empire, the Empire of Alexander the Great, the Umayyad Caliphate, the Persian Empire, the Roman Empire, the Byzantine Empire. The Ottoman Empire was created across Mediterranean, North Africa and into South-Eastern Europe and existed during the time of European colonization of the other parts of the world.

After the Portuguese *Reconquista* period when the Kingdom of Portugal fought against the Muslim domination of Iberia, in the 12th and 13th centuries, the Portuguese started to expand overseas. European colonialism began in 1415, with Portugal's conquest of the Muslim port of Ceuta, Northern Africa. In the following decades Portugal braved the coast of Africa establishing trading posts, ports and fortresses. Colonialism was led by Portuguese and Spanish exploration of the Americas, and the coasts of Africa, the Middle East, India, and East Asia.

On June 7, 1494, Pope Alexander VI divided "newly discovered" lands outside Europe between Spain and Portugal along a north-south meridian 370 leagues west of the Cape Verde islands (off the west coast of Africa). This division was never accepted by the rulers of England or France.

The latter half of the sixteenth century witnessed the expansion of the English colonial state throughout Ireland.[2] Despite some earlier attempts, it was not until the 17th century that Britain, France and the Netherlands successfully established overseas empires outside Europe, in direct competition with Spain and Portugal and with each other. In the 19th century the British Empire grew to become the largest empire yet seen.

Before the expansion of the Bantu languages and their speakers, the southern half of Africa is believed to have been populated by Pygmies and Khoisan speaking people, today occupying the arid regions around the Kalahari and the forest of Central Africa. By about 1000 AD Bantu migration had reached modern day Zimbabwe and South Africa. The Banu Hilal and Banu Ma'qil were a collection of Arab Bedouin tribes from the Arabian peninsula who migrated westwards via Egypt between the 11th and 13th centuries. Their migration strongly contributed to the Arabization and Islamization of the western Maghreb, which was until then dominated by Berber tribes. Ostsiedlung was the medieval eastward migration and settlement of Germans. The 13th century was the time of the great Mongol and Turkic migrations across Eurasia. Between the 11th and 18th centuries, the Vietnamese expanded southward in a process known as nam ti¿n (southward expansion).

More recent examples of internal colonialism are the movement of ethnic Chinese into Tibet and Eastern Turkistan, ethnic Javanese into Western New Guinea and Kalimantan, Brazilians into Amazonia, Israelis into the West Bank and Gaza, ethnic Arabs into Iraqi Kurdistan, and ethnic Russians into Siberia and Central Asia. The local populations or tribes, such as the aboriginal people in Canada, Australia, Argentina, Brazil, Japan, Siberia and the United States, were usually far overwhelmed numerically by the settlers.

The end of the 18th and early 19th century saw the first era of decolonization when most of the European colonies in the Americas gained their independence from their respective metropoles. Spain and Portugal were irreversibly weakened after the loss of their New World colonies, but Britain (after the union of England and Scotland), France and the Netherlands turned their attention to the Old World, particularly South Africa, India and South East Asia, where coastal enclaves had already been established. The German Empire (now Republic), created by most of Germany being united under Prussia (omitting Austria, and other ethnic-German areas) also sought colonies in German East Africa. Territories in other parts of the world were also added to the trans-oceanic, or extra-European, German colonial empire. Italy occupied Eritrea, Somalia and Libya. During the First and the Second Italo-Ethiopian War, Italy invaded Abyssinia, and in 1936 the Italian Empire was created.

The industrialization of the 19th century led to what has been termed the era of New Imperialism, when the pace of colonization rapidly accelerated, the height of which was the Scramble for Africa.

In 1823, the United States, while expanding westward for the Pacific, had published the Monroe Doctrine in which it gave fair warning to western European expansionists to stay out of American affairs. Originally, the document targeted the spread of colonialism in Latin America and the Caribbean, deeming it oppressive and intolerable. By the end of the 19th century, interpretation of the Monroe Doctrine by individuals such as Theodore Roosevelt, viewed it as an American responsibility to ensure Central American, Caribbean, and South American economic stability that would allow those nations to repay their debts to their colonizers. In fact, under Roosevelt's presidency in 1904, the Roosevelt Corollary to the Monroe Doctrine was added to the original document in order to justify colonial expansionist policies and actions by the U.S. under Roosevelt (Marks, 1979)

In this case imperialism would now, for the first time in American history, begin to manifest itself across the bordering waters and incorporating the Philippines, Guam, Cuba, Puerto Rico, and Hawaii as American territories.

America was successful in "liberating" the territories of Cuba, Puerto Rico, Guam, and the Philippines. U.S. government replaced the existing government in Hawaii in 1893; it was annexed into the American union as an offshore territory in 1898. Between 1898 and 1902, Cuba was a territory of the United States along with Puerto Rico, Guam, and the Philippines, which were all colonies gained by the United States from Spain. In 1946, the Philippines was granted independence from the United States and Puerto Rico still to this day remains a territory of the United States along with American, Samoa, Guam, and The U.S. Virgin Islands. In Cuba, the Platt Amendment was replaced in 1934 by the Treaty of Relations which granted Cuba less intervention by U.S. government on matters of economy and international relations. 1934 would also be the year that, under the presidency of Franklin D. Roosevelt, that the Good Neighbour Policy was adopted in order to limit American intervention in South and Central America.

During the 20th century, the overseas colonies of the losers of World War I were distributed amongst the victors as mandates, but it was not until the end of World War II that the second phase of decolonization began in earnest.

Neo-colonialism— The term neo-colonialism has been used to refer to a variety of things since the decolonization efforts after World War II. Generally it does not refer to a type of colonialism but rather colonialism by other means. Specifically, the accusation that the relationship between stronger and weaker countries is similar to exploitation colonialism, without the stronger country having to build or maintain colonies. Such accusations typically focus on economic relationships and interference in the politics of weaker countries by stronger countries.

Post-colonialism— Post-colonialism refers to a set of theories in philosophy and literature that grapple with the legacy of colonial rule. In this sense, postcolonial literature may be considered a branch of Post-modern literature concerned with the political and cultural independence of peoples formerly subjugated in colonial empires. Many practitioners take Edward Said's book *Orientalism* (1978) to be the theory's founding work. Edward Said analyzed the works of Balzac, Baudelaire and Lautréamont, exploring how they were both influenced by and helped to shape a societal fantasy of

European racial superiority. Post-colonial fictional writers interact with the traditional colonial discourse, but modify or subvert it; for instance by retelling a familiar story from the perspective of an oppressed minor character in the story.

In **A Critique of Postcolonial Reason (1999)**, Spivak explored how major works of European metaphysics (e.g., Kant, Hegel) not only tended to exclude the subaltern from their discussions, but actively prevented non-Europeans from occupying positions as fully human subjects. Hegel's *Phenomenology of Spirit* (1807) is famous for its explicit ethnocentrism, in considering the Western civilization as the most accomplished of all, while Kant also incorporated some elements of racism in his work.

Impact of colonialism and colonization— Debate about the perceived negative and positive aspects (spread of virulent diseases, unequal social relations, exploitation, enslavement, infrastructures, medical advances, new institutions, technological advancements etc.) of colonialism has occurred for centuries, amongst both colonizer and colonized, and continues to the present day. The questions of miscegenation; the alleged ties between colonial enterprises, genocides— see the Herero Genocide and the Armenian Genocide— and the Holocaust; and the questions of the nature of imperialism, dependency theory and neo-colonialism (in particular the Third World debt) continue to retain their actuality.

Slave trade— Slavery has existed to varying extents, forms and periods in almost all cultures and continents. Between the 7th and 20th centuries, Arab slave trade (also known as slavery in the East) took approximately 18 million slaves from Africa via trans-Saharan and Indian Ocean routes. Between the 15th and the 19th centuries, the Atlantic slave trade took up to 12 million slaves to the New World.

From 1654 until 1865, slavery for life was legal within the boundaries of the present United States. According to the 1860 U.S. census, nearly four million slaves were held in a total population of just over 12 million in the 15 states in which slavery was legal. Of all 1,515,605 families in the 15 slave states, 393,967 held slaves (roughly one in four), amounting to 8% of all American families.

In 1807, the United Kingdom became one of the first nations to end its own participation in the slave trade. Between 1808 and 1860, the British West Africa Squadron seized approximately 1,600 slave ships and freed 150,000 Africans who were aboard. Action was also taken against African leaders who refused to agree to British treaties to outlaw the trade, for example against "the usurping King of Lagos", deposed in 1851. Anti-slavery treaties were signed with over 50 African rulers. In 1827, Britain declared the slave trade piracy, punishable by death.

Social change— Now let us come to the meaning of word 'social change'. This is one of the most popular concepts in sociology. Change is the law of nature. What exists today shall not remain the same tomorrow. A society is always subject to incessant change. Caste, family, kinship system and religion have not remained the same throughout the history of India because these institutions have been subjects to considerable changes in course of time. Individuals may strive for stability, societies may create the illusion of permanence, the quest for certainty may continue unabated, yet the fact remains that society is an ever changing phenomenon, growing, decaying, renewing and accommodating itself to changing conditions and experiencing vast modifications in the course of time. Our understanding of it will not be complete unless we take into consideration this changeable nature of society, study how differences emerge and discover the direction of change.

Social change refers to modifications of social structures and processes over time. In India, the traditional caste system based on the theory of pollution and purity has undergone considerable transformations. The rule of law has largely replaced the caste panchayats which enforced caste-based customs and regulations. The traditional joint family system supported by ancestral property has undergone radical changes. The process of democracy has significantly altered the power structures and led to the empowerment of new power elites drawn from the dalits and other backward classes. The emergence of the 'information society' and globalization has created a vast new middle class with an appetite for latest consumer goods. Industrialization, demographic transition, urbanization, modernization, westernization and numerous technological changes have significantly altered the nature and functions of most Indian social institutions.

Dictionary of Sociology and Related Sciences (Fairchild 1966:277) has defined social change as 'variations or modifications in any aspect of social process, pattern or form....Social change may be progressive or regressive, permanent or temporary, planned or unplanned, unidirectional or multidirectional, beneficial or harmful.' Social change may be swift and radical as in the case of the French or Russian revolutions, or it may be slow and gradual as in the case of secularization and modernization. All societies evolve over a period of time, and social change is part of the process of growth. Herein the term social change is employed to refer to change not only in social structure, but also in cultural system or order which has occurred in Indian society over the years. Since the context of change is historical in nature, we have tried to use this term in a broad historical perspective rather than in a limited sociological or anthropological sense.

M. N. Srinivas (1977) is the leading sociologist of India who has tried to explain the dynamics of change in a historical perspective through the use of the concepts like sanskritization, westernization, and secularization. In his view these are the three major comprehensive processes that have altered and articulated the social and cultural patterns of Indian society. Sanskritization refers to the process by which the low caste are able to rise to a higher position in the social hierarchy by adopting the symbols of higher status, thus taking over, as far as possible, the customs, rites, beliefs, and ways of life of the higher castes. However, mobility associated with sanskritization results only in positional changes in the system and does not lead to any structural change. Sanskritization may be a historical process of cultural change but its relevance to contemporary society is limited. In the age of mass political participation and caste-based power politics, numerical superiority is far more important than ritual superiority.

Westernization refers to the complex, multi-layered process of diffusion of western ideas, legal and philosophical systems, Western ways of life and culture in Indian society with the onset of colonization of India. The twice-born castes were the first to sense the trend of change and took the advantage of the new opportunities. Western education, legal system and the development of modern transport and communication accelerated the process. One only needs to look at the Indian railway or other system of mass transportation, cable television channels to have sense of impact of westernization on our way of life, music, fashion, dance, art, and even attitudes. Western ideas have eroded the concept of pollution and purity and lifted the ritual ban on many vocations. The rule of law has replaced caste-based rules in traditional society. Modern education has fostered the concepts of equality, social justice, and human dignity. Although caste, ethnicity, and class distinctions survive, there is a greater awareness of the worth and dignity of the individual now than in ancient or medieval period.

Secularization is yet another concept which is useful in the analysis of social change in India. In the past, Srinivas has indicated, the strength of a belief lay in its sacerdotal importance displayed by ritualistic ceremonies.

The only standard of reference was tradition and the only authority was the Sanskritic literature in terms of which a belief or practice would be evaluated and validated. But the introduction of western education, the British legal system, and various ideological movements either changed or abolished many customs once thought to be part of religion. Traditional ideals of ritual cleanliness and pollution and purity have given way to the rules of reasoned or rational hygiene. Rituals are not only omitted or abolished but are also telescoped with others. All this 'meant that religious customs had to satisfy the test of reason and humanitarianism became broader, deeper, and more powerful, and the years since the achievement of independence have seen a remarkable increase- a genuine leap forward- in the extension of both'. The growth of towns and cities, increased spatial mobility, the struggle for political freedom, declaration of India as a secular state, constitutional recognition of the equality of all citizens before law, and the introduction of universal adult suffrage have given added impetus to the process of secularization. Above all, secularization is a process of rationalization based on science which provides the only validation for most human actions in modern society.

The British Raj

British Raj (*râj*, lit. "reign" in Hindustani[3]) primarily refers to the British rule in the Indian subcontinent between 1858 and 1947;[4] it can also refer to the *period* of dominion, and even the *region under the rule*.[5] The region, commonly called **India** in contemporary usage, included areas directly administered by the United Kingdom,[6] as well as the princely states ruled by individual rulers under the paramountcy of the British Crown. After 1876, the resulting political union was officially called the **Indian Empire** and issued passports under that name. The system of governance was instituted in 1858, when the rule of the British East India Company was transferred to the Crown in the person of Queen Victoria (and who, in 1876, was proclaimed Empress of India), and lasted until 1947, when the British Indian Empire was partitioned into two sovereign dominion states, the *Union of India* (later the Republic of India) and the *Dominion of Pakistan* (later the Islamic Republic of Pakistan and the People's Republic of Bangladesh).

India under the British *Raj*
Crown Rule, 1858–1947

The British Indian Empire, 1909

Capital	Calcutta (1858-1912)
	New Delhi (1912-1947)
Language(s)	Hindustani, English and many others

Emperor/ Empress of India (1876-1947)	
- 1858-1901	Victoria[1]
- 1901-1910	Edward VII
- 1910-1936	George V
- 1936	Edward VIII
- 1936-1947	George VI
Viceroy[2]	
- 1858-1862	The Viscount Canning
- 1862-1863	The 8th Earl of Elgin
- 1864-1869	Sri John Lawrence
- 1869-1872	The Earl of Mayo
- 1872-1876	The Lord Northbrook
History	
- Established	August 2, 1858
- Disestablished	August 15, 1947

Notes:

1. Reigned as Empress of India from May 1, 1876, before that as Queen of the United Kingdom.
2. Governor-General and Viceroy of India.

Geographical extent of the Raj— The British Raj extended over all regions of present-day India, Pakistan, and Bangladesh. In addition, at various times, it included Aden Colony (from 1858 to 1937), Lower Burma (from 1858 to 1937), Upper Burma (from 1886 to 1937), British Somaliland (briefly from 1884 to 1898), and Singapore (briefly from 1858 to 1867). Burma was directly administered by the British Crown from 1937 to 1948.

Among other countries in the region, Ceylon (now Sri Lanka), was ceded to the United Kingdom in 1802 under the Treaty of Amiens. Ceylon was a British Crown Colony, but not part of British India. The kingdoms of Nepal and Bhutan, having fought wars with the British, subsequently signed treaties with them, were recognized by the British as independent states.[7] The Kingdom of Sikkim was established as a princely state after the *Anglo-Sikkimese Treaty* of 1861. However, the issue of sovereignty was left undefined.[8] The Maldive Islands were a British protectorate from 1887 to 1965, but not part of British India.

In the beginning of 17th century, Europeans, particularly British, started trading in the subcontinent. Merchants of the East India Company never imagined that British presence in the subcontinent could mean anything more than peaceful trading. French arrived in the middle of the 17th century, signalling the beginning of militarization. Within 100 years the French were a spent force and the British possessed the most efficient military power in the subcontinent.

As Mughal power declined, British influence increased. Indian rulers proved very indisciplined when it came to facing British army and therefore, there was no problem in defeating Indian cavalry. In 1775, the Company was found to be corrupt and a regulatory act gave the government control over Company officials. In 1784 the Indian Act left the Company solely in-charge of commerce. Motivated by imperialism, the British began to annex states, offering troop protection against aggressive neighbours in return of loyalty and sizeable subsidies. By 1818, Bengal, Bihar, Orissa, and a tract of land north of the Ganges running up to Delhi were firmly in British hands.

Sikh vs. British: British could not take over Punjab because Sikhs held a dominant force under the ruler Ranjit Singh. Punjab had been the home of the Sikhs since the late 15th century. In 1799, Lahore was taken over by Sikh emperor Ranjit Singh and under his rule, Punjab was virtually harmless from British invasion. After Ranjit Singh's death in 1839, British finally moved in and Sikh empire began to collapse.

Kashmir Conspiracy: The consequences of the first Sikh war (1846) had major repercussions for another state, Kashmir. Before being taken by Ranjit Singh, it had been ruled alternatively by Mughals and Afghans. Kashmir was then 90% Muslim, but after the siege of Multan in 1819 Ranjit Singh wanted to reward one of his leaders, Gulab Singh, a Hindu. He was duly granted the estate of Jammu.

In 1841 Gulab Singh allowed British troops to march through his territory on their way to do battle in Afghanistan. During the Sikh wars, he had refused to help the Sikhs, and was once again rewarded, this time by the British. The prize was worth his treachery: in 1846, he received Kashmir by the treaty of Amritsar. The granting of the control of Kashmir to a Hindu began a struggle which has not finished to this day.

Sindh and the Indus: British first stepped on Sindhi soil in 1809 when a diplomatic mission visited the Talpur Mirs. The British saw the importance of the Indus River, believing it could be an important commercial highway. In 1839, they seized Karachi, Sukkur and Bukkur. By 1843, Sir Charles Napier had secured the province of Sindh for the British.

North West Frontier Province: At the far northwest of the Punjab, this was the tribal highland area belonging to the Pathans. Since the Punjab annexation, there had been a bitter and bloody struggle between the Pathans and the British. Beyond settled areas, the British initially tolerated a degree of tribal independence, but used hostage taking, blockades, subsidies and punitive expeditions to ensure the area's security. With North West Frontier under control, British went on to capture northern Pakistan such as Gilgit, Hunza and Chitral. From the fear of Russian intrusion, the British fenced a border between Afghanistan and NWFP, the famous Durand Line, in 1893.

Baluchistan: To the west, Baluchistan with its borders to Persia and Afghanistan was of great strategic importance. The routes through Bolan Pass to Quetta and beyond were vital. Again the British faced the tribal problem, solved by the same kinds of measures used to subdue the Pathans. By the 1890s Baluchistan was largely pacified and stabilised.

The British Raj: The Indian Mutiny erupted in isolated areas in 1857. There were bloody uprisings in Meerut, Delhi, Kanpur and Lucknow. British reprisals were exceptionally brutal. The soldiers petitioned the last Mughal Bahadur Shah Zafar, who was officially up to this time the sovereign ruler of the Mughal Empire, to be their figurehead. The British exiled him to Burma where he died in 1862.

Control now passed from the East India Company to the Crown and the Company was dissolved. The Crown's representative in India was now the Viceroy, who had almost absolute authority.

India prospered during the British rule. Agricultural output was increased manifold. The railway network was setup, which provided a major contribution to the boom. Trade was expanded and industrial development was on the rise.

On the political front, after the mutiny, most factions of Indian society expressed absolute loyalty to the Raj. And despite the fact that the British tried to blame the Muslims for the mutiny, support from the Muslim westernized elite did not diminish. Some Muslims saw that they had difficult times ahead, wondering how they should assimilate to developments under the British while still holding on to their traditions.

Sir Syed Ahmad Khan: Sir Syed Ahmad Khan (1818-1898) emerged as the main advocate of reforming Muslim society towards progress, representing a feeling that a rejection of the British would only result in the Muslims of India disappearing into oblivion. He wanted advantages for Muslims and was keen for the reform of Muslim education. He stressed that science was not anti-Islamic. In 1875, the British gave him a grant to found the Mohammadan Anglo-Oriental College which later became Aligarh University. From here, a stream of educated Muslims went into government services.

Indian National Congress: In 1885, the Indian National Congress was formed. The party began to fight for devolution of power into Indian hands. Although some leading Muslims were members, it was viewed with suspicion by most, including Sir Syed, as being a Hindu body which would only ever represent Hindu interests.

All India Muslim League: In 1906, All India Muslim League was formed to promote feelings of loyalty to the British and advance Muslim political interests. They petitioned the Viceroy that in any political move, Muslim interests be taken into account. The 1909 India Councils Act rewarded Muslim loyalty. The act gave Muslims separate electorates, where they could elect their own representatives to the Legislative Council. Some people claim that this move foreshadowed the birth of Pakistan.

Turnaround: Muslims began to feel isolated and their fears were boosted by European attacks on Muslim countries such as the fight against Turkey in the First World War. They saw Britain leading a Christian crusade against

Islam. More and more Muslims decided to transfer to the Congress party. In 1916, the Muslim League and the Congress signed the Lucknow Pact: Congress accepted separate Muslim electorates in return for League support in its cause to drive out the British.

Mohammad Ali Jinnah: Mohammad Ali Jinnah (1875-1948) was initially a Congress member and endeavoured to bring about the political union of Muslims and Hindus. He left Congress in 1920, but the turning point came when Congress leaders ignored Muslim demands for one third of the seats in any future parliaments. Jinnah never trusted Congress after several exclusions of Muslim interest in Congress decisions. He worked furiously to amass Muslim support for the League to show the world that the League and the League only was the true representation of India's Muslims.

Pakistan Resolution: In March 1940, Jinnah submitted the Lahore Resolution, also known as Pakistan Resolution. In it was the essence of Pakistan: "The Muslims and the Hindus belong to two different religious philosophies: they neither intermarry nor interdine.... Muslims are a nation and according to any definition of a nation they must have their homelands, their territory, their state."

The idea of separate Muslim state was gaining favour, despite opposition from the Congress. It led to terrible violence as Muslims and Hindus turned on each other in an atmosphere of unease about the future.

The Indian independence movement—As independence approached, the violence between Hindus and Muslims in the provinces of Punjab and Bengal continued unabated. With the British army unprepared for the potential for increased violence, the new viceroy, Louis Mountbatten, advanced the date for the transfer of power, allowing less than six months for a mutually agreed plan for independence. In June 1947, the nationalist leaders, including Nehru and Abul Kalam Azad on behalf of the Congress, Jinnah representing the Muslim League, B. R. Ambedkar representing the Untouchable community, and Master Tara Singh representing the Sikhs, agreed to a partition of the country along religious lines. The predominantly Hindu and Sikh areas were assigned to the new India and predominantly Muslim areas to the new nation of Pakistan; the plan included a partition of the Muslim-majority provinces of Punjab and Bengal.

The first step toward Indian independence and western-style democracy was taken with the appointment of Indian councillors to advise the British viceroy, and with the establishment of provincial Councils with Indian members the councillors' participation was subsequently widened in legislative councils. From 1920 leaders such as Mohandas Karamchand Gandhi began mass movements to campaign against the British Raj. Subash Chandra Bose was another freedom fighter who formed army forces against the British rule. Bhagat Singh was also an Indian freedom fighter, considered to be one of the most influential revolutionaries of the Indian independence movement. He is often referred to as Shaheed Bhagat Singh (the word shaheed means "martyr"). Veerapandiya Kattabomman was also another freedom fighter who started his freedom movement against British rule by refusing to pay tax to British Government. Revolutionary activities against the British rule also took place throughout the Indian sub-continent, and these movements succeeded in bringing Independence to the Indian sub-continent in 1947. One year later, Gandhi was assassinated. However, he did live long enough to free his homeland.

Independence and partition— Along with the desire for independence, tensions between Hindus and Muslims had also been developing over the years. The Muslims had always been a minority, and the prospect of an exclusively Hindu government made them wary of independence; they were as inclined to mistrust Hindu rule as they were to resist the Raj. In 1915, Mohandas Karamchand Gandhi came onto the scene, calling for unity between the two groups in an astonishing display of leadership that would eventually lead the country to independence. The profound impact Gandhi had on India and his ability to gain independence through a totally non-violent mass movement made him one of the most remarkable leaders the world has ever known. He led by example, wearing homespun clothes to weaken the British textile industry and orchestrating a march to the sea, where demonstrators proceeded to make their own salt in protest against the British monopoly. Indians gave him the name Mahatma, or Great Soul, first suggested by the Bengali poet Rabindranath Tagore. The British promised that they would leave India by 1947.

British Indian territories gained independence, after being partitioned into the Union of India and Dominion of Pakistan. Following the division of pre-partition Punjab and Bengal provinces, riots broke out between Sikhs, Hindus and Muslims in several parts of India, including Punjab, Bengal and Delhi, leaving some 500,000 dead. Also, this period saw one of the largest mass migrations ever recorded in modern history, with a total of 12 million Hindus, Sikhs and Muslims moving between the newly created nations of India and Pakistan.

Many millions of Muslim, Sikh, and Hindu refugees trekked across the newly drawn borders. In Punjab, where the new border lines divided the Sikh regions in half, massive bloodshed followed; in Bengal and Bihar, where Gandhi's presence assuaged communal tempers, the violence was more limited. In all, anywhere between 250,000 and 500,000 people on both sides of the new borders died in the violence.[9] On August 14, 1947, the new Dominion of Pakistan came into being, with Muhammad Ali Jinnah sworn in as its first Governor General in Karachi. The following day, August 15, 1947, India, now a smaller *Union of India*, became an independent country with official ceremonies taking place in New Delhi, and with Jawaharlal Nehru assuming the office of the Prime Minister, and the viceroy, Louis Mountbatten, staying on as its first Governor General.

References

Allan, J. T., Wolseley Haig, and H. H. Dodwell (1934), *The Cambridge Shorter History of India*. Cambridge: Cambridge University Press.

Andrews, Kenneth R. (1984) *Trade, Plunder and Settlement: Maritime Enterprise and the Genesis of the British Empire, 1480–1630.*

Ankerl, Guy (2000), *Coexisting Contemporary Civilizations: Arabo-Muslim, Bharati, Chinese, and Western*.

Armitage, David, (1999) 'Greater Britain: A Useful Category of Historical Analysis?' *American Historical Review,* 104, 427–45. in JSTOR

Armitage, David (2000) *The Ideological Origins of the British Empire*.

Beer, George Louis(1913*) The Old Colonial System, 1660-1754* full text online

Brendon, Piers (2007) "A Moral Audit of the British Empire." *History Today*, (Oct 2007), Vol. 57 Issue 10, pp 44–47, online at EBSCO

Brendon, Piers (2008) *The Decline and Fall of the British Empire, 1781-1997* (2008)

Chand, Tara (1961), *History of the Freedom Movement in India*, Vol. I, New Delhi: Publications Division.

Chandra, Bipan et al. (1972), *Freedom Struggle*, New Delhi: National Book Trust.

Chandra, Bipan *et al*. (1989), *India's Struggle for Independence*, New Delhi: Penguin Books.

Desai, A. R. (1976), Social Background of Indian Nationalism, Bombay: Popular Prakashan.

Dutt, R. C. (1976), Economic History of India (Under Early British Rule, 1757-1857), Vol. I, Delhi: Publications Division.

Dutt, R. Palme (1949), India Today, Bombay, People's Publishing House Ltd.

Gopal, S. (1965), British Policy in India, 1858-1905, London: Cambridge University Press.

Hutchins, Francis G. (1967), *The Illusion of Permanence: British Imperialism in India*, New Jersey: Princeton University Press.

Mahajan, Sucheta (2000), *Independence and partition: the erosion of colonial power in India*, New Delhi [u.a.]: Sage.

Majumdar, R. C. (1951), *The History and Culture of the Indian People, New York: The Macmillan Co.*

Majumdar, R.C. (1963), *History of the Freedom Movement in India,* Vol. II, Calcutta: Firma K.L. Mukhopadhyay.

Majumdar, R.C., H.C. Raychaudhuri, and Kalikinkar Dutta (1960), *An Advanced History of India.* London: Macmillan.

Marshall, P.J. (1998) "The British in Asia: Trade to Dominion, 1700-1765," in *The Oxford History of the British Empire:* Vol. 2, The Eighteenth Century" ed. by P. J. Marshall, pp 487-507.

Marx, Karl and F. Engels (eds.) (1965), *On Colonialism*, Moscow: Progress Publishers.

Olson, James S. and Robert S. Shadle (1996) Historical Dictionary of the British Empire online edition

Osterhammel, Jürgen (1997) *Colonialism: A Theoretical Overview*, Princeton, N J: M. Wiener.

Porter, A. N. (1994) *Atlas of British Overseas Expansion*

Prakash, Gyan (1990) "Writing Post-Orientalist Histories of the Third World: Perspectives from Indian Historiography," *Comparative Studies in Society and History* 32, 2: 383-408 in JSTOR

Ray, Rajat Kanta *(1998)* "Indian Society and the Establishment of British Supremacy, 1765-1818," in *The Oxford History of the British Empire: vol. 2, The Eighteenth Century" ed. by P. J. Marshall, pp 508-29.*

Richardson, David (1998) "The British Empire and the Atlantic Slave Trade, 1660-1807," in P.J. Marshall, ed. *The Oxford History of the British Empire*: Volume II: The

Rose, J. Holland, A. P. Newton and E. A. Benians (gen. eds.), *The Cambridge History of the British Empire*, 9 vols. (1929–61); Vol. 1: "The Old Empire from the Beginnings to 1783" 934pp online edition Volume I

Rothermund, Dietmar (1993), *An Economic History of India: From Pre-Colonial Times to 1991.*

Said, Edward (1978), *Orientalism.*

Seal, Anil (1968), *The Emergence of Indian Nationalism* (Competition and Collaboration in the Later Nineteenth Century), London: Cambridge University Press.

Smith, Vincent (1981), *The Oxford History of India,* London: Oxford University Press.

Spear, Percival (1990), *The History of India,* Vol. 2, London: Oxford University Press.

Srinivas, M. N. (1977), *Social Change in Modern India*, New Delhi: Orient Longman.

Tyrrell, Ian (1999) "Making Nations/Making States: American Historians in the Context of Empire," *Journal of American History,* Vol. 86, No. 3, (Dec.), pp. 1015-1044 in JSTOR.

Ward, J.R. (1998) "The British West Indies in the Age of Abolition," in P.J. Marshall, ed. *The Oxford History of the British Empire*: Volume II: The Eighteenth Century, pp 415-39.

Whaites, Alan (2007), "States in Development," DFID, London.

Notes

1. Colonialism, Stanford Encyclopedia of Philosophy.
2. Anderson, Benedict, Under Three Flags: Anarchism and the Anti- Colonial Imagination, Verso, New York, 2005.
3. Oxford English Dictionary, 2nd edition, 1989: from Skr. *râj*: to reign, rule; cognate with L. *rçx*, *rçg-is*, OIr. *rî*, *rîg* king (see RICH).
4. Oxford English Dictionary, 2nd edition, 1989. "b. spec. the British dominion or rule in the Indian sub-continent (before 1947). In full, *British Raj*.
5. Oxford English Dictionary, 2nd edition, 1989. Examples: 1955 *Times* 25 Aug. 9/7. It was effective against the British Raj in India, and the conclusion drawn here is that the British knew that they were wrong. 1969 R. MILLAR *Kut* xv. 288 Sir Stanley Maude had taken command in Mesopotamia, displacing the raj of antique Indian Army commanders. 1975 H. R. ISAACS in H. M. Patel et al. *Say not the Struggle Nought Availeth* 251. The post-independence régime in all its incarnations since the passing of the British Raj. For the latter usage, see: Google Scholar references: ("British Raj" in the primary sense of "British India," *i.e.* "regions of India under British rule").
6. First the United Kingdom of Great Britain and Ireland then, after 1927, the nited Kingdom of Great Britain and Northern Ireland.
7. "Nepal." Encyclopædia Britannica, 2008 and "Bhutan." Encyclopædia Britannica, 2008.
8. "Sikkim." Encyclopædia Britannica, 2007. Encyclopædia Britannica Online. 5 Aug 2007 <http://www.britannica.com/eb/article-46212>.
9. Khosla, G. D. (2001), "Stern Reckoning", in Page, David; Anita Inder Singh & Penderal Moon *et al., The Partition Omnibus: Prelude to Partition/the Origins of the Partition of India 1936-1947/Divide and Quit/Stern Reckoning,* Delhi and Oxford: Oxford University Press, p. 299.

Chapter- 2

Society and Polity of Pre-British India

In order to highlight the impact of colonialism on Indian economy, polity, culture and society, it is important that some light should be shed on a long chequered history of India in general although briefly. This is necessitated in view of the fact that the knowledge of ancient and medieval period would help us understand as to what happened to India during the period following the European settlements and subsequent occupation of the country. One must know the nature of the state of affairs which prevailed in India before the establishment of Pax Britannica. Changes encountered and experienced during the British period can be easily and clearly understood, if viewed against the backdrop of past scenario. Let us begin with the ancient past in a chronological order.

Stone age— Isolated remains of Homo erectus in Hathnora in the Narmada Valley in Central India indicate that India might have been inhabited since at least the Middle Pleistocene era, somewhere between 200,000 to 500,000 years ago.[1] Most traces of the out of Africa migration along the shores of the Indian Ocean seem to have been lost. Due to flooding in the post-Ice Age period, recent finds in Tamil Nadu (at c. 75,000 years ago, before and after the explosion of the Toba volcano) indicate the presence of the first anatomically modern humans in the area.

The Mesolithic period in the Indian subcontinent covered a time span of around 25,000 years, starting around 30,000 years ago. More extensive settlement of the subcontinent occurred after the end of the last Ice Age, or approximately 12,000 years ago. The first confirmed permanent settlements appeared 9,000 years ago in the Rock Shelters of Bhimbetka in modern Madhya Pradesh, India.

Early Neolithic culture in South Asia is represented by the Mehrgarh findings (7000 BCE onwards) in present day Baluchistan, Pakistan. Traces of a Neolithic culture have been found submerged in the Gulf of Khambat in India, radiocarbon dated to 7500 BCE.[2] The Edakkal Caves has one of the earliest examples of Stone Age writing. Late Neolithic cultures sprang up in the Indus Valley region between 6000 and 2000 BCE and in southern India between 2800 and 1200 BCE.

The north-western part of the Subcontinent has been inhabited continuously for at least two million years.[3] The ancient history of the region includes some of South Asia's oldest settlements and some of its major civilizations.[4] The earliest archaeological site in the Subcontinent is the Palaeolithic hominid site in the Soan River valley. Village life began with the Neolithic site of Mehrgarh, while the first urban civilization of the region began with the Indus Valley Civilization.[5]

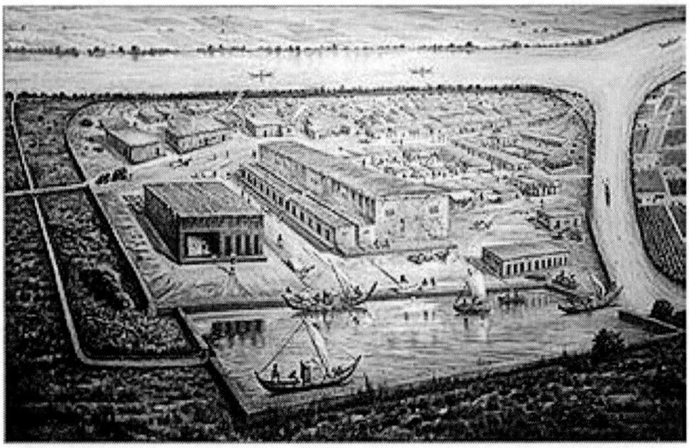

Ancient Lothal as envisaged by the Archaeological Survey of India.

Bronze Age— The known history of India begins with the Indus Valley Civilization, which spread and flourished in the north-western part of the Indian subcontinent, from c. 3300 to 1300 BCE. This marked the beginning of Bronze Age on the Indian subcontinent. It was centred on the Indus River and its tributaries which extended into the Ghaggar-Hakra River valley, the Ganges-Yamuna Doab, Gujarat, and northern Afghanistan.[6]

The civilization is primarily located in modern day India (Gujarat, Haryana, Punjab and Rajasthan states) and today's Pakistan (Sindh, Punjab, and Baluchistan provinces). Historically part of Ancient India, it is one of the world's earliest urban civilizations along with Mesopotamia and Ancient Egypt. Inhabitants of the ancient Indus river valley, the Harappans, developed new techniques in metallurgy and produced copper, bronze, lead and tin."

The Mature Harappan period flourished from about 2600 BCE to 1900 BCE and it marked the beginning of the urban civilization on the subcontinent. The ancient civilization included urban centres such as Dholavira, Kalibangan, Rupar, Rakhigarhi, Lothal in modern day India and Harappa, Ganeriwala, Mohenjo-daro in modern day Pakistan. The civilization is noted for its cities built of brick, road-side drainage system and multi-storied houses. This Bronze Age civilization collapsed at the beginning of the second millennium BCE and was followed by the Iron Age Vedic period, which extended over much of the Indo-Gangetic plains and which witnessed the rise of major kingdoms known as the Mahajanapadas. In one of these kingdoms Magadha, Mahavira and Gautama Buddha were born in the 6th century BCE, who propagated their Shramanic philosophies among the masses.

Vedic period— The Vedic period is characterized by Indo-Aryan culture associated with the texts of Vedas, sacred to Hindus, which were orally composed in Vedic Sanskrit. The Vedas are some of the oldest extant texts, next to those of Egypt and Mesopotamia. The Vedic period lasted from about 1500 BCE to 500 BCE, laid the foundations of Hinduism and other cultural aspects of early Indian society. The Aryas established Vedic civilization all over North India, and increasingly so in the Gangetic Plain. This period succeeded the prehistoric Late Harappan during which immigrations of Indo-Aryan speaking tribes overlaid the existing civilizations of local people whom they called Dasyus.

Early Vedic society consisted of largely pastoral groups, with late Harappan urbanization having been abandoned. After the Rigveda, Aryan society became increasingly agricultural, and was socially organized around the four Varnas. In addition to the principal texts of Hinduism the Vedas, the core themes of the Sanskrit epics Ramayana and Mahabharata are said to have their ultimate origins during this period. Early Indo-Aryan presence probably corresponds, in part, to the presence of Ochre Coloured Pottery in archaeological findings.[7]

The kingdom of the Kurus corresponds to the Black and Red Ware and Painted Grey Ware culture and the beginning of the Iron Age in Northwestern India, around 1000 BCE with the composition of the Atharvaveda, the first

Vaishali was the capital of "Licchavi," world's second republic only after Arwad.

Indian text to mention iron, as [yma ayas, literally "black metal." The Painted Grey Ware culture spanning much of Northern India was prevalent from about 1100 to 600 BCE. The Vedic Period also established republics (such as Vaishali) which existed as early as the sixth century BC and persisted in some areas until the fourth century AD. The later part of this period corresponds with an increasing movement away from the prevalent tribal system towards establishment of kingdoms, called *Maha Janapadas*.

Excavation of the site of Nalanda University near Rajgir in Nalanda District

Mahajanapadas and Magadha Empire: History of Hinduism, Buddhism and Jainism

The Mahajanapadas were the sixteen most powerful kingdoms and republics of the era, located mainly across the fertile Indo-Gangetic plains, however there were a number of smaller kingdoms stretching the length and breadth of Ancient India (Majumdar, 1951).

Nalanda University is considered "one of the first great universities in recorded history." It was the centre of Buddhist learning and research in the world from 450–1193 CE.

In the later Vedic Age, a number of small kingdoms or city states had covered the subcontinent, many mentioned during Vedic, early Buddhist and Jaina literature as far back as 1000 BCE. By 500 BCE, sixteen monarchies and 'republics' known as the *Mahajanapadas*— Kasi, Kosala, Anga, Magadha, Vajji (or Vriji), Malla, Chedi, Vatsa (or Vamsa), Kuru, Panchala, Machcha (or Matsya), Surasena, Assaka, Avanti, Gandhara, Kamboja— stretched across the Indo-Gangetic plains from modern-day Afghanistan to Bengal and Maharashtra. This period was that of the second major urbanization in India after the Indus Valley Civilization (Majumdar, 1951).

Many smaller clans mentioned within early literature seem to have been present across the rest of the subcontinent. Some of these kings were hereditary; other states elected their rulers. The educated speech at that time was Sanskrit, while the dialects of the general population of northern India are referred to as Prakrits. Many of the sixteen kingdoms had coalesced to four major ones by 500/400 BCE, by the time of Siddhartha Gautama. These four were Vatsa, Avanti, Kosala and Magadha.[8]

Hindu rituals at that time were complicated and conducted by the priestly class. It is thought that the Upanishads, later Vedic texts dealing mainly with incipient philosophy, were composed in the later Vedic Age and early in this period of the *Mahajanapadas* (from about 600 - 400 BCE). Upanishads had a substantial effect on Indian philosophy, and were contemporary to the development of Buddhism and Jainism, indicating a golden age of thought in this period.

It is believed that in 537 BCE, that Siddhartha Gautama attained the state of "enlightenment", and became known as the 'Buddha'- the enlightened one. Around the same time, Mahavira (the 24th Jain Tirthankara according to Jains) propagated a similar theology, that was to later become

Jainism.[9] However, Jain orthodoxy believes it predates all known time. The Vedas are believed to have documented a few Jain Tirthankars, and an ascetic order similar to the sramana movement.[10]

Buddhism and Jainism had doctrines inclined towards asceticism, and were preached in Prakrit, which helped them gain acceptance amongst the masses. They have profoundly influenced practices that Hinduism and Indian spiritual orders are associated with namely, vegetarianism, prohibition of animal slaughter and ahimsa (non-violence). While the geographic impact of Jainism was limited to India, Buddhist nuns and monks eventually spread the teachings of Buddha to Central Asia, East Asia, Tibet, Sri Lanka and South East Asia (Majumdar, 1951).

Persian and Greek Invasions

Much of the northwestern Indian Subcontinent (present day Eastern Afghanistan and Pakistan) came under the rule of the Persian Achaemenid Empire in c. 520 BCE during the reign of Darius the Great, and remained so for two centuries thereafter. In 326 BCE, Alexander the Great conquered Asia Minor and the Achaemenid Empire, reaching the north-west frontiers of the Indian subcontinent. There, he defeated King Puru in the Battle of the Hydaspes (near modern-day Jhelum, Pakistan) and conquered much of

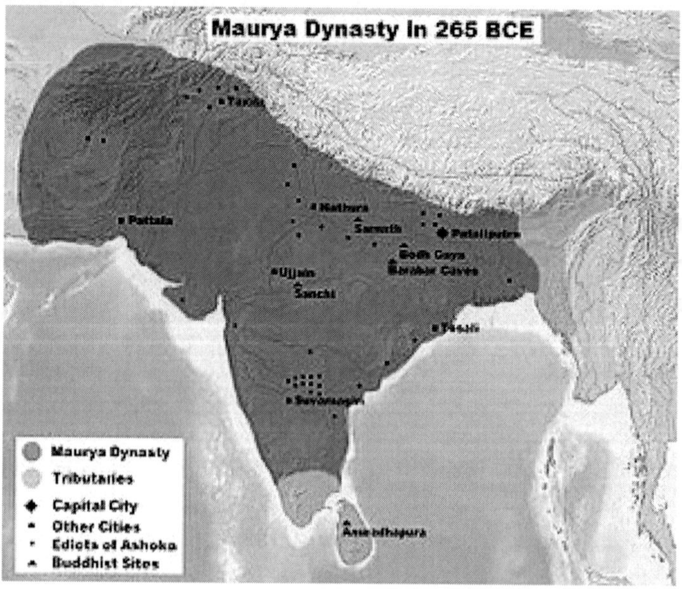

Maurya Empire under Ashoka the Great

the Punjab.[11] Alexander's march East put him in confrontation with the Nanda Empire of Magadha and Gangaridai Empire of Bengal. His army, exhausted and frightened by the prospect of facing larger Indian armies at the Ganges River, mutinied at the Hyphasis (modern Beas) and refused to march further east. Alexander, after the meeting with his officer, Coenus, was convinced that it was better to return.

The Persian and Greek invasions had important repercussions on Indian civilization. The political systems of the Persians were to influence future forms of governance on the subcontinent, including the administration of the Mauryan dynasty. In addition, the region of Gandhara, or present-day eastern Afghanistan and north-west Pakistan, became a melting pot of Indian, Persian, Central Asian and Greek cultures and gave rise to a hybrid culture, Greco-Buddhism, which lasted until the 5th century CE and influenced the artistic development of Mahayana Buddhism.

Maurya period— The Maurya Empire (322–185 B.C), ruled by the Mauryan dynasty, was geographically extensive, powerful, and a political military empire in ancient India. The great Maurya Empire was established by Chandragupta Maurya and this empire was flourished by Ashoka the Great. At its greatest extent, the Empire stretched to the north along the natural boundaries of the Himalayas, and to the east stretching into what is now Assam. To the west, it reached beyond modern Pakistan, annexing Baluchistan and much of what is now Afghanistan, including the modern Herat and Kandahar provinces. The Empire was expanded into India's central and southern regions by the emperors Chandragupta and Bindusara, but it excluded a big portion of unexplored tribal and forested regions near Kalinga which was won by Ashoka the Great (Majumdar, 1951).

Early Middle Kingdoms: The Golden Age

Middle kingdoms of India— The middle period was a time of notable cultural development. The Satavahanas, also known as the Andhras, was a dynasty which ruled in Southern and Central India starting from around 230 BCE. Satakarni, the sixth ruler of the Satavahana dynasty, defeated the Sunga dynasty of North India. Gautamiputra Satakarni was another notable ruler of the dynasty. Kuninda Kingdom was a small Himalayan state that survived from around the 2nd century BCE to roughly the 3rd century CE. The Kushanas invaded north-western India about the middle of the 1st century CE, from Central Asia, and founded an empire that eventually stretched from Peshawar to the middle Ganges and, perhaps, as far as the Bay of Bengal. It also included ancient Bactria (in the north of modern

Afghanistan) and southern Tajikistan. The Western Satraps (35-405 CE) were Saka rulers of the western and central part of India. They were the successors of the Indo-Scythians and contemporaneous with the Kushans who ruled the northern part of the Indian subcontinent, and the Satavahana (Andhra) who ruled in Central India.

Different empires such as the Pandyan Kingdom, Chola Dynasty, Chera Dynasty, Kadamba Dynasty, Western Ganga Dynasty, Pallavas and Chalukya Dynasty dominated the southern part of the Indian peninsula, at different periods of time. Several southern kingdoms formed overseas empires that stretched across South East Asia. The kingdoms warred with each other and Deccan states, for domination of the south. Kalabhras, a Buddhist kingdom, briefly interrupted the usual domination of the Cholas, Cheras and Pandyas in the South.

Northwestern hybrid cultures— The north-western hybrid cultures of the subcontinent included the *Indo-Greeks*, the *Indo-Scythians*, the *Indo-Parthians*, and the *Indo-Sassanids*. The first of these, the Indo-Greek Kingdom, founded when the Greco-Bactrian king Demetrius invaded the region in 180 BCE, extended over various parts of present-day Afghanistan and Pakistan. Lasting for almost two centuries, it was ruled by a succession of more than 30 Greek kings, who were often in conflict with each other. The Indo-Scythians was a branch of the Indo-European (Sạkas Scythians), who migrated from southern Siberia first into Bactria, subsequently into Sogdiana, Kashmir, Arachosia, Gandhara and finally into India; their kingdom lasted from the middle of the 2nd century BCE to the 1st century BCE. Yet another kingdom, the Indo-Parthians (also known as Pahlavas) came to control most of present-day Afghanistan and northern Pakistan, after fighting many local rulers such as the Kushan ruler Kujula Kadphises, in the Gandhara region. The Sassanid Empire of Persia, who was contemporaries of the Guptas, expanded into the region of present-day Pakistan, where the mingling of Indian and Persian cultures gave birth to the Indo-Sassanid culture.

Roman trade with India— Roman trade with India started around 1 CE following the reign of Augustus and his conquest of Egypt made it India's biggest trade partner in the West. The trade started by Eudoxus of Cyzicus in 130 BCE kept increasing, and according to Strabo (II.5.12.), by the time of Augustus up to 120 ships were setting sail every year from Myos Hormos to India. So much gold was used for this trade, and apparently recycled by the Kushans for their own coinage, that Pliny (NH VI.101) complained about the drain of specie to India:

> "India, China and the Arabian peninsula take one hundred million sesterces from our empire per annum at a conservative estimate: that is what our luxuries and women cost us. For what percentage of these imports is intended for sacrifices to the gods or the spirits of the dead?"
>
> —**Pliny, Historia Naturae 12.41.84.**

These trade routes and harbour are described in detail in the 1st century CE Periplus of the Erythraean Sea.

Gupta dynasty— In the 4th and 5th centuries, the Gupta Dynasty unified northern India. During this period, known as India's Golden Age of Hindu renaissance, Hindu culture, science and political administration reached new heights. Chandragupta I, Samudragupta, and Chandragupta II were the most notable rulers of the Gupta dynasty. The earliest available Puranas are also thought to have been written around this period. The empire came to an end with the attack of the Huns from central Asia. After the collapse of the Gupta Empire in the 6th century, India was again ruled by numerous regional kingdoms. A minor line of the Gupta clan continued to rule Magadha after the disintegration of the empire. These Guptas were ultimately ousted by the Vardhana king Harsha, who established an empire in the first half of the seventh century.

The White Huns, who seem to have been part of the Hephthalite group, established themselves in Afghanistan by the first half of the fifth century, with their capital at Bamiyan. They were responsible for the downfall of the Gupta dynasty, and thus brought an end to what historians consider a golden age in northern India. Nevertheless, much of the Deccan and southern India were largely unaffected by this state of flux in the north.

Late Middle Kingdoms: The Classical Age

The classical age in India began with the Guptas and the resurgence of the north during Harsha's conquests around the 7th century, and ended with the fall of the Vijayanagar Empire in the South, due to pressure from the invaders to the north in the 13th century. This period produced some of India's finest art, considered the epitome of classical development, and the development of the main spiritual and philosophical systems which continued to be in Hinduism, Buddhism and Jainism. King Harsha of Kanauj succeeded in reuniting northern India during his reign in the 7th century, after the collapse of the Gupta dynasty. His kingdom collapsed after his death (Smith, 1981; 1990).

From the 7th to the 9th century, three dynasties contested for control of northern India: the Pratiharas of Malwa, the Palas of Bengal and the Rashtrakutas of Deccan. The Sena dynasty would later assume control of the Pala Empire, and the Pratiharas fragmented into various states. These were the first of the Rajputs, a series of kingdoms which managed to survive in some form for almost a millennium until Indian independence from the British. The first recorded Rajput kingdoms emerged in Rajasthan in the 6th century, and small Rajput dynasties later ruled much of northern India. One Rajput of the Chauhan clan, Prithvi Raj Chauhan, was known for bloody conflicts against the encroaching Islamic Sultanates. The Shahi dynasty ruled portions of eastern Afghanistan, northern Pakistan, and Kashmir from the mid-seventh century to the early eleventh century. Whilst the northern concept of a pan-Indian empire had collapsed at the end of Harsha's empire, the ideal instead shifted to the south.

The Chalukya Empire ruled parts of southern and central India from 550 to 750 from Badami, Karnataka and again from 970 to 1190 from Kalyani, Karnataka. The Pallavas of Kanchi were their contemporaries further to the south. With the decline of the Chalukya empire, their feudatories, Hoysalas of Halebidu, Kakatiyas of Warangal, Seuna Yadavas of Devagiri and a southern branch of the Kalachuri divided the vast Chalukya empire amongst themselves around the middle of 12th century. Later during the middle period, the Chola kingdom emerged in northern Tamil Nadu, and the Chera kingdom in Kerala. By 1343, all these kingdoms had ceased to exist giving rise to the Vijayanagar Empire. Southern Indian kingdoms of the time expanded their influence as far as Indonesia, controlling vast overseas empires in Southeast Asia. The ports of South India were involved in the Indian Ocean trade, chiefly involving spices, with the Roman Empire to the west and Southeast Asia to the east.[12] Literature in local vernaculars and spectacular architecture flourished till about the beginning of the 14th century when southern expeditions of the sultan of Delhi took their toll on these kingdoms. The Hindu Vijayanagar dynasty came into conflict with Islamic rule (the Bahmani Kingdom) and the clashing of the two systems, caused a mingling of the indigenous and foreign culture that left lasting cultural influences on each other. The Vijaynagar Empire eventually declined due to pressure from the first Delhi Sultanates who had managed to establish themselves in the north, centred around the city of Delhi by that time.

The Islamic Sultanates

After the Arab invasion of India's ancient western neighbour Persia, expanding forces in that area were keen to invade India, which was the richest classical civilization, with a flourishing international trade and the only known diamond mines in the world. After resistance for a few centuries by various north Indian kingdoms, short lived Islamic empires (Sultanates) were established and spread across the northern subcontinent over a period of a few centuries. But, prior to Turkic invasions, Muslim trading communities had flourished throughout coastal South India, particularly in Kerala, where they arrived in small numbers, mainly from the Arabian peninsula, through trade links via the Indian Ocean. However, this had marked the introduction of an Abrahamic Middle Eastern religion in Southern India's pre-existing dharmic Hindu culture, often in puritanical form. Later, the Bahmani Sultanate and Deccan Sultanates flourished in the south.

Delhi sultanate— In the 12th and 13th centuries, Turkics and Pashtuns invaded parts of northern India and established the Delhi Sultanate at the beginning of the 13th century, in the former Rajput holdings. The subsequent Slave dynasty of Delhi managed to conquer large areas of northern India, approximate to the ancient extent of the Guptas, while the Khilji Empire was also able to conquer most of central India, but were ultimately unsuccessful in conquering and uniting most of the subcontinent. The Sultanate ushered in a period of Indian cultural renaissance. The resulting "Indo-Muslim" fusion of cultures left lasting syncretic monuments in architecture, music, literature, religion, and clothing. It is surmised that the language of Urdu (literally meaning "horde" or "camp" in various Turkic dialects) was born during the Delhi Sultanate period as a result of the intermingling of the local speakers of Sanskritic prakrits with the Persian, Turkic and Arabic speaking immigrants under the Muslim rulers. The Delhi Sultanate is the only Indo-Islamic empire to stake a claim to enthroning one of the few female rulers in India, Razia Sultan (1236-1240).

A Turko-Mongol conqueror Timur began a trek starting in 1398 to invade the reigning Sultan Nasir-ud-Din Mahmud of the Tughlaq Dynasty in the north Indian city of Delhi. The Sultan's army was defeated on December 17, 1398. Timur entered Delhi and the city was sacked, destroyed, and left in ruins.

Colonial era— Vasco da Gama's maritime success to discover for Europeans a new sea route to India in 1498 paved the way for direct Indo-European commerce. The Portuguese soon set up trading-posts in Goa, Daman, Diu and Bombay. The next to arrive were the Dutch, the British—who set up a trading-post in the west-coast port of Surat in 1619—and the

French. The internal conflicts among Indian Kingdoms gave opportunities to the European traders to gradually establish political influence and appropriate lands. Although these continental European powers were to control various regions of southern and eastern India during the ensuing century, they would eventually lose all their territories in India to the British islanders, with the exception of the French outposts of Pondicherry and Chandernagore, the Dutch port of Travancore, and the Portuguese colonies of Goa, Daman, and Diu.

In 1526, Babur, a Timurid descendant of Timur and Genghis Khan, swept across the Khyber Pass and established the Mughal Empire, which lasted for over 200 years. The Mughal Dynasty ruled most of the Indian subcontinent by 1600; it went into a slow decline after 1707 and was finally defeated during the 1857 War of Independence also called the Indian Rebellion of 1857. This period marked vast social change in the subcontinent as the Hindu majority were ruled over by the Mughal emperors, most of them showed religious tolerance, liberally patronising Hindu culture. The famous emperor Akbar, who was the grandson of Babur, tried to establish a good relationship with the Hindus. However, later emperors such as Aurangzeb tried to establish complete Muslim dominance and as a result several historical temples were destroyed during this period and taxes imposed on non-Muslims. During the decline of the Mughal Empire, which at its peak occupied an area similar to the ancient Maurya Empire, several smaller empires rose to fill the power vacuum or themselves were contributing factors to the decline. The Mughals were perhaps the richest single dynasty to have ever existed. In 1739, Nader Shah defeated the Mughal army at the huge Battle of Karnal. After this victory, Nader captured and sacked Delhi, carrying away many treasures, including the Peacock Throne (Smith, 1981; 1990).

During the Mughal era, the dominant political forces consisted of the Mughal Empire and its tributaries and, later on, the rising successor states-including the Maratha confederacy- who fought an increasingly weak and disfavoured Mughal dynasty. The Mughals, while often employing brutal tactics to subjugate their empire, had a policy of integration with Indian culture, which is what made them successful where the short-lived Sultanates of Delhi had failed. Akbar the Great was particularly famed for this. Akbar declared "Amari" or non-killing of animals in the holy days of Jainism. He rolled back the *Jazia Tax* for non-Muslims. The Mughal Emperors married local royalty, allied themselves with local Maharajas, and attempted to fuse their Turko-Persian culture with ancient Indian styles, creating unique

Indo-Saracenic architecture. It was the erosion of this tradition coupled with increased brutality and centralization that played a large part in their downfall after Aurangzeb, who unlike previous emperors, imposed relatively non-pluralistic policies on the general population, that often inflamed the majority Hindu population (Allan, Haig and Dodwell, 1934).

Post-Mughal regional kingdoms— The post-Mughal era was dominated by the rise of the Maratha suzerainty as other small regional states (mostly post-Mughal tributary states) emerged, and also by the increasing activities of European powers. The Maratha Kingdom was founded and consolidated by Shivaji. By the 18th century, it had transformed itself into the Maratha Empire under the rule of the Peshwas. By 1760, the Empire had stretched across practically the entire subcontinent. This expansion was brought to an end by the defeat of the Marathas by an Afghan army led by Ahmad Shah Abdali at the Third Battle of Panipat (1761). The last Peshwa, Baji Rao II, was defeated by the British in the Third Anglo-Maratha War.

Mysore was a kingdom of southern India, which was founded around 1400 CE by the Wodeyar dynasty. The rule of the Wodeyars was interrupted

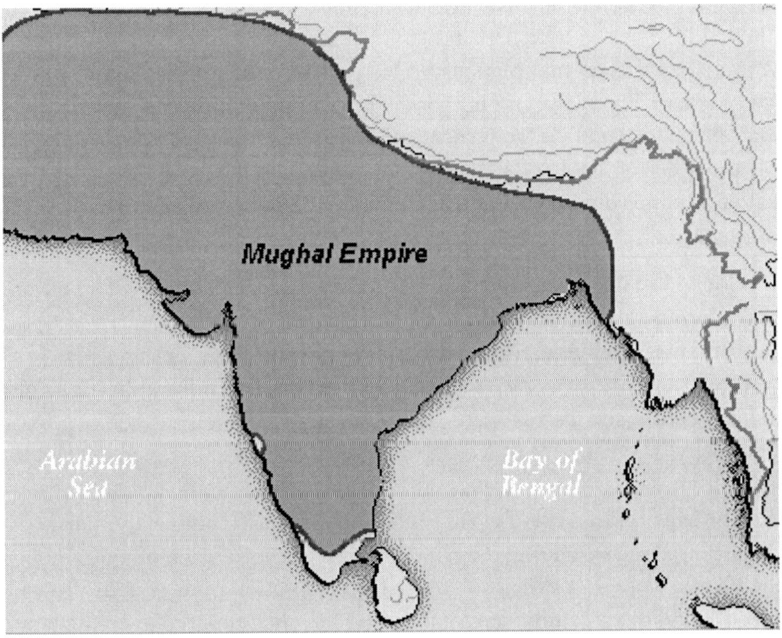

Approximate extent of the Mughal Empire in the 17th century.

by Hyder Ali and his son Tipu Sultan. Under their rule Mysore fought a series of wars sometimes against the combined forces of the British and Marathas, but mostly against the British with some aid or promise of aid from the French. Hyderabad was founded by the Qutb Shahi dynasty of Golconda in 1591. Following a brief Mughal rule, Asif Jah, a Mughal official, seized control of Hyderabad declaring himself Nizam-al-Mulk of Hyderabad in 1724. It was ruled by a hereditary Nizam from 1724 until 1948. Both Mysore and Hyderabad became princely states in British India.

The Punjabi kingdom, ruled by members of the Sikh religion, was a political entity that governed the region of modern day Punjab. This was among the last areas of the subcontinent to be conquered by the British. The Anglo-Sikh wars marked the downfall of the Sikh Empire. Around the 18th century modern Nepal was formed by Gorkha rulers, and the Shahs and the Ranas very strictly maintained their national identity and integrity.

The social, religious and economic conditions of the Indians were very bad in the 18th century. As we all know that after the death of Aurangzeb there was complete anarchy in the country. When Aurangzeb was alive he himself could not manage such a huge empire because of lack of transportation and communication in those days. But the condition deteriorated after his death due to lack of able successors. Aurangzeb never allowed his sons to take part in administration because of his suspicious nature. This was a great blunder on his part for which India had to pay a heavy price. There was no authority, no administration, no law and no security in the country after the death of this great Mughal emperor. Anarchy was the order of the day. The strong prevailed over the weak. Thus, we see that before the rule of the English Company, Indians had very bad time in every way.

Social life in 18th century was marked by pains and poverty. There was no uniformity of culture and social patterns all over the country. People were divided by religion, region, tribe, language and caste. The upper classes lived a lavish life whereas the lower classes lived a miserable life. The higher classes and castes were over-conscious of their supremacy and superiority. The entire wealth of the country was concentrated in the hands of the higher classes while the masses lacked the basic necessities of the life. The Muslim concept of equality and fraternity had completely vanished. The different castes among the Hindus were jealous of each other's rights. The people were so much absorbed in the celebration of marriages, feasts, festivals and other family ceremonies that they had no urge to create new social values.

The social system in the 18th century had two aspects. One aspect was a grading on the basis of official power and position. The second aspect was a grading on the basis of religion. The first was a reflection of the political system whereas the second comprised the castes and sub-castes among the Hindus.

Caste system— During those days when British were new to India it came to their observation that the Hindu society was divided into four parts namely the Brahmans, the Kshatriyas, the Vaishyas and the Shudras. The Brahman was the priest as well as the teacher and guide. In the Hindu society both the ignorant and the educated were superstitious and the Brahmanas exploited the innate human fear of the unknown. The hereditary occupation of the Kshatriyas was to involve in battles and wars for the sake of the country. The kings, ministers and soldiers generally belonged to this class. Now the question arises whether the Kshatriyas were doing justice to their occupation or not? To this point Nagari Dass, the Hindi poet has observed that the Kshatriyas were greedy and selfish. They never did any good to anybody and were not compassionate. If they saw a beautiful woman in the house of poor man, their strength of arm lay only in their effort to grab her for themselves. The Vaishyas were the community of businessmen. They had two broad divisions. One branch took to trade and the other to agriculture. It was the former who were somewhat typical of their class. They were the usurers and the sole aim of their life was to live on the interest of the money that they gave as loans. A Bania was notorious for his love for money. He was looked down upon by the society for that reason. The Shudras comprised the mass of the people. Their sole duty was to render service to the three upper classes. Below these four castes were the Antyajas. They had to live at the distance from higher class and still rendered their services to them. The lowest of the low were the Hadis, Doms and Chandalas.

The Brahmans, Kshatriyas and Vaishyas were all divided and sub-divided into a large number of castes and sub-castes. Each caste formed an endogamous group and only in this endogamous group that inter-dining was permissible. If a person was found to break his own social customs he was excommunicated. The Panchayat would not readmit him in his caste until he humbled himself publicly. The marriage had to be in the same caste in order to prevent the intermixture of blood and maintain the purity of descent.

In the 18th century, the people were very sensitive about the concept of roti (bread) and beti (daughter). Inter-dining among the people of different castes was non-existent. Only the Sikhs had their institution of Langar which was open to all. People of different castes could worship the same gods, observe the same manners and customs, but would not eat together.

The question of permissible and forbidden food was an important one. As a rule, the Brahmans had to abstain from meat and intoxicating liquors. The caste prescribed different codes for different groups. Meat was not a staple diet in India. Abstinence from meat was generally practiced in the areas dominated by Jain influence. The classes that came into contact with them were generally vegetarian, while others took meat as a luxury and delicacy. The Kshatriyas, Rajputs and Jats and other lower classes all ate meat.

Occupation was another decisive factor in the formation of caste. In spite of the general taboos the artisan classes were sometimes compelled to intermingle with the twice-born. Those who practiced the professions of barber, weaver, embroiderer, dyer, printer, gardener, potter, ivory worker, etc. were sometimes paid directly for the services rendered by them. More often they were paid by fixed quantity of grain at the harvest time or some clothes or some money on the occasions of celebration in the family. There were certain occupations which were open to all. Trading, agriculture and even military service could be taken up by anybody who was eligible for it. Caste regulations were strictly enforced by caste councils and panchayats. Anyone found violating it had to pay fines, suffer penances (Prayaschitta) and sometimes he could be expelled from the caste. Caste was a major dividing line in pre-British India. We can also say that caste was an element of disintegration in the India of 18th century or precisely pre-British India. The credit goes to Englishmen for eliminating this evil from the soil of this country.

Family and marriage— The family system in the 18th century was primarily patriarchal. The male member dominated the family. Inheritance was through the male line. However, we see that in Kerala, the family was matrilineal. Outside Kerala, women were subjected to nearly complete male control. They were expected to live as mothers and wives only. But few exceptions we see here and there also. Ahilya Bai administered Indore with great success from 1766 to 1796. Many other Hindu and Muslim women played an important role in the politics of that time. The status of a woman in a family depended entirely on her capacity to give births to sons and hence they were prepared to make any sacrifice for that purpose. A daughter occupied a peculiar position in the family. Although she was considered

Lakshmi (the Goddess of prosperity) but her birth was not welcome. She had no share in her father's and brother's property.

In the pre-British India, the percentage of Muslims was quite large. In the 18th century it became difficult to differentiate between the practices of a Muslim family and a Hindu family although the Muslims conformed to the Shariat. A polygamous household was the fashion among the royalty and the nobility. The first wife enjoyed the privileges of seniority. She was considered to be the head of the female establishment and she was given precedence over all the other wives. However, the children of the subsequent wives enjoyed equal status. The mother in a Muslim family had a status of her own. The father was the head of the family but he did not have the absolute power in a Muslim family. The Muslim women had their right to give or withhold her consent to marriage, but she could not exercise her right in the 18th century. In certain cases a marriage in Islam could be even a temporary contract which could only serve the purpose of sexual gratification. Due to the influence of Hinduism, divorce in Muslim families was looked down upon and respectable people preferred to put up with all the differences and conflicts in the family than to become objects of public discussion by trying to get a divorce. Muslim parents had to give dowries to their daughters which proved a huge financial burden. The son in a Muslim family was a source of much more pleasure than a daughter. The reason was mainly economic as the father of the girls was considered to be a poor man.

Purdah system was practiced in Muslim society. Muslim women were kept in seclusion. The family dwelling was divided into a Zenanah (woman's quarter) and a Mardanah (man's quarter). This arrangement was done because of political insecurity in those days. But in the 18th century it was made a point of prestige to have the women of the family concealed in the house. The seclusion of women, both among Muslims and Hindus, was mainly confined to the higher classes. Women of the lower class had to appear in the public because they had to work and earn. As they had to work for their men-folk, they could not be kept veiled. Those who lived in the villages had to till the land and carry the grains to the market, while those in the towns had to pay the price of their existence by performing all the household duties in other houses.

The custom of female infanticide was very much prevalent among the Rajputs. Child marriage was prevalent in society. Child marriage was done for social security rather than as a sign of backwardness. The instability in the 18th century created great anxiety among the parents about the honour of their daughters and hence they were married at an early age. Purdah system was prevalent among both the Hindus and the Muslims. There was complete insecurity and lawlessness during those days and that's why the women were not given the education. Their physical and mental health also suffered. The custom of Sati mostly prevailed in Bengal, Central India and Rajputana. In the south, it was uncommon. The Peshwas discouraged Sati in their dominion with limited success. Polygamy prevailed among the upper classes of Uttar Pradesh and Bengal. Remarriage of widows was considered bad although it prevailed in some places. The Peshwas imposed a tax called Patdam on remarriage of widows. The lot of the Hindu widows was pitiable. All sort of restrictions were imposed on their clothing, diet, movements, etc. They were expected to give up all the pleasures of the earth and serve the members of her husband's or brother's family. Raja Sawai Jai Singh of Amber and the Maratha General Parshuram Bhau tried to promote widow remarriage but failed. Untouchability was prevalent in society. The untouchables were denied certain basic privileges of living. They could not use the tanks and wells of the higher castes in villages. They had their own separate wells and tanks from which they could fetch water. If by some reason their wells or tanks become contaminated and become unsuitable for drinking purpose, they could not think of approaching the wells or tanks of the elite classes. It was considered a sin and for this they were supposed to pay a heavy price. Such was the condition of untouchables in those days. These untouchables if they touched a Brahmana by mistake, then the Brahmana would rush to have a bath.

The people performed many superstitious rites. The upper class Hindus resorted to human sacrifices on certain occasions. It was believed that the Goddess Kali requires human blood or heads and for the satisfaction of this Devi, a human victim was slaughtered. Self-immolation was another form of human sacrifice. In some cases, one could drown oneself in a river in order to escape a disease. In some cases life could be taken by way of mortification and penance. In some cases one's child was sacrificed. Under peculiar conditions parents took a vow to offer their first born child to the Ganges. Another superstitious rite was self-torture. Many devotees pierced their tongues and arms with pointed rods. This was done in the belief that good results could follow self-torture.

Slavery— Now let us discuss about the institution of slavery before the arrival of Englishmen in India. As we all know like in other countries slavery prevailed in India also. In ancient Rome, slavery was quite dominant. It was considered a luxury to own slaves. But we see the same case with

India also. Broadly speaking slaves could be divided into two parts, domestic slaves and serfs tied to the land. The second category of the slaves was transferred with the sale of the land to the buyer. In some cases economic distress, natural calamities, extreme poverty and famines compelled parents to sell their children. The Rajputs, the Kshatriyas and Kayasthas usually kept slave women for domestic work. Slaves in India were treated better than the slaves in Europe and America. They were usually treated as hereditary servants of the family and were allowed to marry among themselves.

The practice of slavery increased with the coming of the Europeans in India, particularly the Portuguese, the Dutch and the English. The European companies purchased slaves in the open market. There were reports of Europeans at Surat, Madras and Calcutta purchasing Abyssinian slaves and employing them for domestic work.

Among the Muslims, celibacy did not find any recognition as a virtue. Except for the Sufi saints, marriage was an obligation to be fulfilled by every Muslim. Among the orthodox Muslims, marriages did not take place between Sunni and Shiah. In Islam it is given that one could not have more than four wives and they were to be treated in a very equitable manner. The number of wives almost determined the social status of men. The leading noblemen kept regular harems while the lower class was mainly monogamous because they did not have enough money to support more than one wife. No age limit was fixed for marriage, but Muslims generally favoured early marriages that may be due to the influence of Hinduism. As a rule, boys were not allowed to see the girls before they were married. Occasionally there were inter-communal marriages. Farrukh-siyar was married to the daughter of Raja Ajit Singh. We did not find any other reference to inter-communal marriage.

Religious Institutions of Hindus

The Hindus continued to believe in the trinity of Brahma, Vishnu and Mahesh- the three major powers of creation, sustenance and destruction. The worship of Brahma was not popular because he was alleged to have been cursed by a god on account of some sin. Siva and Vishnu, along with their female counterparts- Parvati and Lakshmi claimed the devotion of almost entire Hindu society. Their worship represented three distinct forms of belief and practice. The followers of Siva were called Shaivites. The followers of Vishnu were called Vaishnavites. The people who worshipped the female counterpart (Sakti) of Lord Siva were called Saktas. However, these divisions did not make any difference in the basic concepts of Hinduism.

The worship of Siva was generally the religion of the common people. His ritual could be performed without a priest. He appeared to be more terrible than benevolent and consequently more feared and revered than loved. His third eye could rain fire on the people who neglected him. He was the patron of craftsmen, cartwrights, smiths, potters, hunters and washermen. He was also the head of the armies, the god of the fighters in any mode of warfare. His name, Har Har Mahadev, was a war-cry. Thieves and free-booters were devoted to him. The beggars and Faqirs showed their affinity with him by wearing long and matted hair or by shaving their heads clean. He was omnipotent but he was supposed to live on high mountains, dense forests and solitary places. The Rajputs were predominantly the followers of Siva. They built temples dedicated to Siva even outside Rajasthan-Gujarat and Bundelkhand. The image of Siva in the form of Lingam was carved out of stone and water was poured over it to give bath to the god.

Vishnu was the ideal god for the householder. He was the god recommended to him by the priestly class. The ascendancy of Vishnu over the other gods is shown by a painting of the Rajasthani School dated 1740 A.D. Vishnu is seated on a throne in heaven with Lakshmi on his knee. He is attended by the other gods, among whom Siva appears on the right as an ascetic along with Ganesh. On the left are seen Indra and Brahma with his four heads. It was both fashionable and respectable to be a devotee of Vishnu. His image was a complete image of a well-formed human being

Both Siva and Vishnu held very prominent positions in the religious thought of Hindus. It was not necessary to be either follower of Siva or Vishnu. Harihara was a god representing both of them. Hari was the name of Vishnu and Hara of Siva. They could both be worshipped in this combined form.

The third important sect of the Hindus was the Saktas. They believed that the goddesses were more benevolent and powerful than the gods. In the difficult circumstances, the worshippers turn to the goddesses with the greater devotions than to the gods. Mahadevi, the Great goddess, was worshipped under thousand forms. All over northern India, the goddesses were worshipped as the great mothers. These goddesses were sometimes very gracious and bounteous like Gauri whom the young girls worshipped in the hope of getting good husbands and a happy married life. The Rajputs took their inspirations and courage from Durga.

The Hindus also worshipped Ganesa or Ganapati. Ganesha was the god of good luck and fortune. The Hindus worshipped Siva, Vishnu, Shakti, Ganesha and the sun. This five-fold reverence was called Panchayatan Puja and was the most popular form of worship. Ganesha was believed to be the remover of all evil and was worshipped everywhere at the beginning of all auspicious ceremonies. In Rajasthan Ganesa was called Vinayak.

The worship of Surya was also prevalent in the 18th century. As we are aware of the fact that the sun supports the life on this earth, so Sun-God was highly revered by the Hindus. Sun worship was in the blood of the Hindu people. Every morning the sun was saluted and offered water in the form of Arghya by the householders. As we have seen in all ancient civilizations, sun god was highly respected because he gives good harvest to the poor farmers and brings prosperity and surplus food grains. In Mesopotamian civilization, temples were constructed for sun-god as a mark of reverence to him. Down the ages this tradition continued in the annals of Indian History. Gayatri Mantra was composed during the Rig Vedic period. It was chanted for the invocation of sun-god. Even to this day, we see people reciting this mantra on holy occasions for getting the grace of God.

The agricultural people had deep belief in the forces of nature. They always used to become victims to the extremities of weather. They had to bear the harshness and bitterness of nature. So, out of fear the timid Indians started worshipping these forces of nature to seek their blessings. The rivers Ganga and Jamuna were worshipped as the Great Mothers. Their entire course in the plains was clotted with holy cities. Tree worship was very common. Pipal was considered as the Brahman among trees. Tulsi plant was held very sacred by the Hindus. Spirit worship was another major element in Hindu belief. Separate religious communities well organized within the fold of Shaivism and Vaishnavism. All these sects had developed in the medieval India but this also continued till the advent of the British. We see proto-Siva figurines even in the Indus Valley Civilization. The Shaiva worship continued in all the ages with several developments taking place from time to time.

Islamic Beliefs in Pre-British India

The beliefs and practices of the Muslims in the 18th century were influenced by three main factors viz., the decline of the Mughal Empire, the wide prevalence of the doctrine of Wahdat-ul-Wujud (unity of Existence) and the influence of Hinduism. The Muslim state was supposed to be Islamic state and Muslim rulers were responsible for the maintenance of the Shariat.

However, his responsibility was hypothetical. The Muslims of the 18th century had neither the wish nor the power to follow the Shariat.

Wahdat-ul-Wujud emphasised on the tolerance of the beliefs and practices of non- Muslims. Islam and other religions are all one. There was opposition to the doctrine of Wahdat-ul-Wujud. Shaikh Ahmad of Sirhind declared that those who believed in Wahdat-ul-Wujud were undermining the Shariat. Besides this, we see there were many religious reformers. He tried hard to bring Islam to the masses of India by translating the Quran into Persian.

The orthodox Muslims were involved in acute sectarianism. The party system at the Mughal court was strongly influenced by Shiah-Sunni differences. For example, we can see that Mirza Mazhar Jani Janan was murdered by Shias because he was suspected to having made derogatory remarks about Tadhiahs. Thus, we see that there existed many evils in the religious life of the Muslims.

Economic Condition under the British Rule

India of the 18th century was a land of contrasts. Extreme poverty existed side by side with extreme riches and luxury. The nobles were rich and powerful. While the nobles lived in luxury and comfort, the peasants were oppressed and impoverished. The increasing revenue demands of the state along with the oppression of officials were a headache to the peasants. The greed and rapacity of the nobles added more to the burden of the farmers. The marches and counter-marches of the rival armies spoilt the crops in those days. The destruction brought about by foreign invaders made the life of the people wretched. Many prosperous cities which were the centres of flourishing industry were sacked and devastated. Delhi and Mathura were plundered by Ahmed Shah Abdali. Agra was plundered by the Jats. Surat and other cities of Gujarat and the Deccan were plundered by the Maratha Chiefs. Sarhind was plundered by the Sikhs. On account of the disintegration of the Mughal Empire in the 18th century, there was practically no law and order. It is pointed out that by the close of the 18th century, the urban centres had become a "dead place" (Dutt, 1976; Rothermund 1993).

In the 18th century, when the Mughal dynasty was on its decline, everywhere there was anarchy and chaos in the ambience. Political disintegration had set in. It was not possible for a man to prosper amid conditions of insecurity and oppression. This destroyed the creative and cooperative spirit of man. The 18th century India saw glory in war and chivalry. It turned a deaf ear to peace, stability and economic development.

Everywhere we see there were battles and violence. For example, the Anglo-Mysore wars, the battles of Plassey and Buxar, the Anglo-Maratha wars and the Anglo-Sikh wars. All these wars never ensured any future for the nation, but it surely claimed a heavy toll of lives. India should have learnt a lesson of unity and stand for development.

Ghulam Hussain, a historian of Bengal, calls the 18th century as an age of senseless, slothful princes and of ignorant grandees. The administration was wretched in those days and every part of the country had gone to ruin. The urban inhabitants who were educated and enlightened saw no ray of hope for the country. They were discouraged and their hearts were broken. But they became optimistic when the British landed on the Indian shores. They were developed. They were determined to fight against the traditional evils; such as illiteracy, sati-system, purdah system, superstitions and blind-baseless beliefs of the ancient –oriental world. These white men gave some hope to the urban middle-class men of India who always stood by the side of Europeans. This we see in the revolt of 1857 when the middle-class Indians supported the British in their fight against the reactionary forces. These middle-class elite believed that India had to fight a long battle against the social evils prevalent in the Indian society. Their true enemy were these evils and not the Englishmen who left no leaf unturned to educate and modernise the poor Indians. Of course the Englishmen were harsh towards us. But let us first put this question to ourselves that weren't we cruel towards our women. Vivekananda says that, "that society or nation can never progress in which women are not respected".

In the 18th century, wars, invasions and other calamities created havoc and cities like Lahore, Delhi, Agra and Mathura in the North and large tracts of the country in the Deccan were destroyed. However, this adversity was compensated by the appearance of Europeans on the coasts of India. They purchased Indian goods in return for gold and silver and gave a stimulus to industry

The traditional handicraft industry was highly developed in India. There was a group of specialist at each step in the process of production of finished goods. In industrial organisation and techniques, India was more advanced than the Western countries. The products of Indian industry fulfilled not only the needs of Asian and African countries but there was also a great demand in the markets of Europe. They reached the Western countries by sea and land routes (Bipan et al., 1972; 1989).

The Indian merchants were well established all along the ports of the Persian Gulf and the Red Sea. They were also met in considerable numbers in Kandahar, Kabul, Balkh, Bukhara, Kashgar, etc., in Afghanistan and Central Asia. Peter, the Great, once wrote: "The commerce of India is the commerce of the world and he who can exclusively control it is the dictator of Europe." Indian goods found their way into the East-Asian countries viz., Burma, Malaya, Indonesia, China and Japan.

But there was a decline in the internal trade of the country. That was partly due to the absence of a strong power in the country. There were too many states and there was not much of law and order. There was no safety on the roads. The states did nothing to give protection to the merchants carrying on inland trade. In some cases, the petty feudal chiefs molested and plundered the merchants on the highways. There were too many feudal dues to be paid in the course of internal trade (Dutt, 1976; Rothermund 1993).

The upper classes in India demanded luxury articles. Its volume was considerable. The rich created a great volume of demand for luxury goods as they loved good things of life. The nobles desired expensive and fine quality articles. The producers of high quality luxury goods worked in their homes or in the workshops in the towns. Some village artisans who had acquired special skill in certain crafts also produced expensive articles for the use of nobility.

As most of the craftsmen were poor, they were forced to work for merchants. These merchants gave money to the craftsmen for implements and raw materials. The merchants also gave them wages for getting finished goods. But these merchants or middlemen misappropriated the funds. They kept a major or portion of profit with them and thus very little was saved for the hard working craftsmen. The middlemen took the finished products from the craftsmen and sold them at higher prices in the markets. So, to ward away this expensiveness, the nobles held direct dealings with the artisans. In this way, the middlemen could not make profit.

The Indian village was a self-sufficient economic unit. The agricultural surplus went to the king in the form of land revenue. The farmer after meeting the government demand, had little surplus left with him for purchasing the goods of the urban industry. There was very little exchange between the village and the town. The traditional Indian business class could never develop like its European counter-type (Dutt, 1976; Rothermund 1993). The main factors responsible for this were as follows:

(a) Lack of capital,

(b) Rigidity of caste restrictions, and

(c) Lack of economic interaction between the village and the town.

The tradesmen, bankers and moneylenders constituted the Indian mercantile community. They utilised their income in giving loans to the members of the ruling class. However, they lacked the spirit of enterprise.

Merchant ships which were in the port towns and boats playing on the country's rivers were all manufactured in the country. There was a flourishing boat-building industry at Dacca, Allahabad, Lahore, Thatta, Masulipatam, Pulicat, Calicut, Surat, Bassein and Goa. In the art of ship-building, India was ahead of European nations. Parkinson writes, "In ship-building, they probably taught the English far more than they learnt from them." The important ship-building centres were Goa, Bassein, Surat, Masulipatam, Satgaon, Dacca and Chittagong.

Textile industry was also in a flourishing condition. The important centres of textile industry were Dacca and Murshidabad in Bengal, Patna in Bihar, Surat, Ahmedabad and Broach in Gujarat, Chanderi in Madhya Pradesh, Burhanpur in Maharashtra, Jaunpur, Varanasi, Lucknow and Agra in Uttar Pradesh, Multan and Lahore in the Punjab, Masulipatam, Aurangabad, Chicacole and Vishakhapatnam in Andhra Pradesh, Bangalore in Mysore Karnataka) and Coimbatore and Madurai in Madras. Kashmir was a centre of woollen manufactures. India was self-sufficient in agricultural and industrial goods required for the consumption of her population. The imported materials included raw silk, ivory, coral, tortoise-shell and amber in addition to metals (Bipan et al., 1972; 1989).

India had been famous for her cotton products since ancient days. There was a large consumption of Indian manufactures in Rome in ancient times. India was rich in silk and cotton stuffs. The Indian craftsmen excelled in making beautiful silk clothes. Cotton yarn was exported from the Coromandal coast. Among other articles of export, indigo was of importance. Limited quantities of iron and steel were exported from Masulipatam. Gujarat exported precious stones, marble, drugs, opium, hing, etc.

The Indian merchants financed the trade and industry of India. They were not confined to port towns but were spread in all cities and towns of the country. Multan in the Punjab and the three Sindh towns of Bukkur, Sukkur and Rohri were important centres of inland trade in the North-West. Khattris, Lohanas and Bhatias were a community of merchants. Lahore, Delhi and Agra were great commercial centres. Malda, Rangpur and Kasimbazar were important trade centres in Bengal. Ajmer, Jodhpur,

Pali and Jaisalmer were trade centres in Rajasthan. But these were old centres. Ahmedabad in Gujarat and Poona and Nagpur in the Maratha country rose in importance after 1750. Hyderabad, Bangalore and Tanjore were flourishing centres of trade and commerce.

In the 18th century, financiers also thrived quite well. The Jagat Seths of Bengal, the Nathjis of Gujarat and the Chettis of the South were famous financiers. The Jagat Seths possessed a capital of 10 crore of rupees in the first half of the 18th century. In those days, Marathas used to invade Bengal from time to time. During their first invasion of Bengal, the Marathas carried away from their Kothi two crore of rupees but even that loss did not affect their resources appreciably. The Nathjis in Surat had similarly vast resources. The single family of Nathu Kothari Chettis monopolised business and was regarded the richest. Their business extended to Burma, Malaya and the Eastern Islands. The Chettis acted as bankers and supplied the British merchants with cash for their bills of exchange on Madras, Bombay and Calcutta. The big bankers performed all the functions of a modern bank viz., receiving deposits, giving loans and issuing Hundis. There were small bankers who gave loans to artisans and other producers. Every village had its own moneylender. These moneylenders used to give loans for agricultural works and also to fulfil their other requirements. If the resources of all the bankers, financiers and moneylenders in India in the 18th century are taken into account, the total capital resources of the country was quite good. The view of Tara Chand is that the peasant in the 18th century was better off than his successor in the 19th century. This was because of mainly two reasons. The 18th century peasant had larger size of land holding and also the average productivity of land was higher at that time (Chand, 1961).

In the later Mughal period, the most important item of agricultural produce was foodgrains. Wheat, rice, gram and millet were the crops grown in Deccan. Khafi Khan states that Jowar and Bajra were the main support of the people of the Deccan and were extensively grown. Millet was also major food constituent of the North. As we see today that wheat is extensively grown in Uttar Pradesh, but this was not the case in those days. Wheat was not an important crop in Uttar Pradesh at that time. Along with foodgrains, cotton and sugar were the most widely grown crops. Tobacco, opium and indigo were the other commercial crops. When the British came to India, they asked the Indians to grow Indigo on 3/20th part of their land. This system is also known as Tinkathia system. In this way, the British exploited the poor peasants to serve their own purpose. This system was mostly prevalent in Champaran in Bihar.

There were wide variations of prices of food grains. Generally, food grains were cheaper in Bengal than in Northern India. Those were cheaper in Northern India than in Gujarat. The prices of commodities of daily consumption were very low. The prices in India showed two types of fluctuations viz., regional and periodical. The former was the result of the difficulties and heavy cost of transportation. Every region and even every village tried to be self-sufficient in food supply. If the rains were deficient and crops failed, he could not supplement his stock from outside. In the same locality from year to year, price fluctuations were very wide. The price level affected mostly the wage earners. In the villages, the agricultural labourers were paid, by giving them a share in the produce of the farm on which they worked. Money wages were paid to ordinary and skilled labourers employed in the town. By the middle of the 18th century, an ordinary labourer in Calcutta was paid 6 paise daily and skilled worker was paid 10 paise daily.

European travellers have mentioned the poverty of the Indian masses. Their view was based on the scantiness of clothing, miserable dwellings, poor utensils and lack of furniture and lack of nourishing diet to support life. A European writer has written that in Northern India, the people had no clothes to cover their body except a little cloth bound about their middle. The view of Tara Chand is that as far as the poor classes of the people were concerned, they had few wants and those were fulfilled from what the country produced. There was no general starvation. There was also no inadequate nourishment except in periods of famine, nor did they have any surplus to accumulate even in normal years. It is true that their clothing was scanty and dwellings were poor. But they never felt necessary to have more than this and also they were concerned to improve their living conditions (Chand, 1961). Life was simple and so those simple and few wants were easily met. That's why the struggle for existence was not hard. Their simplicity and contentment had its own advantages but it had one great drawback also. The common people did not feel the urge for improvement and hence did not struggle for economic progress.

The country's economic progress was also retarded because of the luxurious life style of the upper classes. The princes, nobles and the provincial chiefs lived in grand style and in great luxury. Mughal nobility was notorious for living a lavish life. A lot of money was spent on delicacies like costly imported fruit, on servants and retainers, on horses and elephants, on marriages and dowries and on building fort-like houses. A large part of the income was spent on jewellery, costly dresses and horses and elephants.

Each noble kept hundreds of servants for his stables and his household. A large sum of money was spent on making presents to the king. There was a rule that after the death of a noble, all his accumulated wealth would go to the royal treasury. The result was that there was no intention to save the gold and money but to spend them nicely whatever they had. Under the circumstances, there was no accumulation of capital. There was no opportunity for profitable investment of savings. The result was that even if some nobles accumulated large fortunes, they spent them in marriages, dowries and buildings rather than in investment in business or industry.

The British East India Company had been given permission by the Mughal emperor Jahangir in 1617 to trade in India. Gradually their increasing influence led the *de-jure* Mughal emperor Farrukh Siyar to grant them *dastaks* or permits for duty free trade in Bengal in 1717. The Nawab of Bengal Siraj-ud-Daulah, the *de facto* ruler of the Bengal province, opposed British attempts to use these permits. This led to the Battle of Plassey in 1757, in which the 'army' of East India Company, led by Robert Clive, defeated the Nawab's forces. This was the first political foothold with territorial implications that the British acquired in India. Clive was appointed by the Company as its first 'Governor of Bengal' in 1757. After the Battle of Buxar in 1764, the Company acquired the civil rights of administration in Bengal from the Mughal Emperor Shah Alam II; it marked the beginning of its formal rule, which was to engulf eventually most of India and extinguish the Mughal rule and dynasty itself in a century.[13] The East India Company monopolized the trade of Bengal. They introduced a land taxation system called the Permanent Settlement which introduced a feudal like structure in Bengal. By the 1850s, the East India Company controlled most of the Indian sub-continent, which included present-day Pakistan and Bangladesh. Their policy was sometimes summed up as Divide and Rule, taking advantage of the enmity festering between various princely states and social and religious groups. During the British Raj, famines in India, often attributed to failed government policies, were some of the worst ever recorded, including the Great Famine of 1876–78, in which 6.1 million to 10.3 million people died and the Indian famine of 1899–1900, in which 1.25 to 10 million people died. The Third Plague Pandemic started in China in the middle of the 19th century, spreading plague to all inhabited continents and killing 10 million people in India alone. Despite persistent diseases and famines, the population of the Indian subcontinent, which stood at about 125 million in 1750, had reached 389 million by 1941.

In the 18th century, the servants of the English Company penetrated into all parts of the country. The Nawab of Bengal, Mir Kasim, had granted the Europeans many privileges in inland trade. They were given free passes called Dastaks which they misutilised. By a Firman of 1717, the English Company had been given the privilege of free seaborne trade. After the battle of Plassey of 1757, the Company started taking the advantage of the chaotic condition in the country and started abusing the privilege by extending the same to the private trade of all kinds. In this way, the Company instigated the Battle of Buxar of 1764. Even after the battle of Buxar, the Company continued to make huge profits. The battle of Buxar was won by the English Company. The Company installed a puppet on the throne. The British dealt with the Indians even more harsh than they used to do previously. The weavers were compelled to enter into engagements to work for the English Company and for a breach of the contract, they were punished with fine, imprisonment, flogging, etc. Even the highest officials of the Company were engaged in private trade which brought them huge sums of money. Vansittart tells us that the English compelled the natives to buy or sell at just what rates they pleased. It was estimated that between 1757 and 1766, the English East India Company and its employees received six millions pounds from Indians as gifts. Clive himself was guilty of this offence. Political corruption and exorbitant land taxes enabled the English Company to transfer large sums of money annually to Great Britain. There was a regular drain of wealth from India to Great Britain (Andrews, 1984; Brendon, 2008).

The first major movement against the British Company's high handed rule resulted in the Indian Rebellion of 1857, also known as the "Indian Mutiny" or "Sepoy Mutiny" or the "First War of Independence". After a year of turmoil, and reinforcement of the East India Company's troops with British soldiers, the British overcame the rebellion (Majumdar, 1963; Gopal, 1965).

The nominal leader of the uprising, the last Mughal emperor Bahadur Shah Zafar, was exiled to Burma, his children were beheaded and the Mughal line abolished. In the aftermath all power was transferred from the East India Company to the British Crown, which began to administer most of India as a colony; the Company's lands were controlled directly and the rest through the rulers of what it called the Princely states. There were 565 princely states when the Indian subcontinent became independent from Britain in August 1947.

References

Allan, J. T., Wolseley Haig, and H. H. Dodwell (1934), *The Cambridge Shorter History of India*.

Andrews, Kenneth R. (1984) *Trade, Plunder and Settlement: Maritime Enterprise and the Genesis of the British Empire, 1480–1630.*

Brendon, Piers (2008) *The Decline and Fall of the British Empire, 1781-1997* (2008)

Chand, Tara (1961), *History of the Freedom Movement in India*, Vol. I, New Delhi: Publications Division.

Chandra, Bipan *et al.* (1972), *Freedom Struggle*, New Delhi: National Book Trust.

Chandra, Bipan *et al.* (1989), India's Struggle for Independence, New Delhi: Penguin Books.

Dutt, R. C. (1976), *Economic History of India* (Under Early British Rule, 1757-1857), Vol. I, Delhi: Publications Division.

Gopal, S. (1965), *British Policy in India, 1858-1905*, London: Cambridge University Press.

Majumdar, R. C. (1951), *The History and Culture of the Indian People, New York: The Macmillan Co.*

Majumdar, R.C. (1963), *History of the Freedom Movement in India*, Vol. II, Calcutta: Firma K.L. Mukhopadhyay.

Krishna Reddy (2003), *Indian History*, New Delhi: Tata McGraw Hill.

Rothermund, Dietmar (1993), *An Economic History of India: From Pre-Colonial Times to 1991*.

Smith, Vincent (1981), *The Oxford History of India,* London: Oxford University Press.

Spear, Percival (1990), *The History of India,* Vol. 2, London: Oxford University Press.

Notes

1. "Mudur, G.S (March 21, 2005), "Still a mystery", *KnowHow* (The Telegraph) and "The Hathnora Skull Fossil from Madhya Pradesh, India", *Multi Disciplinary Geoscientific Studies. Geological Survey of India.* 20 September 2005.
2. Gaur, A. S.; K. H. Vora (July 10, 1999), "Ancient shorelines of Gujarat, India, during the Indus civilization (Late Mid-Holocene): A study based on archaeological evidences", *Current India Science* 77 (1): 180–185.
3. Murray, Tim (1999). *Time and archaeology*. London; New York: Routledge. pp. 84.
4. Possehl, G. L. (October 1990), "Revolution in the Urban Revolution: The Emergence of Indus Urbanization", *Annual Review of Anthropology,* 19: 261–282 and Kenoyer, Jonathan Mark; Kimberley Heuston (May 2005), *The Ancient South Asian World*. Oxford University Press.
5. Feuerstein, George; Subhash Kak; David Frawley (1995), *In search of the cradle of civilization: New light on ancient India*. Wheaton, Illinois: Quest Books. pp. 147 and Kenoyer, J. Mark (1998), *The Ancient Cities of the Indus Valley Civilization,* Oxford University Press.

6. *Indian Archaeology: A Review.* 1958-1959 Excavations at Alamgirpur, Delhi: Archaeological Survey of India, pp. 51–52 and Kenoyer, Jonathan (15 September 1998), *Ancient Cities of the Indus Valley Civilization,* USA: Oxford University Press. pp. p. 96.
7. Krishna Reddy (2003), *Indian History*, New Delhi: Tata McGraw Hill.
8. Krishna Reddy (2003), *Indian History,* New Delhi: Tata McGraw Hill, pp.A 107
9. Mary Pat Fisher (1997), In: Living Religions: An Encyclopedia of the World's Faiths I.B.Tauris : London- *Jainism's major teacher is the Mahavira, a contemporary of the Buddha, and who died approximately 526 BCE, Page 114.*
10. Mary Pat Fisher (1997), In: Living Religions: An Encyclopedia of the World's Faiths I.B.Tauris : London *"The extreme antiquity of Jainism as a non-vedic, indigenous Indian religion is well documented. Ancient Hindu and Buddhist scriptures refer to Jainism as an existing tradition which began long before Mahavira", Page 115.*
11. Fuller, J.F.C. (February 3, 2004). "Alexander's Great Battles". *The Generalsb-p of Alexander the Great* (Reprint ed.). New York: Da Capo Press. pp. 188–199
12. Miller, J. Innes. (1969), *The Spice Trade of The Roman Empire*: 29 B.C. to A.D. 641, Oxford University Press. Special edition for Sandpiper Books, 1998.
13. Prakash, Om, "The Transformation from a Pre-Colonial to a Colonial Order: The Case of India" (PDF), *Global Economic History Network,* Economic History Department, London School of Economics, 3–40.

Chapter- 3

The Coming of European Colonialism in India

This chapter is primarily devoted to the discussion on arrival of Europeans in the Indian subcontinent and the process of expansion of their rule or empire. In addition, it also deals with the process of integration of princely states in India till 1947-48.

Colonial India

Portuguese India	1502-1961
Dutch India	1605-1825
Danish India	1696-1869
French India	1759-1954
British Empire in India	
East India Company	1612-1757
Company rule in India	1757-1857
British Raj	1858-1947
British rule in Burma	1826-1948
British India	1612-1947
Princely states	1765-1947
Partition of India	1947

The Portuguese— The colonial era in India began in 1502, when the Portuguese established the first European trading centre at Kollam in the present day Kerala. The closing of traditional trade routes in western Asia by the Ottomans and rivalry with the Italian states set Portugal in search of an alternate sea route to India. The first successful voyage to India was by Vasco da Gama in 1498, when he arrived in Calicut. Rivalry between

European powers saw the entry of the Dutch, British and French among others from the beginning of the 17th century.

In 1498 the Portuguese were the first European to set foot in India, landing near the city of Calicut in the present-day State of Kerala in South India. The pursuit of trade and competition between European powers saw the entry of the British and French, among others, into India. The fractured, debilitated kingdoms of the Indian subcontinent were gradually taken over by the Europeans or indirectly controlled by puppet rulers. By the 19th century, the British had assumed direct and indirect control over most of India.

The Portuguese established a chain of outposts along India's west coast and on the island of Ceylon in the early 16th century. They built the St. Angelo Fort at Kannur to guard their possessions in North Malabar. Goa was their prized possession and, the seat of Portugal's viceroy who governed Portugal's empire in Asia. Portugal's northern province included settlements at Daman, Diu, Chaul, Baçaim, Salsette, and Mumbai. Bombay (Mumbai) was given to the British crown in 1661 as part of the dowry of Catherine of Braganza. The rest of the northern province, with the exception of Daman and Diu, was lost to the Marathas in the early 18th century. Dadra and Nagar Haveli were acquired by the Portuguese in 1779. Dadra and Nagar Haveli were occupied by the Republic of India in 1954, and Goa, Daman, and Diu were annexed to India in 1961.

The Dutch—The Dutch East India Company established trading posts on different parts along the Indian coast. For some while, they controlled the Malabar southwest coast (Cranganore/Cranganor/Kodungallor, Cochin de Cima/Pallipuram, Cochin, Cochin de Baixo/Santa Cruz, Quilon (Coylan), Cannanore, Kundapura, Kayankulam, Ponnani) and the Coromandel southeastern coast (Golkonda, Bimilipatnam, Jaggernaikpoeram/Kakinada, Palikol, Pulicat, Porto Novo/Parangippettai, Negapatnam) and Surat (1616-1795). They conquered Ceylon, nowadays Sri Lanka (1658-1796), from the Portuguese. The Dutch also established trading stations in Travancore and coastal Tamil Nadu as well as at Rajshahi in present-day Bangladesh, Pipely, Hugli-Chinsura, and Murshidabad in present-day West Bengal, Balasore (Baleshwar or Bellasoor) in Orissa, and Ava, Arakan, and Syriam in present-day Myanmar Burma). Ceylon was lost at the Congress of Vienna in the aftermath of the Napoleonic Wars, where the Dutch having fallen subject to France, saw their colonies raided by Britain. The Dutch later became less involved in India, as they had the Dutch East Indies (now Indonesia) as their prized possession.

The French— Following the Portuguese, British, and Dutch, the French also established trading bases in India. Their first establishment is in Pondicherry on the Coromandel Coast in southeastern India, in 1674. Subsequent French settlements are Chandernagore in Bengal, northeastern India in 1688, Yanam in Andhra Pradesh in 1723, Mahe in 1725, and Karaikal in 1739. The French were constantly in conflict with the Dutch, and later on mainly with the British in India. At the height of French power in the mid-18th century, the French occupied most of southern India and the area lying in today's northern Andhra Pradesh (including State of Telangana) and Orissa. Between 1744 and 1761, the British and the French repeatedly attacked and conquered each others forts and towns, in south-eastern India, and in Bengal in the northeast. After some initial French successes, the British decisively defeated the French in Bengal in the Battle of Plassey in 1757, and in the southeast in 1761 in the Battle of Wandiwash, after which the British East India Company was the supreme military and political power in Southern India as well as in Bengal. In the following decades it gradually increased the size of the territories under its control. The enclaves of Pondicherry, Karaikal, Yanam, Mahé and Chandernagore were returned to France in 1816, and were integrated with the Republic of India after its independence in 1947.

Danish and other external powers— Denmark was a minor colonial power to set foot in India. It established trading outposts in Tranquebar, Tamil Nadu (1620), Serampore, West Bengal (1755) and the Nicobar Islands (1750s). At one time, the main Danish and Swedish East Asia companies together imported more tea to Europe than the British did. Their outposts lost economic and strategic importance, and Tranquebar, the last Danish outpost, was sold to the British in 1845. Other colonial nations such as Belgium, Italy and Germany did not set foot in India. The Spanish did not have territorial rights to India due to the Line of Demarcation drawn by Pope Alexander VI in 1493 with the *Bull Inter caetera*, ceding the eastern hemisphere to Portugal. The Japanese briefly occupied the Andaman and Nicobar Islands during World War II.

The British in India

In 1600, Queen Elizabeth I of England accorded a charter, forming the East India Company to trade with India and eastern Asia. The British landed in India in Surat in 1612. Permission was granted by the ruling sovereign, Jehangir, to open up outposts in Calcutta and Madras. The British soon took advantage of their position by actively supporting the kingdoms militarily and gradually entering their politics. In the period 1740-1763, when England and France are also at war in Europe (Seven Years' War) and North America (French and Indian Wars), the British and the French fight the Carnatic Wars in India on the behalf of the Indian rulers. During the last of these wars, Robert Clive decisively defeated the French and greatly extended British rule. By early 19th century, the French were almost defeated and the British East India Company indirectly ruled most of India through puppet kings. In 1857, an insurrection in the army sepoys ensued in the popular Revolt of 1857 (Sepoy Mutiny). This mobilised resistance, though short-lasting, was caused due to the widespread resentment due to British discriminatory and religious policies. As a result of this, India formally became a crown possession. At the height of British power in the closing part of the 19th century, the British Empire stretched from Burma (now Myanmar) to Afghanistan, covering almost the entire undivided Indian subcontinent consisting of modern day India, Pakistan and Bangladesh. Areas also under occupation were Bhutan (for a short period) and Ceylon (now Sri Lanka). The British rule in India ended with the independence of India and Pakistan in 1947.

In 1757, Mir Jafar, the commander in chief of the army of the Nawab of Bengal, secretly connived with the British, asking logistic support to overthrow the Nawab in return for trade grants. The British forces, whose sole duty until then was guarding their British East India Company property, were numerically inferior to the Bengali armed forces. At the Battle of Plassey on 23 June 1757, fought between the British under the command of and the Nawab, Mir Jafar's forces betrayed the Nawab and helped defeat him. Jafar was installed on the throne as a British subservient ruler (Stanley, 1989: 180). The battle transformed British perspective as they realized their strength and potential to conquer smaller Indian kingdoms, and marked the beginning of the imperial or colonial era.

Company Rule, 1757-1857

Although the British East India Company had *administered* its factory areas in India—beginning with Surat early in the 17th century, and including by the century's end, Fort William near Calcutta, Fort St George in Madras and the Bombay Castle—its victory in the Battle of Plassey in 1757 marked the real beginning of the Company rule in India. The victory was consolidated in 1764 at the Battle of Buxar (in Bihar), when the defeated Mughal emperor, Shah Alam II, granted the Company the *Diwani* ("right to collect land-revenue") in Bengal, Bihar, and Orissa. The Company soon expanded its territories around its bases in Bombay and Madras. The Anglo-Mysore Wars (1766–1799) and the Anglo-Maratha Wars (1772–1818) gave it control over most of India south of the Narmada River.

Earlier, in 1773, the British Parliament granted regulatory control over East India Company to the British government and established the post of Governor-General of India, with Warren Hastings as the first incumbent. In 1784, the British Parliament passed Pitt's India Act which created a Board of Control for overseeing the administration of East India Company. Hastings was succeeded in 1784 by Cornwallis, who promulgated the 'Permanent Settlement of Bengal' with the zamindars.

A multiplicity of motives underlay the British penetration into India: commerce, security, and a purported moral uplift of the people. The "expansive force" of private and Company trade eventually led to the conquest or annexation of territories in which spices, cotton, and opium were produced. British investors ventured into the unfamiliar interior landscape in search of opportunities that promised substantial profits. British economic penetration was aided by Indian collaborators, such as the bankers and merchants who controlled intricate credit networks. British rule in India would have been a frustrated or half-realized dream had not Indian counterparts provided connections between rural and urban centres. External threats, both real and imagined, such as the Napoleonic Wars (1796-1815) and Russian expansion toward Afghanistan (in the 1830s), as well as the desire for internal stability, led to the annexation of more territory in India.

Political analysts in Britain wavered initially as they were uncertain of the costs or the advantages in undertaking wars in India, but by the 1810s, as the territorial aggrandizement eventually paid off, opinion in London welcomed the absorption of new areas. Occasionally the British Parliament witnessed heated debates against expansion, but arguments justifying military operations for security reasons always won over even the most vehement critics.

At the turn of the 19th century, Governor-General Wellesley began what became two decades of accelerated expansion of Company territories (Ramusack, 2004). This was achieved either by *subsidiary alliances* between the Company and local rulers or by direct military annexation. The subsidiary alliances created the Princely States (or *Native States*) of the Hindu Maharajas and the Muslim Nawabs, prominent among which were: Cochin (1791), Jaipur (1794), Travancore (1795), Hyderabad (1798), Mysore (1799), Cis-Sutlej Hill States (1815), Central India Agency (1819), Kutch and Gujarat Gaikwad territories (1819), Rajputana (1818), and Bahawalpur (1833). The annexed regions included the *North Western Provinces* (comprising Rohilkhand, Gorakhpur, and the Doab) (1801), Delhi (1803), and Sindh (1843). Punjab, Northwest Frontier Province, and Kashmir, were annexed after the Anglo-Sikh Wars in 1849; however, Kashmir was immediately sold under the Treaty of Amritsar (1850) to the Dogra Dynasty of Jammu, and thereby became a princely state. In 1854 Berar was annexed, and the state of Oudh two years later (Ludden, 2002: 133).

The East India Company also signed treaties with various Afghan rulers and with Ranjit Singh of Lahore to counterbalance the Russian support of Persia's plans in western Afghanistan. In 1839, the Company's effort to more actively support Shah Shuja as *Amir* in Afghanistan, led to the First Afghan War (1839-42) and resulted in a military disaster for it. As the British expanded their territory in India, so did Russia in Central Asia with the taking of Bukhara and Samarkand in 1863 and 1868 respectively, and thereby setting the stage for the Great Game of Central Asia.

The British soon forgot their own rivalry with the Portuguese and the French and permitted them to stay in their coastal enclaves, which they kept even after independence in 1947. The British, however, continued to expand vigorously well into the 1850s. A number of aggressive governors-generals undertook relentless campaigns against several Hindu and Muslim rulers. Among them were Richard Colley Wellesley (1798-1805), William Pitt Amherst (1823-28), George Eden (1836-42), Edward Law (1842-44), and James Andrew Brown Ramsay (1848-56; also known as the Marquess of Dalhousie). Despite desperate efforts at salvaging their tottering power and keeping the British at bay, many Hindu and Muslim rulers lost their territories: Mysore (1799, but later restored), the Maratha Confederacy (1818), and Punjab (1849). The British success in large measure was the result not only of their superiority in tactics and weapons but also of their ingenious relations with Indian rulers through the "subsidiary alliance" system, introduced in the early nineteenth century. Many rulers bartered away their real responsibilities by agreeing to uphold British paramountcy in India, while they retained a fictional sovereignty under the rubric of Pax Britannica. Later, Dalhousie espoused the "doctrine of lapse" and annexed outright the estates of deceased princes of Satara (1848), Udaipur (1852), Jhansi (1853), Tanjore (1853), Nagpur (1854), and Oudh (1856).

European perceptions of India, and those of the British especially, shifted from unequivocal appreciation to sweeping condemnation of India's past achievements and customs. Imbued with an ethnocentric sense of superiority, British intellectuals, including Christian missionaries, spearheaded a movement that sought to bring Western intellectual and technological innovations to Indians. Interpretations of the causes of India's cultural and spiritual "backwardness" varied, as did the solutions. Many argued that it was Europe's mission to civilize India and hold it as a trust until Indians proved themselves competent for self-rule.

Indian Rebellion of 1857

The rebellion began with mutinies by *sepoys* of the Bengal Presidency Army; in 1857 the Presidency consisted of present-day Bangladesh, and the Indian states of West Bengal, Bihar and UP. However, most rebel soldiers were from the UP region *Northwest Provinces* (especially, Ganga-Jumna Doab) and Oudh, and many came from landowning families. Within weeks of the initial mutinies—as the rebel soldiers wrested control of many urban garrisons from the British—the rebellion was joined by various discontented groups in the hinterlands, in both farmed areas and the backwoods. The latter group, forming the *civilian rebellion*, consisted of feudal nobility, landlords, peasants, rural merchants, and some tribal groups (Metcalf and Metcalf, 2006: 101).

After the annexation of Oudh by the East India Company in 1856, many sepoys were unhappy on account of losing their perquisites as landed gentry in the Oudh courts and also for fear of rise in land-revenue payments that the annexation might cause. Some Indian soldiers, misreading the presence of missionaries as a sign of official intent, were persuaded that the East India Company was masterminding mass conversions of Hindus and Muslims to Christianity. Changes in the terms of their professional service may also have created resentment. As the extent of British jurisdiction expanded with British victories in wars and with annexation of territory, the soldiers were now not only expected to serve in less familiar regions (such as Lower Burma after the Second Burmese War in 1852-53), but also make do without the "foreign service," remuneration that had previously been their due (Bandyopadhyay 2004: 171).

The civilian rebellion was more multifarious in origin. The rebels consisted of three groups: feudal nobility, rural landlords called *taluqdars*, and the peasants. The nobility, many of whom had lost titles and domains under the Doctrine of Lapse, which derecognised adopted children of princes as legal heirs, felt that the British had interfered with a traditional system of inheritance. Rebel leaders such as Nana Sahib and the Rani of Jhansi belonged to this group; the latter, for example, was prepared to accept British paramountcy if her adopted son was recognized as the heir. The second group, the *taluqdars* had lost half their landed estates to peasant farmers as a result of the land reforms that came in the wake of annexation of Oudh. As the rebellion gained ground, the *taluqdars* quickly reoccupied the lands they had lost, and paradoxically, in part due to ties of kinship and feudal loyalty, did not experience significant opposition from the peasant farmers, many of whom too now joined the rebellion to the great dismay of the British. Heavy land-revenue assessment in some areas by the British may have resulted in many landowning families either losing their land or going into great debt with money lenders, and providing ultimately a reason to rebel; money lenders, in addition to the British, were particular objects of the rebels' animosity. The civilian rebellion was also highly uneven in its geographic distribution, even in areas of north-central India that were no longer under British control. For example, the relatively prosperous Muzaffarnagar district, a beneficiary of a British irrigation scheme, and next door to Meerut where the upheaval began, stayed mostly calm throughout (Brown 1994: 92).

Effects on Economy

In the second half of the 19th century, both the direct administration of India by the British crown and the technological change ushered in by the industrial revolution, had the effect of closely intertwining the economies of India and Great Britain (Stein, 2001: 259).

In fact many of the major changes in transport and communications (that are typically associated with Crown Rule of India) had already begun before the Mutiny. Since Dalhousie had embraced the technological change then rampant in Great Britain, India too saw rapid development of all those technologies. Railways, roads, canals, and bridges were rapidly built in India and telegraph links equally rapidly established in order that raw materials, such as cotton, from India's hinterland could be transported more efficiently to ports, such as Bombay, for subsequent export to England. Likewise, finished goods from England were transported back just as efficiently, for sale in the burgeoning Indian markets (Oldenburg, 2007). However, unlike Britain itself, where the market risks for the infrastructure development were borne by private investors, in India, it was the taxpayers—primarily farmers and farm-labourers—who endured the risks, which, in the end, amounted to £50 million. In spite of these costs, very little skilled employment was created for Indians. By 1920, with the fourth largest railway network in the world and a history of 60 years of its construction, only ten percent of the "superior posts" in the Indian Railways were held by Indians. The Indian railways system, by 1900, provided India with social savings of 9% of India's national income (about 1.2 billion rupees).

The rush of technology was also changing the agricultural economy in India: by the last decade of the 19th century, a large fraction of some raw materials—not only cotton, but also some food-grains—were being exported to faraway markets. Consequently, many small farmers, dependent on the whims of those markets, lost land, animals, and equipment to money-lenders.[1] More tellingly, the latter half of the 19th century also saw an increase in the number of large-scale famines in India. Although famines were not new to the subcontinent, these were particularly severe, with tens of millions dying, and with many critics, both British and Indian, laying the blame at the doorsteps of the lumbering colonial administrations.[2]

Taxes in India decreased during the colonial period for most of India's population; with the land tax revenue claiming 15% of India's national income during Mogul times compared with 1% at the end of the colonial period. The percentage of national income for the village economy increased from 44% during Mogul times to 54% by the end of colonial period. India's per capita GDP decreased from $550 in 1700 to $520 by 1857, although it had increased to $618 by 1947.[3]

British India and the Native States

There were as many as 568 states in India before independence. A Princely State (also called Native State or Indian State) was a *nominally sovereign* entity of British rule in India that was not directly administered by the British, but rather by an Indian ruler under a form of indirect rule such as suzerainty or paramountcy (Ramusack, 2004: 57-59).

India under the British *Raj* or the British Indian Empire consisted of two divisions: British India and the *Native States* or ***Princely states***. In its Interpretation Act of 1889, the British Parliament adopted the following definitions (Copland, 1997: 15-16).

The expression *British India* shall mean all territories and places within Her Majesty's dominions which are for the time being governed by Her Majesty through the Governor-General of India, or through any Governor or other officer subordinate to the Governor-General of India. The expression *India* shall mean British India together with any territory of a Native Prince or Chief under the suzerainty of Her Majesty, exercised through the Governor-General of India, or through any Governor or other officer subordinate to the Governor-General of India (52 & 53 Vict. cap. 63, sec. 18). In general the term "British India" had been used (and is still used) to also refer to the regions under the rule of the British East India Company in India from 1600 to 1858. The term has also been used to refer to the "British in India."

Suzerainty over 175 Princely States, some of the largest and most important, was exercised (in the name of the British Crown) by central government of British India under the Viceroy; the remaining, approximately 500, states were dependents of the provincial governments of British India under a Governor, Lieutenant-Governor, or Chief Commissioner (as the case might have been). A clear distinction between "dominion" and "suzerainty" was supplied by the jurisdiction of the courts of law: the law of British India rested upon the laws passed by the British Parliament and the legislative powers those laws vested in the various governments of British India, both central and local; in contrast, the courts of the Princely States existed under the authority of the respective rulers of those states (Ashton, 1982: 29-57).

Princely status and titles— The Indian rulers bore various titles— including Maharaja ("great king"), Badshah ("emperor"), Raja ("king"), Nawab ("governor"), Nizam, Wâli, and many others. Whatever the literal meaning and traditional prestige of the ruler's actual title, the British government translated them all as "prince," in order to avoid the implication that the native rulers could be "kings" with status equal to that of the British monarch. Some Hindu rulers used the title Thakur or its variant Thakore.

More prestigious Hindu rulers (mostly existing before the Mughal Empire, or having split from such old states) often used the title "Raja," or a variant such as "Rana," "Rao," "Rawat" or "Rawal." Also in this 'class' were several Thakur sahibs and a few particular titles, such as Sar Desai.

The most prestigious Hindu rulers usually had the prefix "maha" ("great", compare for example Grand duke) in their titles, as in *Maharaja, Maharana, Maharao*, etc. The states of Travancore and Cochin had queens regnant styled Maharani, generally the female forms applied only to sisters, spouses and widows, who could however act as regents.

There were also compound titles, such as (Maha)rajadhiraj, Raj-i-rajgan, often relics from an elaborate system of hierarchical titles under the Mughal emperors. For example, the addition of the adjective *Bahadur* raised the status of the titleholder one level.

Furthermore most dynasties used a variety of additional titles, such as Varma in South India. This should not be confused with various titles and suffixes not specific to princes but used by entire (sub) castes.

The Sikh princes concentrated at Punjab, usually adopted Hindu type titles when attaining princely rank; at a lower level Sardar was used.

Muslim rulers almost all used the title "Nawab" (the Arabic honorific of *naib*, "deputy," used of the Mughal governors, who became de facto autonomous with the decline of the Mughal Empire), with the prominent exceptions of the Nizam of Hyderabad & Berar, the Wâli/Khan of Kalat and the Wâli of Swat. Other less usual titles included Darbar Sahib, Dewan, Jam, Mehtar (unique to Chitral) and Mir (from Emir).

Precedence and prestige— However, the actual importance of a princely state cannot be read from the title of its ruler, which was usually granted (or at least recognised) as a favour, often in recognition for loyalty and services rendered historically by the Mughal emperor, and later by the British rulers succeeding it as paramount power (first the HEIC, de facto; later the British crown, and ultimately assuming the style Emperor of India as successor to the emperor of the abolished Mughal realm). Although some titles were raised once or even repeatedly, there was no automatic updating when a state gained or lost real power. In fact, princely titles were even awarded to holders of domains (mainly jagirs) and even zamindars (tax Collectors), which were not states at all. Various sources give significantly different numbers of states and domains of the various types. Even in general, the definition of titles and domains are clearly not well-established. There is also no strict relation between the levels of the titles and the classes of gun salutes, the real measure of precedence, but merely a growing percentage of higher titles in classes with more guns.

The gun salute system was used to set unambiguously the precedence of the major rulers in the area in which the British East India Company was active, or generally of the states and their dynasties. Princely rulers were entitled to be saluted by the firing of an odd number of guns between three and 21, with a greater number of guns indicating greater prestige. (There were many minor rulers who were not entitled to any gun salutes, and as a rule the majority of gun-salute princes had at least nine, with numbers below that usually the prerogative of Arab coastal Sheikhs also under British protection.) Generally, the number of guns remained the same for all successive rulers of a particular state, but individual princes were sometimes granted additional guns on a personal basis. Furthermore, rulers were sometimes granted additional gun salutes within their own territories only, constituting a semi-promotion.

While the states of all these rulers (about 120) were known as salute states, there were far more so-called non-salute states of lower prestige, and even more princes (in the broadest sense of the term) not even acknowledged as such. On the other hand, the dynasties of certain defunct states were allowed to keep their princely status — they were known as Political Pensioners. Though none of these princes were awarded gun salutes, princely titles in this category were recognized as among certain vassals of salute states, and were not even in direct relation with the paramount power.

After independence, the (Hindu) Maharana of Udaipur displaced the Nizam of Hyderabad as the most senior prince in India, and the style *Highness* was extended to all rulers entitled to 9-gun salutes. When these dynasties had been integrated into the Indian Union they were promised continued privileges and an income, known as the Privy Purse, for their upkeep. Subsequently, when the Indian government abolished the Privy Purse in 1971, the whole princely order ceased to exist under Indian law, although many families continue to retain their social prestige informally; some descendants are still prominent in regional or national politics, diplomacy, business and high society.

At the time of Indian independence, only five rulers— the Nizam of Hyderabad, the Maharaja of Mysore, the Maharaja of Jammu and Kashmir state, the Maharaja Gaekwad of Baroda and the Maharaja Scindia of Gwalior— were entitled to a 21-gun salute. Five more rulers— the Nawab of Bhopal, the Maharaja Holkar of Indore, the Maharana of Udaipur, the Maharaja of Kolhapur and the Maharaja of Travancore— were entitled to 19-gun salutes. The most senior princely ruler was the (Muslim) Nizam of Hyderabad, who was entitled to the unique style *Exalted Highness*. Other princely rulers entitled to salutes of 11 guns (soon 9 guns too) or more were entitled to the style *Highness*. No special style was used by rulers entitled to lesser gun salutes.

As **paramount ruler,** and successor to the Mughals, the British *King-Emperor* of India, for whom the style of Majesty was reserved, was entitled to an 'imperial' 101-gun salute— in the European tradition also the number of guns fired to announce the birth of a (male) heir to the throne.

All princely rulers were eligible to be appointed to certain British orders of chivalry associated with India, The Most Exalted Order of the Star of

India and The Most Eminent Order of the Indian Empire. Even women could be appointed as "Knights" (instead of Dames) of these orders. Rulers entitled to 21-gun and 19-gun salutes were normally appointed to the highest rank possible (Knight Grand Commander of the Order of the Star of India).

Many Indian princes served in the British army (as others in local guard or police forces), often rising to the high official ranks; some even served while on the throne. Many of these were appointed as ADC etc., either to the ruling prince of their own house (in the case of relatives of such rulers) or indeed to the British King-Emperor. Many also saw action, both on the subcontinent and on other fronts, during both World Wars.

It was also not unusual for members of princely houses to be appointed to various colonial offices, often far from their native state, or to enter the diplomatic corps.

Organisation of British India: Native States

Following the Indian Rebellion of 1857, the Act for the Better Government of India (1858) made changes in the governance of India at three levels: in the imperial government in London, in the central government in Calcutta, and in the provincial governments in the presidencies (and later in the provinces).

In London, it provided for a cabinet-level Secretary of State for India and a fifteen-member Council of India, whose members were required, as one prerequisite of membership, to have spent at least ten years in India and to have done so no more than ten years before. Although the Secretary of State formulated the policy instructions to be communicated to India, he was required in most instances to consult the Council, but especially so in matters relating to spending of Indian revenues. The Act envisaged a system of "double government" in which the Council ideally served both as a check on excesses in imperial policy-making and as a body of up-to-date expertise on India. However, the Secretary of State also had special emergency powers that allowed him to make unilateral decisions, and, in reality, the Council's expertise was sometimes outdated. From 1858 until 1947, twenty seven individuals would serve as Secretary of State for India and direct the India Office; these included: Sir Charles Wood (1859-1866), Marquess of Salisbury (1874-1878) (later three time Prime Minister of Britain), John Morley (1905- 1910) (initiator of the Minto-Morley Reforms), E. S. Montagu (1917-1922) (an architect of the Montagu-Chelmsford reforms), and Frederick Pethick-Lawrence (1945-1947) (head of the 1946 Cabinet

Mission to India). The size of the advisory Council would be reduced over the next half-century, but its powers would remain unchanged; in 1907, for the first time, two Indians would be appointed to the Council.

In Calcutta, the Governor-General remained head of the Government of India and now was more commonly called the Viceroy on account of his secondary role as the Crown's representative to the nominally sovereign princely states; he was, however, now responsible to the Secretary of State in London and through him to British Parliament. A system of "double government" had already been in place in the East India Company rule in India from the time of Pitt's India Act of 1784. The Governor-General in the capital, Calcutta, and the Governor in a subordinate presidency (Madras or Bombay) was each required to consult his advisory council; executive orders in Calcutta, for example, were issued in the name of "Governor-General-in-Council" (i.e., the Governor-General with the advice of the Council). The Company's system of "double government" had its critics, since, from the time of the system's inception, there had been intermittent feuding between the Governor-General and his Council; still, the Act of 1858 made no major changes in governance. However, in the years immediately thereafter, which were also the years of post-rebellion reconstruction, the Viceroy Lord Canning found the collective decision-making of the Council to be too time-consuming for the pressing tasks ahead. He therefore requested the "portfolio system" of an *Executive Council* in which the business of each government department (the "portfolio") was assigned to and became the responsibility of a single Council member. Routine departmental decisions were made exclusively by the member, however, important decisions required the consent of the Governor-General and, in the absence such consent, required discussion by the entire Executive Council. This innovation in Indian governance was promulgated in the Indian Councils Act of 1861.

If the Government of India needed to enact new laws, the Councils Act allowed for a *Legislative Council*—an expansion of the Executive Council by up to twelve additional members, each appointed to a two-year term—with half the members consisting of British officials of the government (termed *official*) and allowed to vote, and the other half, comprising Indians and domiciled Britons in India (termed *non-official*) and serving only in an advisory capacity. All laws enacted by *Legislative Councils* in India, whether by the Imperial Legislative Council in Calcutta or by the provincial ones in Madras and Bombay, required the final assent of the Secretary of State in London; this prompted Sir Charles Wood, the second Secretary of State, to describe the Government of India as "a despotism controlled from home" (Moore, 2001: 426). Moreover, although the appointment of Indians to the Legislative Council was a response to calls after the 1857 rebellion, most notably by Sir Sayyid Ahmad Khan, for more consultation with Indians, the Indians so appointed were from the landed aristocracy, often chosen for their loyalty, and far from representative. Even so, the "tiny advances in the practise of representative government were intended to provide safety valves for the expression of public opinion which had been so badly misjudged before the rebellion" (Bayly, 1990: 195). Indian affairs now also came to be more closely examined in the British parliament and more widely discussed in the British press.

Although the Great Uprising of 1857 had shaken the British rule in India, it had not derailed it. After the rebellion, the British became more circumspect. Much thought was devoted to the causes of the rebellion, and from it three main lessons were drawn. At a more practical level, it was felt that there needed to be more communication and camaraderie between the British and Indians; not just between British army officers and their Indian staff, but in civilian life as well. The Indian army was completely reorganised: units composed of the Muslims and Brahmins of the United Provinces of Agra and Oudh, who had formed the core of the rebellion, were disbanded. New regiments, like the Sikhs and Baluchis, composed of Indians who, in British estimation, had demonstrated steadfastness, were formed. From then on, the Indian army was to remain unchanged in its organisation until 1947 (Spear, 1990: 147-148).

It was also felt that both the princes and the large land-holders, by not joining the rebellion, had proved to be, in Lord Canning's words, "breakwaters in a storm." They too were rewarded in the new British Raj, by being officially recognised in the treaties each state now signed with the Crown. At the same time, it was felt that the peasants, for whose benefit the large land-reforms of the United Provinces had been undertaken, had shown disloyalty, by, in many cases, fighting for their former landlords against the British. Consequently, no more land reforms were implemented for the next 90 years: Bengal and Bihar were to remain the realms of large land holdings (unlike the Punjab and Uttar Pradesh) (Spear 1990: 147-148).

Lastly, the British felt disenchanted with Indian reaction to social change. Until the rebellion, they had enthusiastically pushed through social reform, like the ban on *sati* by Lord William Bentinck. It was now felt that traditions and customs in India were too strong and too rigid to be changed easily; consequently, no more British social interventions were made, especially in matters dealing with religion, even when the British felt very strongly about the issue (as in the instance of the remarriage of Hindu child widows).

The doctrine of lapse—A controversial aspect of Company rule was the doctrine of lapse, a policy under which lands whose feudal ruler had died (or otherwise become unfit to rule) without an heir would become directly controlled by the Company. This policy went counter to Indian tradition where unlike Europe it was far more the accepted norm for a ruler to appoint his own heir.

The doctrine of lapse was pursued most vigorously by the Governor-General Sir James Ramsay, 10th Earl (later 1st Marquess) of Dalhousie. Dalhousie annexed seven states, including the Maratha states of Nagpur, Jhansi, Satara and Awadh (Oudh), whose Nawabs he had accused of misrule. Resentment over the annexation of these states turned to indignation when the heirlooms of the Maharajas of Nagpur were auctioned off in Calcutta. Dalhousie's actions contributed to the rising discontent amongst the upper castes which played a large part in the outbreak of the Indian rebellion of 1857. The last Mughal Badshah (emperor), whom many of the mutineers saw as a figurehead to rally around, was deposed following its suppression.

In response to the unpopularity of the doctrine, it was discontinued with the end of Company rule and the formation of the Indian Empire, and no further states were absorbed in such a way.

Colonial governance— By the beginning of the 20th century, the four largest states— Hyderabad State, Mysore, Jammu and Kashmir, and Baroda— were directly under the authority of the Governor-General of India, in the person of a British Resident. Two agencies, Rajputana Agency and Central India Agency, oversaw 20 and 148 princely states, respectively. The remaining princely states had political officers, or Agents, who answered to the administrators of India's provinces. Five princely states were then under the authority of Madras, 354 under Bombay, 26 of Bengal, 2 under Assam, 34 under Punjab, 15 under Central Provinces and Berar and 2 under United Provinces.

By the early 1930s, the British took over the state whose king had died (Doctrine of Lapse). Most of the princely states under the authority of India's provinces were organised into new agencies, answerable to the Governor-general, on the model of the Central India—and Rajputana agencies: the Eastern States Agency, Punjab States Agency, Baluchistan Agency, Deccan States Agency, Madras States Agency and the Northwest Frontier States

Agency. The Baroda residency was combined with the princely states of northern Bombay Presidency into the Baroda, Western States and Gujarat Agency. Gwalior was separated from the Central India Agency and placed under its own Resident, and the states of Rampur and Benares, formerly under the authority of the United Provinces, were placed under the Gwalior Residency in 1936. The princely states of Sandur and Banganapalle in Mysore Presidency were transferred to the authority of the Mysore Resident in 1939.

Political Integration of India

The early history of British expansion in India was characterised by the co-existence of two approaches towards the existing princely states. The first was a policy of annexation, where the British sought to forcibly absorb the Indian princely states into the provinces which constituted their Empire in India. The second was a policy of indirect rule, where the British assumed suzerainty and paramountcy over princely states, but conceded some degree of sovereignty to them. During the early part of the nineteenth century, the policy of the British tended towards annexation, but the Indian Rebellion of 1857 forced a change in this approach, by demonstrating both the difficulty of absorbing and subduing annexed states, and the usefulness of princely states as a source of support. In 1858, the policy of annexation was formally renounced, and British relations with the princely states thereafter were based on indirect rule, whereby the British exercised paramountcy over all princely states with the British crown as ultimate suzerain, but at the same time respected and protected them as allies. The exact relations between the British and each princely state were regulated by individual treaties, and varied widely, with some states having significant autonomy, some being subject to significant control in internal affairs, and some being in effect the owners of a few acres of land with little autonomy.

During the 20th century, the British made several attempts to integrate the princely states more closely with British India, creating the Chamber of Princes in 1921 as a consultative and advisory body, transferring the responsibility for supervision of smaller states from the provinces to the centre in 1936, and creating direct relations between the Government of India and the larger princely states superseding political agents. The most ambitious was a scheme of federation in the Government of India Act 1935, which envisaged the princely states and British India being united under a federal government. This scheme came close to success, but was abandoned in 1939 as a result of the outbreak of the Second World War. As a result, in the 1940s, the relationship between the princely states and the crown remained regulated by the principle of paramountcy and the various treaties between the British crown and the states (Ramusack, 1978).

Neither paramountcy nor these arrangements could continue after Indian independence. The British took the view that because they had been established directly between the British crown and the princely states, they could not be transferred to independent India. At the same time, they imposed obligations on Britain that it was not prepared to continue to carry out, such as the obligation to maintain troops in India for the defence of the princely states. The British government therefore decided that paramountcy, together with all treaties between them and the princely states, would come to an end upon the transfer of power (Copland, 1993: 387-388).

Reasons for integration— The termination of paramountcy would have in principle meant that all rights that flowed from the states' relationship with the British crown would return to them, leaving them free to negotiate relationships with the new states of India and Pakistan "on a basis of complete freedom". Early British plans for the transfer of power, such as the offer produced by the Cripps Mission, recognised the possibility that some princely states might choose to stand out of independent India. This was unacceptable to the Congress, which regarded the independence of princely states as a denial of the course of Indian history, and consequently regarded this scheme as a "Balkanization" of India. The Congress had traditionally been less active in the princely states because of their limited resources which restricted their ability to organise there and their focus on the goal of independence from the British, and because Congress leaders, in particular Gandhi, were sympathetic to the more progressive princes as examples of the capacity of Indians to rule themselves. This changed in the 1930s as a result of the federation scheme contained in the Government of India Act 1935 and the rise of socialist Congress leaders such as Jayaprakash Narayan, and the Congress began to actively engage with popular political and labour activity in the princely states. By 1939, the Congress' official stance was that the states must enter independent India, on the same terms and with the same autonomy as the provinces of British India, and with their people granted responsible government. As a result, it insisted on the incorporation of the princely states into India in its negotiations with Mountbatten (Moore, 1983).

A few British leaders, particularly Lord Mountbatten, the last British viceroy in India, were also uncomfortable with breaking links between independent India and the princely states. The development of trade, commerce and communications during the 19th and 20th centuries had bound the princely states to British India through a complex network of interests. Agreements relating to railways, customs, irrigation, the use of ports, and other similar agreements would disappear, posing a serious threat to the economic life of the subcontinent. Mountbatten was also persuaded by the argument of Indian leaders such as V. P. Menon that the integration of the princely states into independent India would to some extent assuage the wounds of partition. The result was that Mountbatten personally favoured and worked towards the accession of princely states to India following the transfer of power, as proposed by the Congress.

Accepting integration— The rulers of the princely states were not uniformly enthusiastic about integrating their domains into independent India. Some, such as the kings of Bikaner and Jawhar, were motivated to join India out of ideological and patriotic considerations, but others insisted that they had the right to join either India or Pakistan, to remain independent, or form a union of their own. Bhopal, Travancore and Hyderabad announced that they did not intend to join either dominion. Hyderabad went as far as to appoint trade representatives in European countries and commencing negotiations with the Portuguese to lease or buy Goa to give it access to the sea, and Travancore pointed to the strategic importance to western countries of its thorium reserves while asking for recognition. Some states proposed a subcontinent-wide confederation of princely states, as a third entity in addition to India and Pakistan. Bhopal attempted to build an alliance between the princely states and the Muslim League to counter the pressure being put on rulers by the Congress (Lumby 1954: 226-227; Copland, 1997).

A number of factors contributed to the collapse of this initial resistance and to nearly all princely states agreeing to accede to India. An important factor was the lack of unity among the princes. The smaller states did not trust the larger states to protect their interests, and many Hindu rulers did not trust Muslim princes, in particular Hamidullah Khan, the Nawab of Bhopal and a leading proponent of independence, whom they viewed as an agent for Pakistan. Others, believing integration to be inevitable, sought to build bridges with the Congress, hoping thereby to gain a say in shaping the final settlement. The resultant inability to present a united front or agree on a common position significantly reduced their bargaining power in negotiations with the Congress. The decision by the Muslim League to stay out of the Constituent Assembly was also fatal to the princes' plan to build an alliance with it to counter the Congress, and attempts to boycott the Constituent Assembly altogether failed on 28 April 1947, when the states of Baroda, Bikaner, Cochin, Gwalior, Jaipur, Jodhpur, Patiala and Rewa took their seats in the Assembly (Copland, 1997: 237).

Many princes were also pressured by popular sentiment favouring integration with India, which meant their plans for independence had little support from their subjects. The King of Travancore, for example, definitively abandoned his plans for independence after the attempted assassination of his dewan, Sir C. P. Ramaswamy Aiyar. In a few states, the chief ministers or dewans played a significant role in convincing the princes to accede to India. The key factors that led the states to accept integration into India were, however, the efforts of Lord Mountbatten, the last Viceroy of British India, and Vallabhbhai Patel and V. P. Menon, who were respectively the political and administrative heads of the Indian Government's States Department, which was in charge of relations with the princely states.

Mountbatten's role— Mountbatten believed that securing the states' accession to India was crucial to reaching a negotiated settlement with the Congress for the transfer of power. As a relative of the British Emperor, he was trusted by most of the princes and was a personal friend of many, especially the Nawab of Bhopal, Hamidullah Khan. The princes also believed that he would be in a position to ensure the independent India adhered to any terms that might be agreed upon, because Jawaharlal Nehru and Patel had asked him to become the first Governor General of the Dominion of India. Mountbatten used his influence with the princes to push them towards accession. He declared that the British Government would not grant dominion status to any of the princely states, nor would it accept them into the British Commonwealth, which meant that the states would sever all connections with the British crown unless they joined either India or Pakistan. He pointed out that the Indian subcontinent was one economic entity, and that the states would suffer most if the link was broken. He also pointed to the difficulties that princes would face maintaining order in the face of threats such as the rise of communal violence and communist movements.

Mountbatten stressed that he would act as the trustee of the princes' commitment, as he would be serving as India's head of state well into 1948. He engaged in a personal dialogue with reluctant princes, such as the Nawab of Bhopal, who he asked through a confidential letter to sign the Instrument of Accession making Bhopal part of India, which Mountbatten would keep locked up in his safe. It would be handed to the States Department on

15 August only if the Nawab did not change his mind before then, which he was free to do. The Nawab agreed, and did not renege over the deal (Gandhi 1991: 413-414).

At the time, several princes complained that they were being betrayed by Britain, who they regarded as an ally, and Sir Conrad Corfield resigned his position as head of the Political Department in protest at Mountbatten's policies. Mountbatten's policies were also criticised by the opposition Conservative Party. Winston Churchill compared the language used by the Indian government with that used by Adolf Hitler before the invasion of Austria. Modern historians such as Lumby and Moore, however, take the view that Mountbatten played a crucial role in ensuring that the princely states agreed to accede to India (Lumby 1954: 236; Moore, 1983: 347).

Pressure and diplomacy— Vallabhbhai Patel as Minister for Home and States Affairs had the responsibility of welding the British Indian provinces and the princely states into a united India. By far the most significant factor that led to the princes' decision to accede to India was the policy of the Congress and, in particular, of the two key figures in the States Department, Sardar Vallabhbhai Patel and V. P. Menon. The Congress' stated position was that the princely states were not sovereign entities, and as such could not opt to be independent notwithstanding the end of paramountcy. The princely states, it declared, must therefore accede to either India or Pakistan. In July 1946, Nehru pointedly observed that no princely state could prevail militarily against the army of independent India. In January 1947, he said that independent India would not accept the Divine Right of Kings, and in May 1947, he declared that any princely state which refused to join the Constituent Assembly would be treated as an enemy state. Other Congress leaders, such as C. Rajagopalachari, argued that as paramountcy "came into being as a fact and not by agreement", it would necessarily pass to the government of independent India, as the successors of the British (Lumby 1954: 218-219).

Patel and Menon, who were charged with the actual job of negotiating with the princes, took a more conciliatory approach than Nehru. The official policy statement of the Government of India made by Patel on 5 July 1947 made no threats. Instead, it emphasised the unity of India and the common interests of the princes and independent India, reassured them about the Congress' intentions, and invited them to join independent India "to make laws sitting together as friends than to make treaties as aliens" (Menon, 1956: 114). He reiterated that the States Department would not attempt to establish a relationship of domination over the princely states. Unlike the

Political Department of the British Government, it would not be an instrument of paramountcy, but a medium whereby business could be conducted between the states and India as equals.

Instruments of accession— Patel and Menon backed up their diplomatic efforts by producing treaties that were designed to be attractive to rulers of princely states. Two key documents were produced. The first was the Standstill Agreement, which confirmed that the agreements and administrative practices that existed as between the princely state in question and the British would be continued by India. The second was the Instruments of Accession, by which the ruler of the princely state in question agreed to the accession of his kingdom to independent India, and to granting India control over specified subject matters. The nature of the subject matters varied depending on the acceding state. The states which had internal autonomy under the British signed an Instrument of Accession which only ceded three subjects to the government of India—defence, external affairs, and communications, each defined in accordance with List 1 to Schedule VII of the Government of India Act 1935. Rulers of states which were in effect estates or talukas, where substantial administrative powers were exercised by the Crown, signed a different Instrument of Accession, which vested all residuary powers and jurisdiction in the government of India. Rulers of states which had an intermediate status signed a third type of Instrument, which preserved the degree of power they had under the British.

The Instruments of Accession implemented a number of other safeguards. Clause 7 provided that the princes would not be bound to the Indian constitution as and when it was drafted. Clause 8 guaranteed their autonomy in all areas in which authority was not expressly ceded to the Government of India. This was supplemented by a number of promises. Rulers who agreed to accede would receive guarantees that their extra-territorial rights, such as immunity from prosecution in Indian courts and exemption from customs duty, would be protected, that they would be allowed to democratize slowly, that none of the eighteen major states would be forced to merge, and that they would remain eligible for British honours and decorations. In discussions, Lord Mountbatten reinforced the statements of Patel and Menon by emphasizing that the documents gave the princes all the "practical independence" they needed. Mountbatten, Patel and Menon also sought to give princes the impression that if they did not accept the terms put to them then, they would subsequently have to accede on substantially less favourable terms. The Standstill Agreement was also used as a negotiating tool, as the States Department categorically ruled out signing a Standstill Agreement with princely states that did not sign an Instrument of Accession (Menon, 1956: 114).

The accession process— The limited scope of the Instruments of Accession and the promise of a wide-ranging autonomy and the other guarantees they offered, gave sufficient comfort to many rulers, who saw this as the best deal they could strike given the lack of support from the British, and popular internal pressures. Between May 1947 and the transfer of power on 15 August 1947, the vast majority of states signed Instruments of Accession. A few, however, held out. Some simply delayed signing the Instrument of Accession. Piploda, a small state in central India, did not accede until March 1948. The biggest problems, however, arose with a few border states, such as Jodhpur, which tried to negotiate better deals with Pakistan, with Junagadh, which actually did accede to Pakistan, and with Hyderabad and Kashmir, which declared that they intended to remain independent.

The ruler of Jodhpur, Hanwant Singh, was antipathetic to the Congress, and did not see much future in India for him or the lifestyle he wished to lead, and entered into negotiations with Jinnah, who was the designated head of state for Pakistan, along with the ruler of Jaisalmer. Jinnah was keen to attract some of the larger border states, hoping thereby to attract other Rajput states to Pakistan and compensate for the loss of half of Bengal and Punjab. He offered to permit Jodhpur and Jaisalmer to accede to Pakistan on any terms they chose, giving their rulers blank sheets of paper and asking them to write down their terms, which he would sign. Jaisalmer refused, arguing that it would be difficult for him to side with Muslims against Hindus in the event of communal problems. Hanwant Singh came close to signing. However, the atmosphere in Jodhpur was in general hostile to accession to Pakistan. Mountbatten also pointed out that the accession of a predominantly Hindu state to Pakistan would violate the principle of the two-nation theory on which Partition was based, and was likely to cause communal violence in the State. Hanwant Singh was persuaded by these arguments, and somewhat reluctantly agreed to accede to India (Copland, 1960: 260).

Although the states were in theory free to choose whether they wished to accede to India or Pakistan, Mountbatten had pointed out that "geographic compulsions" meant that most of them must choose India. In effect, he took the position that only the states that shared a border with Pakistan could choose to accede to it.

The Nawab of Junagadh, a princely state located on the south-western end of Gujarat and having no common border with Pakistan, chose to accede to Pakistan ignoring Mountbatten's views, arguing that it could be reached from Pakistan by sea. The rulers of two states that were subject to the suzerainty of Junagadh—Mangrol and Babariawad—reacted to this by declaring their independence from Junagadh and acceding to India. In response, the Nawab of Junagadh militarily occupied the states. The rulers of neighbouring states reacted angrily, sending their troops to the Junagadh frontier and appealed to the Government of India for assistance. A group of Junagadhi people, led by Samaldas Gandhi, formed a government-in-exile, the *Aarzi Hukumat* ("temporary government").

India believed that if Junagadh was permitted to go to Pakistan, the communal tension already simmering in Gujarat would worsen, and refused to accept the accession. The government pointed out that the state was 80% Hindu, and called for a plebiscite to decide the question of accession. Simultaneously, they cut off supplies of fuel and coal to Junagadh, severed air and postal links, sent troops to the frontier, and reoccupied the principalities of Mangrol and Babariawad that had acceded to India. Pakistan agreed to discuss a plebiscite, subject to the withdrawal of Indian troops, a condition India rejected. On 26 October, the Nawab and his family fled to Pakistan following clashes with Indian troops. On 7 November, Junagadh's court, facing collapse, invited the Government of India to take over the State's administration. The Government of India agreed. A plebiscite was conducted in February 1948, which went almost unanimously in favour of accession to India (Furber 1951: 359).

At the time of the transfer of power, Kashmir was ruled by Maharaja Hari Singh, a Hindu, although the state itself had a Muslim majority. Hari Singh was equally hesitant about acceding to either India or Pakistan, as either would have provoked adverse reactions in parts of his kingdom. He signed a Standstill Agreement with Pakistan and proposed one with India as well, but announced that Kashmir intended to remain independent. However, his rule was opposed by Sheikh Abdullah, the popular leader of Kashmir's largest political party, the National Conference, who demanded his abdication.

Pakistan, attempting to force the issue of Kashmir's accession, cut off supplies and transport links. The chaos in Punjab resulting from Partition had also severed transport links with India, meaning that Kashmir's only links with the two dominions was by air. Rumours about atrocities against the Muslim population of Poonch by the Maharajah's forces caused the outbreak of civil unrest. Shortly thereafter, Pathan tribesmen from the North-West Frontier Province of Pakistan crossed the border and entered Kashmir. The invaders made rapid progress towards Srinagar. The Maharaja of Kashmir wrote to India, asking for military assistance, offering an Instrument of Accession, and setting up an interim government headed by Sheikh Abdullah. The accession was accepted, but Nehru declared that it would have to be confirmed by a plebiscite, although there was no legal requirement to seek such confirmation (Potter 1950: 361).

Indian troops secured Jammu, Srinagar and the valley itself during the First Kashmir War, but the intense fighting flagged with the onset of winter, which made much of the state impassable. Prime Minister Nehru, in a move that baffled political and military strategists, declared a ceasefire and sought U.N. arbitration, arguing that India would otherwise have to invade Pakistan itself, in view of its failure to stop the tribal incursions. The plebiscite was never held, and on 26 January 1950, the Constitution of India came into force in Kashmir, but with special provisions made for it in the Constitution's Article 370. India did not, however, secure administrative control over all of Kashmir. The northern and western portions of Kashmir came under Pakistan's control in 1947, and are today referred to as 'Pakistan-Occupied Kashmir' by the Indian government. In the 1962 Sino-Indian War, China occupied Aksai Chin, the north-eastern region bordering Ladakh, which it continues to control and administer.

Hyderabad was a landlocked state that stretched over 82,000 square miles (over 212,000 square kilometres) in south-eastern India. While 87% of its 17 million people were Hindus, its ruler Nizam Osman Ali Khan was a Muslim, and its politics were dominated by a Muslim elite. The Muslim nobility and the Ittehad-ul-Muslimeen, a powerful pro-Nizam Muslim party, insisted that Hyderabad must remain an independent state and stand on an equal footing to India and Pakistan. Accordingly, the Nizam in June 1947 issued a *firman* announcing that on the transfer of power, his state would be resuming independence. The Government of India rejected the firman, terming it a "legalistic claim of doubtful validity". It argued that the strategic location of Hyderabad, which lay astride the main lines of communication between northern and southern India, meant it could easily be used by "foreign interests" to threaten India, and that in consequence, the issue involved India's peace and security. It also pointed out that the state's people, history and location made it unquestionably Indian, and that its own "common interests" therefore mandated its integration into India.

The Nizam was prepared to enter into a limited treaty with India, which gave Hyderabad safeguards not provided for in the standard Instrument of Accession, such as a provision guaranteeing Hyderabad's neutrality in the event of a conflict between India and Pakistan. India rejected this proposal, arguing that other states would demand similar concessions. A temporary Standstill Agreement was signed as a stopgap measure, even though Hyderabad had not yet agreed to accede to India. By December 1947, however, India was accusing Hyderabad of repeatedly violating the Agreement, while the Nizam alleged that India was blockading his state, a charge India denied (Talbot, 1949: 325-326).

The situation deteriorated further in 1948. The Razakars ("volunteers"), a militia affiliated to the Ittehad-ul-Muslimeen and set up under the influence of Muslim radical Qasim Razvi, assumed the role of supporting the Muslim ruling class against upsurges by the Hindu populace, and began intensifying its activities and was accused of attempting to intimidate villages. The Hyderabad State Congress Party, affiliated to the Indian National Congress, launched a political agitation. Matters were made worse by Communist groups, which had originally supported the Congress but now switched sides and began attacking Congress groups. Attempts by Mountbatten to find a negotiated solution failed and, in August, the Nizam, claiming that he feared an imminent invasion, attempted to approach the UN Security Council and the International Court of Justice. Patel now insisted that if Hyderabad was allowed to continue its independence, the prestige of the Government would be tarnished and then neither Hindus nor Muslims would feel secure in its realm. On 13 September, the Indian Army was sent into Hyderabad in Operation Polo on the ground that the law and order situation there threatened the peace of South India. The troops met little resistance and between 13 and 18 September took complete control of the state. The Nizam was retained as the head of state in the same manner as the other princes who acceded to India. He thereupon disavowed the complaints that had been made to the UN and, despite vehement protests from Pakistan and strong criticism from other countries, the Security Council did not deal further with the question, and Hyderabad was absorbed into India (Eagleton, 1949: 280; Talbot 1949: 326-327).

The Instruments of Accession were limited, transferring control of only three matters to India, and would by themselves have produced a rather loose federation, with significant differences in administration and governance across the various states. Full political integration, in contrast, would require a process whereby the political actors in the various states were "persuaded to shift their loyalties, expectations, and political activities towards a new centre", namely, the Republic of India. This was not an easy task. While some princely states such as Mysore had legislative systems of governance that were based on a broad franchise and not significantly different from those of British India, in others, political decision-making took place in small, limited aristocratic circles and governance was, as a result, at best paternalistic and at worst the result of courtly intrigue. Having secured the accession of the princely states, the Government of India between 1948 and 1950 turned to the task of welding the states and the former British provinces into one polity under a single republican constitution (Furber 1951: 352).

References

Ashton, S.R. (1982), *British Policy towards the Indian States, 1905–1938*, London Studies on South Asia no. 2, London: Curzon Press.

Brown, Judith M. (1984), "The Mountbatten Viceroyalty. Announcement and Reception of the 3 June Plan, 31 May-7 July 1947", *The English Historical Review* 99 (392): 667–668.

Copland, Ian (1987), "Congress Paternalism: The "High Command" and the Struggle for Freedom in Princely India", in Masselos, Jim, *Struggling and Ruling: The Indian National Congress 1885–1985*, New Delhi: Sterling Publishers, pp. 121–140.

Copland, Ian (1993), "Lord Mountbatten and the Integration of the Indian States: A Reappraisal", *The Journal of Imperial and Commonwealth History* 21 (2): 385–408.

Copland, Ian (1997), *The Princes of India in the Endgame of Empire, 1917–1947*, Cambridge, England: Cambridge University Press.

Copland, Ian (2002), *Princes of India in the Endgame of Empire, 1917-1947*, (Cambridge Studies in Indian History & Society). Cambridge and London: Cambridge University Press.

Eagleton, Clyde (1950), "The Case of Hyderabad Before the Security Council", *The American Journal of International Law* 44 (2): 277–302.

Furber, Holden (1951), "The Unification of India, 1947–1951", *Pacific Affairs* 24 (4): 352–371.

Gandhi, Rajmohan (1991), *Patel: A Life,* Ahmedabad: Navajivan Publishing House.

Imperial Gazetteer of India vol. II (1908), The Indian Empire, Historical, Published under the authority of His Majesty's Secretary of State for India in Council, Oxford at the Clarendon Press.

Imperial Gazetteer of India vol. III (1907), *The Indian Empire, Economic (Chapter X: Famine, pp. 475–502*, Published under the authority of His Majesty's Secretary of State for India in Council, Oxford at the Clarendon Press.

Imperial Gazetteer of India vol. IV (1907), *The Indian Empire, Administrative*, Published under the authority of His Majesty's Secretary of State for India in Council, Oxford at the Clarendon Press.

Ludden, David (2002), *India and South Asia: A Short History*, Oxford: Oneworld Publications.

Lumby, E.W.R. (1954), *The Transfer of Power in India, 1945–1947*, London: George Allen and Unwin

Menon, V. P. (1956), *The Story of the Integration of the Indian States*, New York: Macmillan.

Metcalf, Barbara & Thomas R. Metcalf (2006), *A Concise History of Modern India (Cambridge Concise Histories)*, Cambridge and New York: Cambridge University Press.

Moore, R.J. (1983), *Escape from Empire: The Attlee Government and the Indian.*

Oldenburg, Philip (2007), "India: Movement for Freedom", *Encarta Encyclopedia.*

Potter, Pitman B. (1950), "The Principal Legal and Political Problems Involved in the Kashmir Case", *The American Journal of International Law* 44 (2): 361–363.

Ramusack, Barbara N. (1978), *The Princes of India in the Twilight of Empire: Dissolution of a patron-client system, 1914–1939*, Colombus, Ohio: Ohio State University Press.

Ramusack, Barbara N. (1988), "Congress and the People's Movement in Princely India: Ambivalence in Strategy and Organisation", in Sisson, Richard; Wolpert, Stanley, *Congress and Indian Nationalism*, Berkeley: University of California Press, pp. 377–403.

Ramusack, Barbara N. (2004), *The Indian Princes and Their States*, The New Cambridge History of India III.6, Cambridge, England: Cambridge University Press.

Talbot, Phillips (1949), "Kashmir and Hyderabad", *World Politics* 1 (3): 321–332.

Wolpert, Stanley (1989), *A New History of India* (3rd ed.), Oxford University Press.

Notes

1. Ian J. Kerr, Engines of Change: The Railroads that Made India, page 9 (2006)
2. (Stein 2001, p. 260) Quote: "The British knew about Indian famines well before the East India Company assumed political responsibility for India. Peter Mundy, an early seventeenth-century Company agent, reported a devastating series of bad harvests and food shortages in Gujarat and elsewhere in western India which drove cultivators and artisans to migrate, some making their way a thousand miles to the southern tip of India, where they continue to live. Mundy described the responses of the Mughal governor of the province, ... he noted with appreciation the free food distributions ordered by Emperor Shah Jahan."
3. Angus Maddison, *The World Economy*, pages 109-112, (2001).

Chapter- 4

Governance and Legal System

Before the British came to India there was no definite system of governance, as there did not exist any written laws. Customary practices, system of age-old belief, traditional practices and religious scriptures considerably influenced the system of governance and distribution of justice. The arrival of the British on the Indian political scene introduced various kinds of secular laws and bureaucratic system of governance in course of time. The prevailing system of laws and governance of modern India is very much based on the foundation of the British system of governance. Even the Constitution of modern India is heavily based on the Government of India Act of 1935. Here let us briefly dwell on the development of British system of governance and legal system in India.

The Governor-General of India (or, from 1858 to 1947, the Viceroy and Governor-General of India) was the head of the British administration in India, and later, after Indian independence, the representative of the monarch and *de facto* head of state. The office was created in 1773, with the title of Governor-General of the Presidency of Fort William. The officer had direct control only over Fort William, but supervised other British East India Company officials in India. Complete authority over all of British India was granted in 1833, and the official became known as the Governor-General of India.

In 1858, the territories of the East India Company came under the direct control of the British Crown. The Governor-General headed the central

Government of India which administered the Provinces of British India, including the Punjab, Bengal, Bombay, Madras, the United Provinces, and others.[1] However, much of India was not ruled directly by the British government: outside the provinces of British India there were hundreds of nominally sovereign princely states or "native states", whose relationship was not with the British government, but directly with the monarch. To reflect the Governor-General's role as the representative of the monarch to the feudal rulers of the princely states, from 1858 the term Viceroy and Governor-General of India (known in short as the Viceroy of India) was applied to him.

The title of Viceroy was abandoned when India and Pakistan gained their independence in 1947, but the office of Governor-General continued to exist in both new dominions until they adopted republican constitutions in 1950 and 1956 respectively.

Until 1858, the Governor-General was selected by the Court of Directors of the East India Company, to whom he was responsible. Thereafter, he was appointed by the Sovereign on the advice of the British government; the Secretary of State for India, a member of the UK Cabinet, was responsible for instructing him on the exercise of his powers. After 1947, the Sovereign continued to appoint the Governor-General, but did so on the advice of the Indian government, rather than the British one.

Governors-General served five-year terms, but could be removed earlier. After the conclusion of a term, a provisional Governor-General was sometimes appointed until a new holder of the office could be chosen. Provisional Governors-General were often chosen from among the provincial Governors.

Many parts of India were governed by the East India Company, which nominally acted as the agent of the Mughal Emperor. In 1773, motivated by corruption in the Company, the British government assumed partial control over the governance of India with the passage of the Regulating Act. A Governor-General and Council were appointed to rule over the Presidency of Fort William in Bengal. The first Governor-General and Council were named in the Act; their successors were to be elected by the East India Company's Court of Directors. The Act provided for a five-year term for the Governor-General and Council, but the Sovereign had the power to remove any of them.

The Charter Act, 1833 replaced the Governor-General and Council of Fort William with the Governor-General and Council of India. The power to elect the Governor-General was retained by the Court of Directors, but the choice became subject to the Sovereign's approval.

After the Indian Rebellion of 1857, the East India Company was abolished, and its territories in India were put under the direct control of the Sovereign. The Government of India Act 1858 vested the power to appoint the Governor-General in the Sovereign. The Governor-General, in turn, had the power to appoint all lieutenant governors in India, subject to the Sovereign's approval.

India and Pakistan acquired independence in 1947, but Governors-General continued to be appointed over each nation until republican constitutions were written. Louis Mountbatten, 1st Earl Mountbatten of Burma remained Governor-General of India for some time after independence, but the two nations were otherwise headed by native Governors-General. India became a secular republic in 1950; Pakistan became an Islamic one in 1956.

Functions— The Governor-General originally had power only over the Presidency of Fort William in Bengal. The Regulating Act, however, granted them additional powers relating to foreign affairs and defence. The other Presidencies of the East India Company (Madras, Bombay and Bencoolen) were neither allowed to declare war on nor make peace with an Indian prince without receiving the prior approval of the Governor-General and Council of Fort William.

The powers of the Governor-General in respect of foreign affairs were increased by the India Act 1784. The Act provided that the other Governors under the East India Company could not declare war, make peace or conclude a treaty with an Indian prince unless expressly directed to do so by the Governor-General, or by the Company's Court of Directors.

While the Governor-General thus became the controller of foreign policy in India, he was not the explicit head of British India. This status only came with the Charter Act 1833, which granted him "superintendence, direction and control of the whole civil and military Government" of all of British India. The Act also granted legislative powers to the Governor-General and Council.

After 1858, the Governor-General functioned as the chief administrator of India and as the Sovereign's representative. India was divided into numerous provinces, each under the head of a Governor, Lieutenant Governor or Chief Commissioner or Administrator. Governors were appointed by the British government, to whom they were directly responsible; Lieutenant Governors, Chief Commissioners, and Administrators, however, were appointed by and were subordinate to the Governor-General. The Governor-General also oversaw the most powerful princely rulers: the Nizam of Hyderabad, the Maharaja of Mysore, the Maharaja (Scindia) of Gwalior, the Maharaja of Jammu and Kashmir and the Gaekwad (Gaekwar) Maharaja of Baroda. The remaining princely rulers were overseen either by the Rajputana Agency and Central India Agency (which were headed by representatives of the Governor-General), or by provincial authorities.

Once India acquired independence, however, the Governor-General's role became almost entirely ceremonial, with power being exercised on a day-to-day basis by the Indian cabinet. After the nation became a republic, the non-executive President of India continued to perform the same functions.

Council of India— The Governor-General was always advised by a Council on the exercise of his legislative and executive powers. The Governor-General, while exercising many functions, was referred to as the "Governor-General in Council."

The Regulating Act 1773 provided for the election of four counsellors by the East India Company's Court of Directors. The Governor-General had a vote along with the counsellors, but he also had an additional vote to break ties. The decision of the Council was binding on the Governor-General.

In 1784, the Council was reduced to three members; the Governor-General continued to have both an ordinary vote and a casting vote. In 1786, the power of the Governor-General was increased even further, as Council decisions ceased to be binding.

The Charter Act 1833 made further changes to the structure of the Council. The Act was the first law to distinguish between the executive and legislative responsibilities of the Governor-General. As provided under the Act, there were to be four members of the Council elected by the Court of Directors. The first three members were permitted to participate on all occasions, but the fourth member was only allowed to sit and vote when legislation was being debated.

In 1858, the Court of Directors ceased to have the power to elect members of the Council. Instead, the one member who had a vote only on legislative questions came to be appointed by the Sovereign, and the other three members by the Secretary of State for India.

The Indian Councils Act 1861 made several changes to the Council's composition. Three members were to be appointed by the Secretary of State for India, and two by the Sovereign (The power to appoint all five members passed to the Crown in 1869). The Governor-General was empowered to appoint an additional six to twelve members (changed to ten to sixteen in 1892, and to sixty in 1909). The five individuals appointed by the Indian Secretary or Sovereign headed the executive departments, while those appointed by the Governor-General debated and voted on legislation.

In 1919, an Indian legislature, consisting of a Council of State and a Legislative Assembly, took over the legislative functions of the Governor-General's Council. The Governor-General nonetheless retained significant power over legislation. He could authorize the expenditure of money without the Legislature's consent for "ecclesiastical, political [and] defense" purposes, and for any purpose during "emergencies." He was permitted to veto, or even stop debate on, any bill. If he recommended the passage of a bill, but only one chamber cooperated, he could declare the bill passed over the objections of the other chamber. The Legislature had no authority over foreign affairs and defence. The President of the Council of State was appointed by the Governor-General; the Legislative Assembly elected its President, but the election required the Governor-General's approval.

Style and title— The Governor-General (including when he was Viceroy from 1858 to 1947) used the style Excellency and enjoyed precedence over all other government officials in India. He would be referred to as 'His Excellency' and addressed as 'Your Excellency'. From 1858 to 1947, Governors-General were known as "Viceroys" (from the French roi, meaning "king"). Wives of Viceroys were known as Vicereines (from the French reine, meaning "queen"). The Vicereine would be referred to as 'Her Excellency' and would also be addressed as 'Your Excellency'. Neither title was employed while the Sovereign was in India.

When the Order of the Star of India was founded in 1861, the Viceroy was made its Grand Master *ex officio*. The Viceroy was also made the *ex officio* Grand Master of the Order of the Indian Empire upon its foundation in 1877.

Most Governors-General and Viceroys were peers. Of those that were not, Sir John Shore was a baronet, and Lord William Bentinck was entitled to the courtesy title "Lord" because he was the son of a Duke. Only the first and last Governors-General – Warren Hastings and Chakravarti Rajagopalachari – as well as some provisional Governors-General, had no special titles at all.

Flag— From around 1885, the Governor-General was allowed to fly a Union Flag augmented in the centre with the "Star of India" surmounted by a Crown. This flag was not the Governor-General's personal flag; it was also used by Governors, Lieutenant Governors, Chief Commissioners and other British officers in India. When at sea, only the Governor-General flew the flag from the mainmast, while other officials flew it from the foremast.

From 1947 to 1950, the Governor-General of India used a dark blue flag bearing the royal crest (a lion standing on a crown), beneath which was the word "India" in gold majuscules. The same design is still used by many other Governors-General. This last flag was the personal flag of the Governor-General only.

Residence— Government House served as the Governor-General's residence during most of the nineteenth century. The Governor-General of Fort William resided in Belvedere House, Calcutta until the early nineteenth century, when Government House was constructed. In 1854, the Lieutenant Governor of Bengal took up residence there. Now, the Belvedere Estate houses the National Library of India.

Richard Wellesley, 1st Marquess Wellesley, who is reputed to have said that "India should be governed from a palace, not from a country house," constructed a grand mansion, known as Government House, between 1799 and 1803. The mansion remained in use until the capital moved from Calcutta to Delhi in 1912. Thereafter, the Lieutenant Governor of Bengal, who had hitherto resided in Belvedere House, was upgraded to a full Governor and transferred to Government House. Now, it serves as the residence of the Governor of the Indian state of West Bengal, and is referred to by its Hindi name Raj Bhavan.

After the capital moved from Calcutta to Delhi, the Viceroy occupied a newly-built Viceroy's House, designed by Sir Edwin Lutyens. Though construction began in 1912, it did not conclude until 1929; the home was not formally inaugurated until 1931. The final cost exceeded £877,000 (over £35,000,000 in modern terms) – more than twice the figure originally allocated. Today the residence, now known by the Hindi name of "Rashtrapati Bhavan," is used by the President of India.

Throughout the British administration, Governors-General retreated to the Viceregal Lodge *(see Rashtrapati Niwas)* at Shimla each summer to escape the heat, and the government of India moved with them. The Viceregal Lodge now houses the Indian Institute of Advanced Study.

Beginnings of Self-government

The first steps were taken toward self-government in British India in the late 19th century with the appointment of Indian counsellors to advise the British viceroy and the establishment of provincial councils with Indian members; the British subsequently widened participation in legislative councils with the Indian Councils Act of 1892. Municipal Corporations and District Boards were created for local administration; they included elected Indian members.

The Government of India Act of 1909— also known as the Morley-Minto Reforms (John Morley was the secretary of state for India, and Gilbert Elliot, fourth earl of Minto, was viceroy)— gave Indians limited roles in the central and provincial legislatures, known as legislative councils. Indians had previously been appointed to legislative councils, but after the reforms some were elected to them. At the centre, the majority of council members continued to be government-appointed officials, and the viceroy was in no way responsible to the legislature. At the provincial level, the elected members, together with unofficial appointees, outnumbered the appointed officials, but responsibility of the governor to the legislature was not contemplated. Morley made it clear in introducing the legislation to the British Parliament that parliamentary self-government was not the goal of the British government.

The Morley-Minto Reforms were a milestone. Step by step, the elective principle was introduced for membership in Indian legislative councils. The "electorate" was limited, however, to a small group of upper-class Indians. These elected members increasingly became an "opposition" to the "official government". The Communal electorates were later extended to other communities and made a political factor of the Indian tendency toward group identification through religion.

World War I and its aftermath— World War I would prove to be a watershed in the imperial relationship between Britain and India. 1.4 million Indian and British soldiers of the British Indian Army would take part in the war and their participation would have a wider cultural fallout: news of Indian soldiers fighting and dying with British soldiers, as well as soldiers from dominions like Canada and Australia, would travel to distant corners of the world both in newsprint and by the new medium of the radio. India's international profile would thereby rise and would continue to rise during the 1920s. It was to lead, among other things, to India, under its own name, becoming a founding member of the League of Nations in 1920 and participating, under the name, "Les Indes Anglaises" (The British Indies), in the 1920 Summer Olympics in Antwerp. Back in India, especially among the leaders of the Indian National Congress, it would lead to calls for greater self-government for Indians (Brown, 1994: 197-98).

In 1916, in the face of new strength demonstrated by the moderate nationalists with the signing of the Lucknow Pact and the founding of the Home Rule leagues, and the realization, after the disaster in the Mesopotamian campaign, that the war would likely last longer, the new Viceroy, Lord Chelmsford, cautioned that the Government of India needed to be more responsive to Indian opinion. Towards the end of the year, after discussions with the government in London, he suggested that the British demonstrate their good faith– in light of the Indian war role– through a number of public actions, including awards of titles and honors to princes, granting of commissions in the army to Indians, and removal of the much-reviled cotton excise duty, but most importantly, an announcement of Britain's future plans for India and an indication of some concrete steps. After more discussion, in August 1917, the new Liberal Secretary of State for India, Edwin Montagu, announced the British aim of "increasing association of Indians in every branch of the administration, and the gradual development of self-governing institutions, with a view to the progressive realization of responsible government in India as an integral part of the British Empire." Although the plan envisioned limited self-government at first only in the provinces– with India emphatically within the British Empire– it represented the first British proposal for any form of representative government in a non-white colony (Brown, 1994: 203-204).

Earlier, at the onset of World War I, the reassignment of most of the British army in India to Europe and Mesopotamia had led the previous Viceroy, Lord Harding, to worry about the "risks involved in denuding India of troops." Revolutionary violence had already been a concern in British India, and outlines of collaboration with Germany were being identified by British intelligence; consequently in 1915, to strengthen its powers during what it saw was a time of increased vulnerability, the Government of India passed the Defence of India Act, which allowed it to intern politically dangerous dissidents without due process and added to the power it already had– under the 1910 Press Act– both to imprison journalists without trial and to censor the press. Now, as constitutional reform began to be discussed in earnest, the British began to consider how new moderate Indians could be brought into the fold of constitutional politics and simultaneously, how the hand of established constitutionalists could be strengthened. However, since the Government of India wanted to check the revolutionary problem, and since its reform plan was devised during a time when extremist violence had ebbed as a result of increased governmental control, it also began to consider how some of its war-time powers could be extended into peace time (Brown, 1994: 197-98).

Edwin Montagu, left, the Secretary of State for India, whose report led to the Government of India Act of 1919, also known as the Montford Reforms or the Montagu-Chelmsford Reforms.

Consequently in 1917, even as Edwin Montague announced the new constitutional reforms, a sedition committee chaired by a British judge, Mr. S. A. T. Rowlatt, was tasked with investigating revolutionary conspiracies and the German and Bolshevik links to the violence in India, with the unstated goal of extending the government's war-time powers. The Rowlatt committee presented its report in July 1918 and identified three regions of conspiratorial insurgency: Bengal, the Bombay presidency, and the Punjab. To combat subversive acts in these regions, the committee recommended that the government use emergency powers akin to its war-time authority, which included the ability to try cases of sedition by a panel of three judges and without juries, exaction of securities from suspects, governmental overseeing of residences of suspects, and the power for provincial governments to arrest and detain suspects in short-term detention facilities and without trial (Spear 1990: 190).

With the end of World War I, there was also a change in the economic climate. By year's end 1919, 1.5 million Indians had served in the armed services in either combatant or non-combatant roles, and India had provided £146 million in revenue for the war. The increased taxes coupled with disruptions in both domestic and international trade had the effect of approximately doubling the index of overall prices in India between 1914 and 1920. Returning war veterans, especially in the Punjab, created a growing unemployment crisis and post-war inflation led to food riots in Bombay, Madras, and Bengal provinces, a situation that was made only worse by the failure of the 1918-19 monsoon and by profiteering and speculation. The global influenza epidemic and the Bolshevik Revolution of 1917 added to the general jitters; the former among the population already experiencing economic woes, and the latter among government officials, fearing a similar revolution in India (Ludden, 2002: 208).

To combat what it saw as a coming crisis, the government now drafted the Rowlatt committee's recommendations into two Rowlatt Bills. Although the bills were authorised for legislative consideration by Edwin Montagu, they were done so unwillingly, with the accompanying declaration, "I loathe the suggestion at first sight of preserving the Defence of India Act in peace time to such an extent as Rowlatt and his friends think necessary." In the ensuing discussion and vote in the Imperial Legislative Council, all Indian members voiced opposition to the bills. The Government of India was nevertheless able to use of its "official majority" to ensure passage of the bills early in 1919. However, what it passed, in deference to the Indian opposition, was a lesser version of the first bill, which now allowed extra-judicial powers, but for a period of exactly three years and for the prosecution solely of "anarchical and revolutionary movements," dropping entirely the second bill involving modification of the Indian Penal Code. Even so, when it was passed the new Rowlatt Act aroused widespread indignation throughout India and brought Mohandas Gandhi to the forefront of the nationalist movement.

Meanwhile, Montague and Chelmsford themselves finally presented their report in July 1918 after a long fact-finding trip through India the previous winter. After more discussion by the government and parliament in Britain, and another tour by the Franchise and Functions Committee for the purpose of identifying who among the Indian population could vote in future elections, the Government of India Act of 1919 (also known as the Montagu-Chelmsford Reforms) was passed in December 1919. The new Act enlarged both the provincial and imperial legislative councils and repealed the Government of India's recourse to the "official majority" in unfavourable votes. Although departments like defence, foreign affairs, criminal law, communications and income-tax were retained by the Viceroy and the central government in New Delhi, other departments like public health, education, land-revenue and local self-government were transferred to the provinces. The provinces themselves were now to be administered under a new diarchic system, whereby some areas like education, agriculture, infrastructure development, and local self-government became the preserve of Indian ministers and legislatures, and ultimately the Indian electorates, while others like irrigation, land-revenue, police, prisons, and control of media remained within the purview of the British governor and his executive council. The new Act also made it easier for Indians to be admitted into the civil service and the army officer corps.

A greater number of Indians were now enfranchised, although, for voting at the national level, they constituted only 10% of the total adult male population, many of whom were still illiterate. In the provincial legislatures, the British continued to exercise some control by setting aside seats for special interests they considered cooperative or useful. In particular, rural candidates, generally sympathetic to British rule and less confrontational, were assigned more seats than their urban counterparts. Seats were also reserved for non-Brahmins, landowners, businessmen, and college graduates. The principal of "communal representation," an integral part of the Minto-Morley reforms, and more recently of the Congress-Muslim League Lucknow Pact, was reaffirmed, with seats being reserved for Muslims, Sikhs, Indian Christians, Anglo-Indians, and domiciled Europeans, in both provincial and Imperial legislative councils (Brown, 1994: 205-07). The Montagu-Chelmsford reforms offered Indians the most significant opportunity yet for exercising legislative power, especially at the provincial level; however, that opportunity was also restricted by the still limited number of eligible voters, by the small budgets available to provincial legislatures, and by the presence of rural and special interest seats that were seen as instruments of British control. Its scope was, however, severely dissatisfactory to the Indian political leadership, famously expressed by Annie Beasant as something "unworthy of England to offer and India to accept" (Chhabra, 2005: 2).

1930s: The Government of India Act (1935)

In 1935, after the Round Table Conferences, the British Parliament approved the Government of India Act of 1935, which authorised the establishment of independent legislative assemblies in all provinces of British India, the creation of a central government incorporating both the British provinces and the princely states, and the protection of Muslim minorities. At this time, it was also decided to separate Burma from British India in 1937, to form a separate crown colony. The future Constitution of independent India would owe a great deal to the text of this act (Low 1993). The act also provided for a bicameral national parliament and an executive branch under the purview of the British government. Although the national federation was never realised, nationwide elections for provincial assemblies were held in 1937. Despite initial hesitation, the Congress took part in the elections and won victories in seven of the eleven provinces of British

India, and Congress governments, with wide powers, were formed in these provinces. In Great Britain, these victories were to later turn the tide for the idea of Indian independence (Low 1993: 40, 156).

World War II— With the outbreak of World War II in 1939, the viceroy, Lord Linlithgow, declared war on India's behalf without consulting Indian leaders, leading the Congress provincial ministries to resign in protest. The Muslim League, in contrast, supported Britain in the war effort; however, it now took the view that Muslims would be unfairly treated in an independent India dominated by the Congress. The British government— through its Cripps' mission— attempted to secure Indian nationalists' cooperation in the war effort in exchange for independence afterwards; however, the negotiations between them and the Congress broke down. Gandhi, subsequently, launched the "Quit India" movement in August 1942, demanding the immediate withdrawal of the British from India or face nationwide civil disobedience. Along with all other Congress leaders, Gandhi was immediately imprisoned, and the country erupted in violent demonstrations led by students and later by peasant political groups, especially in Eastern United Provinces, Bihar, and western Bengal. The large war-time British Army presence in India led to most of the movement being crushed in a little more than six weeks; nonetheless, a portion of the movement formed for a time an underground provisional government on the border with Nepal. In other parts of India, the movement was less spontaneous and the protest less intensive, however it lasted sporadically into the summer of 1943 (Bandopadhyay, 2004: 418-420).

With Congress leaders in jail, attention also turned to Subhas Bose, who had been ousted from the Congress in 1939 following differences with the more conservative high command; Bose now turned to the Axis powers for help with liberating India by force. With Japanese support, he organised the Indian National Army, composed largely of Indian soldiers of the British Indian army who had been captured at Singapore by the Japanese. From the onset of the war, the Japanese secret service had promoted unrest in South east Asia to destabilise the British War effort, and came to support a number of puppet and provisional governments in the captured regions, including those in Burma, the Philippines and Vietnam, the Provisional Government of Azad Hind (Free India), presided by Bose (Lebra 1977: 31). Bose's effort, however, was short lived; after the reverses of 1944, the reinforced British Indian Army in 1945 first halted and then reversed the Japanese U Go offensive, beginning the successful part of the Burma Campaign. Bose's Indian National Army surrendered with the recapture of

Singapore, and Bose died in a plane crash soon thereafter. The trials of the INA soldiers at Red Fort in late 1945 however caused widespread public unrest and nationalist violence in India (Chaudhury 1953: 349).

Post-war developments: Transfer of power— In January 1946, a number of mutinies broke out in the armed services, starting with that of RAF servicemen frustrated with their slow repatriation to Britain. The mutinies came to a head with mutiny of the Royal Indian Navy in Bombay in February 1946, followed by others in Calcutta, Madras, and Karachi. Although these latter mutinies were rapidly suppressed, they found much public support in India then gripped by the Red Fort Trials, and had the effect of spurring the new Labour government in Britain to action, and leading to the Cabinet Mission to India led by the Secretary of State for India, Lord Pethick Lawrence, and including Sir Stafford Cripps, who had visited four years before (Judd, 2004: 172).

Also in early 1946, new elections were called in India in which the Congress won electoral victories in eight of the eleven provinces. The negotiations between the Congress and the Muslim League, however, stumbled over the issue of the partition. Jinnah proclaimed August 16, 1946, Direct Action Day, with the stated goal of highlighting, peacefully, the demand for a Muslim homeland in British India. The following day Hindu-Muslim riots broke out in Calcutta and quickly spread throughout India. Although the Government of India and the Congress were both shaken by the course of events, in September, a Congress-led interim government was installed, with Jawaharlal Nehru as united India's prime minister.

Later that year, the Labour government in Britain, its exchequer exhausted by the recently concluded World War II, and conscious that it had neither the mandate at home, the international support, nor the reliability of native forces for continuing to control an increasingly restless India, decided to end British rule of India, and in early 1947 Britain announced its intention of transferring power no later than June 1948.[2] [3]

Development of Legal System

The roots of the present day human institutions lie deeply buried in the past. This is also true about the country's law and legal system. The legal system of a country at any given time cannot be said to be creation of one man for one day; it represents the cumulative effect of the endeavour, experience, thoughtful planning and patient labour of a large number of people throughout generations.

Ancient India represented a distinct tradition of law, and had an historically independent school of legal theory and practice. Law in ancient India meant "Dharma" in the broader sense. The Vedas, regarded as divine revelation, were the supreme source of authority for all codes which contained what was then understood as law or dharma. The traditional records have governed and moulded the life and evolution of the Hindu community from one age to another. These are supposed to have their source in the Rigveda. The *Arthashastra*, dating from 400 BC and the *Manusmriti*, from 100 AD, were influential treatises in India, texts that were considered authoritative legal guidance. Manu's central philosophy was tolerance and pluralism, and was cited across Southeast Asia (Glenn, 2000). The Judiciary, the Executive, and the Legislature were the same person- the King or the Ruler of the Land. But the villages had considerable independence, and had their own panchayat system to resolve disputes among its members. Only a bigger feud merited a trans village council.

Justice was administered in ancient India, stated as above, according to the rules of civil and criminal law as provided in the *Manusmriti*. There was a regular system of local courts from which an appeal lay to the superior court at the capital, and from there to the King in his own court. The King's Court was composed of himself, a number of judges, and his domestic chaplain who directed his conscience; but they only advised and the decision rested with the King. Arbitrators in three gradations existed below the local courts: first of kinsmen, secondly of men of the same trade, and thirdly, of townsmen. An appeal lay from the first to the second, from the second to the third, and from the third to the local court. Thus under this system there were no less than five appeals. Decision by arbitration, generally of five *(Panches),* was very common when other means of obtaining justice were not available. The village headman was the judge and magistrate of the village community and also collected and transmitted the Government revenue. This tradition in India continued beyond the Islamic conquest of India, and through to the Middle Ages.

Early in this period, which finally culminated in the creation of the Mauryan and Gupta Empire, relations with ancient Greece and Rome were not infrequent. The appearances of similar fundamental institutions of international law in various parts of the world show that they are inherent in international society, irrespective of culture and tradition (Alexander 1952: 289-300).

These Hindu traditions, along with Islamic law, were supplanted by the common law when India became part of the British Empire (Glenn,

2000). Islamic law "the Sharia" was applied only to the Muslims of the country. But this tradition, along with Islamic law, was supplanted by the common law when India became part of the British Empire. The history of Modern Judicial System in India starts from there.

Legal system in India during the British period— As said before, India has one of the oldest legal systems in the world. Its law and jurisprudence stretches back centuries, forming a living tradition which has grown and evolved with the lives of its diverse people. The modern judicial system in India started to take shape with the control of the British in India during the 17th century. The present judicial system in India owes much to the judicial system developed during the time of the British. The history of the present judicial system may be traced back to the year 1726, when a Charter was issued by King George I for bringing about important changes in the judicial administration of the Presidency Towns of Bombay, Calcutta and Madras. The system of appeals from India to the Privy Council in England was introduced by this Charter in 1726.

Beginning with the Mayor's Court, established in 1727 for civil litigation in Bombay, Calcutta, and Madras, justice in the interior came under the Company's jurisdiction. In 1772 an elaborate judicial system, known as *adalat*, established civil and criminal jurisdictions along with a complex set of codes or rules of procedure and evidence. Both Hindu pundits and Muslim *qazis* (sharia court judges) were recruited to aid the presiding judges in interpreting their customary laws, but in other instances, British common and statutory laws became applicable. In extraordinary situations where none of these systems was applicable, the judges were enjoined to adjudicate on the basis of "justice, equity, and good conscience." The legal profession provided numerous opportunities for educated and talented Indians who were unable to secure positions in the Company, and, as a result, Indian lawyers later dominated nationalist politics and reform movements.

The British Parliament enacted a series of laws, among which the Charter Act of 1813 is important one which recognized British moral responsibility by introducing just and humane laws in India, foreshadowing future social legislation, and outlawing a number of traditional practices such as sati and *thagi* (or thugee, robbery coupled with ritual murder).

In order to bring about better management of the affairs of the East India Company, the East India Company Regulating Act of 1773 was promulgated by the King. This Act subjected the East India Company to the control of the British Government and made a provision for His Majesty by Charters or Letters Patent to establish the Supreme Court of Judicature at Fort William at Calcutta, superseding the then prevalent judicial system. The Supreme Court of Judicature at Fort William was established by a letter patent issued on March 26, 1774. This Court, as a court of record, had full power and authority to hear and determine all complaints against any of His Majesty's subjects for any crimes and also to entertain, hear and determine any suits or actions against any of His Majesty's subjects in Bengal, Bihar and Orissa. Two more Supreme Courts, conceived along the same lines as that of the Supreme Court of Calcutta, were established at Madras and Bombay by King George III through Charters issued on 26th December, 1800 and on 8th December, 1823 respectively.

The role of the Privy Council has been a great unifying force and the instrument and embodiment of the rule of law in India. The Judicial Committee of the Privy Council was made a Statutory Permanent Committee of legal experts to hear appeals from the British Colonies in the year 1833 by an Act passed by the British Parliament. Thus, the Act of 1833 transformed the Privy Council into a great imperial court of unimpeachable authority.

The Indian High Court's Act of 1861 reorganized the then prevalent judicial system in the country by abolishing the Supreme Courts at Fort William, Madras, and Bombay, and also the then existing Sadar Adalats in the Presidency Towns. The High Courts were established having civil, criminal, admiralty, vice-admiralty, testimony, intestate, and matrimonial jurisdiction, as well as original and appellate jurisdiction.

Provincial autonomy was established in India with the establishment of the Government of India Act, 1935, which introduced responsibility at the provincial level and sought the Union of British Indian Provinces with the rulers of Estate in a federation. As a federal system depends largely upon a just and competent administration of the law between governments themselves, the 1935 Act provided for the establishment of the Federal Court, forerunner of the Supreme Court of India. The Federal Court was the second highest Court in the judicial hierarchy in India.

The Federal Court was the first Constitutional Court and also the first all-India Court of extensive jurisdiction, and it had Original Jurisdiction in matters where there was dispute between the provinces or federal States. It was also the Appellate Court for the judgments, decrees, or final orders of the High Courts. Thus, the Federal Court of India had original, appellate and advisory jurisdiction. The doctrine of precedent in India also had its roots in Federal Court as the law declared by the Federal Court and Privy Council has been given binding affect on all the courts in British India.

The most abiding impacts of the British rule in India were manifested in the fields of administration. The British Rulers introduced Rule of Law in their territories. Even the meanest subject enjoyed personal liberty according to the Rule of Law. The principle of habeas corpus provided that no person could be arrested or kept in prison without a written order from the local executive or the judicial authority, even if the viceroy when desired. Even the Government servant, if the acts done in their official capacity could be sued in the court of Law. The natural upshot of the Rule of Law was the Equality before the Law, which subsequently followed the Rule of Law. The Equality before the Law appeared as a novel feature in the caste ridden society.

The British rulers further established a codification of law. The Code of Civil Procedure, the Code of Criminal Procedure laid down in clear, precise and in exact terms, the law applicable to all citizens, high and low breed and irrespective of caste, creed and religion. The British rulers also set up a gradation of courts, civil and criminal for the trial of the petty and heinous crimes with the right to appeal at the High Courts and even an appeal to Committees of Privy Council in civil suits.

The legal system introduced by the British Government in India had several shortcomings. It was very expensive and the rich had the opportunity to wear out the poor and uneducated. The British legal system stimulated the growth of the falsehood, chicanery, and deceit. The inordinate delay in the decision of the case was one of the significant negative features of the Legal system of the British. The lawyer class in the British legal system was interested in delaying and prolonging cases and pleading for clients who could afford to pay them. Even the Governments of independent India, later was not be able to remove all the shortcomings of the British legal system. The worst aspects of the legal system in the British time were the special procedures for the trial of the European in the criminal cases. The Ilbert Bill highlighted the injustice involved in the racial discrimination in judicial matters but no remedial measures were provided.

The organisation of an Indian Civil Service, which worked according to the codified rules and with efficiency and impartiality, was a striking feature of the administration. The administrative system established by the British was completely different from the personal rules and regulations of a dictator monarch. The ICS officers, under the British administrative system worked as Collectors, Magistrates, and Judges and maintained a high standard of impartiality and integrity.

However highly applauded the system of Indian Civil Service had several drawbacks. In spite of the repeated resolutions of the British Parliament and announcements by the British Crown about the recruitments to the ICS on the basis of Competitive Examination free from racial discrimination, the British system of Indian Civil Service was completely aimed to constitute as a close preserve of the Europeans. In this way the British Government wanted to strengthen their own position in the politics and administrative field of India. Various measures like holding of examination in London, reducing the average age limit of the examination etc.were adopted to keep the Indians out of the Civil services or to participate in the administrative system directly. Therefore the British impact on the law and administration was immense and was directed to fortify the British administration in India.

The system of law which presently operates in India is largely based on English common law because of the long period of British colonial influence during the British Raj period. Much of contemporary Indian law shows substantial European and American influence. Various acts and ordinances first introduced by the British are still in effect in their modified forms today. During the drafting of the Indian Constitution, laws from Ireland, the United States, Britain, and France were all synthesized to get a refined set of Indian laws, as it currently stands. Indian laws also adhere to the United Nations guidelines on human rights law and the environmental law. Certain international trade laws, such as those on intellectual property, are also enforced in India.

Indian civil law is complex, with each religion having its own specific laws which they adhere to. In most states, registering of marriages and divorces is not compulsory. There are separate laws governing Hindus, Muslims, Christians, Sikhs and followers of other religions. The exception to this rule is in the state of Goa, where a Portuguese uniform civil code is in place, in which all religions have a common law regarding marriages, divorces and adoption.

Abolition of Sati Act, 1829— Since the practice of sati had been one of important evils of Hindu society for long and was abolished through legislative measures during the British regime, there is need to have some discussion on this subject here. By about the 10th century sati was known across much of the subcontinent. It continued to occur, usually at a low frequency and with regional variations, until the early 19th century.

Sati is a funeral practice among some Hindu communities in which a recently widowed woman would either voluntarily or by use of force and coercion immolate herself on her husband's funeral pyre. This practice is now rare and outlawed in modern India. Some instances of voluntary self-immolation by both women and men that may be regarded as at least partly historical accounts are included in the Mahabharata and other works. However, large portions of these works are relatively late interpolations into an original story, rendering difficult their use for reliable dating. Also, neither immolation nor the desire for self-immolation is regarded as a custom in the Mahabharata.

Voluntary death at funerals has been described in northern India before the Gupta Empire. The original practices were called anumarana, and were uncommon. Anumarana was not comparable to later understandings of sati, since the practices were not restricted to widows— rather, anyone, male or female, with personal loyalty to the deceased could commit suicide at a loved one's funeral. These included the deceased's relatives, servants, followers, or friends.

Sati often emphasized the marriage between the widow and her deceased husband. For instance, rather than mourning clothes, the to-be sati was often dressed in marriage robes or other finery. In the preliminaries of the related act of Jauhar (in Rajasthan), both the husbands and wives have been known to dress in their marriage clothes and re-enact their wedding ritual, before going to their separate deaths. Sati was supposed to be voluntary, but it is known that it has often been forced. Setting aside the issue of social pressures, many accounts exist of women being physically forced to their deaths.

There are no reliable figures for the numbers who died by sati across the country. A local indication of the numbers is given in the records kept by the Bengal Presidency of the British East India Company. The total figure of known occurrences for the period 1813 to 1828 is 8,135;[4] another source gives a comparable number of 7,941 from 1815 to 1828,[5] thus giving an average of about 507 to 567 documented incidents per year in that period. Raja Ram Mohan Roy estimated that there were ten times as many cases of Sati in Bengal compared to the rest of the country.[6] Bentinck, in his 1829 report, states that 420 occurrences took place in one (unspecified) year in the 'Lower Provinces' of Bengal, Bihar and Orissa, and 44 in the 'Upper Provinces' (the upper Gangetic plain).[7]

In the Lower Gangetic plain, the practice may have reached a high level fairly late in history. Based on available evidence and the existing reports of the occurrences of it, the greatest incidence of sati in any region and period, in terms of total numbers, occurred in Bengal and Bihar in the late 18th and early 19th centuries.[8] This was during the earlier period of British rule, and before its formal abolition. The Bengal Presidency kept records from 1813 to 1829. The frequency increased in periods of hardship and famine. Ram Mohan Roy suggested that it was more prevalent in Bengal than in the rest of the subcontinent. An unusually large number of the surviving reports for this period are from Bengal, also suggesting that it was most common there.

By the end of the 18th century, the practice had been banned in territories held by some European powers. The Portuguese banned the practice in Goa by about 1515, though it is not believed to have been especially prevalent there.[9] The Dutch and the French also banned it in Chinsurah and Pondicherry. The British who by then ruled much of the subcontinent, and the Danes, who held the small territories of Tranquebar and Serampore, permitted it until the 19th century.

Attempts to limit or ban the practice had been made by individual British officers in the 18th century, but without the backing of the British East India Company. The first formal British ban was imposed in 1798, in the city of Calcutta only. The practice continued in surrounding regions. Toward the end of the 18th century, the evangelical church in Britain, and its members in India, started campaigns against sati. Leaders of these campaigns included William Carey and William Wilberforce, and both appeared to be motivated partly by a desire to convert Indians to Christianity. These movements put pressure on the Company to ban the act, and the Bengal Presidency started collecting figures on the practice in 1813.

From about 1812, the Bengali reformer Raja Rammohan Roy started his own campaign against the practice. He was motivated by the experience of seeing his own sister-in-law being forced to commit sati. Among his actions, he visited Calcutta cremation grounds to persuade widows not to so die, formed watch groups to do the same, and wrote and disseminated articles to show that it was not required by scripture. On 4 December 1829, the practice was formally banned in the Bengal Presidency lands, by the then governor, Lord William Bentinck. The ban was challenged in the courts, and the matter went to the Privy Council in London, but was upheld in 1832. Other Company territories also banned it shortly after.

Sati remained legal in some princely states for a time after it had been abolished in lands under British control. Jaipur, banned the practice in 1846. Nepal continued to practice Sati well into the 20th century. On the Indonesian island of Bali, sati was practiced by the aristocracy as late as 1905, until Dutch colonial rule pushed for its termination.

Some of the important legislations of the British days are as follows: Abolition of Sati Act, 1829; Hindu Widows Remarriage Act, 1856; The Converts' Marriage Dissolution Act, 1866; The Indian Christian Marriage Act, 1872; The Kazis Act, 1880; The Indian Divorce Act, 1869; Indian Contract Act, 1872; Indian Trusts Act of 1882; Indian Penal Code, 1860; The Anand Marriage Act, 1909; The Child Marriage Restraint Act, 1929; The Parsi Marriage and Divorce Act, 1936; The Hindu Women's Right to Property Act, 1937; The Widow Remarriage Act, 1856; the Native Marriage Act, 1872; Child Marriage Restraint Law, 1929; Hindu Marriage Act, 1955; Indian Divorce Act, 1869 and1936; Dissolution of Muslim Marriages Act, 1939; The Muslim Marriage Act, 1939; The Indian Succession Act, 1925; The Hindu Succession Act, 1925; The Shariat Act, 1937; The Dissolution of Muslim Marriages Act, 1939 and several others.

References

Alexander, C.H. (1952), *International Law in India*, The International and Comparative Law Quarterly, Vol. 1, No. 3. (July), pp. 289-300.

Brown, Judith M. (1994), *Modern India: The Origins of an Asian Democracy*, Oxford and New York: Oxford University Press.

Glenn, H. Patrick (2000). *Legal Traditions of the World*. Oxford University Press.

Hyam, Ronald (2007), *Britain's Declining Empire: The Road to Decolonization 1918-1968*, Cambridge University Press.

Metcalf, Barbara & Thomas R. Metcalf (2006), *A Concise History of Modern India (Cambridge Concise Histories)*, Cambridge and New York: Cambridge University Press.

Sarkar, Sumit (1983), *Modern India: 1885-1947*, Delhi: Macmillan India Ltd.

Viswanatha, S.T. (1925), *International Law in Ancient India*.

Notes

1. The term British India is mistakenly used to mean the same as the British Indian Empire, which included both the Provinces and the Native States.
2. Hyam 2007, p. 106, Quote: By the end of 1945, he and the Commander-in-Chief, General Auckinleck were advising that there was a real threat in 1946 of large scale anti-British Disorder amounting to even a well-organised rising aiming to expel the British by paralysing the administration. Quote: ...it was clear to Attlee that everything depended on the spirit and reliability of the Indian Army:

"Provided that they do their duty, armed insurrection in India would not be an insoluble problem. If, however, the Indian Army was to go the other way, the picture would be very different... Quote:...Thus, Wavell concluded, if the army and the police "failed" Britain would be forced to go. In theory, it might be possible to revive and reinvigorate the services, and rule for another fifteen to twenty years, but: It is a fallacy to suppose that the solution lies in trying to maintain status quo. We have no longer the resources, nor the necessary prestige or confidence in ourselves.

3. Brown 1994, p. 330, Quote: "India had always been a minority interest in British public life; no great body of public opinion now emerged to argue that war-weary and impoverished Britain should send troops and money to hold it against its will in an empire of doubtful value. By late 1946 both Prime Minister and Secretary of State for India recognized that neither international opinion nor their own voters would stand for any reassertion of the *raj*, even if there had been the men, money, and administrative machinery with which to do so." Sarkar 1983, p. 418 Quote: "With a war weary army and people and a ravaged economy, Britain would have had to retreat; the Labour victory only quickened the process somewhat." Metcalf & Metcalf 2006, p. 212 Quote: "More importantly, though victorious in war, Britain had suffered immensely in the struggle. It simply did not possess the manpower or economic resources required to coerce a restive India."
4. Sakuntala Narasimhan, Sati: widow burning in India, quoted by Matthew White, "Selected Death Tolls for Wars, Massacres and Atrocities Before the 20th Century", p.2.
5. Sakuntala Narasimhan, Sati: widow burning in India.
6. Modern History Sourcebook: On Ritual Murder in India, 1829 by William Bentinck.
7. John Ovington, A Voyage to Surat: Since the Mahometans became Masters of the Indies, this execrable custom is much abated, and almost laid aside, by the orders which nabobs receive for suppressing and extinguishing it in all their provinces. And now it is very rare, except it be some Rajah's wives, that the Indian women burn at all.
8. The Times of India, "Woman commits 'sati' in UP village", May 19, 2006.
9. To Cherish and to Share: The Goan Christian Heritage Paper presented at the 1991 Conference on Goa at the University of Toronto by: John Correia Alfonso S.J. from: "South Asian Studies Papers", no 9; Goa: Goa Continuity and Change; Edited by Narendra K. Wagle and George Coelho; University of Toronto Centre for South Asian Studies 1995.

Chapter- 5

Emergence of new Land Relationships and Industrial Development

The British rule in India had a very distressing impact on Indian economy- both agrarian and industrial. The Britishers introduced their own system of collection of rent from peasants and landlords to increase their revenue collection. Little attention was paid to rural or agricultural development. No tangible attempt was made to contain or minimize the problems of recurrence of drought and famines in their country. Millions often became unfortunate victims of hunger, malnutrition and disease. The land tax was so exorbitant that the peasants were subjected to massive exploitation by the state and its agencies. Similarly well-developed cottage industries of India too suffered a lot. The Britishers were interested more in running their own industries back home rather than in safeguarding the interests of Indian industries. India had to survive merely as a dependent economy during the whole of British rule. Some of the important works on this subject are those of Marx and Engels (1965), Dutt (1949), (Chand 1961), Majumdar (1963), Chandra (1972; 989), Desai (1976), Dutt (1976), Andrews (1984), Rothermund (1993) and a host of others. This fact has been elaborated in the subsequent discussion.

Land Revenue Settlements

Starting in 1772, the Company began a series of land revenue "settlements," which would create major changes in landed rights and rural economy in India. In 1793, the Governor-General Lord Cornwallis promulgated the permanent settlement in the Bengal Presidency, the first socio-economic regulation in colonial India. It was named *permanent* because it fixed the land tax in perpetuity in return for landed property rights for a class of intermediaries called zamindars, who thereafter became owners of the land. It was hoped that knowledge of a fixed government demand would encourage the *zamindars* to increase both their average outcrop and the land under cultivation, since they would be able to retain the profits from the increased output; in addition, the land itself would become a marketable form of property that could be purchased, sold, or mortgaged. However, the *zamindars* themselves were often unable to meet the increased demands that the Company had placed on them; consequently, many defaulted, and by one estimate, up to one-third of their lands were auctioned during the first three decades following the permanent settlement. In southern India, Thomas Munro, who would later become Governor of Madras, promoted the *Ryotwari* system, in which the government settled land-revenue directly with the peasant farmers, or *Ryots*. Based on the utilitarian ideas of James Mill, who supervised the Company's land revenue policy during 1819-1830, and David Ricardo's Law of Rent, it was considered by its supporters to be both closer to traditional practice and more progressive, allowing the benefits of Company rule to reach the lowest levels of rural society (Peers 2006: 47; Brown 1994: 65). However, in spite of the appeal of the *Ryotwari* system's abstract principles, class hierarchies in southern Indian villages had not entirely disappeared—for example village headmen continued to hold sway— and peasant cultivators came to experience revenue demands they could not meet.

Land revenue settlements constituted a major administrative activity of the various governments in India under Company rule. In all areas other than the Bengal Presidency, land settlement work involved a continually repetitive process of surveying and measuring plots, assessing their quality, and recording landed rights, and constituted a large proportion of the work of Indian Civil Service officers working for the government. After the Company lost its trading rights, it became the single most important source of government revenue, roughly half of overall revenue in the middle of the 19th century (Brown 1994: 64). Since, in many regions, the land tax assessment could be revised, and since it was generally computed at a high level, it created lasting resentment which would later come to a head in the rebellion which rocked much of North India in 1857 (Metcalf and Metcalf, 2006:79).

Zamindari or permanent settlement— One of Lord Cornwallis' major achievements was the Permanent Settlement (1793) of land revenue in Bengal. For a quarter century after the grant (1765) of Diwani Rights to the

John Company, the revenue settlement had been on an annual basis, though a permanent system was also anticipated.

On 10 February 1790, the Governor-General announced a decennial settlement. Three years later it was approved by the Court of Directors and made permanent as of 22 March 1793. It constituted Regulation 1 in the series of regulations passed by the Calcutta Supreme Council on 1 May and collectively known as the Cornwallis Code.

Under the new dispensation, the zamindars were recognized as proprietors of land. Land revenue was to be fixed, there being no enhancement of dues to the government, nor could be zamindar in return expect any remissions or postponement of dues.

Cornwallis argued that these measures would encourage landlords to obtain the maximum produce as well as reclaim waste land, ensure a permanent income to the government, and save time and effort hitherto wasted on annual settlements. By accepting the hereditary status of zamindars, however, the settlement completely ignored the interests of cultivators who were thus thrown to the mercy of big landlords.

The Governor-General's views were opposed by most of his advisors, including John Shore and Charles Grant. Shore wanted a proper survey to be carried out before a perpetual assessment was made; Grant was doubtful about the zamindar's proprietary rights to the land without an exhaustive study of the records. Ironically, Shore who succeeded Cornwallis was to bear witness to the first results of the Permanent Settlement he had so steadfastly opposed.

The changes it brought about proved to be more of social disorders. The loss of rights of peasants, growth of sub-infeudation, conflicts between old and new houses, absenteeism, pressure of the sale laws, inadequate law courts and police system, exclusion of the natives from the important offices, decline of trade and commerce and industries— all contributed to an extremely tense and unstable social environment. Within that atmosphere, the zamindars failed to stand for improvement. Instead of becoming improving landlords they turned out to be tyrannical and unproductive.

In actual fact the Settlement was the result of a complex causation in which ideas too played a role to the extent that these were relevant to mundane interests and provided a decent appearance to them. Cornwallis not only legitimised a heavy tribute in the form of rent; he also made its collection rigid and harsh. His ideas represented British ruling classes' immediate interests as well as their false view of Bengal's social reality. Viewed in its purely commercial and financial aspects, the settlement resulted in considerable loss of future revenues. As an administrative measure, its completion required a stronger statutory base and more vigorous executive management than were forthcoming. But looking at the measure solely from a political point of view, it was the means of allaying apprehensions and removing doubts amongst a class of Indians.

Ryotwari settlement— Not long after Cornwallis introduced the Permanent Settlement in Bengal, the question of extending it to other territories, acquired by the John Company from time to time presented itself. The capture of Baramahal and Dindigul from Tipu Sultan in the Third Mysore War, and the cession of the Northern circars in 1794 as a jagir brought the issue to the fore. In 1799 Tanjore and Coimbatore and in 1801 Malabar and the territory of the Nawab of Arcot had been annexed to Madras Presidency. Among the first officials to be associated with land revenue settlement in these areas were Alexander Read and Lionel Place. Thomas Munro was one of Read's assistants; in 1800 he had been transferred from Kanara to the Deccan districts ceded by the Nizam of Hyderabad.

While these officials were busy sorting out the complex revenue affairs under their charge, Lord Wellesley, the Governor-General, issued a peremptory order to the Madras Government to introduce the Bengal system of Permanent Settlement in its newly acquired dominion. The directive was not well received, for as Munro and his assistants gained in experience, they became extremely critical of the Bengal system. Moreover, they were able to sell their new ideas to the local administration. In particular, William Bentinck, the Governor of Madras (1803-7), was attracted by what they were doing and ruled that further progress with zamindari settlement be stayed. Later (1808), permission was accorded to experiment with village panchayats, apart from the Ryotwari system.

The Ryotwari system had a staunch champion in Munro. As a result of earlier experiences in Tanjore, Hodgson, who was then powerful in the Madras Board of Revenue, was keen on village panchayats. In 1808-9, the Ryotwari experiment was tried in most of the districts, but much to Hodgson's discomfiture reports regarding village leases were uniformly unfavourable.

In Madras, by 1818, the suppression of landed aristocrats, the poligars, the establishment of judicial courts and the improvement of the revenue system had been ensured. However, in the bargain they had claimed a heavy toll. As soon as Munro became governor in May 1820 the system was declared generally operative in all parts of the Madras Presidency, barring areas already under the Permanent Settlement. As to the latter, every opportunity was taken of getting back, on account of lapses or by means of purchase, the zamindari mootahs and such other tenures as existed, with a view to introducing the new system therein.

The central characteristic of Munro's system was that the government demand on land was now permanently fixed and each cultivator could take or reject the field he was offered if he thought its rent to be excessive. Munro reduced the assessment from roughly half (45 or 50 or 55 percent) to one-third of the estimated produce; even so, in many cases the latter represented the entire economic rent and was thus, by definition, oppressive.

Two other factors impinged on the situation: first, the cultivator had to pay a fixed sum of money irrespective of the actual yield or the prevalent price; secondly, the rent was not calculated through local bodies, as in the North-Western Provinces, but by low-paid agents who made unjust extortions and used oppressive methods. It is to Munro's credit that he strove all through his seven-year administration to lower the assessments and keep the evils of the system under constant check.

In the Bombay area the Maratha system of farming out the revenue was adopted to start with. The districts were farmed out to Desais and later to Patels of villages. The Collector or his agent, the Mamlatdar or Kamavisdar, had to make the best possible deal with the Desai for the annual revenue and, provided the amount was duly paid, kept out of the way as far as the Desai's methods were concerned. After 1819, the Ryotwari system was introduced and the talti or village accountant, appointed directly by the Bombay Government, superseded the Desai or Patel. Apart from the Madras and Bombay (including Sind) Presidencies, the Ryotwari system, with such modifications as local conditions demanded, was also prevalent in Berar, Assam, Burma and Coorg.

Mahalwari settlement— The question of introducing a settlement of land revenue in the ceded and conquered provinces came to the fore in the opening years of the nineteenth century. The provinces included territory ceded by the Nawab of Awadh and his tributary, the Nawab of Faizabad, in 1801 2 and conquered by the British in 1803 as a result of Lord Lake's victories over the Marathas. Later they were known as the North-Western Provinces.

On the basis of a recommendation of the Board of Commissioners, Holt Mackenzie had his minutes of 1819, in which he recommended a settlement with village communities after a systematic survey and inquiry. While undertaking operations, a record of the rights was to be prepared—village communities being represented by headmen called lambardars (viz. persons having a "number" in the Collector's register of persons liable to pay land revenue to the state).

With all ideas of the Bengal system finally abandoned in 1821, Mackenzi's minutes became the basis for a new settlement. In essence, his plea was that revenue be fixed at a moderate rate and the settlement be made with the landlords (viz. zamindars) or peasant proprietors where they existed and with the village communities where they held land in common tenancy. Landlords or talukdars who claimed rights of land were generally granted compensation from the government treasury, the sum being later collected from the village zamindars. As the revenue settlement was to be made village by village and estate by estate and as an estate is called a "Mahal", it came to be known as the Mahalwari Settlement. The basis of the settlement was the "net produce" or that portion of the gross produce of land which remained after deducting the expenses of cultivation including the profits of stock (invested capital) and wages of labour.

Regulation 7 of 1822 and the settlement were a failure because inquiries needed for a system of record of rights made no progress; detailed investigations relating to produce of individual fields "proved vexatious and futile"; state demand computed at 80 percent and above was both severe and impracticable. William Bentinck's Regulation 9 of 1833, however, became the true basis of the land settlement in northern India. Moreover, government demand was reduced to two-thirds of the gross rental, and the settlement took 30 years to be completed. R. M. Bird, the Lt. Governor of North-Western Provinces, implemented the settlement, and is rightly known as "the father of land settlement in northern India". Subsequently, the system was introduced in the Central Provinces, the Punjab, etc.

Rural indebtedness and growth of landless labour— Causes of the impoverishment and indebtedness of the peasantry were:

1. Impoverishment of the peasantry in zamindari areas due to the oppression of the peasants by the zamindars.
2. Their impoverishment in Ryotwari Mahalwari areas due to the excessive revenue demand of the government.
3. Very little investment by the government to improve agriculture.

4. Rigid manner of revenue collection.
5. The impoverished peasant was driven then to borrow money at high rates of interest from the moneylender. And this further worsened his economic position and finally he was deprived of his land.

By the early 20th century, rural indebtedness grew unprecedently. The total rural debt of India at the beginning of the 20th century was Rs.300 crores. But, according to the Central Banking Enquiry Committee of 1929, the magnitude of rural indebtedness was about Rs.900 crores. Following the Great Depression, the burden of debt in British India alone was estimated to have increased to Rs.1200 crores.

Rural credit policy— The peasant became an easy prey to the moneylender in the absence of state protection in the form of a rural credit policy. In fact, there existed a credit policy of the government which funded only microscopic needs of the peasant. Even this was formulated in the wake of a number of struggles. The widespread riots that took place in 1875 in the Bombay presidency made even the sceptic authorities of the government realise the seriousness of the situation. A point to be noted here is that one could find anti-moneylender elements in many other uprisings in India in the 19th century. Even in the 1857 revolt, the wrath of the peasants was occasionally directed against the moneylenders. The Santhal Rebellion in the mid-1850s was of course immediately aimed at the money lending community.

Government legislations— The Deccan Riots of 1875 led to the legislation of a series of acts regarding this problem and opening of credit banks. The Land Improvements Act (1883), Agriculturists' Loan Act (1884), the Deccan Agriculturist's Relief Act (1879) and Punjab Land Alienation Act (1902) were some of the acts passed to protect the debtor from the moneylender and ensure government loans to the peasant. In the 20th century, quite a number of acts were passed in the legislature on agricultural indebtedness, like Redemption of the Mortgage Act,1935; Usurious Loans Act,1935; Assam Moneylenders Act,1934; Punjab Debtor's Protection Act,1936; U.P. Agriculturist's Relief Act, 1934; and U.P. Usurious Loans Amendment Act(which assured that the rate of interest on secured loans should not exceed 7%), etc.These acts, which were passed in the wake of rural unrest, however, were not fool-proof and had several loopholes, allowing the usurer to continue his ruthless exploitation.

Responsibility of British policies— In this context, one fact should be made clear regarding the impact of British economic policies on rural indebtedness. Not that exploiters and exploited were absent in the past, but what happened was that the character of the relationship between them changed substantially as a result of British legislation. With the establishment of courts, the moneylenders who were part of a rural society, secured increased power. Land became a valuable and saleable commodity. They changed any amount of interest, and if the tenants failed to pay it, they got the right to grab the land. Espousing the cause of rural indebtedness, the Indian economists claimed that the moneylender of the time was the direct product of British economic doctrines.

Causes for the rise of moneylenders and transfer of land were

1. The new revenue policy
2. The new legal system
3. Frequent occurrence of famines and scarcity of food
4. The growing commercialization of agriculture.

Due to the impoverishment of the large section of peasant proprietors, the class of land labourers rapidly grew. The condition of even the poor-peasant owners who still owned their lands, or sub-tenants, was so bad that there was no appreciable difference between them and the land labourers. The class of agricultural labourers combined with the large mass of poor peasants formed the large majority of the agricultural population. Their number increased enormously due to a process of steady impoverishment of the upper peasantry and expropriation of their land.

Thus, on the one hand, the lands of the unprotected proprietors began to be concentrated in the hands of a few moneylenders. And on the other hand, the large masses of the peasantry began to roll down the social ladder first as tenants-at-will and then as agricultural labourers. In this process the political influence and the power of the British government played a major role, as the protagonists of the moneylenders.

The proportion of agricultural labourers to agricultural population was the highest in the Ryotwari areas and lowest in the joint or Mahalwari areas. This was so, because in the Ryotwari areas it was easier for the moneylenders to usurp the lands of the cultivators or force them to become agricultural labourers due to the easiness in the transfer of the land in these areas. But this was more difficult in the Mahalwari areas because the "joint village" was the owner of the whole estate, and the co-shares cannot get rid of the responsibility which is the condition of ownership.

Commercialization of agriculture— Commercial agriculture, that is, the production of crops for sale rather than for own consumption, grew because of a variety of reasons: One basic reason was the constant need of the peasants under the new land systems to find ways of getting money to meet the mounting demands upon them by the state. The peasants started growing only particular crops. The land in groups of villages was solely used, because of its special suitability, for the cultivation of a single agricultural crop such as cotton, jute, wheat, sugarcane and oil seeds. Another basic reason for the rapid growth in the cultivation of cash crops was that the British government of India encouraged this. With the rise of modern industries in England, the necessity of raw materials for those industries grew. The British government in India pursued economic policies which expanded the area for growth of such raw materials as needed by the British industries. The government gradually improved the means of transport which made commerce in agriculture more widespread. Thus the government accelerated the commercialization and specialization of Indian agriculture.

The commercialization and specialization of agriculture also disrupted the unity of agriculture and industry in the traditional Indian village. Thus the older rural framework of India, weakened by the new land system, was shattered by the spread of commercial agriculture. The commercialization adversely affected even the economic position of the agriculturist. He now produced for the Indian and world market, and so he became subject to all vicissitudes of even the erratic market. He had to compete with formidable international rivals like the big agrarian trusts of America, Europe and Australia which produced on a mass scale by means of all modern agricultural machinery, while he himself cultivated his small strip of land by means of the labour power of bullocks and the primitive plough. Further, the commercialization made him dependent, for the sale of his product, on the middlemen, the merchants. The merchant by his superior economic position took full advantage of the poverty of the peasant. The poor peasant had to sell his product to the middleman at the harvest time to meet the revenue claims of the state and also the claims of the moneylender. This transaction originating in sheer necessity brought a less amount to the peasant than it would have if he waited. The middleman thus appropriated a very large share of the profit.

Plantation industries— Growth of plantation industries such as indigo, rubber, tea and coffee during the 19th century was a significant development in the British Indian economic history. Factors that attracted foreign capital to India were:

1. Prospects of high profits.
2. Availability of extremely cheap labour.
3. Ready and cheap availability of raw materials.
4. Providing ready market by India and its neighbours for many goods.
5. World demand for many Indian products such as the jute and manganese.
6. Willingness of the colonial government and officials to provide all help and show all favours.

The reasons for the domination of Indian modern industries by foreign capital and not Indian capital were

1. British enterprises' use of their close connections with British suppliers of machinery and equipment, shipping and insurance companies, banks, marketing agencies, government officials and political leaders.
2. Government's policy of favouring foreign capital as against Indian capital.
3. Government's railway policy of discriminating against Indian enterprises by fixing freight rates in such way which made the import and distribution of foreign goods easier and cheaper, and the distribution of Indian goods more difficult and costly.

The advantages and disadvantages of the foreign-owned industries to Indians were

1. The only advantage that the Indians got out of these industries was the creation of unskilled jobs.
2. But the disadvantages far outweighed the advantages. The Indian workers in these enterprises were extremely low paid and had to work under extremely harsh conditions for long hours.
3. Moreover, most of their technical staff was foreign and hence the huge salaries earned by them went out of the country.
4. And also these industries purchased most of their equipment abroad.

Many features of Indian industrial development were

1. Slow and painful progress of Indian industries and their inability

to compensate even for the displacement of the indigenous handicrafts in terms of production as well as employment. The main reasons for this feature of Indian industrial development were the British policy of artificially restricting and slowing down the growth of Indian industries by not giving them any protection and financial help in their period of infancy.

2. Almost complete absence of heavy or capital goods industries, without which there can be no rapid and independent development of industries.
3. It also suffered from extreme regional lopsidedness. Indian industries were concentrated only in a few regions and cities of the country. This uneven economic development not only led to wide regional disparities in income also affected the level of national integration.
4. An important social consequence of even this limited industrial development of the country was the birth and growth of two new social classes, the industrial capitalist class and the modern working class, which, though formed a very small part of the Indian population, represented new technology, a new system of economic organisation, new social relations, new ideas and a new outlook.

Stagnation and deterioration of agriculture— Overcrowding of agriculture and increase in sub-infeudation led to subdivision and fragmentation of land into small holdings, which in turn made it difficult to effect improvements in agriculture. Non-availability of resources to improve agriculture was due to the extreme poverty of the peasantry. Absence of any incentive to improve agriculture for the cultivator, who was rack-rented by both the government and landlord; and neglect of peasant and agriculture by the government by giving step-motherly treatment to public works and agricultural improvement led to a further decline in the agriculture sector.

Famines in India

India has suffered from famines since time immemorial. It appears that in earlier times, a major famine occurred once in every 50 years. From the beginning of the 11th century to the end of the 17th century, there were 14 famines almost all of which were confined to small local areas. The frequency of famines increased during the 19th century. In a period of about 90 years from 1765 to 1858, the country experienced 12 famines and four "severe scarcities". Between 1860 and 1908, famine or scarcity prevailed in one part of the country or the other in 20 out of a total of 49 years. There was not only an increase in the frequency of famines, there was also a change in their nature. Now let us discuss the major famines which occurred in India from time to time. These are as follows:

Bengal famine of 1769-70— There was a dreadful famine in Bengal in 1769-70 which claimed a third of the population of the province. Practically no relief measures were undertaken by the English East India Company. As a matter of fact, the servants of the Company made huge profits by buying up rice and selling the same at high prices. There was scarcity in Madras in 1781-1782. There was a severe famine in the whole of Northern India in 1784. There was the repetition of a famine in Madras in 1792. There was a famine in North-Western Provinces and Oudh in 1803. The Guntur famine of 1833 took away a heavy toll of life. Two lakhs of people out of a total population of 5 lakh, died of starvation. When in 1837, famine visited the upper reaches of the Ganges and the Jamuna, the local Government laid down the principle that while the state found work for the able-bodies, the whole community must look after the helpless and infirm. The measures adopted were wholly insufficient. Heavy mortality resulted and violent riots broke out.

Famine of 1860-61—There was a famine in North-Western Provinces in 1860-61. The genesis of the famine lay in the disturbances of 1857 in the course of which villages in North-Western Provinces were plundered and burnt so that the local stores of grains were destroyed. Moreover, the cultivation was interrupted during the next two years due to the punishments meted out to the villages and heavy fines imposed on them for their alleged complicity in the crimes of 1857. During the two years preceding the famine, rainfall was deficient. The result was that the people of North-Western Provinces were completely unprepared to face the drought of 1860. However, the drought was not widespread, but no attempt was made by the state to control the prices of foodgrains or guarantee a minimum wage and employment to labour. The poorer classes deserted their famine-stricken villages to find work in the neighbourhood. In spite of that, there were a minimum of two lakh deaths". It was for the first time that a special enquiry was held to look into the causes and intensity of the famine. Colonel Baird Smith was deputed to examine those matters but his report did not lead to the formulation of general principles of famine relief.

Famine of 1865-66— The scarcity in the Deccan districts of Bombay in 1862 was local and mild in character. The famine of 1865-66 covered a vast area. The districts of Bihar bordering on either bank of the Ganges, North Bengal, Orissa and districts in Madras Presidency lying along the

Bay of Bengal were affected. The blackest portion of the tract comprised the three districts of Orissa division. There was a terrible loss of 1.3 million lives in Orissa. There was also a famine in Bengal and Bihar at the same time. The relief given by the Government was extremely inadequate and ill-organised. The wages paid to the labourers varied from 6 paise in Champaran and Monghyr for an adult and 3 paise for a child to 9 paise for an adult and 3 paise for a child in Shahabad.

This calamity proved a turning point in the history of Indian famines as it was followed by the investigations and report of a Committee presided over by Sir George Campbell which laid the foundations of a definite famine policy. The Campbell Committee made recommendations which in certain respects anticipated those of the Royal Commission of 1880. The report of the Committee produced a change of outlook. Sir John Lawrence who was the Governor-General at that time, blamed himself bitterly for having accepted the facile assurances of the Bengal Government and when famine again appeared elsewhere in 1868, declared that his object was "to save every life" and that district officers would be held responsible if preventable deaths occurred. The old doctrine that the public would be responsible for the relief of the helpless and infirm was entirely abandoned. Money was borrowed in order to finance additional railways and canals.

Famine of 1868-1870— A famine of great severity overtook Northern India in 1868-70. The drought in 1868 covered parts of the Punjab, North-Western Provinces, Central India and Central Provinces, but the main fury of the famine fell on Rajputana. It was during this famine in North-Western Provinces that a clear departure was made from the previous policy and the Lieutenant-Governor instructed the local officers that "every district officer would be held personally responsible that no deaths occurred from starvation which could have been avoided by arrangement on his part or that of his subordinates."

Famine of 1873-74— The famine of 1873-74 in Bengal and Bihar occupies a unique position in the history of famines in India. The famine was actually very severe but the tragedy was avoided on account of a new food policy adopted by the local Government. The timely arrival of imports helped to keep down the prices of foodgrains and saved the people from the rigours of famine. The relief policy of the Bengal Government during this famine differed from its earlier policy. Liberal wages were given for relief works. The policy on relief works was to offer employment to any one who sought it at the normal rate of wages and get full normal work from him. However, later on the wages were reduced and the work was increased.

Famine of 1876-78—The great famine of 1876-78 ravaged the country for three years and was a great calamity of its kind in respect of the area and the population affected and the duration and intensity of the distress. In all, a total area of 2,05,600 sq. miles covering a population of 36.4million was affected. The Government of India felt that famine relief would involve a great financial strain and sent Sir Richard Temple to Bombay and Madras "to consult with the Government of the two Presidencies" and impress upon them the need for economy in relief expenditure. The Government of India made every effort to practise the most severe economy so that the deaths from the famine could be prevented. The Government tried its best to save the human lives. The Government had learnt from the history of past famines to provide efficient assistance for the suffering people without incurring disastrous expenditure. The financial considerations began to weigh so heavily with the Government that the earlier policy of "saving every life whatever the cost" was completely given up. That added to the gravity of the natural calamity and made this famine one of the most disastrous in the annals of the Indian famines.

The Government of India appointed a strong Commission under General Sir Richard Strachey which reported in 1880, suggesting measures of a preventive or protective character. It held that the state should give relief in times of famine but it should not be spendthrift. Care was taken that the structure of the society must not be impaired otherwise the Indians might again rise in revolt. The Commission insisted on the urgent need of proper statistical collection of facts relating to the condition of agricultural community. Relief should be administered on the following basic principles:

(1) The Government recognized that the grant of relief was the duty of the state and not of the general public. Raw grain or money might be distributed in villages and cooked food might be given at centres. Relief in villages required very careful organisation. For this purpose, distressed tracts must be divided into circles and each circle must be placed under a competent officer. Non-officials might be asked to volunteer assistance.

(2) The Government should trust private trade to supply and distribute food, giving it every possible facility. It should prohibit the export of grain because it was necessary to conserve the resources of the country. Supplies of food in distressed areas should be carefully watched.

(3) The Commission recommended that in times of famine landlord should be assisted by loans on easy terms to open works on their estates which would offer employment to labourers and poorer tenants. Loans should also be given for purchases of seed grain and bullocks.

(4) The cost of relief must be localised. For this, famine expenditure must come from local taxation. The representative members of the tax-paying body should be given the responsibility of administration and providing all needful funds. There was always a limit beyond which provincial revenues could not supply famine relief and must be assisted from Imperial funds. In ordinary times also, the Central Government should assist local Governments to undertake water storage and other protective works.

(5) In times of excessive drought, facilities should be given for the migration of cattle to grassy forest areas where abundant pasturage was procurable.

The recommendations of the Commission were generally accepted. Steps were taken to create new resources by which in normal times a surplus of revenue could be secured to meet the extra-ordinary charges thrown on the state by famine. It was finally decided that Rs.15 million should always be entered in the budget under the head "Famine Relief and Insurance".

As a result of scanty rainfall, the rabbi crop of 1664 was deficient in 5 districts of the Southern and South-Eastern parts of Punjab. In 1884-85, there was scarcity in some parts of Madras. In 1886-87, there was scarcity in Central Provinces on account of a long break of rains in August and September. In 1888-89, there was a famine in North Bihar, in the tributary states of Orissa and in Ganjam district in the Madras Presidency. There was scarcity in Kumaon and Garhwal in 1890. In 1890-92, there were scarcities in Madras, Bombay and Bengal.

The great famine of 1896-97 affected almost every province, though in varying degrees of intensity. The total population affected was estimated at 34 millions. Extensive relief measures were undertaken and in many parts of the country the people were relieved in their own homes. The total cost of relief was estimated at Rs.7.27 crores.

The famine was followed by the appointment of a Commission presided over by Sir James Lyall, ex-Lieutenant-Governor of the Punjab. He found it most difficult to compare degrees of distress with those observed in previous famines as conditions had largely changed with the expansion of railways. The Commission largely adhered to the views expressed by the Strachey Commission .The Commission observed, "In the late years, owing to high prices, there has been a considerable increase in the incomes of the land-holding and cultivating classes and their standard of comfort and expenditure has also risen. During recent famines they have shown greater powers of resistance. The poorer professional classes suffer severely from rise of prices but do not come on relief. The wages of day labourers and skilled artisans have not risen. The rise in prices of food has not been accompanied by a rise in the wages of labour. On the contrary, as competition falls off, the rate of wages offered falls frequently below the customary rate."

Famine of 1900— Before the proposals of the Lyall Commission were fully considered by the Government, India was visited in 1900 by a drought the greatest in extent and intensity which had been experienced for 200 years. The area affected amounted to more than 400,000 sq. miles with a population of about 60 million. It embraced the greater part of the Bombay Presidency, the Central Provinces, Berar and much of the Punjab, the States of Kathiawar and Rajputana, the Nizam's dominions, Baroda and the Central Indian principalities. The loss in crops alone amounted to 50 millions pounds in British India and 30millions pounds in the Indian States. The fodder famine destroyed all kinds of cattle. In the matter of saving human lives and relieving distress, the results achieved were not very flattering. The highest number of deaths, viz., 7,45,376 was recorded in Bombay, followed by 1,87,686 in the Central Provinces, 1,27,409 in the Punjab and 1,25,926 in Berar. William Digby put the mortality due to famine and famine diseases at 3.25 million. This was in spite of the fact that Rs.16.5 crores were spent on relief work.

The Government appointed a Commission under the Presidency of Sir Anthony MacDonnel. Their report was published in 1901. It summarised the accepted principles of relief and suggested variations. It emphasised the benefits of a policy of "moral strategy", early ascertainment and publication of suspensions of revenue and rents, early distribution of seed and cattle and the sinking of temporary wells. It recommended the appointment of a Famine Commissioner in a province where relief operations were expected to be extensive.

There was a famine in Deccan Districts of Bombay Presidency in 1905-6. It affected 23,000 sq. miles and 3million people out of a total area of 24,000 sq. miles and a total population of 7 millions in those districts. A famine of considerable severity was experienced in the United Provinces of Agra and Oudh in 1907-8 as a result of failure of rains.

On account of various factors, there was a rise of prices in foodgrains in 1918 and there was also a failure of rains. An extremely severe, widespread and deadly epidemic of influenza added to the general distress. Relief measures were taken by the Government and the distress ended with the abundant rains of 1919.

The Bengal famine (1943)— There was a famine in Bengal in 1943. It has been called a tragedy in unpreparedness. Due to neglect, the food situation in India had been allowed to grow from bad to worse. In spite of the low standard of living of the people of India, the country was unable to feed the population from domestic production of cereals. No steps were taken in India at the beginning of the World War II to meet any dislocation in production, supply and distribution of food that War might cause. When imports of rice from Burma stopped due to its occupation by the Japanese, shortage of food took place in Bengal. The country, the people and the administration, both at the Centre and in the provinces were found unprepared to meet to the challenge. The result was chaos which gave anti-social elements an opportunity to make individual fortunes and hold their countrymen ransom while a million and a half poor died due to sheer hunger.

It has been rightly said that both man and God joined hands to produce the tragedy in Bengal. The famine might be called "more man-made than an act of God." Man merely exploited the situation created by nature and World War II. The root cause of the famine is to be found in the series of crop famines that Bengal experienced from 1938 and in the conditions created by the War. There was the stoppage of normal imports from Burma, dislocation of trade and movements of foodgrains on account of controls and the nearness of Bengal to the theatre of War in the East, the building up of provincial and even district barriers against the movement of grains and other essential supplies, the increase in the demand for food on account of the demand from the army and refugees from Burma and the rise in prices. None of these was a man-made factor. The fault was with the Government which did not take into consideration the change in circumstances in Bengal and did nothing to control the situation so long as Lord Linlithgow was the Governor-General and Viceroy of India. It was only when Lord Wavell took over from him as Governor-General that the situation was tackled on a war footing. However, the famine took a heavy toll of life in Bengal. From July to December 1943, the death rate rose by 108.3 percent. The view of K.P.Chattopadhyaya is that as many as 3.5 million people died during the famine. The estimate of the Famine Enquiry Commission was 1.5 million deaths. Almost the whole of Bengal, in greater or less degree, was affected by the famine and suffered loss of life. The British was always on a war footing to fight against this natural menace and find a remedy to it.

Impact of British Rule on Indian Industry

On some intensely debated issues, an agreement is still to emerge, especially as regards the impact of British capital and British government on the development (or underdevelopment) of Indian industry. One stream of thought associates the distorted pattern of India's industrial evolution with the colonial factor; the other minimises it and seeks explanation in the low level of the Indian economy.

1. The first view dwells on the laissez faire economics of the Raj and the missed opportunities of industrialization in the nineteenth century. It delineates the throttling system of monopoly that flourished in the high noon of empire, in around 1900, and then goes on to show how the shaking up of the structure after 1914 opened the way to a limited degree of industrialization under Indian initiative in the 1920s and 1930s.
2. As opposed to this stream of thought, the second school emphasises the technological backwardness of the Indian economic structure as the major factor blocking the sustained growth of investment in large-scale industry. By and large, however, the explanation of backwardness is no longer sought in the other worldly values of Indian civilization, the Hindu religious ethic, or the institution of caste. Instead of resorting to uncritical generalizations about values and customs, economic historians now pay closer attention to demand and supply factors.

Issues involved— A series of questions crop up regarding the history of industry in India:

1. Why did the linking of Indian capital to industry come so late?
2. How was the sophisticated and highly evolved world of the bazaar, so completely shut out from the European preserves of modern banks, export-import houses, plantations and factories?
3. What were the circumstances in which European enterprise carved out the exclusive sphere of corporate industrial operations for itself?

4. What benefits did this European enterprise confer on the country in terms of economic growth?
5. How is it that Bombay was the one region where Indian enterprise was able to carve out an early role in that exclusive sphere?
6. Such questions are closely related to the basic question— why was the Indian economy unable to effect an industrial revolution?
7. Was it too backward around 1800 for it to take off in the course of the nineteenth century?
8. Or did under-development "develop" in India as a result of what is referred to as "deindustrialization" in the course of that century?

Machine-based industries— The machine age began in India with the starting of cotton mills, jute and coal mining industries in the 1850s. The development of other mechanical industries such as rice, flour and timber mills, leather tanneries, woollen textiles, paper and sugar mills, iron and steel works, and some mineral industries during the second half of the 19th century and beginning of the 20th century contributed further to the growth of modern industries in India.

In the beginning, modern business and industry in British India was predominantly European. In the late nineteenth century, an Indian-owned complex of modern industry had sprung up in Bombay and Ahmedabad, but this was an exception. The tea plantations, the coal mines, the jute mills, etc., had developed in eastern India under European enterprise, roughly between the 1850s and the1880s. Because of circumstances specific to the Bombay Presidency, the cotton mills there developed under Parsi and Gujarati enterprise before and after the Civil War in the United States. There were three distinct phases in the development of large-scale industry in colonial India. These phases overlap to some extent, but are distinct enough to be roughly identified as: (1) 1850-1914; (2) 1914-39; and (3) 1939-47.

First phase— The first phase was dominated by the European managing agencies. It saw the development of light manufacturing, and planting and mining industries, which relied heavily on markets abroad. The tea and jute industries of eastern India were almost pure export-led industries, and the greater part of the cotton textile industry of Bombay also catered to markets in the Far East. There was no serious competition as yet with the industries of Britain, in the domestic market of India. The coal industry, while depending on the domestic market, was principally consumed by the railways running to the colonial ports. Steel, which did promise a revolutionary breakthrough based on the domestic market, was produced in too small a quantity to make any perceptible difference to the total value of industrial production. The industries of the period developed in areas of natural advantage, based on rudimentary technology, easily imported from Britain.

Second phase— Coming to the second time span, certain new features strike us. This second phase of industry, distinguished from the earlier one by its orientation to the domestic market and from the succeeding one by its simpler technology, saw the development of deadly competition with the industries of the advanced West, for the possession of the mass market for consumer's goods within the country. There sprang up, by the side of the older cotton textiles industry, a new range of light manufactures, all protected by war, tariff and depression. The production of cotton textiles, sugar, paper, etc., surged ahead within the sheltered domestic market, helped by the relatively simple technology. By the end of the period, Manchester cotton textiles, Java sugar and foreign paper of all sorts except newsprint, were more or less eliminated by burgeoning manufacturing units owned by Indian businessmen and industrialists. One critical development that went beyond these changes was the Greater Extensions Programme of Tata Iron and Steel Company (1916-24), the completion of which for the first time, made the steel industry a considerable one.

Third phase— Without this development, the third phase, marked by the beginning of the capital goods industry, would not have been possible at all. Industrial growth during the inter-war period had slowly created a market for the heavy engineering and chemical industries. It was, however, the technological leap of the Second World War that enabled Indian industry to launch out on these new and complex lines. The production of basic and heavy capital goods was hampered by formidable technological problems arising from the absence of essential equipment, machinery and technical know how. The problem dictated a new pattern of co-operation between the big Indian houses and several multinational corporations by the time of independence.

Deindustrialization— The industries which were worst affected by the policies of the British were the cotton weaving and spinning industries, silk and woollen industries, pottery, glass, paper, metals, shipping, oil-pressing, tanning and dyeing industries. The poor state of the Indian handicraft industry can be ascribed to the following causes:

1. Influx of foreign goods with the adoption of the policy of one-way free trade by the British.

2. The construction of railways which enabled the British manufacturers to reach the remotest villages of the country.
3. The oppression practised by the East India Company and its servants on the craftsmen in forcing them to sell their goods below the prevailing wage.
4. The loss of European markets to Indian manufacturers due to the imposition of high import duties and other restrictions on the import of Indian goods.
5. The gradual disappearance of Indian rulers and their courts, who were the main customers of town handicrafts.
6. Rise in the prices of raw materials due to the British policy of exporting raw materials.

The downslide in Indian industries resulted in the following

1. Depopulation and ruin of towns and cities which were famous for their manufactures.
2. Increase in unemployment due to the absence of the growth of modern industries.
3. Breaking of the union between agriculture and domestic industry in the countryside which in turn led to the destruction of the self-sufficient village economy.
4. Overcrowding of agriculture by the ruined artisans, thus adding to the general pressure on land.

Course of deindustrialization— The statistical evidence available on employment in the secondary sector of the economy seems to indicate that, despite the emergence of factories and mines, the proportion of the population dependent on industry declined significantly in the course of the nineteenth century. The emergence of modern industry did not offset the decline in artisan industries. There is only one set of survey figures for comparing the proportion of people dependent on industries around 1800 with the corresponding figure in 1900.

1. These are the figures recorded by Buchanan Hamilton, during his survey of the Gangetic districts of Bihar in 1809.
2. The result is suggestive: the proportion of people deriving their sustenance from industry declined from 18.6 percent in 1809 to 8.5 percent in 1901.

Much of the decline was due to a drastic fall in the number of weavers and spinners in the , in the course of the century. Doubt has been expressed on the accuracy of Hamilton's survey; but it is the only survey made at the beginning of the nineteenth century; and its results are more reliable than other estimates based on mere guesswork. In view of the impressions of contemporary observers, which accord closely with the above statistical account, it is reasonably certain that employment and total output in industry declined in the nineteenth-century India, despite the emergence of modern factories. There is evidence, however, to show that this deindustrialization was arrested around the beginning of the twentieth century.

References

Andrews, Kenneth R. (1984) *Trade, Plunder and Settlement: Maritime Enterprise and the Genesis of the British Empire, 1480–1630.*

Brown, Judith M. (1994), *Modern India: The Origins of an Asian Democracy*, Oxford and New York: Oxford University Press.

Chand, Tara (1961), *History of the Freedom Movement in India*, Vol. I, New Delhi: Publications Division.

Chandra, Bipan et al. (1972), *Freedom Struggle*, New Delhi: National Book Trust.

Chandra, Bipan *et al.* (1989), *India's Struggle for Independence*, New Delhi: Penguin Books.

Desai, A. R. (1976), *Social Background of Indian Nationalism*, Bombay: Popular Prakashan.

Dutt, R. C. (1976), *Economic History of India* (Under Early British Rule, 1757-1857), Vol. I, Delhi: Publications Division.

Dutt, R. Palme (1949), *India Today*, Bombay, People's Publishing House Ltd.

Majumdar, R.C. (1963), *History of the Freedom Movement in India*, Vol. II, Calcutta: Firma K.L. Mukhopadhyay.

Marx, Karl and F. Engels (eds.) (1965), *On Colonialism*, Moscow: Progress Publishers.

Metcalf, Barbara & Thomas R. Metcalf (2006), *A Concise History of Modern India (Cambridge Concise Histories)*, Cambridge and New York: Cambridge University Press.

Peers, Douglas M. (2006), *India under Colonial Rule 1700-1885*, Harlow and London: Pearson Longmans.

Rothermund, Dietmar (1993), *An Economic History of India: From Pre-Colonial Times to 1991*.

Chapter- 6

Caste and Class in British India

As the British rule had an all pervasive impact on Indian society, culture, polity and economy for a long time, this chapter proposes to cover the nature of impact on the caste system under the influence of the British rule. The discussion is also necessary because caste system has been one of the characteristic features of the Indian society since ancient days. This institution of caste has always determined the conduct and social status of individuals in society as well as the division of labour in general to a large extent.

In the ancient days, Brahmin was at the apex of caste. But with the advent of the British as the political head of society, things changed. The British brought with them their own traditional form of government. As the Englishmen were Christians, they could not have much sympathy with the institutions of the Hindus. The British introduced a system of education which did not demand of the learners any change of religion. They also followed a policy of non-interference. Later on, with the incoming of the modern industrial organisation and the growth of industrial cities, large number of people settled down in cities, forgetting the ties of caste-system (Ghurye, 1961: 178-211).

The fluidity of the caste system was affected by the arrival of the British. Prior to that, the relative ranking of castes differed from one place to another. The castes did not constitute a rigid description of the occupation or the social status of a group. Since the British society was divided by class, the British attempted to equate the Indian caste system to the class system. They saw caste as an indicator of occupation, social standing, and intellectual ability. During the initial days of the British East India Company's rule, caste privileges and customs were encouraged, but the British law courts disagreed with the discrimination against the lower castes (Alavi, 1998). However, British policies of divide and rule as well as enumeration of the population into rigid categories during the 10 year census contributed towards the hardening of caste identities (Corbridge, 2000).

During the period of British rule, India saw the rebellions of several lower castes, mainly tribals that revolted against British rule. These were:

1. Halba rebellion (1774-79)
2. Bhopalpatnam Struggle (1795)
3. Bhil rebellion (1822–1857)
4. Paralkot rebellion (1825)
5. Tarapur rebellion (1842-54)
6. Maria rebellion (1842-63)
7. First Freedom Struggle (1856-57)
8. Bhil rebellion, begun by Tantya Tope in Banswara (1858)
9. Koi revolt (1859)
10. Gond rebellion, begun by Ramji Gond in Adilabad (1860)
11. Muria rebellion (1876)
12. Rani rebellion (1878-82)
13. Bhumkal (1910)

Early in the history of the British rule the practice of the rulers over the three presidencies was not uniform. In Bengal one of the Regulations, while recognizing the integrity of caste organisation, allowed suits for restoration of caste to be entertained by the ordinary courts.[1] It was held that a person expelled from club or voluntary associations was quite different from the case where a person was excommunicated from caste.[2] In Bombay, there was a regulation that no court shall interfere in any caste question.

Under the old regime of caste certain sections of Hindu society which were regarded as untouchables were devoid of many of the civil rights. The question of removing their disabilities came up for consideration before the British administrators. In 1856 the Government of Bombay had to consider the case of a Mahar boy, who was refused admission to the Government School at Dharwar. The principle involved in the case occupied the attention of the Government for about two years. Finally in 1858 it was announced in a press-note that "although the Governor-in-Council does not contemplate the introduction of low-caste pupils into schools, the expenses of which are shared with Government by local contributors and patrons who object to such a measure, he reserves to himself the full right of refusing the support of Government to any partially aided school in which the benefits of education are withheld from any class of persons on account of caste or race, and further resolves that all schools maintained at the sole cost of Government shall be open to all classes of its subjects without distinction."[3]

John Wilson wrote in 1877: "Few, if any, of the Antyaja are found in Government schools. This is to be ascribed not only to the Brahminical fear of contamination and the general caste prejudices of the people, but to the want of firmness on the part of the Government educational authorities as has been the case in some instances of the agents of the missionary bodies".[4] In a press-note of 1915 we still find the complaint that the evil of untouchability could not be removed even after coming in contact with Western civilization and English education. It further refers that depressed class boys were not allowed to enter the schoolroom but were accommodated outside the room on the verandah. In 1923 the Government issued a resolution that no grants would be paid to any aided educational institution which refused admission to the children of the Depressed Classes. By the time the practice of segregating the Depressed Class boys was fast disappearing especially in the Central Division of the presidency. In many local Board and Municipal schools Depressed Class pupils are now allowed to sit in their classes like boys and girls of the caste Hindus.

While the Bombay Government was thus enforcing the right of the Depressed Class to equal treatment, the Madras Government had on its Statute-book so late as the end of 1923 a law empowering village Magistrates to punish the offenders of the lower castes by imprisonment in the stocks though the Government had definitely pledged itself in 1914 to discontinue this inhuman practice.[5] In 1925 a Bill was introduced in the Madras legislative Council to put under statute the principle of a resolution passed in the previous session of the Council throwing open all public roads, streets, or pathways, giving access to any public office, well, tank, or place of public resort, to all classes of people including the Depressed.

Various non-Brahmin castes other than the Depressed Classes were also subjected to many disabilities. The British did not consider those disabilities as lawful. Yet the services were mainly manned by Brahmin and allied castes, who were the first to profit by English education. This drew the attention of some of the non-Brahmin leaders and sympathetic officers of the Government to demand special treatment to those half-submerged classes. As a response, Chatfield, the Director of Public

Instruction in Bombay, allowed in 1878 some concessions in the matter of fees in primary schools to the boys of some of these castes. Later on were instituted scholarships in secondary schools and colleges for boys from some of them.

The early non-Brahmin leaders had urged upon the Government the necessity of special representation for their members both in the administrative bodies as well as in the services. For a petty long time this appeal remained unheeded. Their cry was, however, taken up by the late Maharaja of Kolhapur.[6] A strong case for it was made by him at the time when Montague came to India to consult the people and the Government of India as regards the future form of Government. In the reformed constitution framed by Montague and Lord Chelmsford special representation through mixed electorates was conceded to the non-Brahmins. Under those provisions the whole Hindu populace in the Bombay Presidency was divided into three sections: Brahmins and allied castes, the intermediate classes formed by Marathas and others, and the backward classes including the so called untouchable.[7] A Resolution of the Government of Bombay Finance Department, dated 17th September, 1923, expressly prohibited recruitment to the lower services from the advanced class of Brahmins and others till a certain proportion of the posts is held by members of the intermediate and backward classes, wherein the absolute restriction on the recruitment from the advanced classes was removed.[8] The Government wanted to see certain castes represented in the services of the Province. That's why for these services the applicants had to state his caste and sub-caste.

In those days, British administrators followed the age-old practice of using caste names as a convenient mode of description of persons. The police Reports while giving details about offenders also mention their caste. The person sending his parcel by post had to sign and fill his caste on it. This was not done to show his occupation. There is a separate entry provided to describe ones profession. Perhaps the caste-entry has been inserted to enable the officers concerned to form a rough estimate of the moral character of the person.

The Britishers in India tried to understand the working of the caste institution in the country. This unique institution of caste had arisen the intellectual curiosity of the Britishers and it is through their efforts that we can understand the growth and origin of this institution. Some of the early officials like Elliot, Dalton, Sherring, and Nesfield, showed their interest in the subject by collecting information and publishing it with their comments. Later officials adopted the method of utilizing the decennial census for collecting information and indulging in the theories of the origins of caste.[9] This procedure reached its culmination in the Census of 1901 under the guidance of Sir Herbert Risley. Risley says that in this caste-ridden society a person, when questioned about his caste, may offer a bewildering variety of replies:" He may give the name of a sect, of a sub-caste, of an exogamous sect or section, of a hypergamous group; he may mention some titular designation which sounds finer than the name of his caste; he may describe himself by his occupation or by the province or tract of country from which he comes."[10] Various ambitious castes wanted to raise their status. For this, they invited conferences of their members, and formed councils to take steps to see that their status was recorded in the way they thought was honourable to them. Other castes which could not do this, resented this "stealthy" procedure. Thus, mutual conflict was set on foot. "The leaders of all but the highest castes frankly looked upon the Census as an opportunity for pressing and perhaps obtaining some recognition of social claims which were denied by persons of castes higher than their own".[11] It has been pointed out to me by an Indian gentleman that the last few years, and especially the occasion of the present census, have witnessed an extraordinary revival of the caste spirit in certain aspects. For numerous caste 'Sabhas' have sprung up, each keen to assert the dignity of the social group which it represents'.[12]

In the old regime one caste used to request the sovereign refrain another caste from carrying a procession through a particular street or from using a particular mark. Such cases are on record in the Diaries of the Peshwas. The British Government discouraged such interference in caste affairs and thus removed some of the occasions for a demonstration of the bitter caste-spirit. On the other hand, the Census officials gave an intelligible picture of caste by means of nice grading of contemporary groups to avoid bitter caste-spirit.

One of the disabilities of the Hinduism is that the low-caste Hindus were denied access to Hindu temples. They are required to step outside the temple proper in the compound and satisfy themselves that they have had a glimpse of the idol of God. A devout Hindu feels very strongly that his homage and prayer to God must be paid in full sight of the idol of God. Hindu religion is not an established church. There are temples for the idols of God maintained by private individuals or by public trusts. The latter sometimes receive grants from the State. The famous temple of Parvati at Poona is one such. The Depressed Classes want to visit the temple as other caste-Hindus do. The trustees refuse to allow them the right. The Government of Bombay, who makes a substantial grant towards the maintenance of the temple, did not think it necessary to intervene as a matter of public policy. It is curious to see that an institution which is maintained by the public money must impose restrictions on a person because of his caste or creed. It is duty of the Government to see that all classes of the Hindus should have access to the temple and in case this is not implemented, grants of money from public funds should be stopped.

Middleton, one of the two Superintendents of Census Operations of 1921, had made some remarks about the effects of the British Administration on caste in the Punjab. He observes: "I had intended pointing out that there is a very wide revolt against the classification of occupational castes; that these castes have been largely manufactured and almost entirely preserved as separate castes by the British Government. Our land records and official documents have added iron bonds to the old rigidity of caste. Caste in itself was rigid among the higher castes, but malleable amongst the lower. We pigeon-holed every one by caste, and if we would not find a true caste for them, labelled them with the name of a hereditary occupation. We deplore the caste-system and its effects on social and economic problems, but we are largely responsible for the system (which we deplore. Left to themselves such castes as Sonar and Lohar would rapidly disappear and no one would suffer.......Government's passion for labels pigeon-holes has led to a crystallization of the caste system, which, except amongst the aristocratic castes, was really very fluid under indigenous rule..... If the Government would ignore caste it would gradually be replaced by something very different amongst the lower castes."[13] The situation in the Punjab cannot be taken as typical of other provinces.

During British rule, the common man was controlled by the opinion of the caste. In 1925, an eminent social worker of Gujarat gives description about the aspect of caste. She observes: "On our side of the country, I mean in Gujarat, the greatest hindrance to all social reforms is the caste. If I want to educate my girl, the caste would step in and say you should not do it. If I wish to postpone my children's marriage till they are sufficiently grown up, the caste would raise its hand and forbid me. If a widow chooses to marry again and settle respectably in her home the caste would threaten to ostracize her. If a young man wishes to go to Europe for bettering his own or the country's prospects, the caste would, though, perhaps nowadays give him a hearty send-off, yet close its doors on him when he returns. If a respectable man of the so-considered Untouchable class is invited to a house, the caste would deliver its judgement against that householder and condemn him as unfit for any intercourse." [14]

In some of the Provinces, a definite percentage of posts in the various services were filled from the members of the non-Brahmin or the intermediate castes, provided they have the minimum qualifications. This was originally the demand of the leaders of the non-Brahmin movement. And it is the most obvious remedy against caste-domination. But the obvious is not necessarily the wisest. Restriction on the numbers of the able members of the Brahmin and the allied castes does not sound right. Even among the Brahmins, there are highly qualified and talented men who deserve services. By giving reservation for low-caste people, the talented upper caste men are denied justice just for no fault. Non- Brahmins, when they fail to acquire a seat in civil services because of lack of adequate merit, get a job only on the ground of birth. Caste never serves the nation, only the merit does. Caste is a mere handicap to the country.

The Government of Bombay, in their memorandum submitted to the Indian Statutory Commission, 1928 (p.94), complain that the District School Boards, where the non-Brahmins have had a majority, "have almost in every case attempted to oust the Brahmins regardless of all consideration of efficiency." The result was the pampering of caste at the cost of efficiency and justice.

On the whole, the British rulers of India, who have throughout professed to be the trustees of the welfare of the country, never seem to have given much thought to the problem of caste, in so far it affects the nationhood of India. Nor have they shown willingness to take a bold step rendering caste harmless. They took only those measures which would ensure the safety of British domination.

It may be argued that, if the British masters of India did not take any steps to minimize the evil effects of caste, it must be said to their credit that they did not at least consciously foster the institution. But, when the uprising of 1857 was suppressed, it does not appear to be true from utterances of some responsible British officers. The uprising opened the eyes of the administrators of the country as well as of the students of British Indian history to the potentialities of caste. It was almost the unanimous opinion of persons connected with the Government of India that the deep causes of the Rising were to be found in the fact that the Bengal Army was composed largely of the higher castes, viz., the Brahmins and the Rajputs. Lord Elphinstone was of the opinion that men of different castes should be enlisted in the army, while Major-General H.T. Tucker went further and insisted on the necessity of keeping the country under British domination through the policy of separating the nationalities into different caste-bodies. Lord Ellenborough advised the same, but clearly pointed out that the recommendation was based solely on the ground of British interests and not on the consideration of efficiency of the Army. He lamented the fact that if the suggested procedure were adopted "we must abandon the hope of ever again seeing a native army composed like that we have lost. It was an army which, under a General that it loved and trusted, would have marched victorious to the Dardanelles."[15] Ever since then the Indian Army has been studiously purged of the higher castes. The British had learnt the lesson from the Rising that the safety of the British domination in India was very closely connected with keeping the Indian people divided on the lines of caste. Some officials like Sir Lepel Griffin thought that caste was useful in preventing rebellion,[16] while James Kerr, the Principal of the Hindu College at Calcutta, wrote the following in 1865: "It may be doubted if the existence of caste is on the whole unfavourable to the permanence of our rule. It may even be considered favourable to it, provided we act with prudence and forbearance. Its spirit is opposed to national union.[17] The maxim of "divide and rule" began to be preached by historians and journalists alike.[18] Because the Rising was largely the work of soldiers of the high castes of Brahmins and Rajputs, there was a clamour in England that the high-caste sepoys should be exterminated.[19] Since the Rising, the British became suspicious of the high castes. The valuable lesson learnt after paying a bloody price was not going to be lost. The British decided to follow the principle of "divide and rule".

The British brought with them a casteless culture and a literature full of thoughts on individual liberty. With the introduction of English education many of the intelligent minds of the country came in closer contact with the religion of the rulers and with some outstanding personalities amongst them. As a result some Indians like Raja Ram Mohan Roy and Devendranath Tagore started movements, which aimed at giving a new dimension to religion and practising the brotherhood of man. The Brahmo Samaj had not only monotheism to preach but also to establish a brotherhood wherein man shall not be divided from man because of caste. The Bombay Prarthana Samaj, inspired by the ideals of Brahmo Samaj in Bengal, attacked caste-system vehemently. While this movement of repudiating caste was being fostered, other capable Hindu minds thought of remodelling Hindu society as enshrined in the Vedas. Swami Dayanand Saraswati had given the slogan: "Back to the Vedas". Swami Dayanand preached that the four- fold division of the Hindu people should be substituted for the manifold division and sub-division of contemporary caste. The one important innovation that this school of thought carried out in its programme of reconstruction was that even the fourth class of the Hindu society, viz., the Sudras, could study the Vedas.[20] The Arya Samaj movement of Swami Dayanand could achieve success in its aim. But, we do not see this in the case of the Prarthana Samaj of Bombay. Its high- caste leaders, when about to arrange for the marriages of their sons or daughters, did not make any effort to practise the ideal they preached. Even we come to see that some of the eminent leaders of the Samaj while openly denouncing caste, busied themselves with the affairs of the caste-groups in which they were born. This shows that it is difficult to free one from the tentacle of caste. An old Tamil proverb supports this fact which goes like this: "even an ascetic is not free from love for his caste." Arya Samaj became more popular than the Prarthana Samaj due to the following reasons:

First, the Arya Samaj tried to revive the ancient purity of the Vedic society and thus appealed to the traditional sentiment of the people.

Secondly, the sincerity of the members of the Arya Samaj was much better demonstrated in actual practice, and

Thirdly, its chief centre of activity was transferred to the Punjab, where caste has been flexible.

In some rural areas and small towns, the caste system is still very rigid. Caste is also a factor in the politics of India.

Movements against caste took the form of a militant nature. In 1873 Jyotirao Phule of Poona, though a man of Mali caste and of comparatively little education, started an association of members called the Satyashodhak Samaj with the purpose of asserting the worth of man irrespective of caste. He carried out a revolt against the tyranny of the caste system. He urged the non-Brahmin castes not to engage any Brahmin priest to conduct their marriage ritual, which he tried to reduce to a very simple procedure. He knew the necessity of educating the people of non-Brahmin castes. He had started primary schools both for boys and girls of the non-Brahmin castes as early as 1848. In 1851, Phule started a primary school for the untouchables in Poona.

Phule waged a war against the caste system which denied ordinary human rights to one and all the members of Hindu society. It was not merely a non-Brahmin movement to cast off the domination of the Brahmins. In his writings he demanded representation for all classes of the Hindus in all the local bodies, the services, and the institutions.[21] The movement did not receive any support from the Brahmins in general. Only stray individuals like Ranade showed sympathy with it. Even among the non-Brahmins the progress of Phule's ideas was slow. It was the late Maharaja of Kolhapur who infused new life into the agitation, so much so that Montague and Chelmsford, in their Indian Political reforms, had to grant the demands.[22]

It would be interesting to know the ideas of the late Maharaja of Kolhapur, who did so much for the recognition of the non-Brahmin movement. On the eve of the announcement of the Indian reforms he said: "If castes remain as they are Home Rule in the sense, it is meant, will result in nothing but a kind of oligarchy. This of course does not mean, I may tell once more, that I am against Home Rule. Surely we want it. Under the present circumstances, however, we must have the protection and guidance of the British Government until the evil of caste-system becomes ineffective. To prevent Home Rule from culminating in oligarchy, we must have communal representation at least for 10 years. It will teach us what our rights are. Once we know them, communal representation can be dispensed with."[23]

Rao Bahadur A.B. Latthe, the biographer of the late Maharaja of Kolhapur, realized that the case for special representation of lower castes couldn't be sanctioned on the plea urged by his late hero. It seeks other grounds. He observes, "Unless, among the Hindus, caste disappears altogether, there is little chance of avoiding political expedients, like communal electorates though their harmful results are obvious".[24]

There were other leaders of the non-Brahmins who insisted on strict reservation of posts in the various services for non-Brahmins. They were at pains to proclaim that their movement was not inspired by any anti-Brahmin classes must have an adequate share of state-support in the form of reserved posts.

Nevertheless, these arguments are opposed to the principle of nationality and social justice. Only a microscopic minority recognized the evils of these demands. They propounded that communalism must be abandoned. The Chairman of the Reception Committee of the meeting of the Madras non-Brahmin party in 1924 made a strong appeal "to abandon the communal policy pursued hitherto and transform the party into an organisation representing the forces working for reform along constitutional lines into which everyone without distinction of caste, religion, or colour would have free admission."[25]

What are the interests which the leaders of the non-Brahmin movement wish to safeguard by means of special representation? If there are any such interests, are they same for all the castes? These are the questions which it is not at all easy for the leaders of the movement to answer. The economic interest of the artisans, the tenant-farmers, land-lords, and mill-workers are not identical.

The non-Brahmins castes can be regarded as one group only in social matters because the attitude of the Brahmins as regards food, social intercourse and religious instruction towards them has been uniform. There has been enough awakening in the country because the Brahmins stopped imposing legal restrictions in these matters. Even the Tamilnad Congress Committee decided in 1925 that "the gradation of merit based on birth should not be observed in Indian social life".[26] The Brahmins became liberal in their attitude during the last forty years mainly due to education and social reform campaign but not because of communal representation.

Reserved representation is thus not necessary. It is harmful because it tends to create the distinction based on birth. The Government had helped in dissolving tribal bonds by ensuring the needs of the social life to all the people alike. The co-operation in the satisfaction of the needs of common life may be based on both territorial contiguity and affinity of interests. When we say that there should be special representation for some castes, it means the negation of such co-operation. In advanced countries, there is a strong sense of unity. There is no representation of different interests, even when they can be divided into different groups with conflicting interests. Thus we have not heard of "labour" claiming special representation in the British Parliament. Where it is a question of engendering a feeling of unity the people must be made to co-operate irrespective of their caste. It is only by such activity that the feeling of nation-community can be created. To allow special representation is to encourage the rise of communal feeling.

Certain types of non-Brahmin leaders find it easy to secure a seat on the legislature or a local body through the door of reserved representation, and that is the main reason, perhaps, why they are so strong in claiming it.[27] But they fail to see that their example would be soon followed by many non-Brahmin castes and their chances of an easy seat would be very much diminished. This is not a mere imagination. This will be clear to anyone who has followed the history of the demand for special representation or reservation in Indian political life. Different castes have always been clamouring for special representation. In this way, national life will be reduced to an absurdity. As it is, the non-Brahmins in the Bombay

Presidency, wherever they could have their way, have shown unmistakable tendency to be anti-Brahmin and to harass their Brahmin employees in the matter of transfers, etc.[28] So, the time had come when the British Government had to protect the interests of the Brahmins against the majority party, i.e., the non-Brahmin classes. All points considered, special representation is unnecessary and harmful. It has been mentioned above that the non-Brahmins demanded reservation of posts in the various services. This feature has latterly been so far insisted upon by the party that a journalist described it as "immediately and on the surface a movement to secure a larger share of offices in the administration."[29]

There are two reasons by which reservations of posts can be supported. First, that the Brahmins and other castes, which have a strong majority in the personnel of the services, can and do harass the populace simply because they are non-Brahmins. Secondly, the dominant castes do not allow fresh vacancies for the non-Brahmins in government services. The former allegation is sometimes made, but our experience does not lead us to believe that such harassment exists on an appreciable scale. Even if it did exist, there is enough general awakening to stop the offenders from doing so. Caste feeling is such that one prefers his own caste-fellows and may use influence in their favour to the detriment of other castes. If proper precaution can be taken against such a contingency, there would be no scope for the principle of the reservation of posts. Such precaution can be effectively taken if all the recruitment to all the public services is made on the results of competitive examinations held by a board consisting of persons well-known for their casteless views.

The problem of the depressed classes deserves special treatment. Among these classes are castes that follow the skilled occupation of tanning, shoe-making and working in bamboo and cane. These are considered so low by the other Hindus that they were not allowed to approach other castes within a measurable distance. They have thus been segregated most effectively for centuries. Their ideas of cleanliness have lagged very far behind those of caste-Hindus. Education has never been a luxury enjoyed by them. Utterly looked down by the higher sections of society they have had no desire to imitate them. To alter the habits of these people, education is essential. Some aspects of these habits also depend on the economic position of these classes. To better the economic position of the depressed classes is thus necessary in order to bring about a real change in their social status.

In the Maratha region since the time of Jyotirao Phule, reformers began their campaign for education of the members of the depressed classes.

Individual workers like Messrs. V.R. Shinde and A. V. Thakkar have done much not only to rouse the feeling of the caste-Hindus against the unjust doctrine of untouchability but also to prepare the depressed classes for better treatment by spreading education amongst them. The problem of the removal of untouchability was made a national one through the efforts of Mahatma Gandhi. The campaign was benefited by the efforts made by Christian and Mohammedans missionaries to convert the depressed classes to their faiths. The high-caste Hindus sensed a real danger to their faith. They did not want the untouchables to drive away into the folds of other faiths. To stop this conversion, the higher castes changed their attitudes towards the Untouchables. "Kulin Brahmins of Nabadwip, Shantipur, Krishnagar, Kustia and other places accepted and drank water from the hands of Nam Shudras, washer-men, boat-men, dais and other untouchables and drank the water amidst scenes of great enthusiasm. Young Brahmins and old Bhattacharyas, Mukherjis, Banerjis, Chatterjis, Maitras, all took part in the interesting function."[30] The untouchables were not allowed to pass through the roads of Vaikam in Travancore in 1924, but the high-caste Hindus tried to remove this prohibition. While the trustees of Hindu temples have closed the temple doors to the untouchables, individual owners of private temples have allowed free access for all classes of Hindus to the temples under their management. There were people who were in favour of untouchability. In the beginning of 1925 a number of merchants of Bombay, among whom were included some of the leading public men, were convened a meeting of orthodox Hindus. Almost every speaker condemned the attitude of Gandhi towards untouchability and declared that the Hindu religion was in danger at his hands. It is the duty of those who have no belief in untouchability to preach its abolition and to demonstrate their belief through their own conduct.

As we have seen the attitude of high-caste Hindus in general, so it becomes necessary to demand some representation for the untouchable classes in the local and legislative bodies. The classes which have been living in misery since ages, have not produced a sufficient number of men who can organize them to take care of their rights by public agitation. Untouchability can be removed if the habits and customs of the untouchable castes are changed. Education of these classes is a crying necessity. Poverty and established practice create hurdles for them to receive education. Under the circumstances, stipends should be provided for their members at all stages of education.

The growth of city life with its migratory population has given rise to hotels and restaurants. The nature of office work has forced city people to put aside their old ideas of purity. Caste-Hindus have to eat articles of food prepared by Christians, Musalmans, or Persians, because Hindu restaurants have not been easily or equally accessible during office hours. In Hindu hotels, they have to take their meals in the Company of people of almost any caste-as the hotel-keeper cannot manage to reserve accommodation for members of different castes. Initially all these were done under the pressure of necessity, but later it became a routine feature. In cities, we come to see that people do not follow caste restrictions about food, but they do not tend to observe all these ideals when they go to their villages. The force of custom and sentiment is so great that they follow a dual standard of life. They find it difficult to break with their village folk. This is especially true of all formal occasions. To accelerate this change, special dinners have been arranged by some associations where at persons sit in a row irrespective of caste. But in Poona a handful of people like M.G. Ranade and others were subjected to social tyranny because they had taken tea at a Christian missionary's place.

In those parts of India, where the untouchables were kept at a great distance, certain exigencies of modern life have forced high-caste Hindus to change their attitude. "In towns, where private scavenging and sweeping are enforced, the scavengers and sweepers have not only to go near the houses but have sometimes to enter into them for scavenging. This has done away with distance pollution."[31]

There is much more freedom in the matter of choice of occupation today than under the old regime. Many of those occupations, like those of draftsmanship and cabinet-making, have come to be looked upon with greater esteem and are better remunerated than their older proto-types. Draftsmanship is partially allied to clerkship (in so far as it involves desk-work in an office) and largely to the ancient designers avocation. Recruits to this profession, therefore, hail both from the higher castes of Brahmins and also the lower castes. Occupations such as tailoring and shoemaking were not respectable in olden days because it was more tedious. Now, the new machinery has made it easy. So, it is held in esteem. Therefore, more and more members of very high castes take them up. Dislocation of the old economic order and provision of facilities for training in arts and crafts have led to the redefining of division between occupations. The total result is that in 1930 many members of the Brahmin caste were seen engaged in almost any of the occupations, excepting those of casual labourer, sweeper and scavenger. Many members of the various artisan castes are teachers, shopkeepers, bank clerks, shop assistants, and architects. It is ignorance that has ceased the occupational freedom of Indians.

Formerly, marriage outside one's caste was not to be thought of. But, today many educated young men and women are prepared to break through the bonds of caste if mutual love or attraction demands it. Many members of younger generation have managed their own matrimonial affairs although they may belong to two different castes. A large majority of such marriages, known as inter-caste or mixed marriages, is formed by couples where the female partner, belongs to a caste lower than that of the male partner. The case, where the male partner belongs to a lower caste, is not altogether rare. As for the older generation, it may be said without exaggeration that, there was very little scopes of inter marriage. When, therefore, elderly persons arrange the marriages of their wards they hardly ever think of going beyond their caste. If they venture to ignore the limits of narrowest division, he is looked up to as a reformer. It would be hard to point out examples of marriages between members of separate castes arranged for their children by the elderly guardians. It is enthusiasm of youth alone that is prepared to break the bounds of castes for the purpose of marriage.

When the city of Bombay began to attract large numbers of people from rural areas, the immigrants began to congregate according to their castes. The Brahmin castes of the Maratha country are mostly vegetarians, while the other castes are usually non-vegetarians. The Brahmins had the motives of escaping bad odours given out by fish and flesh when they were being dressed. So, every large caste tried to live in isolation from other castes. This practice, we see even in villages where special parts of the village were reserved for different castes. With the quickening of caste-consciousness and the fostering of caste-patriotism, philanthropic persons have been building houses and chawls to be rented only to their caste-members at moderate rents. Charity, which was intended to further the educational interests of caste, has found expression also in providing free hostels to the student members of the caste. As a result, in those areas of Bombay, which are largely inhabited by the middle classes, we find today whole chawls, which are occupied by members of one or two castes with close affinity. The buildings are rented at moderate or even nominal rents to the members of a particular caste, and even hostels giving free accommodation to the students of a particular caste. Buildings meant for members of a particular caste generally bear prominent boards announcing the fact of their reservation. Even the colleges and the University are infested with endowments from which scholarships are to be paid to students of certain specified castes.

In business there was a tendency to restrict the holding of shares to the members of a particular caste. The Brahmins of Madras started a fund called the "Triplicane Fund", shares in which could be held only by Brahmins. Those responsible for starting it included gentlemen of "culture, education and learning". Such being the case, we regret that one of the rules of the Fund is so narrowly conceived as to exclude all that are not Brahmins from the right of holding shares. It is just this type of exclusiveness that furnishes interested parties like the 'ministerialists' their best nutrient. Those who decry the excesses of communalism should themselves first set the example of a healthy, wholesome, non-communal outlook in the practical affairs of life".[32]

One feature of the Hindu society is that every caste forms its own association comprising all members of the caste speaking the same language. In the old regime the caste panchayat or council was usually restricted to the confines of village or the town. "In the large majority of cases, the caste- consciousness is limited by the bounds of the village and its organisations do not extend beyond the village area.[33] The functions of those new organisations are: (1) to further the general interests of the caste; (2) to start funds to provide studentships for the needy and deserving students of the caste, usually at the secondary and college stage of education, and sometimes even to help them to proceed to foreign countries for higher academic qualification; (3) to help poor people of the caste; (4) and sometimes to try to regulate certain customs of the caste by resolutions passed at the annual meeting of the members of the caste. All these objects, excepting that of providing studentships, could not be always achieved permanently. Sometimes an ad hoc committee would take up the work and carry it out. The Kayasth Prabhus of Poona and many other castes of the Maratha country protested from time to time to the court of the Peshwa against certain restrictions which other castes wanted to enforce upon them to show them low. Relief of the poor was not usually a duty undertaken by a caste. When a caste decided to apply some of its funds to charitable purposes, it handed over the money to the local priest to be used by him for benevolent purposes. The funds were used to build temples and rest-houses, dig wells and tanks, and to endow free feeding at the temples for a certain number of Brahmins and at the public feeding houses for travellers and others in need. This type of charity was most often accepted without reference to caste. Only the artisan castes, which strong guild- like organisations, had some standing provision for helping the indigent among its members.[34] Occasionally a caste would relieve its own poor by feeding them through the headman. The funds for this purpose were available from the residue of the fines imposed on the defaulting members of caste.

It is interesting to note that the Brahmins of South India assembled the Brahmins of four quarters and decided to put a stop to the practice of taking money for a bride prevailing among them. The oil-mongers of Kanchi proposed to bind themselves by certain conditions about donations to temples and to observe them as "jatidharma", i.e., duty which every member owed to his caste.

From the discussion of the non-Brahmin and depressed class movements it will be evident that the old hierarchy of caste is no longer accepted. Many are the castes that employ priests of their own caste. Some of the castes, the goldsmiths of the Maratha country, for example, have already started asserting their dignity by refusing to take food at the hands of castes, other than the Brahmin. In this process it is the lower caste that starts the movement in order to raise its own status. To add to this the old profession of a teacher, and the more or less new profession of a Government clerk, are coveted by many more castes than was the practice in the old regime. There is struggle for these petty jobs.

To sum up, social and religious privileges and disabilities born of caste are no longer recognised in law and only partially in custom. Only the depressed classes are labouring under certain customary and semi-legal disabilities. Caste no longer rigidly determines an individual's occupation, but continues to guide about one's marriage. One has still to depend very largely on one's caste for help at critical periods of one's life, like marriage and death. One's closest companions and friends are mainly delimited by the circle of one's caste. The difference between the old regime and contemporary society lies in this that whereas under the ancient organisation the facts mentioned above were almost universally true, but today these restrictions are followed only partially. We can see the attitudes of exclusiveness and distrust, between caste and caste, still preserving in the minds of the educated. Caste distinctions are very common and command the services of even the most highly educated persons to further their object of helping the members of their castes. As long as endogamy is prescribed and practised, it encourages the aggrandisement of the members of one's caste. For, the better the economic prospects for the youths of the caste the greater the chances of getting well-to-do husbands for one's daughters. The rule of endogamy is in a way the fundamental factor of contemporary caste.

In the desire to help one's caste-fellows many forget the principles of social justice and do injustice to the members of other castes. Unfortunately many leaders in civic life are associated with the movement of amelioration of their respective castes. The conduct of these leaders in the matter of marriages of their wards usually in their own caste creates an environment of betrayal among the populace. The people feel that their leaders who preach them to rise above the bounds of caste-system are themselves totally helpless to do so. At about the end of the British rule in India, this evil of caste-system has loosened its grip on the minds of the Indians, mostly because of social awakening and modern education.

Even under the changed situation the Indian caste system describes the social stratification and social restrictions in the Indian subcontinent, in which social classes are defined by thousands of endogamous hereditary groups, often termed as *jâtis* or castes. Within a jâti, there exist exogamous groups known as gotras, the lineage or clan of an individual, although in a handful of sub-castes like Shakadvipi, endogamy within a gotra is permitted and alternative mechanisms of restricting endogamy are used (e.g. banning endogamy within a surname).

Although generally identified with Hinduism, the caste system is also observed among followers of other religions in the Indian subcontinent, including some groups of Muslims and Christians. The Indian Constitution has outlawed caste-based discrimination, in keeping with the socialist, secular, democratic principles that founded the nation. Caste barriers have mostly broken down in large cities, though they persist in rural areas of the country, where 72% of India's population resides. Nevertheless, the caste system, in various forms, continues to survive in modern India strengthened by a combination of social perceptions and divisive politics (Bayly, 1999).

Growth of Middle Class

By the Charter Act of 1833 the East India Company was transformed from a business organisation into a political institution. As the Company was debarred from functioning as a business organisation and trade in India was thrown open to the Europeans, many European capitalists came to India and invested their capital. This increased the Indian import and export trade manifold. In this commercial growth, the share of the Indians was negligible.

Whatever share the Indians had, the major portion of it was in the hands of the Marwaris, Mughals and the Parsis. Next to these three communities came the Bengalis. With the spread of trade and commerce there was the rise of naibs, gomasthas, brokers and accountants and with the rise in the number of cases and spread of education there was increase in the number of the lawyers, teachers, doctors and other professionals. People of these different professions constituted the middle class which became a very strong section of the society. The most important effect of the British administration was the end of the importance, social status and power of the former ruling classes and the rise of new social divisions.

As an inevitable result of the establishment of British rule in India, particularly as a result of close contact with European merchants and missionaries, there was a great change in the social attitude and mentality of the Indians. This change began from the second half of the 18th century and continued all through the 19th century. The impact of Western education and culture on Indian society continued to grow deeper and wider. The resultant change began at first in Bengal and then spread to other parts of India.

In place of former social divisions new class divisions began to rise. Despite differences in wealth, education and profession, people belonging to different communities formed a new class which came to be known as the middle class. The middle class in the West had brought about the end of feudalism and the authority of the Church thereby establishing social, economic and individual liberty and economic individualism and freedom of competition. The Indian middle class had contributed to these fields in appreciable measure though they did not succeed in equal measure. However, in the spread of nationalism among the Indians and in winning freedom of the country the contribution of the middle class was quite significant

There were two factors that contributed to the rise of the middle class in India, viz.

1. The end of the feudalist mentality and behaviour due to the abolition of the former ruling class, and
2. Rise of new land-owning, mercantile and intellectual classes.

The rise of the middle class was also due to the trade, commerce and industrial activities of the Europeans in India. Naturally, Calcutta, Bombay and Madras were the first to see the rise of the middle class. These cities were the first to get the opportunity of Western education and outlook as also the taste of Western city life. Merchants, industrial entrepreneurs, capitalists, technologists and people who were experts in the export and import trade first made Calcutta the centre of their activities. Naturally of the three presidencies Calcutta had greatest importance.

Though the middle class emerged first in towns and cities, gradually this class also began to grow in villages. As a result of the Permanent Settlement the number of large estate holders was only twenty thousand whereas that of small landholders was one lakh thirty thousand in Bengal. The owners of big estates came over to towns for luxurious living while the small landholders continued to remain in villages and they formed the nucleus of rural middle class. To this class were added the naibs, gomasthas, moneylenders and darogas of the villages.

In order to meet administrative necessities the British had to encourage the spread of English education and educated Indians were appointed in the service of the Company. These service holders and contractors who undertook to construct roads, buildings, etc. others who took to service under merchants added to this numbers to the urban middle class. Contractors, small scale business men, dalals, Banias, etc., although not highly educated, earned enough money and came to be known as the baboo class who lived a riotous life of lavish expenditure.

It has to be mentioned here that the British did not desire the growth of statesmen, intellectuals, persons who could give leadership to the nation, or persons fit for high military posts. Rise of persons of such capabilities from among the Indians was undesirable from the point of view of quiet British rule over India.

However equipped with a Western education and emboldened by their exposure the middle class became conscious of their rights and status and of the need for progress. The obstacles put in the way of their self-expression by the ruling class made them nationally conscious and set the stage for a national movement. It became clear to the middle class that the only means of social, political and economic emancipation of the Indians was the end of foreign rule.

Caste and Untouchability

Untouchability is the social practice of ostracizing a (usually) minority endogamous group by regarding them as "ritually polluted" and segregating them from the mainstream by social custom or legal mandate. The excluded group could be one that did not accept the norms of the excluding group and historically included foreigners, nomadic tribes, law-breakers and criminals. This exclusion was a method of punishing law-breakers and also protected against contagion from strangers. A member of the excluded group is known as an untouchable.[35] The term is commonly associated with treatment of the Dalit class in India, Nepal, Pakistan and Bangladesh. Untouchability has been made illegal in post-Independence India but prejudice continues.

If this is the lot of the Sudras, what is the treatment reserved for the 'untouchables' who are outside the caste system, and placed even lower than the Sudras in society? In the 1500s, during the rule of the Marathas and the Peshwas in today's Maharashtra state, 'untouchables' were not allowed within the gates of the capital city Poona between 3.00 pm and 9.00 am. The reason was that during this time their bodies were likely to cast long shadows, with the attendant danger that the shadow of an 'untouchable' might fall on a Brahmin and pollute him. An 'untouchable' had to carry an earthen pot around his neck so his spittle may not pollute the earth. In Maharashtra an 'untouchable' wore a black thread either in his neck or on his wrist for ready identification, while in Gujarat a horn had to be worn for identification.

The 'untouchables' constitute 15% of the total population of the sub-continent and have been referred to as Depressed Classes, Scheduled Castes and Scheduled Tribes. Local names for the 'untouchable communities' vary in different parts of India: Bhangi, Pakhi, Chandala, etc. Mahatma Gandhi called them Harijans or children of God. Now they are called Dalits, which means suppressed people.

Many people attempted to change the system: Buddhism condemned both the caste system and the practice of untouchability. In South India, the Hindu religious leader Ramanuja (1017-1137 CE) condemned untouchability and adopted many 'untouchables' as his disciples. In Andhra Pradesh Veera Brahmendra Swamy (10th Century CE) condemned the practice while Minister Sri Basaveswara of Mysore State (1131-1167 CE) fought it with great vigour. Minister Brahma Naidu of Palnadu (14 Century, CE) in Andhra Pradesh condemned the practice and appointed an 'untouchable' named Chenna as his army chief. The monotheistic Sikh religion was born in 1496 partly as a reaction to casteism- but soon fell victim to it. Vemana (circa 15th CE) the deist rationalist poet sneered at the practice of untouchability and admonished the people to respect the 'untouchables'. So did Jyotirao Phule (1827-1890 CE) and Ranade (1842-1901) in Maharashtra, and Narayanaguru (1856-1928) in Kerala. Mahatma

Gandhi (1869-1948) who was born into the third caste supported the caste system, but wanted to eradicate untouchability to save Hinduism.

Atheist and humanist reformers like Periyar (1879-1973) and Gora (1902-1975) fought against the indignity of the caste system and introduced inter-dining - thus trying to break one of Hinduism's biggest taboos. 'Untouchable' poets like Gurram Joshua (1895-1971), as well as Humanist writers like the recently departed Mulk Raj Anand (1905-2004) exposed the people to the gravity of the problem. Humanists like Tripuraneni Ramaswamy (1887-1943) questioned the morality of the Gods in Hindu mythology and created new drama that caught the imagination of people, thus inaugurating a new era of rationalism in literature that flourished between the 1930s and the 1980s. Both upper castes and the lower castes need liberation from the oppressive religious ideology which is at the heart of this terrible situation. The Dalits themselves need economic self-sufficiency without which they will be unable to survive. Any long-term solution to this deeply entrenched problem will require a social, cultural and moral transformation of society.

In the 19th Century, the Brahmo Samaj under Raja Ram Mohan Roy, actively campaigned against untouchability and casteism. The Arya Samaj founded by Swami Dayanand also renounced discrimination against Dalits. Sri Ramakrishna Paramahamsa and his greatest disciple Swami Vivekananda who founded the Ramakrishna Mission that participated in the emancipation of Dalits. Upper caste Hindus, such as Mannathu Padmanabhan also participated in movements to abolish Untouchability against Dalits, opening his family temple for Dalits to worship. Narayana Guru, a pious Hindu and an authority on the Vedas, also criticized casteism and campaigned for the rights of lower-caste Hindus within the context of Hinduism.

The first "upper-caste" temple to openly welcome Dalits into their fold was the Laxminarayan Temple in Wardha in the year 1928 (the move was spearheaded by reformer Jamnalal Bajaj).

The caste system has also been criticized by many Indian social reformers. Some reformers, such as Jyotirao Phule and Thass argued that the lower caste people were the original inhabitants of India, and were conquered in the ancient past by "Brahmin invaders." Mahatma Gandhi coined the term "Harijan", a euphemistic word for *untouchable*, literally meaning *Sons of God*. B. R. Ambedkar, born in Hindu Dalit community, was a heavy critic of the caste system. He pioneered the Dalit Buddhist movement in India, and asked his followers to leave Hinduism, and convert to Buddhism.

References

Alavi, Seema (1998). *Sepoys and the Company Tradition and Transition in Northern India 1770-1830*. New Delhi: Oxford University Press India.

Bayly, Susan (1999), Caste*, Society and Politics in India from the Eighteenth Century to the Modern Age*. Cambridge: Cambridge University Press.

Corbridge, Stuart and Harriss, John (2000), *Reinventing India: Liberalization, Hindu Nationalism and Popular Democracy*. London: Polity Press.

Ghurye, G. S. (1961), *Caste, Class and Occupation*. Bombay: Popular Book Depot.

Notes

1. Kikani, L. T., Caste in Court, 1912, p.iii.
2. Kikani, L. T., Caste in Court, 1912, p.7.
3. The Bombay Chronicle, 31st March, 1924.
4. G. S. Ghurye, Indian Caste, vol. ii, p.45.
5. Bombay Chronicle, 1st May, 1925.
6. Memorandum submitted by the Government of Bombay to the Indian statutory Commission, 1928. (1929), p.228.
7. Ibid., p.44
8. This resolution was modified by a later one, dated 5th February, 1925 wherein the absolute restriction on the recruitment from the advanced classes was removed.
9. See Kitts, p.1
10. India Census, 1901, pp.537-8.
11. Bengal Census, 1921, p.346.
12. Madras Census, 1911, p.178.
13. Punjab Census, 1921, pp.434-4.
14. Lady Vidyagaur i Ramanbhai as reported in the Indian Social Reformer (Bombay), 5th September, 1925.
15. Report of the Peel Commission on the Organisation of the Indian Army, 1859, p.14, and Appendix, pp.6, 10, 147.
16. Vide Murdoch, Caste, p.13.
17. Kerr, p.361, footnote
18. Trotter, L. J., History of India under Queen Victoria, vol. ii, (1886), p.91, and The Times of India, 3rd July, 1897 (leading article).
19. Edward Sullivan, Letters on India, (1858), pp.124-5.
20. See the account of the Arya Samaj given by Pandit Harikishan Kaul in the Punjab Census Report, 1911, pp.133-6.
21. Phule, pp.25, 33, 59, 63.
22. This demand for representation in the services was first made in a petition addressed by the artisan castes of Madras to the Board of Revenue in 1840. "All classes of men to the destruction of Brahminical monopoly should be appointed

to public offices without distinction." John Wilson, Indian Caste, vol. ii, p. 89, footnote.

23. Latthe, vol. ii, p.494.
24. The Indian Social Reformer (Bombay), 3rd January, 1925.
25. The Indian Daily Mail (Bombay), 14th October, 1924.
26. The Bombay Chronicle, 2nd May, 1925.
27. N. B. : This was written in about 1930.
28. Indian Social Reformer, 11th February, 1928, p. 229.
29. *Ibid.*
30. Forward (Calcutta), 6th March, 1924.
31. Travancore Census, 1921, p. 106.
32. The Indian Social Reformer (Bombay), 16th October, 1926.
33. Matthai. p. 65.55.
34. Ibid., pp. 65, 68-9.
35. Francis Buchanan, Indian Census Record, 1883.

Chapter- 7

Spread of Modern Education and Westernization

The Pre-British Education

At the outset let us discuss about the educational system of India before the establishment of British rule in the country. The educational system of India was largely traditional in nature. It was based on Puranas, Shastras and Quran. Science and mathematics of the Indian educational system was not so developed. The educational system of both the Hindus and Muslims were equally backward. Neither of them had the idea of progress science had made in the West. They also knew nothing about the new methods of observation, experiment and criticism. Although the Europeans had made their factories near the sea coast in India and established their settlements in these places, the Indians of Gujarat, Konkan, Kerala, Cholamandal, Orissa and Bengal remained intellectually wholly unaffected by their presence. The princes and noblemen of India showed interest in European animals and birds, mirrors, toys and spirits, but they showed no interest in their social, economic or cultural affairs. Although almost every branch of knowledge of Muslims was studied in the Christian universities of Spain, Italy and France, the new discoveries of America remained almost entirely unknown in India till the end of the 18th century. This was not due to lack of schools in India; rather, the real cause was inherent in the poor quality of education. Education was organized on sectarian lines. There were separate systems of education for Hindus and Muslims. The Hindus used the regional language for elementary education and Sanskrit was used for higher learning, while the medium of instruction in the Muslim schools was Persian.

The pupils in the primary schools spent from five to ten years in completing their course which included elements of reading, writing and arithmetic. The aim was to learn letter writing and composing business correspondence- petition, grants, leases, etc. The students were made proficient in accounting, either agricultural or commercial. The emphasis was on tables such as multiplication, weights and measures. Education was purely utilitarian and extremely narrow. The condition of the higher schools of learning was even worse. In those institutions both the students and teachers were Brahmans. Three main types of courses were taught namely grammar and general literature, law and logic. Studies extended two to twelve and even twenty-two years. Most of the schools were in the house of the teacher. The students of law devoted eight to twenty-three years in mastering the various branches of Hindu law and rites. In Bengal the treatise of Jimutavahan was studied. Manu and Mitakashara were taught in other schools. The study of logic required twelve to twenty-two years. In medicine and astronomy studies were based on the ancient texts and their commentaries.

The educational system of the Muslims was not very much better than that of the Hindus. It was intended for the upper classes and did not offer any instruction to the Muslim masses. In all Muslim schools Persian was the medium of instruction. Neither Urdu nor any other Indian spoken language was used. The Muslim masses were steeped in ignorance. There were three types of instructions for Muslims. The first type consisted of memorizing the verses of Quran without understanding the meaning. The second type of instruction was given in Persian schools. It concerned itself mainly with literature, grammar and arithmetic. In poetry, Firdausi, Sadi, Hafiz, Urfi, Jami, Khaqani, etc. were taught. In prose, Gulistan, Waqai Nimat Khan Ali, Bahar-I-Danish etc. were taught. The teaching of rational sciences, including medicine and astronomy, was wholly bookish. Laboratories and observatories were not available. The Muslim mind was soaked in medievalism and it was intellectually quite unprepared to withstand the attack from the West.

Centres of higher education in Sanskrit literature were called Chatuspathis or Tols in Bengal and Bihar. Nadia, Kas, Tirhut and Utkala were reputed centres for Sanskrit education. Institutions for higher education in Persian and Arabic were called Madrasahs. As Persian was the court language, it was learnt both by the Muslims and the Hindus. Azimabad (Patna) was a great centre of Persian education. Elementary education was widespread. Hindu elementary schools were called Pathshalas and those of the Muslims were called Maktabs. The schools were not attached to temples or mosques. The students were given instruction in the three R's of reading, writing and arithmetic. In schools moral education was also given to the children. Students were told to imbibe the qualities of truth, honesty and obedience. Education was mainly popular with the higher castes. Female education received very little attention. During 18th century Urdu spread to all corners of India.

Role of British in Modern Education

It is recognised by both Marxists as well as nationalist historians that the British played a very significant role in the spread of modern education in India, leave aside their ulterior motive of perpetuating the colonial rule for economic reasons. Indirect gains from the British rule in the field of education were undoubtedly enormous (Allan, Haig, and Dodwell, 1934; O'Malley, 1941; Chand, 1961; Majumdar, 1963; Chandra *et al.*, 1972; Desai, 1976; Smith, 1981; Spear, 1990; Rothermund, 1993; Brendon, 2008).

As has been noted by numerous scholars of British rule in India, the physical presence of the British in India was not significant. Yet, for almost two centuries, the British were able to rule two-thirds of the subcontinent directly, and exercise considerable leverage over the Princely States that accounted for the remaining one-third. While the strategy of divide and conquer was used most effectively, an important aspect of British rule in India was the psychological indoctrination of an elite layer within Indian society who were artfully tutored into becoming model British subjects. This English-educated layer of Indian society was craftily encouraged in absorbing values and notions about themselves and their land of birth that would be conducive to the British occupation of India, and furthering British goals of looting India's physical wealth and exploiting its labour.

In 1835, Thomas Macaulay articulated the goals of British colonial imperialism most succinctly: "We must do our best to form a class who may be interpreters between us and the millions whom we govern, a class of persons Indian in blood and colour, but English in taste, in opinions, words and intellect." As the architect of Colonial Britain's Educational Policy in India, Thomas Macaulay was to set the tone for what educated Indians were going to learn about themselves, their civilization, and their view of Britain and the world around them. An arch-racist, Thomas Macaulay had nothing but scornful disdain for Indian history and civilization. In his infamous minute of 1835, he wrote that he had "never found one among them (speaking of Orientalists, an opposing political faction) who could deny that a single shelf of a good European library was worth the whole native literature of India and Arabia". "It is, no exaggeration to say, that all the historical information which has been collected from all the books written in Sanskrit language is less valuable than what may be found in the paltriest abridgments used at preparatory schools in England".

As a contrast to such unabashed contempt for Indian civilization, we find glowing references to India in the writings of pre-colonial Europeans quoted by Swami Vivekananda: "All history points to India as the mother of science and art," wrote William Macintosh. "This country was anciently so renowned for knowledge and wisdom that the philosophers of Greece did not disdain to travel thither for their improvement." Pierre Sonnerat, a French naturalist, concurred: "We find among the Indians the vestiges of the most remote antiquity.... We know that all peoples came there to draw the elements of their knowledge.... India, in her splendour, gave religions and laws to all the other peoples; Egypt and Greece owed to her both their fables and their wisdom.

But colonial exploitation had created a new imperative for the colonial lords. It could no longer be truthfully acknowledged that India had a rich civilization of its own- that its philosophical and scientific contributions may have influenced European scholars- or helped in shaping the European Renaissance. Britain needed a class of intellectuals meek and docile in their attitude towards the British, but full of hatred towards their fellow citizens. It was thus important to emphasize the negative aspects of the Indian tradition, and obliterate or obscure the positive. Indians were to be taught that they were a deeply conservative and fatalist people- genetically predisposed to irrational superstitions and mystic belief systems. That they had no concept of nation, national feelings or a history. If they had any culture, it had been brought to them by invaders- that they themselves lacked the creative energy to achieve anything by themselves. But the British, on the other hand, epitomized modernity- they were the harbingers of all that was rational and scientific in the world. With their unique organisational skills and energetic zeal, they would raise India from the morass of casteism and religious bigotry. These and other such ideas were repeatedly filled in the minds of the young Indians who received instruction in the British schools.

All manner of conscious (and subconscious) British (and European) agents would henceforth embark on a journey to rape and conquer the Indian mind. Within a matter of years, J.N. Farquhar (a contemporary of Macaulay) was to write: "The new educational policy of the Government created during these years the modern educated class of India. These are men who think and speak in English habitually, who are proud of their citizenship in the British Empire, who are devoted to English literature, and whose intellectual life has been almost entirely formed by the thought of the West, large numbers of them enter government services, while the rest practice law, medicine or teaching, or take to journalism or business."

Much of the indoctrination of the Indian mind actually took place outside the formal classrooms and through the sale of British literature to the English-educated Indian who developed a voracious appetite for the British novel and British writings on a host of popular subjects. In a speech before the Edinburgh Philosophical Society in 1846, Thomas Babington (1800-1859), shortly to become Baron Macaulay, offered a toast: "To the literature of Britain . . . which has exercised an influence wider than that of our commerce and mightier than that of our arms . . .before the light of which impious and cruel superstitions are fast taking flight on the Banks of the Ganges!"

However, the British were not content to influence Indian thinking just through books written in the English language. Realizing the danger of Indians discovering their real heritage through the medium of Sanskrit, Christian missionaries such as William Carey anticipated the need for British educators to learn Sanskrit and transcribe and interpret Sanskrit texts in a manner compatible with colonial aims. That Carey's aims were thoroughly duplicitous is brought out in this quote cited by Richard Fox Young: "To gain the ear of those who are thus deceived it is necessary for them to believe that the speaker has a superior knowledge of the subject. In these circumstances knowledge of Sanskrit is valuable. As the person thus misled, perhaps a Brahman, deems this a most important part of knowledge, if the advocate of truth be deficient therein, he labours against the hill; presumption is altogether against him."

In this manner, India's awareness of its history and culture was manipulated in the hands of colonial ideologues. Domestic and external views of India were shaped by authors whose attitudes towards all things Indian were shaped either by subconscious prejudice or worse by barely concealed racism. For instance, William Carey (who bemoaned how so few Indians had converted to Christianity in spite of his best efforts) had little respect or sympathy for Indian traditions. In one of his letters, he described Indian music as "disgusting", bringing to mind "practices dishonourable to God". Charles Grant, who exercised tremendous influence in colonial evangelical circles, published his "Observations" in 1797 in which he attacked almost every aspect of Indian society and religion, describing Indians as morally depraved, "lacking in truth, honesty and good faith" (p.103). British Governor General Cornwallis asserted "Every native of Hindostan, I verily believe, is corrupt".

Several British and European historians attempted to portray India as a society that had made no civilizational progress for several centuries. William Jones asserted that Hindu society had been stationary for so long that "in beholding the Hindus of the present day, we are beholding the Hindus of many ages past". James Mill, author of the three-volume History of British India (1818) essentially concurred with William Jones as did Henry Maine. This view of India, as an essentially unchanging society where there was no intellectual debate, or technological innovation- where a hidebound caste system had existed without challenge or reform- where social mobility or class struggle were unheard of, became especially popular with European scholars and intellectuals of the colonial era.

Naturally, British-educated Indians absorbed and internalized such characterizations of themselves and their past. Amongst those most affected by such diminution of the Indian character was the young Gandhi, who when in South Africa, wished to meet General Smuts and offer the cooperation of the South African Indian population for the Boer war effort. In a conversation with the General, Gandhi appears as just the sort of colonized sycophant the British education system had hoped to create: "General Smuts, sir we Indians would like to strengthen the hands of the government in the war. However, our efforts have been rebuffed. Could you inform us about our vices so we would reform and be better citizens of this land?" to which Gen. Smuts replied: "Mr. Gandhi, we are not afraid of your vices, we are afraid of your virtues". (Although Gandhi eventually went through a slow and very gradual nationalist transformation, in 1914 he campaigned for the British war efforts in World War I, and was one of the last of the national leaders to call for complete independence from British rule.).

British-educated Indians grew up learning about Pythagoras, Archimedes, Galileo and Newton without ever learning about Panini, Aryabhatta, Bhaskar or Bhaskaracharya. The logic and epistemology of the Nyaya Sutras, the rationality of the early Buddhists or the intriguing philosophical systems of the Jains were generally unknown to them. Neither was there any awareness of the numerous examples of dialectics in nature that are to be found in Indian texts. They may have read Homer or Dickens but not the Panchatantra, the Jataka tales or anything from the Indian epics.

Schooled in the aesthetic and literary theories of the West, many felt embarrassed in acknowledging Indian contributions in the arts and literature. What was important to Western civilization was deemed universal, but everything Indian was dismissed as either backward and anachronistic, or at best tolerated as idiosyncratic oddity. Little did the Westernized Indian know what debt "Western Science and Civilization" owed (directly or indirectly) to Indian scientific discoveries and scholarly texts.

Science education— Throughout the 18th century, India lagged behind the Western countries in the field of science and technology. The Indian rulers of the 18th century did not have interest in the development of science and technology. This was big a blunder on the part of the Indians. Even we see in the revolt of 1857 when Indians were numerically stronger than the British, still they could not win against the British because of lack of modern weapons. The Indians of the 18th century never paid attention to the development of science and technology. Their rudimentary weapons were no match against the mighty British Empire. It was with the advent of the English Company that the Indians made progress in the field of science and technology.

When the English East India Company acquired territories in various parts of India, it found that both the Hindus and Muslims had their educational institutions which were linked up with their religion. The Pandits taught Sanskrit to the Hindus in their Pathshalas and the Maulvis taught the Muslims in the Mosques. To begin with, the Company left the Indian system undisturbed and respected the endowments made by the Indian rulers. However, Warren Hastings established the Calcutta Madrasah to educate the young Muslims for responsible offices in the State. The subjects taught were theology, logic, rhetoric, grammar, law, natural philosophy, astronomy, geometry and arithmetic. A few years later, John Owen, Chaplain to the Bengal Presidency, requested the Government to establish schools for the purpose of teaching English to the natives of these provinces. Nobody cared for his request. However, after a few years, another educational institution was set up at Banaras for the preservation and cultivation of the religion and literature of the nation. This institution was set up also to serve the same purpose for the Hindus as the Madrasah for the Muslims and also to supply qualified Hindu Assistants to European Judges.

In 1792-93, which the House of Commons debated the renewal of the Charter of the East India Company, Wilberforce carried a resolution emphasising the adoption of such steps as would lead to the advancement in useful knowledge of the people of India. He suggested the sending of schoolmasters and missionaries to India. The move of Wilberforce was opposed and it was maintained that the Hindus had "as good a system of faith and morals as most people." It was pointed out that it would be madness to give them any kind of learning other than what they possessed.

After a few years, Charles Grant, one of the Directors of the Company, submitted a memorandum in which he lamented the low moral condition of the people of India. He asked the Company to improve their condition by imparting to them knowledge of the English language which was to serve as "a key which will open to them a world of new ideas." As the Muslim rulers had taught Persian to the Indians, in the same way the Englishmen should teach English to the people of India. He was of the opinion that it would be extremely easy for Government to establish schools for Indian children in various parts of provinces. To quote him," The Hindus would, in time, become teachers of English themselves; and the employment of our language in public business, for which every political reason remains in full force, would in the course of another generation, make it very general throughout the country. There is nothing wanting to the success of this plan, but the hearty patronage of Government."

In 1811, Lord Minto regretted the neglect of literature and science in India and suggested improvements in existing colleges in addition to the establishment of new ones. A clause was inserted in the Charter Act of 1813 stipulating that "a sum of not less than one lakh of rupees in each year shall be set apart and applied to the revival and improvement of literature and for the introduction and promotion of knowledge of the sciences among the inhabitants of the British territories in India."

Raja Ram Mohan Roy formed an association for founding an institution where the Hindus were to receive instructions in European languages and sciences. The Hindu College was founded in 1817. In 1818, the Bishop of Calcutta opened an institution which was to serve the double purpose of training young Christians as preachers and of imparting knowledge of the English language to Hindus and Muslims. Raja Ram Mohan Roy opposed the establishment of a Sanskrit College at Calcutta. However, nobody bothered about this protest. The Court of Directors of the Company was happy at the prospect of having qualified Indians to help them in the administration.

Elphinstone in his Minute of 1823 urged the establishment of schools for teaching English and European sciences. He proposed the establishment of a school at Bombay where English might be taught "classically" and where instruction might also be given in that language on history, geography and science. In 1833, he set up a similar school at Poona. In 1834 was started the Elphinstone college at Bombay. It was expected to train a class of persons for high employment in the civil administration of India.

By this time, demand for the study of English had increased tremendously. English books were being sold by thousands. There was practically no demand for Sanskrit and Arabic books. In order to satisfy the popular demand, English classes were attached to the Calcutta Madrasah and the Sanskrit College at Calcutta. The same was done in the Agra College which was established in 1811. In spite of that, the Oriental Colleges were not popular. There started a controversy as to whether instructions should be given through English or through Arabic or Persian. The Anglicists maintained that all instruction should be given through English. The Orientalists insisted on teaching through the oriental languages. To settle the controversy the Government appointed a Committee. Among the Orientalists were many distinguished officers of the Government and their view prevailed for some time. When Lord Macaulay was appointed the chairman of the Committee in 1835, the parties were so evenly balanced that things had come to a deadlock. Lord Macaulay wrote a Minute which turned the scales against the Orientalists. He came to the conclusion that the Government was free to employ its funds in teaching what was better worth knowing than Sanskrit or Arabic. Macaulay stated that, "Neither as the languages of law nor as the languages of religions have Sanskrit or Arabic any peculiar claim to our encouragement", and "it is possible to make natives of the country thoroughly good English scholars". The English Company believed that the barbarism of the Indians could be eliminated only by providing English education.

Lord William Bentinck, the Governor-General, approved of the Minute of Lord Macaulay. A resolution was passed on 7th March 1835 and the following points were emphasised in that resolution:

1 That the great object of the British Government ought to be the promotion of European literature and science amongst the natives of India and that all funds appropriated for the purposes of education would be best employed on English education alone;
2. That while the colleges of oriental learning were not to be abolished, the practice of supporting their students during their period of education was to be discontinued;
3. That Government Funds were not to be spent on the printing of oriental works; and

4. That all the funds at the disposal of the Government would henceforth be spent in imparting to the Indians knowledge of English literature and science.

The Indian Muslims objected to the English education because they believed that the English education was meant to induce the people to become Christians. With a view to removing the misgivings of the Muslims, Lord William Bentinck declared a policy of strict neutrality. In all schools and colleges, interference and injudicious tempering with the religious belief of the students, mingling direct or indirect teaching of Christianity with the system of instruction, ought to be positively forbidden.

A reference may be made to the work done by the Christian Missions in the field of education. In 1716, the Danish missionaries opened an institution for the training of teachers. In 1717, they opened two charity schools at Madras. They were also instrumental in opening English schools at other places. Missionaries like Carey, Marshman and Ward started their work at Serampore in 1793. By 1820, the Missionary societies were doing a lot of work in this field, but their primary object was not to educate the people, but to preach Christianity. The Missionaries realised that the spread of English language would help the spread of Christianity in the country. In Bombay was started the Wilson College and in Madras the Christian College. In 1853 was founded the Saint John's College at Agra. Missionary colleges were also founded at Masulipatam and Nagpur. The Bible Classes were made compulsory in these institutions. According to Dr. Duff, "One great object was to convey, as largely as possible a knowledge of our ordinary improved literature and science to the young persons; but another, and a more vital object was to convey a thorough knowledge of Christianity."

A Government Resolution of 1844 provided that for public employment in every case, preference would be given to those who had been educated in Western science and were familiar with the English language. According to Lord Auckland, "I would make it my principal aim to communicate through the means of the English language a complete education in European literature, philosophy and science to the greatest number of students who may be ready to accept it."

Wood's Despatch of 1854— The first phase in the history of modern education in India ended with Wood's Despatch, 1854. Sir Charles Wood's Despatch to the Court of Directors has been described as, "The Magna Carta of English Education in India." "The despatch stated that the educational system in India was organized for the triple object of (1) spreading western culture, (2) securing properly trained servants for the public administration, and (3) doing their duty to the sovereign by the Indian objects" (Desai, 1976: 147). Both the English language and the Indian languages were to be regarded as the media for the diffusion of European language.

It was decided to establish universities on the model of the London University. Each university was to consist of a Chancellor, Vice-Chancellor and a Senate. The Senate was to manage the university funds and frame regulations for the holding of examinations. Professorships were to be instituted in various branches of learning among which were law, civil engineering and classical oriental languages. Calcutta and Bombay were to have the first universities. A university might be created at Madras also or at any other place in India where a sufficient number of institutions existed from which properly qualified candidates for degrees could be supplied. It was laid down that the affiliated institutions would be periodically visited by Government Inspectors.

The Despatch also recommended the establishment of institutions for training teachers for all classes of schools. The existing Government Schools and Colleges were to be maintained and their number was to be increased if and when necessary. New Middle Schools were to be established. More attention was to be given to elementary education. The system of grants-in-aid was to be started by the Government to help private enterprise. However, these grants were to be given on the principle of religious neutrality. A comprehensive system of scholarship was to be started. Female education was to be encouraged by the government. A Director of Public Instruction was to be appointed in every province. He was to be assisted by Inspectors and Assistants or Deputy Inspectors. According to Dodwell, the men in charge of the Department were primarily administrators and consequently education tended to become a matter of routine administration.

Role of British in female education— At the beginning of the nineteenth century, female literacy was extremely low in relation to male literacy. Their literacy was confined to reading of sacred literature. Female education was very informal and largely limited to practical matters. In the beginning missionaries played much more important role than the British government in spreading modern education among females (Forbes, 1998: 33-38). One can never forget the inviolable truth that a host of reformers and social organisations like the Brahmo Samaj, the Prarthana Samaj, the Arya Samaj, and the Theosophical Society together tried to inculcate the awareness in the mass for the necessity of the female education. Indeed, this spirit of resurgence was one of the salient features of the Bengal Renaissance.

The desire of many Indians of the elite section of the society to learn English, was the motivational force behind the establishment of the Hindu College in 1817. Men like Radhakanta Deb, Rammohan Roy, Babu Buddinath Mukherjee were involved into this joint-venture with Western pillars of support such as David Hare and Sir Edward Hyde East, Chief Justice of the Supreme Court.

Hindu College was succeeded by the growth of the Calcutta School Society to propagate female education. Radhakanta Deb, a member of the administrative body of this society, encouraged female education. Under his patronage, the Calcutta Female Society came into being in 1819. He was aided by the Christian Missionary organisation, the Baptists. Miss Mary Cooke, a western philanthropic mind, came down to Kolkata in 1821, being beckoned by the School Society. Her assignment was to collect funds and set up schools. Mary Cooke allied with the Church Missionary Society and gave shape to thirty schools for "respectable" Hindu girls.

These schools flourished because of the Hindu social enthusiasts. Brahmin scholars emerged to be the faculty of these educational institutions. The Bethune School, owing its origin to the contribution of the British reformer, J.E.Drinkwater Bethune, reached the acme of perfection under the extraordinary guidance of the outstanding man of letters, Pundit Vidyasagar. The Bengali Medium School imparted secular education. The hallmark was that even the "lowest class" girls could access knowledge in this school.

By 1854, there were probably 626 girls' schools all over India. The total population of girls-students amounted to 21,755. As per as the statistics reveal, Bengal was the leading female literate state of the then India, with 228 students. Next, was Madras with a count of 256. Bombay had a small number of only 65, while North West Frontier and the Oudh, could project the handful amount of 17. The concerned institutions were invested with diminutive infrastructure. It should be noted, that although people by that time had started harbouring consent for female education, the larger part of the female community could not avail of the light of education, due to restrictions.

The British's assertion of the "woman question", enlightened society with the fundamental rights of women.. The outcome was the influence of this question on the Indian intelligentsia. The inspired Hindu college

Foundation Committee and the Hindu College graduates, were eager to enjoy the boon of modernization, and to go ahead of their times, by circulating education among women. They understood that an educated woman can expertly handle individual and social matters and can partake of the responsibilities of life with her spouse, efficiently. This ideology probably worked behind the growing demand for educated brides as the right choice. The situation became conducive for the social-correctors to launch their new plans.

Keshab Chandra Sen, the new generation reformer of the Brahmo Samaj, founded by Raja Rammohan, conducted the first Brahmo widow-remarriage in August 1862. His prime objective was the spread of female education. To take care of this major aspect of his projects, he built his Brahma Bandhu Sabha in 1863. He offered immense support to the arrangers of the Bamabodhini Sabha and Bamabodhini Patrika and directed the Bama Hitaisini Sabha (1871) on the route of the moral and material betterment of the wretched feminine group of society. Finally, the Brahmika Samaj was raised in 1865, as the platform for women to share and enhance their religious knowledge, lessons on the art of stitching, and discourse on social affairs.

However, the sensitive issue of women's well-being caused a rift among the members of the Brahmo Samaj in 1866. Keshabchandra Sen, distanced himself from the mainstream activities of the Adi Brahmo Samaj, supervised by Debendranath Tagore. Keshab formed his own organisation called the Navabidhan. He invited Miss Mary Carpenter to Calcutta, to aid him in his mission of female learning. The deficiency of competent teachers attracted her attention. To attain a solution, she made several propositions before the then Governor-General. This facilitated the spawning of the National Indian Association to usher in reconciliation between the British authority and the native Indians, with regard to the course of actions to be followed.

Atmaram Pandurang (1823-1898), enthralled by the motivational activities of Keshab Chandra Sen's Brahmo Samaj, created the Prarthana Samaj in Bombay, or present Mumbai. Prarthana Samaj extended its helping hand to women's education. Arrangements of free libraries and classes were the immediate steps taken. Women and students' associations, continued their social revolution in an ordered manner.

In 1871 Carpenter, Keshab Sen, and another English woman, Annette Akroyd, together started a school. But schism in principles sprouted, and Akryod, joined the Sadharan Brahmo Samaj to open the Hindu Mahila

Vidyalaya (Hindu Girls' School). Personalities like Brajakishore Basu, Shivanath Shastri, Durga Mohan Das, Dwarkanath Ganguly were the gems of this reputed group. In 1878 this school converged with the Bethune School to turn into Bethune College, affiliated to the educational authority of the Calcutta University. Bethune College provided opportunity to the pride of Indian womanhood, the first female graduates, Kadambini Basu and Chandramukhi Basu. These brilliant women obtained their Bachelors Degree from Bethune College. Kadambani Bose (Kadambini Ganguly, after marriage to the great emancipator, Dwarkanath Ganguly), pursued higher education, and emerged to be the first lady doctor of the nation.

In Madras, it was the diligent Annie Besant and her Theosophical Society, which proclaimed aloud, the significance of female learning. Annie, a self-independent women was very much vocal, about the early Vedic society, when education and free mobility of women, in the spheres of society was the order of the day asserted that in ancient limes Hindu women were educated and moved freely in society. She aimed at a revival of this "golden age". Besant's campaign for women's suffrage in 1874, her demonstration of "New Unionism" in her crusade against the misery of the London match-stick factory-girls in 1888, had already won her international acclaim as the Feminist freedom-fighter.

Madame Blavatsky, one of the founders of the Theosophical Society, strongly condemned child marriage, child widowhood, as abominable perverted practice of Hindu beliefs. Besant adored Blavatsky as her ideal, and stressed her views in the article "Education of Women" in the Indian Ladies Magazine. Besant opined that India would degenerate into a future of bleakness and nothingness, if women remain in ignorance. She modelled Indian womanhood on the iconic female figure of the Goddess Durga. Her ardent fervour got its manifestation in the women's college that sprung as per her principles. She pledged her efforts to this reform and founded a women's college based on these principles.

Arya Samaj directed the course of female education in North India. Its chief was the visionary Swami Dayanand Saraswati. Towards the close of the nineteenth century, the broad-minded Arya Samajists realized the necessity of incorporating female participation in the grave task of reforms. An allied body to the Arya Samaj the Jullundar Samaj inaugurated the Arya Kanya Pathshala (Girls' School) in 1890 with a lady principal to regulate the work-process. It was succeeded by the making of the Kanya Mahavidyalaya (Girls' Higher School) of Jullundar. The dormant structures of these academic centres and the elementary girls' school were cemented into conspicuous learning-sites in 1892 by the benevolent Lala Devraj.

Lala Devraj, was that true Karma Yogi or selfless worker who gave space for the growth of girls' school in his family abode. We are bound to salute him with respect, when we discover that this salvager used to sell "waste paper" to collect money, for running the school. Even the food that he used to provide to the instructors, working in the school, was prepared by the equally devoted mother of Lala Devraj. Slowly with time, more and more people started responding to the upheaval of women's improvement. And this premier institution "became a catalyst for various kinds of change relating to women in Punjab."

Meanwhile, Vidyasagar opened up 30 schools in Bengal, for spreading female education in all the corners of Bengal. One must understand that this rising cult of feminity, was a vital aspect of Indian nationalist ideology during the freedom struggle. Had India not been able to honour her womanhood, then how would have the concept of Bharatmata or the Mother India, fettered to the shackles of the British, instigated the agitated mass against the foreign colonisers?

Female education flowered under the increasing impetus generated from the widened mental horizon of the indigenous Mahatmas (great souls), committed to the architecture of a new reformed society, which would pay women the respect and freedom they deserve.

The British wanted their civil servants to have educated wives to further ensure their loyalty. The British believed that the rebellious plots were first hatched in the minds of these uneducated women. So, they found it necessary to educate the women. These educated women would raise their children to become the supporters of English rule. If women were educated, the society could no longer be backward, while men pursued politics, the women took the charge of social reform. Men feared that if they led the social reform movements, it would complicate juncture of time, the women took over the charge of social reform. Men had always feared that education might lead women so far that they may not recognize any boundaries of subjugation, but female educators promised that they would make only professionalized housewives. However, the British had always remained sympathetic towards the Indian women (Forbes, 1998: 60-61)

Role of Christian missionary— The Christian missionaries did extensive work in the field of modern education as they were mainly interested in proselytizing the Indians. "They sincerely believed that their campaign to convert the Indians was a civilizing mission' (Desai, 1976: 139). The Church Missionary Society opened thirty schools for "respectable" Hindu girls. These schools enjoyed the patronage of Hindu gentlemen, but they failed to attract girls from the higher castes. The Church Missionary Society was more successful in South India where it opened its first boarding school for girls in Tirunelveli in 1821. By 1840 the Scottish Church Society could claim six schools for Hindu girls. By mid-century the missionaries in Madras were instructing nearly 8,000 girls, the majority of whom were Christians, in day schools and boarding schools. One of the most important schools for girls was the Hindu Balika Vidyalaya opened in 1849 in Calcutta by J. E. Drinkwater Bethune. Bethune was the legal member of the Governor-General's Council and President of the Council of Education. The girls of this school were transported in a carriage. A Sanskrit verse was inscribed on the carriages which go like this: A daughter's education was a father's religious duty. The school was secular and education was in Bengali. Pandit Vidyasagar was appointed school secretary. When Bethune died in 1851, support for the school declined. In 1863, the school had 93 girls, three-quarters of whom were from the lowest class. This showed that the upper class society were against female education.

When Bethune School was opened between 1849 and 1882, the Indian Education (Hunter) Commission reviewed the progress of education in India. Efforts were made to develop primary schools for girls. But higher education for women and co-education were still contentious issues. Authors of the Hunter Commission Report noticed that 98 percent of school-age girls were not in school. So, they recommended more facilities for girls than for boys. Special scholarships and prizes were reserved for girls. Consequently, in the next two decades higher education expanded rapidly.

The Hunter Commission, 1882— In 1882, Lord Ripon appointed Hunter Commission. The Hunter Commission collected a lot of useful information and made the following recommendations:

1. While advocating the gradual withdrawal of the State from direct support and management of institutions of higher education, the Commission felt that this withdrawal could only be by slow and cautious steps. A college or a secondary school was to be handed over to the Indians provided there was a reasonable prospect that the cause of education would not suffer through the transfer.
2. Provision was to be made for ordinary and special grants to colleges.

3. There were to be alternative courses in the large colleges.
4. Certain general principles were to be followed as regards college fees and exemption from them.
5. New regulations regarding scholarships were to be framed.
6. An attempt was to be made to prepare a model text-book based upon the fundamental principles of natural religion such as may be taught in all Government and non-government colleges.
7. The principal or one of the professors in each Government and aided college was to deliver to each of the college classes, in every session, a series of lectures on the duties of a man and a citizen.
8. Special measures were to be adopted for the encouragement of education among the Mohammedans.
9. All elementary schools were to be inspected and supervised by the Educational Officers of the Government.
10. The Commission put emphasis on physical and mental education of the students.
11. According to the Commission, primary education needed strongest encouragement. A part of the provincial revenues should be exclusively reserved for primary education. Primary education should be given by the state, district boards and municipalities. Secondary education should be encouraged through local or private bodies. All secondary schools should be made over to private management wherever that is possible.

The Government of India accepted the recommendations of the Commission and directed the preparation of an annual report reviewing the progress of education in the country. Higher education progressed at great speed during the next few decades.

In January 1902, Lord Curzon appointed a Commission to enquire into the conditions and prospects of the universities established in British India. The Commission was supposed to recommend such measures as may tend to elevate the standard of university teaching. The Commission made the following recommendations:

1. The legal powers of the older universities should be enlarged and all the universities be recognised as teaching bodies. The local limits of each university should be more accurately defined and steps taken to remove from the Calcutta list the affiliated colleges in C.P., U.P., etc.

2. The Senate, the Syndicate and the Faculties should be recognised and made more representative than before.
3. There should be a properly constituted governing body for each college.
4. Attention should be paid to the residence and discipline of students.
5. The courses and methods of examination in all subjects should be changed according to the suggestions made in the Report.

Universities Act of 1904—The Government of Lord Curzon accepted the recommendations of the Raleigh Commission and embodied them in the Universities Act of 1904.The Act reconstituted the governing bodies of the universities. The Senate of the university was to have not less than 50 and not more than 100 members. The number of elected fellows was fixed at 20 for Universities of Calcutta, Bombay and Madras and 15 for the other two. Statutory recognition was given to the Syndicates with adequate representation of university teachers on them. Conditions for affiliation to the university were clearly laid down and were intended to be rigorously observed. The University was given the power of making provision for the instruction of students through the appointment of university professors and lecturers. The chief purpose of the Act of 1904 was to tighten the hold of the Government on the Universities. New faculties were created to deal with the university curricula and with the methods of university examinations.

Resolution of 1913— A Government Resolution was issued in 1913 and this clarified the policy with regard to higher education. As India would not be able to dispense altogether with the affiliating universities for a long time, it was necessary to restrict the area over which such universities would have control. New teaching and residential universities were to be established within every province. Teaching universities were to be established at Dacca, Aligarh and Banaras. New affiliating universities were to be established at Rangoon, Patna and Nagpur. The outbreak of the World War delayed the implementation of the Resolution, but universities were started at Banaras and Patna in 1916 and 1917.

Calcutta University Commission—The Government of India in the time of Lord Chelmsford appointed the Sadler Commission for the purpose of holding an inquiry into the problems of the Calcutta University. The terms of reference included all aspects of collegiate and university education. Problems of secondary education were not excluded from the scope of inquiry. The Commission was expected to study the organisation and working of other Indian Universities with a view to helping it to formulate the policy of the Calcutta University. The Commission submitted a voluminous Report in 1919 dealing practically with every problem of secondary and university education. The main recommendations of the Sadler Commission were as follows:

1. The intermediate classes of the university were to be transferred to secondary institutions and the stage of admission to the university was to be that of the existing Intermediate Examination.
2. Secondary and Intermediate education was to be controlled by a Board of Secondary Education and not by university.
3. The Government of India should cease to have any special relationship to the University of Calcutta and the Government of Bengal should take its place.
4. The duration of the Degree Course should be three years after the Intermediate stage.
5. The teaching resources of the City of Calcutta were to be organised to create a real teaching university and the project of a university at Dacca was to be carried into effect at the earliest possible moment.
6. Special attention was to be paid to the education of women and a Board was to be created for that purpose.
7. The Government service system being unsuitable for universities, a new organisation of the teaching service in universities was necessary.
8. Problems of vocational and professional training including that of teachers, lawyers, medical men, engineers, architects and agriculturists were to be seriously taken in hand by the university and numerous reforms were suggested for that purpose.
9. The medium of instruction for most subjects up to High School stage was to be the vernacular, but for later stages, it was to be English.
10. The Government of India drafted a Bill to enforce the recommendations of the Commission. However, financial difficulties stood in the way. In 1920, the recommendations of the Commission were forwarded to the Provincial Governments by the Government of India. The Dacca University and Lucknow University were started in 1920 on unitary teaching lines. The

Allahabad University was started in 1921 and Delhi University was started in 1922 on the same lines.

Under the Government of India Act, 1919, the department of education was transferred into the hands of the Indian Ministers responsible to the Provincial Legislatures. However, the Government of India controlled and guided the general policy of higher education. Under the Government of India Act, 1935, entire university education was placed under the control of the Provincial Governments. The only exception was in the case of a university which functioned in two provinces.

Sergeant scheme for education— This scheme was prepared by Sir John Sergeant, the Educational Adviser to the Government of India. It sought to introduce universal, free and compulsory education for boys and girls between the ages of 6 and 14. The scheme was estimated to cost Rs.200 crores a year. This basic education was to consist of two stages, the junior stage covering 5 years and the senior stage covering 3 years. After the primary stage, all the boys and girls were not to be allowed to go to the High Schools. Only those were to be allowed to proceed who were expected to profit from higher education. Approximately, one out of every five was expected to join the High Schools. Schools were to be maintained out of public funds as far as possible. Restrictions were also to be placed on the admission of students into colleges. Intermediate course was to be included in the High School Course, and the college teaching was to last for three years. A national youth movement was to be started throughout the country. The movement was to teach the young men to build their bodies and serve their country.

Westernization

Srinivas (1962), one of the pioneers of sociology in India, has used the term 'westernization' to indicate the change, which took place in India during the British rule in the nineteenth and early twentieth centuries. Westernization implies changes in dress, style of eating, manners, the change in the medium of instruction, etc. Westernization started having its impact on the elite because they studied secular subjects with English as medium of instruction. The Brahmins and other castes with tradition of learning and traditions of science in the courts readily took to secular education with English as a medium of education. Another big change introduced in the Indian society by the new system of education is that the schools were thrown open to all sorts of people in contrast to the traditional schools which were restricted to upper-caste children and which transmitted mostly traditional knowledge. In asmuch as modernization in India has come about due to westernization, therefore, the above-mentioned changes of modernization can be taken to be result of westernization.

The following are the characteristics of westernization

(1) Morally neutral: Modernization is generally considered to be good but this is not so with westernization. Westernization has been for good as well as evil. In fact, westernization is normally neutral.

(2) Limits of Westernization: A distinction has to be drawn between westernization and western culture. All the elements of the western culture didn't originate in the west for example, Christianity originated in Asia, the decimals system originated in India and via Arabia reached west. Gun powder, printing press and paper were invented in China. All these constitute the important elements of western culture though these didn't originate in the west. The manner in which westernization operates in India is mainly the result of British influence. The culture of Germany, France and Russia etc is quite different from the British culture.

(3) Wide, complex and multi level concept: It substances all changes which are consequent upon western technology and modern science. Secondly it has had varying impact upon the different aspect of the culture; hence it is a complex concept. Thirdly westernizations have affected society at different levels.

For example in olden days people used to eat in thalis or on banana leaves in squatting position but now they are using dining table with all its accessories. While westernization has had very wide impact, there has been resistance to it in some sequences. Thus westernization has had variable impact on the Indian society.

(4) Conscious unconscious process: Westernization has not been incorporated willingly everywhere in India. At some places the copying of British manners and customs was deliberate at other places it was a subconscious process.

"British rule produced radical and lasting changes in Indian society and culture. It was unlike any previous period in Indian history as the British brought with them new technology, institutions, knowledge, beliefs, and values. The new technology, and the revolution in communications which this brought about, enabled the British to integrate the country as never before in its history. I have pointed out how the establishment of *Pax Britannica* put an end once and for all to local wars which were endemic in pre-British India and which were a most important source of social mobility for individuals as well as groups." This observation was made by Srinivas (1977: 46).

During the nineteenth century the British slowly laid the foundations of a modern state by surveying land, settling the revenue, creating a modern bureaucracy, army, and police, instituting law courts, codifying the law, developing communications- railways, post and telegraph, roads and canals- establishing schools and colleges, and so on. The British also brought with them the printing press, and the profound and many-sided changes this brought about in Indian life and thought deserve a volume in itself. One obvious result was that books and journals, along with schools, made possible the transmission of modern as well as traditional knowledge to large number of Indians- knowledge which could no longer be the privilege of a few, hereditary groups- while the newspapers made people in different parts of the far-flung country realize they had common bonds, and that events happening in the world outside influenced their lives for good or ill.

Christian missionaries from Europe knew India long before the British arrived there. However, during the early days of the East India Company the entry of European missionaries into India was banned; this ban was lifted in 1813 when the British Parliament permitted them to enter the country under a new system of licensing. This eventually threw the entire subcontinent open to missionary activity.

In the first half of the nineteenth century the British, often with the support of enlightened Indian opinion, abolished such institutions as *sati* (1829), female infanticide, human sacrifice, and slavery (1833). In brief, the Indo-British impact was profound, many-sided, and fruitful. The term "Westernization" is used to characterize the changes brought about in Indian society and culture as a result of over 150 years of British rule, and the term subsumes changes occurring at different levels- technology, institutions, ideology, values.

Westernization results not only in the introduction of new institutions (for example, newspapers, elections, Christian missions) but also in fundamental changes in the old institutions. Thus while India had schools long before the arrival of the British, they were different from British introduced schools in that they had been restricted to upper-caste children, and transmitted mostly traditional knowledge- to mention only two of the most important differences. Other institutions such as the army, civil service, and law courts were also similarly affected.

Implicit in Westernization are certain other value preferences. A most important value, which in turn subsumes several other values, is what may be broadly characterized as humanitarianism, by which is meant an active concern for the welfare of all human beings irrespective of caste, economic position, religion, age, and sex. Equalitarianism and secularization are both included in humanitarianism.

Humanitarianism underlay many of the reforms introduced by the British in the first half of the nineteenth century. The introduction of British civil, penal, and procedural law put an end to certain inequalities that were part of Hindu and Islamic jurisprudence. In pre-British Hindu law, for instance, punishment varied according to the caste of the person committing the offence as well as to that of the victim. In Islamic law the evidence of non-Muslims was inadmissible; and both Hindus and Muslims regarded their codes as divine, though early Hindu jurists gave considerable importance to customary law.

According to O'Malley, two revolutionary results of introducing the British judicial system were the establishment of the principle of equality and the creation of a consciousness of positive rights: "The last was a plant of slow growth owing to the abject submissiveness of the lower classes which prevented them from taking advantage of the system of equal laws and vindicating their rights by legal action." However, not only their "abject submissiveness," but also their illiteracy, extreme poverty, and the intricacies of a highly complex, expensive, cumbersome and slow system of law made it very difficult for most villagers to resort to the courts to have their rights enforced and grievances redressed. Spear has aptly said that "the courts were to the public a great penny in the slot machine whose working passed man's understanding and from which anything might come except justice" (O' Malley, 1941: 59).

The principle of equality found expression in the abolition of slavery, in the opening of the new schools and colleges- in theory at least- to all irrespective of religion, race, and caste. The new economic opportunities were also; in theory, open to all, though castes and other groups who traditionally lived in the big towns and coastal areas enjoyed a considerable advantage over the others.

Humanitarianism resulted in many administrative measures to fight famine, control epidemics, and found schools, hospitals, and orphanages. Christian missionaries played a notable part in humanitarian activity, especially in providing education and medical aid to sections of Indian society most in need of them- Harijans, women, orphans, lepers, and tribal folk. Equally important were their criticisms of such Hindu institutions as caste, Untouchability, the low position of women, child marriage, and polygyny. The British-Western attack resulted in a reinterpretation of Hinduism at both the ideological and institutional levels, and the conversion of the lower castes (especially Harijans) to Islam and Christianity was an important factor in producing a changed attitude among the Hindu elite toward caste and Untouchability.

Traditionally Indians ate their meals sitting on the floor. The food was served either on leaves or on metal (brass, bronze, or silver) plates. Among the upper castes, and especially among Brahmins, eating was a religious act. The food had to be cooked while the women were in a ritually pure state, since it was offered first to the domestic deities before being served to the members of the family. The men and children ate first, adult men being in a ritually pure state while eating. This meant removing their shirts and changing into a silk *dhoti* (silk is ritually superior to cotton) and upper cloth, or a freshly washed cotton *dhoti* and upper cloth. At the end of the meal the dining leaves became impure and were thrown out. The places where the leaves had rested were purified with a solution of cowdung. Now, in the larger towns and cities, the educated and Westernized groups increasingly prefer to eat at tables. The most obvious feature of the change is the new technology-chairs and table, stainless steel utensils, spoons-but it also has other implications. It means a degree of secularization, and the deliberate adoption of a style of life different from the traditional, because it is prestigious or convenient or both. The new mode of eating contributes to an increase in secularization, as the table is not likely to be purified with cowdung solution after meals, and the ritual acts traditionally performed before and after meals tend to be dropped.

In the political and cultural field, Westernization has given birth not only to nationalism but also to revivalism, communalism, "casteism," heightened linguistic consciousness, and regionalism. To make matters even more bewildering, revivalist movements have used Western-type schools and colleges, and books, pamphlets, and journals to propagate their ideas.

While selection, elaboration, and transformation of the elements of British culture do occur, it is essential to add that it is not a deliberate process, while rational choice operating at every stage. There is a seeming spontaneity in borrowing, and elaboration has the appearance of organic growth. But at this juncture it is well to remind ourselves of the historical background of Indo-British contact; by the beginning of the nineteenth century the British were masters of a great part of India, and they had at their disposal overwhelming and organized force with which to impose their will on the Indian population. This gave them a sense of superiority to Indians. As rulers they had their goals and policies which at every stage they attempted to implement through their British representatives in India.

Students of Indian society may be forgiven if they see the British in India in a *varna* idiom. At the top of the social pyramid were the officers of the civil service, the higher ranks of the military, and the biggest and wealthiest among the merchants and bankers. They corresponded to Brahmin, Kshatriya, and Vaishya categories respectively. Only a tiny fraction of the Indian population came into direct, face-to-face contact with the British or other Europeans, and those who came into such contact did not always become a force for change. Indian servants of the British, for instance, probably wielded some influence among their kin groups and local caste groups but not among others. They generally came from the low castes, their Westernization was of a superficial kind, and the upper castes made fun of their pidgin English, their absurd admiration for their employers, and the airs they gave themselves. Similarly, converts to Christianity from Hinduism did not exercise much influence in Indian society as a whole because, first, these also generally came from the low castes, and second, the act of conversion alienated them from the majority community of Hindus. Finally, conversion to Christianity often only changed the faith but not the customs, the general culture, or the standing of the converts in society.

As far as the bulk of the people were concerned, Westernization began to occur indirectly and gradually; the process has become greatly intensified, in many ways, since 1947 when India became independent. The first and most critical step in Westernization was the establishment of *Pax Britannica*, and the revolution in communications that followed. The extension of the administration and trading frontiers broke the centuries-old isolation of groups inhabiting the forested mountains, and provided them with new contacts and opportunities. The development of communications, and the removal of internal customs barriers, integrated the economy of the various regions in the country into a single one. The introduction of steam-powered ships and the building of the Suez Canal (1869) enabled Britain not only to increase her control of India and other parts of her Eastern empire but also to link up the Indian economy with the economy of the world outside. Indigo, jute, cotton, tobacco, tea, and coffee began to be grown in India by European planters for consumption abroad. World prices for these products assumed significance for the living standards of thousands of people in different parts of the country. The advent of plantations marked the beginning of migration of labourers to the two plantation areas- one formed by the mountain regions of Assam and Bengal, the other in the southern parts of the Western Ghats. The Assam area was by far the more important, in terms of the number of workers employed and the value of the crops. Assam attracted labourers not only from neighbouring states but also from modern Madhya Pradesh, Maharashtra, and Madras, whereas the Western Ghats attracted labourers only from the surrounding densely populated areas. Tea plantations were started in 1840, and importation of labourers for work on them began thirteen years later. The movement of labour was greatly facilitated by the abolition of slavery in 1843, which cut the legal knot binding the serfs and slaves, generally from very low or Harijan castes, to the landowners from the higher castes. It is interesting to note in this connection that the labourers on the South Indian plantations came mostly from the Harijan castes, whereas those on the Assam plantations came from "clean" castes, Harijans, and tribes such as Mundas and Santals.

From a geographical point of view the inhabitants of coastal areas, especially those close to the fast-growing port towns, were favourably situated to undergo Westernization. The areas immediately around Calcutta, Bombay, and Madras experienced Westernization for a hundred or more years before interior areas such as the Punjab. Again, people in princely states were generally more sheltered from the new winds of change than people in British India; in a few exceptional states such as Mysore, Travancore, and Baroda, however, the Westernization process, or some aspects of it, made greater headway mainly owing to the power, prestige, and initiative of enlightened though autocratic rulers.

Generally speaking, people living in towns are more exposed to Western influences than are rural folk. The bigger the town the greater is the chance of such exposure, while in the smaller villages such chances are, even today, minimal, though greater than before Independence. But urbanism does not always result in Westernization. Tangri points out that in 1842 schools had to be closed for lack of students in the two north Indian towns of Chaprah and Arrah, with populations of 50,000 each. According to him it was not urbanism as such, but the greater contact with foreign influences in the coastal areas, that was crucial. He also notes that in 1931 Hindus with 10.5 percent of their population in urban areas had 8.4 percent literates, whereas Muslims with 13.5 percent in urban areas had only 6.4 percent literates (Srinivas, 1977: 63-64).

Colonization, westernization and Indian culture— One of the most profound consequences of colonization has been how the political and economic rape of the colonies has also led to what sometimes seems to be an unbridgeable cultural gap between the nations that were the beneficiaries of colonization and those that were the victims of the colonial assault.

The era of colonial pillage and plunder led to the relative stagnation and often precipitous decline of traditional cultural pursuits in the colonies. Not only were certain aspects of the material culture in the colonies lost or destroyed, colonial societies also lost the power of cultural discrimination. Losing almost all sense of cultural continuity, they were also unable to recover (in any adequate measure) the ability to strive for cultural progress on their own terms.

On the one hand, there was a widespread sociological aversion to appreciating and preserving what had precariously survived from the past. On the other hand, there was an irrational and defensive embrace of religious dogmas and practices that had long since lost any significance or practical utility. Robbed of any measure of self-confidence, the colonized intelligentsia either looked upon its heritage with scepticism or disdain, or conversely, sought refuge in fundamentalism, obscurantism, or idealistic myth-making. When a native tradition had the stamp of approval from a 'respected' Western 'authority', it attracted excited and flattering attention. But rarely, and only in relatively isolated cases, was it possible for the colonized cultural intelligentsia to rise above the cultural stereotypes, and critically explore and examine its cultural legacy for any intrinsic (or sustainable) merit.

This is not to say that the struggle for freedom did not awaken the spirit of cultural regeneration in the colonies. Leaders of the National Liberation Movements invariably invested some effort in seeking the cultural rejuvenation of their societies- but there were too many practical impediments that prevented them from achieving anything more than partial success.

Because the domain of culture is extremely broad, and encompasses many facets of civilized social life- the task of post-colonial cultural regeneration was much larger than what even the most well-meaning advocates of de-colonization could have anticipated. And whereas some aspects of culture are immediately apparent to all (or most people in society), there are other more subtle and complex aspects of social culture that are not as readily understood or appreciated by the majority- especially at times (and in situations) when there have been sharp and forcible breaks in cultural continuity.

When people think or speak of culture, they often do so in very simple and general terms. They think most immediately of popular customs- such as traditions and rituals pertaining to birth and death, to puberty and marriage. They think of social celebrations and festivals, forms of greeting and communication, hospitality rites, cuisine, games, sports and entertainment. But by and large, colonial regimes did not interfere excessively in such aspects of human existence. Thus it is often the case that most victims of colonization are relatively ignorant and oblivious of what they may have irrevocably lost (or incorrectly internalized) as a result of colonization.

In particular, they are rarely able to comprehend how the hundred or two hundred years of colonization were not only very destructive in terms of culture, but that they were also precious decades of lost opportunity- when the colonized nations could have been active recipients of the cultural developments that transformed Europe, and perhaps, made additional contributions of their own. Whereas the European colonizers were able to expropriate (and utilize on their own terms) the centuries of progress made in colonized Asia or Africa- only a small elite in the colonies became aware of the new cultural vistas that had opened up in Europe. And very rarely were these colonized elites able to absorb and communicate the most useful and inspiring elements of the new European culture.

In part, this was because the colonial elites were too removed from the colonized masses, or didn't care enough. But this was also because the cruelty of the colonial occupations led many radical nationalists in the colonial world to associate all European culture with the culture of conquest and hegemony, and it became very difficult to separate the positive and more universally appealing aspects of the new European culture from the racist and chauvinistic philosophical developments that dominated the European intellectual space.

Thus, in part by accident, and in part by design, the colonized nations became very removed from the most advanced of the new humanizing trends that were beginning to shape the best of the new European civilization. But quite unfortunately, by the time many of the colonies were liberated, European culture was already in decline- even decaying; so it was Western "pop" culture that drifted to Asian and African shores. But the more enlightened and invigorating classical culture was unable to make much of an impact.

Although prior to liberation, there was indeed a period of cultural renaissance that accompanied the struggles for freedom in the colonies, these evanescent trends could not survive the inexorable march of pop culture that the forces of Western commerce had a vested interest in pushing.

Soon colonized societies had not only forgotten what they had, they had also forgotten how to sustain or renew (or elaborate upon) their fragile heritage. Above all, they had forgotten to dream, to fantasize and to engage in constructive and creatively critical social discourse. Most of all, colonized societies lost the ability to envision a better future that was consistent with their own geography and history. More often than not, even the most advanced social activists in colonized societies fell prey to a semi-mechanistic interpretation of imported ideas of social change that were indeed inspiring and useful, but yet, may have fallen short in key respects.

Cultural and social progress seldom comes about without some measure of struggle- but struggle alone does not guarantee success. For that, theoretical understanding, historical knowledge, critical self-awareness and material practicality (one that takes into account the physical constraints of geography, resource availability, time and environment) all become important.

Unfortunately, many serious proponents of social change in India have been unable to fully comprehend the lasting sociological consequences of colonization, or effectively mine the rich (non-European) pre-colonial heritage for ideas or inspiration. For instance, in the realm of the fine arts, and in the realm of epistemology, Indian civilization has had much to offer. And the Indian people have not been entirely averse to studying nature so that they might mould it for their own benefit. The long history of managing scarce water resources provides numerous examples of Indian creativity and problem-solving. Putting others before self is also not an entirely alien tradition in India.

Colonial rule destroyed not only the character and spirit of the Indian people, it also took away their ability to engage in holistic analysis. It turned Indians into peons and pages- people who were capable of serving the destiny of others- not those who could shape and mould their own destinies. Indians retained the ability to be intelligent about details and particularities, but lost the ability to be intelligent about the big things in life or important things in life. Whereas once, the wisest Indians had spent years and years contemplating about what brings about human happiness, the colonized Indian couldn't even conceive of happiness- let alone plan the happiness of an entire society.

If we look at the case of India, or any other ancient civilization- certain conclusions are inescapable: barring periods when an external (usually dominant) power (such as an invading conqueror) forced its culture on the society it captured and defeated– civilizations have been typically compelled to develop in harmony with their peculiar geographic environment. Geographic conditions and climate have shaped the economic lives of societies, which in turn has influenced their cultural output. Civilized societies have learned to take advantage of natural resources available in abundance, and do without things that were generally inessential to healthy and comfortable living.

Colonization succeeded through the cultivation of local elites who could make a complete break with almost all prior social obligations. Such elites were trained to be loyal to colonial goals- but disloyal to their fellow citizens. They were encouraged to focus on just their own narrow self-interest, and that too in a very sectarian and individualistic manner.

This is not to say that sectarian currents were absent in pre-colonial societies. Caste and religion have the potential of developing along strongly sectarian lines, and it cannot be denied that many older societies (India included) have been plagued by the ills of social segmentation and stratification. But it is also notable how such divisions were cynically exploited by the colonial authorities, and were exacerbated by colonial rule.

References

Allan, J. T., Wolseley Haig, and H. H. Dodwell (1934), *The Cambridge Shorter History of India.*

Brendon, Piers (2008) *The Decline and Fall of the British Empire, 1781-1997* (2008)

Chand, Tara (1961), *History of the Freedom Movement in India,* Vol. I, New Delhi: Publications Division.

Chandra, Bipan et al. (1972), *Freedom Struggle*, New Delhi: National Book Trust.

Desai, A. R. (1976), *Social Background of Indian Nationalism,* Bombay: Popular Prakashan.

Forbes, Geraldine (1998), *Women in Modern India* (The New Cambridge History of India). Cambridge: Cambridge University Press.

Majumdar, R.C. (1963), *History of the Freedom Movement in India*, Vol. II, Calcutta: Firma K.L. Mukhopadhyay.

O'Malley, L. S. S. (1941), 'The Impact of European Civilization', O'Malley, L. S. S (ed.), *Modern India and the West*. London: Oxford University Press.

Rose, J. Holland, A. P. Newton and E. A. Benians (gen. eds.), T*he Cambridge History of the British Empire,* 9 vols. (1929–61); Vol 1: "The Old Empire from the Beginnings to 1783" 934pp online edition Volume I

Rothermund, Dietmar (1993), *An Economic History of India: From Pre-Colonial Times to 1991*.

Smith, Vincent (1981), *The Oxford History of India,* London: Oxford University Press.

Spear, Percival (1990), *The History of India,* Vol. 2, London: Oxford University Press.

Srinivas, M. N. (1977), *Social Change in Modern India,* New Delhi: Orient Longman.

Chapter- 8

Undercurrents of Reformation Movements and New Awakening

Social and Religious Reform Movements

Indian culture and society have got a very long and chequered history, since India is one of the ancient civilizations of the world. Hence, in course of time lots of evil practices had become prominent features of the Indian society. Exposure to modern knowledge and western culture encouraged and awakened the educated Indians to do away with abusive practices with a view to making this country modern, vibrant and forward looking. The Britishers themselves were not much inclined to take any initiative in such sensitive matters directly, as they were afraid of making external interventions in personal or social affairs of the tradition-bound Indian people. Perhaps, they were scared of earning the wrath of native people. They always tended to have peaceful time with them for administrative or some vested reasons. The British did know that religion was very much central to the Indian life. Colonial domination, however, set the change in motion; Indians reshaped the imported ideas and institutions to fit the social and cultural milieu. The impact of imported ideas can be seen first in the Bengal Renaissance, when intellectuals in eastern India were rediscovering their past and engaging in new intellectual activity. Here we are dealing with major evil or bad socio-cultural practices briefly.

Human sacrifice and female infanticide— The problems of human sacrifice and female infanticide first attracted government action in 1802. After an investigation made by the Baptist missionary, William Carey, Lord Wellesley suppressed human sacrifice. Female infanticide was discovered to be more widespread, existing not only among some so-called primitive tribes but also among certain Rajput castes. By a Bengal Regulation (21) of 1795 the practice was declared to constitute murder and the territory to which the Regulation applied was extended in 1804.

Although a number of states prohibited female infanticide, it still proved impossible to stamp out completely. As late as 1870, the government was compelled to pass yet another Act attempting to enforce the registration of births and regular verification of the fact that girl children were still alive. Gradually, however, the practice of infanticide was reduced.

Abolition of Sati— Among other abuses which offended the "universal moral law" was "sati" or sati (meaning, virtuous one). The rite itself should properly be called sahamarana or "accompanying in death". The practice was of long standing in India, and virtuous widows usually gave up their life by allowing themselves to be burnt to death on the funeral pyre of their husbands. In general, the rite was confined to high caste Hindus. Muslim invaders found it particularly objectionable, and the Mughal emperors tried to discourage it.

Although a number of individual British officials interfered at various times to prevent particular cases of sati, there was no official policy. In 1803, Lord Wellesley proposed to abolish it in the Company's territories but he first referred the idea to the Supreme Court in Calcutta. The court's answer was cautious and pedantic. The government, it suggested, would be well advised to be guided by "the religious opinions and prejudices of the natives". The government therefore compromised with half measures. Understandably, the government's attitude was ineffective in reducing the number of satis.

The Governor-General Amherst was convinced that the time was not right for abolishing sati by legislative action. When William Bentinck arrived in 1828, however, there was a change of tempo. The Directors had instructed him to take steps to end the practice of sati, gradually or immediately, using his personal discretion. Bentinck's own temperament inclined him towards instant reform. Rammohan Roy and H. H. Wilson, a leading British orientalist, both submitted that gradual approach would arouse discontent and was much to be preferred, Bentinck himself could anticipate no such discontent from immediate abolition.

On December 4, 1829, sati was declared illegal in the Bengal Presidency (Regulation 17). By this Regulation anyone assisting a voluntary sacrifice was to be held guilty of culpable homicide and anyone using violence to force a widow to burn herself was to be liable to the death sentence. A similar resolution was passed in Madras on February 2, 1830 and action was also taken to make it effective in Bombay. The Regulation aroused considerable agitation in Bengal, and a petition was submitted to Bentinck, protesting strongly against it. The petitioners even went so far as to appeal to the Privy Council in London (January 1830). However, the appeal was dismissed and there was no disturbance in India.

Suppression of Thuggee— The campaign for the suppression of Thuggee was one act of the government that aroused no public hostility, because its practical advantages were plain to everybody. The word "thug" was probably derived from the Sanskrit verb thagna (to deceive), and the men who were called Thugs should more accurately be termed phansidars (noose-holders), because strangulation was the method they used for murdering their victims before robbing them.

The practice of Thuggee was of considerable antiquity. It is mentioned in a 14th century historical account and probably dates back very much further. During the reign of Shah Jahan, the French traveller, de Thevenot reported that the road between Delhi and Agra was infested by Thugs. The British first realised the existence of these brigands towards the end of the 18th century, but they did not begin effective action against them until 1829.

It was William Sleeman who proved the existence of the powerful Thug confederacy operating over the whole of northern India. In 1829, in the course of his reforms, William Bentinck authorised a special department to investigate and destroy the practice of Thuggee, and Sleeman was placed in charge of the whole operation in 1835. In 1839 he was appointed Commissioner for the Suppression of Thuggee and Dacoity. Thus gangs were often protected by petty rajas and landowners, as well as by revenue-farmers who shared their profits. But the British were determined to suppress Thuggee once they had grasped its proportions. They attacked the menace of Thuggee with single-minded energy and stamped it out. Between 1831 and 1837 more than three thousand Thugs were convicted. Five hundred of these saved their skins by becoming "approvers", or informers. By 1860, Thuggee was no more, though the office of Superintendent of Thuggee and Dacoity was maintained until 1904.

Child marriages – Child marriage had long been a thorny topic in British India. British missionaries and officials expressed their horror of pre-puberty marriage. In 1860 the criminal code set the age of consent for married and unmarried girls at ten years. The issue reappeared in the 1880s and in 1891 the criminal code was amended to raise the age of consent to twelve years. An American journalist, Katherine Mayo, published Mother India, which was a devastating attack on Indians and Indian customs. Using hospital records, official accounts and personal interviews, Mayo wrote about Indian society that shocked the American and British reading public. Mayo wrote that Indians were notorious for their ill-treatment of women of all ages. She focused herself particularly on social behaviour of men and gave a vivid account of child brides "raped" by their older husbands. Mayo concluded that these social customs prevailed because of the weakness of the Indian race. That's why these people were not ready to "hold the reins of Government."

Emancipation of women—The general movement of reform became subsidiary to the government's military preoccupations from the end of the 1830s, though there was little reduction in reformist pressures either in Britain or in India. Much of this agitation was concerned with the position of women in Hindu society.

The government was not willing to provide education for women, and did not do so until the end of Company rule. Most schools for girls were the product of missionary activity. In response both to missionary pressure and the infiltration of general ideas of Western liberalism, a certain amount of agitation did, however, grow up over the status of women in general and widows in particular.

A number of Indians proposed legislations to raise the minimum marriage age, and to permit the remarriage of Hindu widows. Although the governments did not prefer to initiate legislation itself and generally resisted attempts to pressurise it into enacting legislations, which it believed would interfere in religious matters. Eventually it allowed itself to be persuaded by Ishwar Chandra Vidyasagar to pass the Hindu Widows Remarriage Act of 1856.

Hindu polygamy was another matter which brought many petitions to the government between 1855 and 1857. The particular offenders were a Brahmin caste in Bengal known as Kulins. Legislation was drafted, but the outbreak of the Mutiny held up proceedings. When the Lieutenant-Governor of Bengal later asked the Government of India to enact the legislation it refused on the grounds that it might set a precedent which might not be approved by others practicing polygamy (principally Muslims) outside Bengal.

The period up to 1857 was one wherein certain essential reforms were achieved as a result of legislative action stimulated by a positive desire for reform. The limits of security, however, made the government distinctly reluctant to go further. Western ideas, both secular and religious, had their effect on Indian intellectuals, and Hindu reform movements emerged in response to both governmental reforms and the government's unwillingness to do more.

In the nineteenth century, the "woman question" loomed large. This was not a question of "what do women want?", but rather "how can they be modernised?" It became the central question in nineteenth-century British India because the foreign rulers had focused their attention on this particular aspect of society. Enamoured with their "civilizing mission," influential British writers condemned Indian religions, culture and society for their rules and customs regarding women. The ideology that emerged to redefine gender relations was an amalgam of new foreign ideas, indigenous concepts and the response of Indian men and women to the foreign presence in their midst.

Not all agreed that gender relations needed modification. A number of Indian intellectuals praised their own culture's treatment of women or compared the conditions of Indian women with those of European women and concluded that females in both countries suffered hardships. Those who accepted the idea that society's ills could be traced to the oppressed condition of women saw female education and female emancipation as the first step towards progress. But both groups – those who extolled gender relations and those convinced of the need for reform – shared an ideology, later linked to the nationalist project that separated the home from the world.

By the last decade of the nineteenth century, there was a recognisable reformist ideology. The shape of this ideology – particularly in its view of women – was retained throughout much of the twentieth century. First and foremost, Indian women were to be pitied. In 1839, Mahesh Chandra Deb spoke to the Society for the Acquisition of General Knowledge about the daily life of young married women: "Suffice it to say that every man who has carefully examined the condition of Hindoo women cannot help pitying the benighted and miserable situation in which they are placed."

Rammohun Roy, Pandit Vidyasagar, Swami Dayananda Saraswati and many others were trained in Hindu classics and India as recovering from a dark age. There had been a "golden age," they argued, when women were valued and occupied positions of high status. This view of the Vedic past had been adopted from the Indologists and useful to refute Mill's version of India. During this "golden age" women were educated, married only after they had reached maturity, moved about freely, and participated in the social and political life of the time. The power of such an idea may well have stifled serious historical research on women's lives until recently.

A number of reformers located the decline during the time of the smritis, that is, to a period when the vast body of law codes such as the Manusmriti, commentaries, epics and puranas were written. These theorists argued that the decline in women's status could be traced to these writings. But most of the reformers blamed Muslim rule. Ignoring the fact that rulers such as Akbar attempted to abolish sati and that Muslim law accorded women a higher status than Hindu law, these writers claimed child marriage, prohibitions on widow marriage, seclusion and restrictions on female education were responses to the Muslim threat to women's safety. Both the "golden age" and the "dark age" are problematic for historians, but these concepts proved useful in the development of an ideology legitimating social reform. It was the postulation of a "dark age" that made self-criticism palatable. The past had been squandered and change and reform were necessary to regain for society its lost vigour.

By the second half of the nineteenth century, there were reform groups in all parts of British India. They focused attention on sati, female infanticide, polygyny, child marriage, purdah, prohibitions on female education, devadasis (temple dancers wedded to the gods), and the patrilocal joint family. Their activity acted as a stimulus and encouragement to reform-minded individuals in other areas, and gradually, reformist organisations with an all-India identity began to emerge.

Across India, there is a long list of reformers who undertook major efforts on women's behalf. In Bengal, Ishwar Chandra Vidyasagar championed female education and led the campaign to legalise widow remarriage, and Keshab Chandra Sen sought to bring women into new roles through schools, prayer meeting, and experiments in living. By the turn of the century, Swami Vivekananda was arguing that women could become a powerful regenerative force.

In North India, Swami Dayananda Saraswati encouraged female education and condemned customs he regarded as degrading to women: marriages between partners of unequal ages, dowry and polygyny. At the same time, Rai Salig Ram (also known as Huzur Maharaj), a follower of the Radhaswami faith, advocated female emancipation in his volumes of prose, Prem Patra. Among Muslims, Khwaja Altaf Husain Hali and Shaikh Muhammad Abdullah introduced education for girls.

In western India, Mahadev Govind Ranade founded the National Social Conference to focus attention on social reforms. At the same time, the Parsee journalist Behramji Malabari captured the attention of the British reading public with his articles in The Times on the evils of child marriage and the tragedy of enforced widowhood for young women. Dhondo Keshav Karve offered a practical solution with his institutions in Poona to educate young widows to become teachers in girls' schools.

In South India, R. Venkata Ratnam Naidu opposed the devadasi system while Virasalingam Pantulu worked for marriage reform. Both sought to increase opportunities for female education. Reformers were found throughout India and among all communities. They addressed a number of issues, most of them relating to marriage and the importance of female education.

What is especially interesting about these nineteenth-century reformers is their activism. Their ideas on gender were rooted in personal experience; during their lives, they attempted to change those with whom they lived. They were not simply reacting to British pressure– these issues were very real and they responded to them with passion. These reformers viewed women as their subjects– to be changed as a consequence of persuasive arguments, social action, education and legislation.

As a consequence of changes set in motion by the British conquest of India, by the end of the nineteenth century, there were a number of women who were educated, articulate, mobile and increasingly involved in public activities. In the rural setting, life was dominated by the household – for both men and women. With increased urbanization and the growth of new professions associated with colonial domination, work was increasingly separated from the home. Paralleling this change was the establishment of new educational, religious and social institutions. As families moved from their village homes to the cities, they increased their contact with "foreigners" and witnessed the erosion of traditional household activity Like boys of an earlier generation, some of these girls attended educational institutions, social gatherings unrelated to family affairs, and new religious ceremonies. These "new women" were part of a modernising movement which sought to modify gender relations in the direction of greater equality between men and women.

Many of the "new women" were educated in their homes and then sent to a girl's school. Parents who cared about female education waited until their daughters were older before arranging their marriages or occasionally allowed young women to continue their education. Women also experienced increased opportunities for the expression of their individuality. Although women in earlier times were certainly not an undifferentiated group, we do not have sufficient records to go beyond generalizations about their lives. Formal education and particularly the development of publications intended for and written by women gave women a voice. It is impossible to enumerate, let alone locate, all the literature from this period, but we know that in Bengal, women produced almost 400 literary works, ranging from poetry to novels and autobiographies, and twenty-one journals. Through their writings, they were able to communicate with each other and develop new social networks.

The term "colonial milieu" may be used to indicate areas of time and place where the indigenous civilizations of Indian subcontinent came into active contact with British culture. A sphere of military and political control was established first, while the zone of cultural interaction evolved slowly from within the conquered territories. Conquest did not necessarily create the colonial milieu for all individuals or for a given region; that was determined by human interaction, by those who found it expedient or necessary to become part of the new colonial world and the culture which it contained. The uneven development of a colonial milieu and the persistence of indigenous forms of socio-religious dissent produced two distinct types of movement within the period of British rule, the one "transitional"-and the other "acculturative". The transitional movements had their origins in the pre-colonial world and arose from indigenous forms of socio-religious dissent, with little or no influence from the colonial milieu, either because it was not yet established or because it had failed to affect the individuals involved in a particular movement. The clearest determinant of a transitional movement was an absence of anglicised individuals among its leaders and a lack of concern with adjusting its concepts and programmes to the colonial world. Transitional movements linked the pre-colonial period with the era of English political domination and, if successful over time, with the colonial milieu. Once in contact with it, transitional movements made limited adjustments to that environment.

Acculturative movements originated within the colonial milieu and were led by individuals who were products of cultural interaction. The founder of such a movement may or may not have been drawn into the world of British culture, but his followers and those who moved into positions of leadership were largely English-educated Indians, influenced by the specific culture of England. Acculturative movements sought an accommodation to the fact of British supremacy to the colonial milieu that such supremacy had created, and to the personal position of its members within the colonial world. The basis of such movements and many of their declared aims rested on the indigenous heritage of social and religious protest. In no way were acculturative movements totally new or without roots in the established cultures of India and the specific subcultures of a given region. Thus, the difference between the transitional and acculturative movements was primarily at their point of origin.

The socio-religious movements of a given area must be examined in relation to British influence and political dominance, in terms of the local and regional culture, and according to patterns of interaction between different religious communities. The historic role of socio-religious movements can only be understood within the context in which they originated and functioned.

Important socio-religious movements which took place during the British rule may be noted thus:

Brahmo Samaj

Raja Rammohun Roy established the Brahmo Samaj at Calcutta in 1828 in order to purify Hinduism and to preach monotheism. The Samaj under him was based on the twin pillars of reason and the ancient Hindu scriptures (only the Vedas and the Upanishads), and incorporated the best teachings of other religions as well.

Raja Rammohun Roy (1772-1833)— Born in 1772 at Radhanagar in Burdwan district in West Bengal, he is unanimously considered as the first "modern man". He was a pioneer of socio-religious and political reform movements in modern India. He passed away at Bristol in England in 1833. He was sent to England by the titular Mughal emperor to plead with the British crown for a larger sum of pension. He studied different languages (Persian, Arabic, Sanskrit, English, French, Latin, Greek, Hebrew, etc.) in order to study the various religious scriptures in their original. He believed in monotheism (Doctrine of the Unity of Godhead) and opposed idol worship. In 1803 he published a Persian treatise called Tuhfat-ul-Muwahidin or "A gift to monotheists" wherein he explains his concept of monotheism. He established the Atmiya Sabha in Calcutta (1815) in order to propagate monotheism and to fight against the evil customs and practices in Hinduism. Later in 1828 he established the Brahmo Samaj at Calcutta in order to purify Hinduism and to preach monotheism.

He laid emphasis on human reason and rationality in all religious matters. He also applied rationality to Christianity, by publishing in 1820 a book entitled "The Precepts of Jesus, the Guide to Peace and Happiness", which embodied the moral and spiritual precepts of Jesus without the narratives of the miracles. Further, he defended Hinduism and its Vedanta philosophy, as found in the Vedas and the Upanishads, from the ignorant attacks of Christian missionaries. He led a life-long crusade against the practice of sati and finally in 1829 he succeeded in persuading Lord William Bentinck to abolish it. He championed women's rights, like right of inheritance and property, and attacked polygamy and the degraded state of widows.

He fought for the introduction and spread of modern education through the medium of English. He made Bengali the vehicle of intellectual intercourse in Bengal. He believed in the unification of divergent groups of Indian society in order to bring about national consciousness in India. He initiated public agitation on political questions like the need for reforms in the British administration, trade and economic policies etc. He also pioneered Indian journalism in order to educate the public on current issues and to represent public opinion before the government.

Brahmo Samaj after Rammohun Roy— Debendranath Tagore (1817-1905) established the Tattvabodhini Sabha (1839) at Calcutta to propagate Rammohun Roy's ideas. Formally he joined the Brahmo Samaj in 1843 and reorganised it. He promoted the systematic study of India's past through the Tattvabodhini Patrika, a Bengali monthly. He remained the undisputed leader of the Brahmo Samaj till 1866 and carried on the socio-religious reform work initiated by Roy.

Keshab Chandra Sen (1838-84) joined the Brahmo Samaj in 1857 and became the right hand man of Debendranath. During this time differences developed between the older and conservative section led by Debendranath and the younger progressive section led by Sen over the issues of social reforms (particularly the caste system) and of the relationship between Hinduism and Brahmoism (while the latter group stood for the complete abolition of the caste system and maintained that Brahmoism is different from Hinduism, the former group wanted to retain caste system, though criticising its rigidity, and asserted that Brahmoism is Hinduism). This led to the secession of Sen's group from the parent body (which had come to be known as the Adi Brahmo Samaj) in 1865 and formation of a new organisation, known as the Brahmo Samaj of India, by it in 1866.

He spread the message of Brahmo Samaj in other parts of India including Bombay and Madras by his tours (once in 1864 and again in 1868). He adopted a much more radical and comprehensive scheme of social reform and issued bhakti into Brahmoism. Further, he formed the 'Indian Reform Association' (1870) and persuaded the British government to enact the Native Marriage Act of 1872 (popularly known as the Civil Marriage Act) which legalised the Brahmo marriages and fixed the minimum age for the groom and the bride at 18 and 14 respectively.

The second schism in Brahmoism occurred in 1878 when a group of Sen's followers, under Ananda Mohan Bose and Shivanatha Shastri, left him and formed the Sadharana Brahmo Samaj. The causes for this split were the question of management of the Samaj and the violation of the Native Marriage Act by Sen himself (he gave his eldest daughter in marriage to the ruler of Cooch Bihar, but neither of them had attained the marriageable age under the Act).

Manav Dharma Sabha

Durgaram Manchharam (1809-78) was a leading figure among the small groups of educated Gujaratis who in the 1830s became strong critics of contemporary society. Participants in this group were Dadoba Panderung, Dinmani Shankar, Dalpatram Bhagubai, and Damodar Das. They founded the Manav Dharma Sabha at Surat in 1844 and held meetings every Sunday that were open to anyone who wished to attend.

As part of its programme, the Manav Dharma Sabha challenged magicians and the reciters of incantations to demonstrate their skills. They also criticised caste, but took no direct action against this institution. The Manav Dharma Sabha had only a short career as an active organisation. It began to shatter in 1846 when Dadoba Panderung returned to Bombay, and ceased to function in 1852 when Durgaram Manchharam left for Rajkot. Although its life was severely limited, this Sabha was directly linked to later developments in Maharashtra and Gujarat as its members carried with them the ideals of the movement and became leaders in similar organisations.

Paramahansa Mandali

Its history was closely linked to the Manav Dharma Sabha and to the leadership of Dadoba Panderung (1814-82). Dadoba outlined his doctrines in Dharma Vivechan (1848). He listed seven principles that became the basis for the new association. They are:

1. God alone should be worshipped;
2. real religion is based on love and moral conduct;
3. spiritual religion is one;
4. every religion should have freedom of thought;
5. our daily words should be consistent with reason;
6. mankind is one caste; and
7. the right kind of knowledge should be given to all.

These principles denied the polytheism of popular Hinduism, the caste system, and the Brahmanical monopoly of knowledge.

In 1849, Dadoba and his friends organised the Paramahansa Mandali at Bombay, a radical socio-religious society that met in secret. Ram BAL Krishna Jayakar became president of the Mandali. All members were required to pledge that they would abandon caste restrictions. Each had to take food and drink prepared by a member of the lower castes. Meetings were held at set times in the homes of various members and sympathisers. They read papers and discussed a variety of social and religious topics. The group soon came to an agreement on two major principles. First, they would not attack any religion and, secondly, they rejected any religion which claimed infallibility.

Branches of this organisation were established in Poona, Ahmadnagar, and Ratnagiri. The Mandali, following the path of the Manav Dharma Sabha with its attempts to reject the caste system, idols, orthodox rituals, and Brahmanical authority, left little behind it in concrete achievements. Its insistence on remaining a secret organisation illustrated an unwillingness to openly challenge Hindu orthodoxy. Yet the ideas seen in the Manav Dharma Sabha and the Paramahansa Mandali appeared once more in the form of a new socio-religious movement.

An off-shoot of the Brahmo Samaj, Prarthana Samaj was founded in 1867 in Bombay by Dr. Atmaram Pandurang (1823-98). In 1870 M. G. Ranade and R. G. Bhandarkar joined it and infused new strength in it. It was reform movement within Hinduism, and concentrated on social reforms like inter-dining, inter-marriage, remarriage of widows, and uplift of women and depressed classes.

Arya Samaj

The Arya Samaj was founded by Swami Dayanand Saraswati (1824-83). Originally known as Mula Shankara, Dayanand was born in 1824 in the town of Tankara in Gujarat. He spent 15 years (1845-60) as a wandering ascetic and later received education from Swami Birajananda at Mathura. He founded the Arya Samaj at Bombay in 1875. The most distinctive feature of Arya Samaj was the suddhi movement, which means the reconversion of those Hindus who had once been willingly or forcibly converted into other religions, but were now willing to come back into the fold of Hinduism. It was considered by the Arya Samajists as a potent instrument for effecting socio-religious and political unity of India. The Arya Samaj, though founded in Bombay, became very powerful in Punjab and its influence to other parts of north India like Uttar Pradesh, Rajasthan, Gujarat, etc.

Swami Dayanand Saraswati considered the Vedas as eternal and infallible. He was against idolatry, ritual and priesthood (in his opinion priests had perverted Hinduism with the help of the Puranas which were full of falsehood). He attacked child marriages and caste system based on birth; encouraged inter-caste marriages and widow remarriage; favoured the spread of western sciences; and organised social services during natural calamities, etc. He started the shuddhi movement. He wrote three books, viz. Satyartha Prakash (in Hindi), Veda-Bhashya Bhumika (partly in Hindi and partly in Sanskrit) and Veda-Bhashya (in Sanskrit) and toured India extensively to spread his teachings.

After the death of Dayanand (1883), serious differences arose between two sections of the Arya Samaj over the question of the system of education to be followed, resulting in a split in 1892. One section, known as the Gurukula section led by Swami Shraddhanand, advocated the adoption of the ancient system of Hindu education and established institutions for boys only, the most important among them being the one at Hardwar. The other one, called the College section led by Lajpat Rai and Hans Raj, stood for the spread of English education, and established a number of Dayanand Anglo-Vedic (DAV) schools and colleges both for boys and girls, the most important being the one at Lahore.

Ramakrishna Mission and Ramakrishna Math

The former is a social service and charitable society, formed by Swami Vivekananda in 1897 at Belur, with the objective of carrying on humanitarian relief and social work through the establishment of schools, colleges, hospitals, orphanages, etc. The latter is a religious order or trust, founded by Vivekananda in 1887 at Baranagar (Belur has become the headquarters of both the Mission and the Math since 1898), with the objective of bringing into existence a band of dedicated monks who would propagate the teachings of Ramakrishna Paramahamsa (the universal message of Vedanta). Though legally two district entities with separate funds and finances, the Mission and the Math are in practice single body, with the members of the Math forming the principal workers of the Mission and the trustees of the Math forming the governing body of the Mission.

Ramakrishna Paramahamsa (1836-1886)— Originally known as Gadodhar Chattopadhyay, he was born in 1836 in Kamarpukur village in Hooghly district in West Bengal. He became a priest in the temple of Goddess Kali at Dakshineshwar near Calcutta (1856). He married Sharadamani, a minor girl, in 1860 (she later came to Dakshineshwar and served him till the end). He sought religious salvation in the traditional way of renunciation, meditation and devotion. He emphasised that there were several roads to god and salvation and that service of man was service of god.

Swami Vivekananda (1863-1902)— Originally known as Narendranath Datta, he was born in 1863 in Calcutta. His first visit to Ramakrishna, his future guru, was in 1881, and made frequent visits to him there after. He established a monastery at Baranagar (1887) after the death of his guru. He made an extensive tour of India which brought him into close contact with the people and enabled him to realise the true condition of India. He also attended the World Parliament of Religions (1893) at Chicago (USA) and raised the prestige of India and Hinduism very high. From USA, he visited Europe and returned to India in 1897. Meanwhile he started publishing two papers- the monthly Prabudha Bharata in English and the fortnightly Udbodhana in Bengali. Later he made his second visit to USA in 1899 and also spoke at the Congress of the History of Religions at Paris (1900). He returned to India in 1900 and soon expired in 1902 due to ill-health.

He popularised his guru's religious message and tried to put it in a form that would suit the needs of contemporary Indian society. He stressed that social action was essential without which knowledge was useless in this world. Further, he condemned the caste system and the current Hindu emphasis on rituals, ceremonies, etc. and urged the people to imbibe the spirit of liberty, equality and free thinking. He proclaimed the essential oneness of all religions. Vedanta according to him was a fully rational system.

Theosophical Society

It was founded in New York (USA) in 1875 by Madam H P Balavatsky (1831-91), a Russian lady, and H S Olcott (1832-1907), an American colonel, with three main objects:

1. To form a universal brotherhood of man.
2. To promote the study of ancient religions and philosophies.
3. To make a systematic investigation into the mystic potencies of life and matter, which is called occultism.

They arrived in India in 1879 and established their headquarters at Adyar, near Madras in 1882. Later Mrs. Annie Besant arrived in India in 1893 and succeeded to the presidentship of the society after the death of Olcott in 1907. The society under Besant concentrated on the revival of Hinduism and its ancient ideas. In order to provide Hindu religious instruction, she founded the Central Hindu School at Varanasi (1898), which was later developed into the Benaras Hindu University by Madan Mohan Malaviya.

Young Bengal movement— Its founder was Henry Vivian Derozio, who was born in Calcutta in 1809 and who taught at the Hindu college between 1826 and 1831. He died of cholera in 1831. His followers were known as the Derozians and their movement as the Young Bengal movement. They attacked old traditions and decadent customs. Also advocated women's rights and their education and educated the public on the current socio-economic and political questions through the press and public associations. They carried on public agitation on public questions like freedom of press, trial by jury, protection of peasants, etc.

Other Hindu Reformers and Social Workers

Pandit Ishwar Chandra Vidyasagar contributed to the uplift of Indian women by struggling in favour of widow remarriage (his efforts bore fruit in 1856 when the British passed the Hindu Widow's Remarriage Act), by opposing child marriage and polygamy, and by campaigning in favour of education of women. He evolved a new technique of teaching Sanskrit and a modern prose style in Bengali. He also admitted non-Brahmin students into Sanskrit College at Calcutta (of which he became the principal in 1851) and introduced the study of Western thought in it.

Gopal Hari Deshmukh was a champion of new learning and social reform in Maharashtra. He was popularly known as Lokhitawadi. He made powerful rationalist attacks on Hindu orthodoxy, and preached religious and social equality.

M. G. Ranade was the famous socio-religious reformer of Maharashtra who was one of the prominent members of the Prarthana Samaj as well as the source of inspiration for the foundation of the Deccan Education Society (1884) by Agarkar. He inaugurated the Indian National Social Conference in 1887. G. K. Gokhale acknowledged him as his guru.

Gopal Ganesh Agarkar was one of the greatest rationalist thinkers from Maharashtra. He advocated the power of human reason. He was totally opposed to any blind dependence on tradition or false glorification of India's past. He founded the Deccan Education Society at Poona in 1884 in association with B G Tilak, V K Chiplunkar and Madhavrao Namjoshi.

Jyotiba Phule, belonging to a low caste from Maharashtra and being aware of the degraded position of the untouchables and non-Brahmins, waged a life-long struggle against upper caste domination and Brahmanical supremacy through his Satyashodak Samaj (1873). He pioneered the widow remarriage movement in Maharashtra and worked for the education of women.

Tulsi Ram, who was popularly known as Shiva Dayal Saheb, founded the Radha Swami Satsang, an esoteric sect, in 1861 at Agra, with the aim of propagating a monotheistic doctrine. According to him, the only means of salvation was the practice of *surat sabdyoga* (union of the human soul with the spirit-current or word) under the guidance of a Sant Satguru or sincere lover of the Supreme Being. His teachings were embodied in two books, each named Sarr Bachan (Essential Utterance). The sect recognises no God of the Hindu pantheon, nor any temples or sacred places except those sanctified by the presence of the guru or his relics.

Shivanarayan Agnihotri, hailing from UP, was educated in the Engineering College at Rurki and later became an active member of the Lahore branch of the Brahmo Samaj. But due to differences with the other leaders of the Samaj, he left it and founded the Deva Samaj in 1887 at Lahore with aims similar to those of the Brahmo Samaj but with an additional element, namely the predominance of the guru. The religious text of this Samaj was Deva Shastra and the teaching devadharma. The guru, claiming supernatural powers, was practically regarded and worshipped as a god by his disciples.

Gopal Krishna Gokhale was a famous moderate nationalist leader who was also a renowned social worker. He founded the Servants of India Society in 1905 at Bombay with the aim of training Indians in different fields for the service of their motherland. Earlier he was an active member of the Deccan Education Society (founded by G. G. Agarkar in 1884 at Poona) but left it after some time due to serious differences with Tilak who was also its member.

N M Joshi, initially a member of Gokhale's Servants of India Society, founded the Social Service League at Bombay in 1911 with the aim of securing for the masses better and reasonable conditions of life and work. He also founded the All India Trade Union Congress in 1920 at Bombay, but left it in 1929 when it showed leaning towards the Soviet Union, and started the Indian Trades Union Federation.

H N Kunzru founded the Seva Samiti at Allahabad in 1914 with the objective of organising social service during natural calamities, and promoting education, sanitation, physical culture, etc. He was also a member of the Servants of India Society earlier.

Shri Ram Bajpai, another member of the Servants of India Society, founded the Seva Samiti Boy Scouts Association in 1914 at Bombay on the lines of the world-wide Baden-Powell Organisation, which at that time banned Indians from joining it. Though later Baden-Powell, after a private visit to India, lifted the colour bar, Bajpai's organisation continued its separate existence, for it had the aim of bringing about the complete Indianization of the Boy Scout movement in India.

Vireshalingam Pantulu was the most prominent social reformer of south India in the second half of the 19th century. He founded the Rajahmundry Social Reform Association in Andhra Pradesh in 1878 with the principal objective of promoting widow remarriage.

The Muslim Reform Movements

The Aligarh movement— It was a movement started by Sir Syed Ahmad Khan (1817-98) for the social and educational advancement of the Muslims in India. Other prominent members of the movement were Altaf Hussain Hali, Dr. Nazir Ahmad, Nawab Muhsin-ul-Mulk, Chirag Ali, etc. Sir Syed fought medieval obscurantism through his journal Tahzib-ul-Akhlaq, and advocated a rational approach towards religion. He rejected blind adherence to religious law and asked for a reinterpretation of the Quran in the light of reason to suit the new trends of the time. In order to promote English education among the Muslims, he founded in 1875 a modern school at Aligarh, which soon developed into the Muhammadan

Anglo-Oriental College (1877) and later into a full fledged university. And in 1866, he founded the Muhammadan Educational Conference as a general forum for spreading liberal ideas among the Muslims. But unfortunately, this movement in the later stages became anti-Congress and anti-Hindu, and pro-British due to some misconceived fears of Hindu domination.

The Deoband movement— It was the movement that began after the foundation of the Dar-ul-Ulum (name of the institution) at Deoband in 1866 by Maulana Husain Ahmad and others with the aim of resuscitating classical Islam and improving the spiritual and moral conditions of the Muslims. The liberal interpretation of Islam by its founders created political awakening among its followers, and some of them like Maulana Abul Kalam Azad played an important role in the national movement.

The Ahrar movement— was a movement founded in 1910 under the leadership of Maulana Muhammad Ali, Hakim Ajmal Khan, Hasan Imam, Maulana Zafar Ali Khan and Mazhar-ul-Haq in opposition to the loyalist politics of the Aligarh movement. Moved by modern ideas of self-government its members advocated active participation in the nationalist movement.

The Ahmadia movement— Also known as the Qadiani movement, it was founded by Mirza Ghulam Ahmad (1837-1908) at Qadiani in Punjab, towards the end of the nineteenth century with the objective of reforming Islam and defending it against the onslaughts of Christain missionaries and the Arya Samajists. It gave religious recognition to modern industrial and technological progress. And it has become the most closely knit and the best organised Muslim group in India.

Other Muslim Reformers

Muhammad Iqbal (1873-1938) emphasised the need for a reconstruction of Muslim religious thought in the light of the problems posed by the modern world; criticised those ascetic elements of religious thought which made man parasitic and indolent, and preached a life of self-assertion and self-realization; influenced the contemporary Muslim religious attitude through his poetry.

Maulana Shibli Numani- founded the institution of Nadwah-ul-Ulama at Lucknow in 1894 with the objectives of recasting Muslim educational system, developing religious sciences, reforming Muslim morals and putting an end to theological controversies with in Islam.

Syed Nazir Husain founded the sect of Ahl-I-Hadis (People of the hadis) in Punjab in the second half of the 19th century. This group considered only the hadis (Sayings of the Prophet) and the Quran as the only and the ultimate authority on Islam, and refused to recognise none of the existing four schools of jurisprudence.

Abdullah Chakralavi founded the sect of Ahl-I-Quran (People of the Quran) in Punjab in the late 19th century. Its members, also known as the "Chakralavis", considered only the Quran as the ultimate authority on Islam.

Ahmad Riza Khan founded the Barelwi School in Punjab in the late 19th century. Its members, known as "Barelwis", preached the revival of many old Islamic practices and vehemently opposed the Deoband School and its preaching.

The Parsi Reform Movements

The refugee Zoroastrians from Iran, known as Parsis, are said to have reached Gujarat in 936 A. D. Their temples and dokmas (towers of silence), where the dead were exposed, were closed to non-Parsis. Over the period the Indian Parsis retained a limited contact with those followers of Zoroastrianism still living in Iran, known as the "Gabars". In 1746 the Indian Parsis got divided into two groups, when a group of them decided to accept the Irani calendar and came to be known as the "Kadmi" (ancient section) as opposed to the "Shahanshahis" (royalists), who retained the calendar used in Gujarat. This major division of the community lasted into the 20th century. A second division was created by the movement of Parsis into Bombay where many of them became wealthy as merchants, ship builders and commercial brokers.

Besides, the Parsi religion was frequently targeted by the Christain missionaries. In this background, Nauroji Furdunji edited in the 1840s the Fam-I-Famshid, a journal aimed at defending the cause of Zoroastrianism. He also wrote a number of pamphlets and published the book, Tarikha Farthest (1850), in which he convincingly argued that Zoroaster pre-dated Jesus Christ. All these events led to the formation of a socio-religious movement designed to codify the Zoroastrian religion and reshape Parsi social life.

In 1851, a small group of educated Parsis from Bombay founded the Rahnumai Mazdayasnan Sabha (Parsis' Reform Society), with funds provided by K. N. Kama. Furdunji Nauroji became its president and

S. S. Bengali, the Secretary. The latter was an ardent writer, whose main subjects were the glories of ancient Iran and popularising the new western knowledge. In 1850, he began publishing a monthly journal, Jagat Mitra (Friend of the World), to further the acceptance of his ideas among literate Parsis. In 1851, he started another journal, Jagat Premi (Lover of the World), for spreading knowledge of ancient Iran. The Sabha also issued its own Journal, Rast Goftar (The Truth Teller), as the main voice of their movement. The leaders of the Sabha criticised elaborate ceremonies at betrothals, marriages and funerals. They opposed both infant marriage and the use of astrology.

But the activities of the Sabha divided the Parsis into two groups – those who advocated radical change, and those who wished only limited alterations in customs and rituals. The latter organised the Raherastanumai Mazdayasnan Sabha in opposition to the radicals. In 1863 M. H. Kama founded the orthodox journal, Suryodaya (Sunrise), edited by M. B. Minocheer. This division between radical and orthodox Parsis continued into the 20th century.

The Sikh Reform Movements

Nirankaris— Baba Dayal Das (1783-1855) was the founder of this movement of purification and return. In the 1840s, he called for the return of Sikhism to its origins and emphasised the worship of God as *nirankar* (formless). Such an approach meant a rejection of idols, rituals associated with idolatry, and the priests who conducted these rituals. Stressing the importance and authority of Guru Nanak and of the Adi Granth, he prohibited eating meat, drinking liquor, lying, cheating, using false weights, etc. Before his death Dayal Das named his son, Baba Darbara Singh (1814-70), as his successor.

Determined to cut all ties with Hinduism, Darbara Singh began to issue hukamnamas (statements describing both doctrine and approved rituals). Under him the Nirankaris had their most rapid period of expansion; for in fifteen years he opened forty new subcentres.

Rattan Chand, younger brother and successor of Darbara Singh, also established new centres and appointed biredars (leaders) for each congregation or sangat. The biredars oversaw these groups and were charged with reciting the hukamnamas every fifteen days. Thus they provided a tie between the head of the Nirankari movement and its members. Between

1909 and 1947, Baba Gurdit Singh, son and successor of Rattan Chand, headed the movement.

The Nirankaris led emphasis on Guru Nanak and on Sikhism before the establishment of the Khalsa by Guru Govind Singh at Anandpur. In this they pursued a path open to both orthodox Sikhs, kesadharis, and to the non-baptised ranks of the sahajdharis, but drew members mainly from the urban non-Jat section of the Sikh community. Their dependence on Guru Nanak and early Sikhism for their model of "pure" religion separated them from another movement, the Namdharis.

Namdharis— Baba Ram Singh (1816-85) was the founder of this movement. In 1841, he became a disciple of Balak Singh of the Kuka movement. Those who accepted Balak Singh's leadership saw him as a reincarnation of Guru Gobind Singh. Before his death, Balak Singh chose Ram Singh as his successor.

In 1857, Ram Singh formally inaugurated the Namdhari movement with a set of rituals modelled after Guru Gobind Singh's founding of the Khalsa. To initiate followers into the new community, Ram Singh used a recitation of Gurbani (hymns from the Granth Sahib), ardas (the Sikh prayer), a flag, and baptism. Every baptised Sikh was required to wear the five symbols (kakka). Instead of the sword, Ram Singh required them to keep a lathi. In addition the Namdharis wore white clothes with a white turban and carried a rosary to further set them apart from all others.

The Namdharis were to abandon the worship of gods, goddesses, idols, graves, tombs, trees and snakes. They were also told to abstain from drinking, stealing, cheating, adultery, falsehood, slandering and blackbiting. Further, the consumption of beef was strictly forbidden, since protection of cattle remained one of the Namdharis' most ardently held values.

The Amritsar Singh Sabha— Shaken by Namdhari unrest, the speeches of Shraddha Ram of Arya Samaj, and by Christian conversions, a small group of prominent Sikhs decided to form the Singh Sabha of Amritsar, which held its first meeting on 1 October 1873. Thakur Singh Sandhawalia became its president and Giani Gian Singh its secretary. The aims of the Sabha were:

1. Restoring of Sikhism to its past purity;
2. Publishing historical religious books, magazines and journals;
3. Propagating knowledge using Punjabi;

4. Returning Sikh apostates to their original faith; and
5. Involving high placed Englishmen in the educational programme of the Sikhs.

It was joined by members of the landed gentry, the aristocracy, and by various types of temple servants – pujaris (who conducted rituals), granthis (who recited the Sikh scriptures), mahants (who administered the gurudwaras), gianis and descendants of the gurus. One of the main activities of the Sabha was the preparation of a definitive text of the Dassam Granth. When this task proved very demanding, a separate organisation, the Gurmat Granth Pracharak Sabha, was founded to finish it. The Sabha published numerous tracts and books and in 1894 organised the Khalsa Tract Society to popularise Punjabi, the Gurmukhi script, and to issue monthly tracts on the Sikh religion.

The Lahore Singh Sabha— Soon the Amritsar Sabha was emulated and rivalled by a new organisation, viz. the Lahore Singh Sabha, which held its first meeting on 2 November 1879. The latter was led by Professor Gurmukh Singh and Bhai Ditt Singh. It announced goals similar to those of the former. The first president of the Lahore Sabha was Diwan Buta Singh, and Bhai Gurmukh Singh served as its secretary.

Differences between the two societies soon came to the forefront. The Lahore Sabha was more democratic and accepted members from all castes including untouchables. Their programme of purifying Sikhism directly opposed the vested interests of the Amritsar Sabha. The career of Bhai Ditt Singh illustrates the type of friction that erupted between the two societies. Ditt Singh, coming from a low-caste, wanted to remove the evils of caste system and the institution of guru from the Sikh community. His tract, Sudan Natak, ridiculed the religious establishment and resulted in a court case.

The Lahore Sabha expanded with local branches in many of the Punjabi towns. The Amritsar Sabha developed its own societies, but its growth was far slower than the Lahore society.

Other sabhas— In 1880 a General Sabha was founded at Amritsar to provide a central organisation for all Singh Sabhas. On 11 April 1883 this was renamed the Khalsa Diwan, Amritsar. It included 36 to 37 different Singh Sabhas as well as the Lahore association. But this effort at unity was short-lived. In 1886 the Lahore Singh Sabha created its own Khalsa Diwan (Sikh Council). Only the Sabhas of Faridkot, Amritsar, and Rawalpindi allied with the original Diwan; the rest turned to the Lahore leadership and to its radical ideology of social and religious change. The Lahore Khalsa Diwan received assistance from the Maharaja of Nabha as its patron, while Sir Attar Singh served as its president and Bhai Gurmukh Singh as its secretary.

The Singh Sabhas continued to expand, new branches were founded that, at times, created their own distinct ideas and programmes. The Bhasur Singh Sabha became a hub of Sikh militancy under the leadership of Bhai Teja Singh. It was aggressive in its missionary zeal and extreme in its ideology. In time it developed into the Panch Khalsa Diwan and competed with other Khalsa Diwans. Not all deviation or enthusiasm by local Singh Sabhas proved as controversial.

The low-caste Sikhs, particularly the Rahtias (untouchable weavers) from the Jullundur Doab, demanded that the Singh Sabhas remove their social and religious liabilities, caste system. Since the Singh Sabha leaders did not respond to their pleas, they turned to the Arya Samaj, which welcomed them and conducted public ceremonies of shuddhi for Rahtias.

Thus, in the 20th century the Singh Sabhas were overwhelmed by other organisations. In the first decade they were supplanted by the Khalsa Diwans and then in the second decade by the struggle for control over the Sikh place of worship.

The Akali Movement— The next important Sikh reform movement was the Akali movement in the 1920s. The main aim of the Akalis was to purify the management of the Sikh gurudwaras or shrines by removing the corrupt and selfish mahants (priests) from them. Their movement led to the enactment of a new Sikh Gurudwaras Act by the British in 1925, and with the help of this Act and sometimes through direct action, they removed the mahants from the gurudwaras and managed them through the Shiromani Gurudwara Prabhandhak Committee (SGPC).

Nature and Limitations of 19th Century Renaissance

1. The socio-religious ferment that characterised this period was religious in character. Secularization was not yet a viable stance, although a few anticipated it. The leaders couched their appeals in religious language and were heard as spiritual persons.
2. By and large, they stayed away from politics. Only a few had opposed British rule and preached for its overthrow.

3. The economic ideas of the reform leaders represented the traditional outlook. They never possessed radical economic ideas, for the time was not ripe to breed such ideas.
4. A lot of difference can be observed in the approach and methods of the leaders in carrying out the reform movement. Roy broke away from the mainstream of traditional Hindu society. Ranade followed the path of gradual reform within Hindu society, Dayanand displayed an attitude of intransigence and rigidity towards foreign influences.

Achievements of renaissance are as follows

1. One should give credit to the 19th century reformers for initiating social and religious awakening in India.
2. It was due to their work that great self-respect, self-confidence and pride were fostered among Indians.
3. The problems of women were highlighted by almost all the reform leaders. Though the result was not spectacular, the road was laid in the proper form.
4. During the first two decades of the 20th century, much attention was paid to the problem of depressed classes in society.

Limitations of renaissance are as follows:

1. At the same time, the religious reform movement was concentrated upon and benefited only a microscopic minority of the Indian population.
2. Further, it started tending to look backward, appeal to past greatness and rely on scriptural authority.
3. The supremacy of the human reason and scientific outlook was undermined.
4. The neglect of medieval Indian history showed serious repercussions both socially and politically, in later periods.
5. One of the main limitations of the Indian renaissance was a lack of unity and a sound organisation. Opposition from orthodox elements was there at every attempt of the reformers. For instance, Radhakanta Dev organised the Dharma Sabha to protest against reforms of Roy, Sayyid Ahmed Khan was attacked by the conservatives of Deoband Movement.

6. Rise of revival during the last decade of the 19th century in the form of Theosophical society, also contributed to the declining zeal of the reform movements.
7. The upsurge of militant nationalism, with its revivalist undertones, strengthened this trend.
8. These movements were carried under constraints inherent in a colonial society. They tended to lean more on alien rulers for helping in their efforts to achieve their ends.
9. Also the reformers lacked mass support as their ideas and programmes never went beyond the reach of middle classes and their problems.
10. On top of all this, feudalism, though moribund, continued to be a major force and its ideology did not show signs of a real break-up.

Rise of Nationalist Movement

The section deals with various factors and forces which were accountable for the rise of anti-colonial movement in India. It was the British colonial policy of discrimination against the natives and economic exploitation without much regard for the welfare of the ruled that created material, moral and intellectual conditions for the rise of anti-colonial movement in India. The discussion of various issues is necessarily brief, because the analysis of a subject of this kind in an exhaustive manner would make this section quite lengthy and cumbersome.

In the case of India, political awakening or movement might seem to imply prior situation in which politics was either dormant or altogether absent, but this was never the case. Pre- British India, like other countries, did have politics. But the traditional politics was not the popular agitational politics of present-day India which involves mass communication, organisation of formal parties, ideological indoctrination, elections and civil disobedience. Rather traditional politics could better be described as administrative-politics consisting of discrete, deferential requests to the ruling authority by individual supplicants for favour or for modifications of administrative politics. Some Indologists have tried to trace the history of nationalism from ancient times but that exercise appears to be a-historical, inasmuch as the concept of "nation" itself is not ancient in origin. It is, however, not to be denied that some elements of nationalistic spirit were derived from the ancient and mediaeval cultures and civilization of this country. India, or let us say parts of the territory of the Indian sub-continent, had fallen prey to several foreign powers prior to the establishment of *Pax-*

Britannica, but never before did the people dare militate collectively against them. Of course, there was resistance-reaction against the Muslims, but the struggle of various rules and chieftains against them did not have a nationalistic character. The struggles lacked a genuine patriotic fervour and outlook. Even in the beginning of the nineteenth century there was scarcely any sign of political consciousness. Hardly any organized attempt was made by the people to resist the British Government's repressive measures and economic exploitation. The later half of the nineteenth century was, in fact, a landmark in the history of Indian nationalism, and it found expression in the mass movement under the banner of the Indian National Congress in the second decade of the 20th century. Peoples from all sections joined the movement, sinking their centuries- old difference, and struggled collectively against the imperial power until they succeeded in attaining Independence in 1947.

With regard to the period of origin of nationalism in India it is argued that the regime of Viceroyalty of Lords Lytton and Ripon was the seed time[1]. Theirs was the period of a policy of distrust and oppression possibly as a result of the Sepoy Mutiny in 1857[2]– a strategy of counter posing natives against natives and increasingly deepening crisis and miseries of the masses. Lack of imagination, political insight and sympathy for the sentiments and aspirations of the people of India on the part of Lord Lytton prepared the ground for the emergence of nationalism. Already numerous political organisations like the British Indian Association of Bengal, the East Indian Association, the Bombay Presidency Association, the Madras Native Association, and the Poona *Sarvajanik Sabha* had appeared on the political scene of India. All these developments made the way smooth for the formal inauguration of the Indian National Congress in 1885. It was the first all-India political party founded in India which came into being under the leadership of Sir A. O. Hume – a retired I. C. S. Officer.[3] The members of this party mostly belonged to middle class section of upper caste Indians. For obvious reasons the Congress leaders at that time mostly hailed from high castes, more particularly the Brahmin caste.[4]

The Congress was evolved as a safety valve for revolutionary discontents. This is evident from a letter that Sir A. O. Hume had written to Sir Auckland Colvin.[5] In the opinion of Daniel Thorner, Sir Hume was blessed privately by the high British officials to form the Congress with a view to guiding public feeling along the peaceful constitutional lines.[6] During its early phase or until the first decade of the twentieth century, the Congress was under the hegemony of the Liberals and was not directly connected with the struggle of the masses; rather, it was hostile to it. The leaders were loyal to the British and used to praise them for establishing "peace and order" in India (called Pax-Britannica).[7] They never advocated independence from Britain but used political weapons to air their grievances and tried to win British popular support for proposed social and economic reforms.[8] The early nationalists were akin to the German nationalists in the sense that "they were isolated between the generally indifferent British administration and the masses of ordinary Indians to whom their preoccupations were as nothing."[9]

With the rise of discontent and disappointment in public life, as a sequel of increasing disregard to the people's interests, non-fulfilment of promises of reforms and repressive measures of the Government, the Congress started showing its disapproval to actions and policies of the Government. The tone of demand and protest, however, remained very moderate. Although the Liberals changed their tone of protest and moved from the demand of administrative reforms to self-government, they did not adopt extra-parliamentary forms of struggle. This was possibly because of their impregnable faith in the efficacy of the methods of constitutional agitation. "As a result of the spread of political disillusionment regarding the principles and methods of the Liberals among the ranks of the Congress, a new group of militant nationalists having a different political ideology and conception of struggle emerged and crystallized within the Congress."[10] This group was known as the Extremists.

During the second decade and onward of the 20th century, the anti-British speeches of the Congress became so strong and vociferous that the colonial masters were compelled to review their attitudes towards the Congress and started taking serious actions against the leaders. This, instead of uprooting or unnerving the Congress, strengthened it as an organisation and helped mobilize the masses against oppressions and atrocities. When Mahatma Gandhi arrived on the political scene of the country "the Congress became a mass movement with which the British had to come to terms."[11] But he, too, initially extended his support to the British Government in India and South Africa.

Economic Exploitation and Westernization

To begin with, the Congress leaders were much impressed by the introduction of railways, postal services, educational institutions, and other modern facilities and amenities of the British rule. A leader like Dadabhai Naoroji considered it to be fortunate to be under the civilizing rule of the

Queen and people of England, and promised a deeper loyalty to the British rule in India.[12] Like him and several other leaders, G. K. Gokhale too supported the regime. Pandit B. N. Dhar in a strongly-worded presidential address observed in 1911: "Peace, order and perfect security of life and property have been secured to us to a degree never known to the old Roman Empire and even now not to be seen anywhere beyond the limits of the British Empire ...I thank God that I am a British subject, and feel no hesitation in saying that the government of India by England ... is the greatest gift of Providence to my race; for England is the only country that knows how to govern those who cannot govern themselves."[13] But with the passing of time and as a result of increasing English education, political consciousness and activities, doubts about the value of material gains from the British Raj began to crop up. The leaders who pledged a deeper loyalty began to be disloyal to and critical of the British Government. They started making public speeches and writing articles and books to explode the myth created by the British that India had made material progress under the British rule.

India's economic backwardness and poverty were not owing to the niggardliness of nature. They were purely man-made. The main interest of the British lay in exploitation of economic resources of India. Ever since the East India Company came into being, they had been virtually plundering the country.[14] While some historians have disputed the argument that India was becoming gradually poorer and poorer under the British suzerainty. There is hardly any dispute on the fact that during the British regime a vast majority of the people always lived on the verge of starvation. As time passed, they found it more and more difficult to secure employment for a living. The British pattern of economic exploitation, the decline of indigenous industries, the failure to replace traditional cottage industries by modern ones, high taxation, the drain of wealth to Britain, and the exploitation of the poor peasants by the *zamindars*, landlords, money-lenders, merchants, and the state, reduced the masses to extreme poverty bit by bit and prevented them from making progress. Ultimately, India's colonial economy came down to a very low economic level.[15] This led Indian leaders to believe that India had suffered more from economic domination than from a political one. A Congress leader once expressed his view that, if given the option to choose between political and economic *Swaraj*, he would certainly prefer the latter.[16]

One of the important developments during the British rule was the establishment of large-scale machine-based industries. The following were the important areas of industrial development: cotton, jute and wool textiles, rice, flour, sugar, paper, glass, matches, cement, iron and steel works, leather tanneries, salt, mica, saltpetre, coal, etc. Apart from development in machine-based industries, development also took place in plantation industries such as indigo, tea and coffee. The industries were mostly controlled and owned by the British capital. Indian capitalists had to struggle hard against the power of British managing agencies and British banks. In many cases even India-owned companies were controlled by foreign owned or controlled managing agencies. It was very hard for the Indian businessmen to get credits from banks most of which were dominated by British financiers.

On the whole the industrial progress in India was exceedingly slow, stunted and lopsided. Industries owned by the natives were developed without government support and often against the British policy. British manufacturers looked upon Indian textile and other industries as their rivals and put pressure on the government of India not to encourage but rather to discourage industrial development. The whole effort of the British imperialists was to slow down the independent industrial development of the country and prevent its industrialization. "British monopoly capital made particularly great efforts to hamper the development of heavy industry, which was the chief requirement for the economic dependence of the country."[17] Besides, industries were concentrated only in a few regions and urban centres of the country, and a large part of the country remained totally neglected.

The development of machine-driven industries brought decay of the traditional industries in India as was the case in Britain and other European countries. A large number of handicraftsmen and artisans were thrown out of their job, and the only alternative left to them to eke out their living was agricultural pursuits. The gradual destruction of rural crafts severed the linkage between agriculture and domestic industry in the countryside, and greatly contributed to the destruction of the village economy which was largely self-sufficient. A vast section of peasantry who were supplementing their income by part-time spinning and weaving had to bank upon cultivation. The rural artisans who depended upon traditional calling had to join the agricultural labour force or to become petty tenants holding tiny plots of land. In this way, the people of India were progressively impoverished under the British rule. The total number of factory workers in the country in 1946 was not more than two percent of the working population. According to the Census of India, 1931, the number of people depending on agriculture increased while the number of dependants on industry decreased.

The economic policies of the colonialists affected the agricultural economy very adversely. They brought transformation in agricultural economy through introduction of new systems of revenue collection. This was done not with a view to augmenting agricultural production or promoting the welfare of tillers of land.[18] Three systems of land revenue were introduced in India by the colonial authorities: *zamindari* (mainly in the northern part of the country), *ryotwari* (in the south and west), and *mahalwari* (in the northwest). In the *zamindari* regions the land was given to the big landlords and in the *ryotwar*i regions the land was acknowledged to be the property of the small peasant proprietors. Under these systems the peasant cultivators were subjected to untold miseries. They were forced to pay exorbitant amounts of rent and for all practical purposes and functioned as tenants at-will. They had to pay many illegal dues and cesses and very often were required to perform forced labour or "*begari.*"

Against the interests of peasants the British Government and its machinery favoured and protected the *zamindars* and landlords who rack-rented them, and the merchants and money lenders, who cheated and exploited them in diverse ways and took away their land from them. Whenever the peasantry or wage labourers struggled against landlords and money lenders' oppression, the police and army suppressed the peasantry summarily in the name of law and order. The Mopla rebellion of the Madras Presidency, the *Tebhaga* movement in the Calcutta Presidency, the Bardoli movement in the Bombay Presidency, the Champaran movement of indigo planters in Bihar and the Oudh Kisan rising are some of the glaring examples of peasant uprisings against the exploitative activities of the British in collaboration with the native allies.[19] The result was the development of discontent with and hatred for the British and their henchmen.

Introduction of a new agrarian economic order, among other factors noted below, gave rise to a new class of people (middle class) which extended whole-hearted support to the ruling authority and was content to serve as its subordinate agency. But the cooperation of this class to the British could not last long, because "the natural instinct of this class was to seek openings in commerce, industry, and the civil service; but here it found itself faced with stiff opposition from the middle classes of Britain that constituted the main power behind British rule in India… it provided the crops of the intelligentsia who became the spearhead of the movement for India's emancipation. But this was a totally unforeseen consequence of the land-laws introduced by the British."[20]

The emergence of a new class was not confined to rural areas only, but it emerged in urban areas as well. In fact, this class was more prominent in towns and cities than in villages. It came into existence as a result of industrialization and urbanization. The people belonging to this class were clearly distinguishable from the rural masses in standards of belief and conduct. One of the most distinctive features of this class was national in character. The new middle class was unknown to the past Indian society, since it was primarily the outcome of the new capitalist economic transformation introduced by the British.[21] The new middle class played a very significant role in the nationalist movement. To quote Niharranjan Ray, "Indian nationalism is mostly, if not exclusively, an urban phenomenon originating in and nourished by the urban elite of India of the nineteenth century and the first four decades of the twentieth century."[22] The anti-British activities of this class not only awakened urban dwellers but also rural masses through public meetings, news papers and personal contacts.

It was Mahatma Gandhi who first took the urban-based middle class movement to peasants and labourers who formed nearly 90 percent of the total population of India. He possibly believed that the middle class people living in towns could make sacrifices only to a limited extent. A revolutionary movement, to be successful, had to be carried on pre-eminently among the peasants and the rural poor, "as they alone could make the requisite sacrifices on a scale large enough to compel the bureaucracy to change its mind and yield to the demand of the people."[23]

The destruction of traditional agrarian economic system, autarkical nature of village, collective life of the people and the establishment of modern trade and industries were proved in one sense a boon for the freedom struggle. Development of a new economic system on an all-India scale had made India's economic life a single whole and inter-linked the economic fate of people inhabiting different parts of the country. If famine or scarcity, for instance, occurred in one part of India, prices and availability of foodstuffs were affected in all other parts of the country, too. This was not usually the case before the 19th century. Similarly, the products of a factory in Bombay were sold far north in Lahore or Peshawar. The life of the workers and capitalists in Madras, Bombay or Calcutta was closely tied with the life of the countless peasants in the countryside. Furthermore, introduction of modern means of transportation and communication had brought different parts of the country together and accelerated the process of cultural diffusion and social interaction, creating a situation for the people to think of themselves as one nation and helping the rise of nationalism on all-India basis. Before the advent of British rule, the people of India thought of themselves in terms of the regions they belonged to, rather than as Indians. Regional feelings were so predominant those days that the British historians had to describe India as a mere geographical expression.

Autocratic Rule and European Ethnocentrism

The British Government was "a great cruel blundering machine, running by its own weight," so observed A. O. Hume.[24] Autocratic nature of the Government is also reflected in the statement of the Governor-General Lord Lytton: "We hold India as a conquering country ... which must be governed in all essentials by the strong, unchallenged hand of the conquering power."[25] Karl Marx has given a detailed description of ill treatment meted out to the Indians by the English.[26] In spite of this fact, the ruling authorities used to justify the continuation of the British rule on the grounds of efficient and just administration and welfare of the people whenever they experienced a threat to the colonial empire.

Torturing of innocent people, the autocratic nature of the Government, and denial of the system of representation to the people awakened the Indians to their humiliating status in the British system, and consequently national consciousness came to the fore. Had the government taken up some milder policy towards the natives, there would not have developed a serious misunderstanding and gap between the ruler and the ruled. The British Government in India, whether imperial or provincial, by their determined opposition to the demands of the people for a share in the system of governance, aroused a spirit of patriotism, a will for self-sacrifice, a zeal for the greatness of their country which had transformed and exalted their lives.[27]

Racism was another important factor which helped the Indians to militate against the British. "Europeans believed that they belonged to a race which god has destined to govern and subdue."[28] A sense of racial superiority is very much obvious in the direction of Governor-General Mayo issued to the Lieutenant-Governor of the Punjab, i.e., "Teach your subordinates that we are British gentlemen engaged in the magnificent work of governing an inferior race."[29] A person like Lord Curzon, who was willing to hang a Briton for murdering an Indian, also believed that the Indians were men of inferior racial breed and incapable of telling the truth.[30] Even the middle and the lower class Europeans, not to speak of the people belonging to the upper echelon, considered themselves "*Sahib*" or gentlemen and remained aloof from the Indians.[31] Indians were kept out of the

European clubs and were very seldom allowed to travel along with the English passengers in the same compartment of a train. Racial arrogance branded all Indians, irrespective of their caste, religion, education, or class, with the badge of inferiority. They were called "nigger" and European masters often used to perpetrate severe cruelties on them. Sir Henry Cotton mentioned abuses, insults, and assaults hurled upon the native population by the British officials as well as non-officials and noted that the more the Indians were educated, the more they were disliked by Englishmen, for they wanted to be treated as equals.[32] Whenever an Englishman was involved in a legal dispute with an Indian, there was hardly any chance of getting justice. "In the administration of justice itself the balance was heavily weighed in favour of Europeans ... There was one scale of justice for European settlers and another for the Indian coolie." [33] The Indian newspapers, especially those patronized by the Government, used to publish very distorted news in favour of the British. All this was not because of partiality by the judges, administrators or journalists, but even more because of ethnic prejudice. H. V. Hodson's view that race or colour was not a problem between the British and the Indian runs counter to the facts of history.[34] Numerous are the instances which are contrary to his contention. A high sense of racial superiority on the part of the English, besides some other factors, led the natives to think of themselves as one or the same people while facing the foreigners. [35]

Western Education and Rise of Political Awakening

The British were highly zealous of spreading their education and culture outside. Statesmen like Lord Macaulay and Sir Cecil Rhodes were of the view that the English culture was the best and the most liberal in the world and if India, South Africa and later on, the entire world were "Anglicized" culturally through British pattern of education, it would pave the way for the social and political unification of the world. The idea of "Anglicizing" the world and thereby building up the empire and forging political and social unity of peoples at the global level under the leadership of the British, is apparent in the will of Sir Cecil Rhodes. He had desired "the extension of British rule throughout the world, the occupation by British settlers of the entire Continent of Africa, the Valley of the Euphrates ... the whole of South Africa ... the ultimate recovery of the United States of America as an integral part of the British Empire, the inauguration of a system of Colonial representation in the Imperial Parliament, which may tend to weld together the disjointed members of the Empire, and finally, the foundation of so great a Power as to hereafter render wars impossible and promote the best interests of humanity."[36] Thus the belief in Britain's role as the Messiah to civilize and unify the world by disseminating the British culture was one of the important reasons for the introduction of modern education in India.

Introduction of modern education was also necessitated by the fact that the Government required a large number of English speaking people to run the vast administrative apparatus. Besides, educated people were needed in industrial and commercial sectors. It was neither possible to get a sufficient number of people from Britain nor was the recruitment of the Superior Britain race profitable either to the rulers or to their countrymen at home.[37] The British held only key posts in the state machinery and business management, and the subordinate posts were given to Indians. The British, therefore, established schools and colleges to serve their own end. Another important reason behind the introduction of modern education was to add strength to the colonial empire with an eye to perpetuating it in India. Lord Macaulay and Lord William Bentinck anticipated, to quote B. N. Pandey, "The introduction of English education would not only turn its recipients into loyal subjects of the British Raj but might eventually induce them to embrace Christianity and thereby unshakably strengthen the foundation of the Empire in India."[38]

In the long run the modern education, however, turned out to be a serious miscalculation in the interest of the Raj. People became aware of the evil effects of foreign rule and education also divulged the secrets of modern Western rationalism. It was the English education through which liberal and democratic ideas of Jeremy Bentham, J. S. Rousseau, Herbert Spencer, and the several other social and political thinkers of the West filtered into India. Thus, leaders were inspired by the dream of a modern, strong, prosperous, united India. It was not a mere accident that the leaders who championed the cause of India's freedom struggle hailed from English educated classes. The Congress leaders like S. N. Banerjee and Sankaran Nair too had admitted the important role of English education in arousing political consciousness in their presidential address.

Lord Salisbury had rightly forewarned the high-ups of his ruling race that the newly educated persons would not be anything else than an opposition in quiet times and rebels in the times of trouble.[39] Salisbury's fear was quite genuine. Sir Henry J. S. Cotton had pointed out that a feeling was fast developing in India chiefly owing to the spread of English education, and the emancipation of India, therefore, had become inevitable ever since a system of English education was introduced.[40] One of the important reasons for discontent among the intelligentsia, besides several others as noted earlier, was that the British Government was reluctant to associate Indians with the administration at the highest level. They were deemed unfit for superior administrative posts. Even in the lesser services the experience of the Indians was mostly unhappy. They suffered from a sense of humiliation and frustration which soon transformed them into one of opposition to the foreign rule. The case of Surendranath Banerjee, among innumerable others, is a notable one.

A part of threat to the British regime came from the half-educated Indian elites. Every educational system has a certain amount of educational wastage. The half-educated products (drop-outs or failures) of the educational institutions of higher learning, who could not get a suitable job in government service or in the professions, could only hope to find odd jobs for which a smattering of English and a nodding acquaintance with the liberal arts were deemed sufficient. Journalists, translators, unemployed educated young and political agitators mostly represented the group of half-educated elites. They enriched their vernacular languages by translating English books or by writing articles, which were indigenous in language and context. The half-educated persons kept themselves more in touch with the common people than those who passed their examinations with good results and obtained lucrative jobs and tried to conform to the standard set by the colonial rulers. In the words of Michael Edwardes: "The institution of higher learning contributed to increased political activity not so much through those who graduated, many of whom could be absorbed by the demands of a growing bureaucracy, as through the high proportion of failures– the wastage often being as high as 60 percent of candidates– who tended to drift into extremist political spheres."[41]

Historians have rightly argued that Indian nationalism is the foster-child of English education. The rationale of argument is that the nationalist movement had been pioneered and successfully led by the English educated people. Through the knowledge of English they were able to know the Western history, politics, and thought which helped them greatly in organizing the Congress on democratic principles and ideals, making the movement puissant and effective. Questioning the prominent role of Western education in the movement, R. Palme Dutt has stated that "the Indian national movement arose from social conditions, from the conditions of imperialism and its system of exploitation and from the social and economic forces generated within Indian society under the conditions of that exploitation... ."[42]

Despite its many disadvantages the alien rule proved to be a blessing in disguise for Indian literature. Abolition of medieval feudalism by the British marked a turning point in the cultural sphere. Poets and writers were no longer bound to display hypocritical reverence and high-sounding praises to the princes and aristocrats. They were set free to move out of the courts to the courtyards. The new formative forces like the press, the emergence of middle class intelligentsia, infusion of modern scientific ideas, and the like gave birth to certain broad features which are easily recognizable in most of the Indian language. The new wave in Indian literature at first became prominent in Bengali and later in Hindi during the second half of the nineteenth century.

The pioneers of the new tradition in Bengali were men like Dinbandhu Mitra, Hem Chandra Banerjee, Bankim Chandra Chatterjee, Ishwar Chandra Vidyasagar, Rajendra Lal Mitra, Raj Narain Bose, Bhudev Mukhopadhya, Madhusudan Dutta, Dwijendra Nath Tagore, Rangalal, Nabin Chandra, etc. Their writings appealed to the dumb millions of India to be ready to liberate the motherland from the immeasurable pathos. The national lyrics of Hem Chandra whom Aurobindo Ghose called "one of the mightiest prophets of Indian nationalism,"[43] championed the legitimate rights of the Indians and inspired all the nationalist leaders. Of all these writers Bankim Chandra Chatterjee exercised the greatest influence and his works hailed the loss of independence in a heart-rending manner and stirred up the imagination of the people and made them devotees to the cause of the nation. He was a hydra-headed genius of his times and his services to the national cause need no emphasis. Rabindra Nath Tagore was another great Bengali genius, Asia's first Noble Prize Winner, who profusely contributed to the growth of national literature. He stressed the importance of "*Atma Shakti*" (self confidence) and criticized those who were begging concessions and reforms from the alien ruler.

The press was yet another instrument through which the leaders and intelligentsia were able to familiarize the masses with the anti-imperialist doctrines and ideologies such as representative form the government, individual liberty, democratic framework of the political and social institutions, misdeeds of the colonial rule, and self-government or Swaraj. In the press they also discovered a powerful weapon to propagate and popularize their programmes, policies, and the means of struggle enunciated by them and the official policies of the government. The extensive exchange of views on programmes and problem relating to different regions of the country led to the creation of a spirit of national collaboration in political and social spheres. The press also assisted in the development of a rich literature and culture provincial in form and national in character. In this way, the Indian press had played a distinct role in accelerating the process of formation of public opinion in India.

Newspapers like the Hindoo Patriot, the Amrita Bazar Patrika, the Bengalee, the Som Prakash, and the Sanjivani in Bengal; the Rast Goftar, the Native Opinion, the Indu Prakash, the Mahratta, and the Kesari in Bombay; the Hindu, the Swadeshmitran, the Andhra Prakashika, and the Kerala Patrika in Madras; the Advocate, the Hindustani, and the Azad in U.P.; the Tribune, the Akhbar-i-Am, and the Koh-i-noor in the Punjab; the Bihar Herald in Bihar, and several others played a very significant part in creating public opinion favourable to the freedom struggle. The role of the press those days was no less than that of a constitutional opposition.

Political awakening in India was not an isolated and solitary event; rather, it was a part of world awakening. The unification movement in Germany and Italy and parliamentary reforms in England during the 19th century exercised considerable influence upon the Indian people. Under the influence of parliamentary reforms in England, Indian leaders asked for similar things in India. Some scholars consider that the nationalist movement of India or other Asian countries was impelled more by the 1905-1907 revolution in Russia and then by the Great October Socialist Revolution than by the national movements in Eastern and Southern Europe. The Russo-Japanese war was another big international event that positively affected the movement. In India it was taken as a war between East and West, and the defeat of the great Russian Power by little Japan was considered the victory of the East over West. This certainly changed the scene of despair into a sign of hope in India. The impact on India's emancipation movement of the Young Turk Movement, introduction of representative institutions in colonies like New South Wales, New Zealand, New Foundland, Barbados and Philippines and the rise of Sinn Fein in Ireland was quite significant.

Socio-cultural Reforms

The nineteenth century socio-cultural reforms, which constituted the core of the Indian Renaissance, had given a great impetus to the rising national consciousness in India.[11] The reformists had created a new outlook, facilitating the process of unification of various religious communities at all-India level through historically progressive techniques. As nationalism generally thrives on past memories and achievements, the renaissance leaders made every effort to discover and popularize the glories of the ancient and medieval Hindus in different spheres of life. The memories of the Vedic past; the reigns of great emperors like Chandra Gupta, Ashoka, and Harsha; the heroic deeds of Prithvi Raj, Rana Pratap, Shivaji and Guru Govind Singh; the epic patriotism of Rani Laxmibai and Kunwar Singh were resuscitated with an intent to infusing a new life and vigour in the masses.[45] At first it was, in fact, the Europeans who studied the language and culture of ancient India and rediscovered past wisdom not only for themselves but also for Indians. Through the labours and appreciation of these scholars the British and the Indians both came to know and value India's culture anew. The basic difference between the purpose of rediscovering the pristine glories of India by the European and Indian scholars was that the former acted out of their academic curiosity, while the latter acted with a view to awakening their countrymen. The revival of India's past glories stirred up the hearts of the Hindus so deeply that they were imbued with a spirit of nationalism and ardent patriotism. The reformists of the twentieth century attempted to combine Hindu revivalism with politics – with an object to give "Indian nationalism a mass appeal and to convert Congress from the narrow expression of minority self-interest into the apparent spokesman of the Indian people."[46] On the basis of the knowledge of their great past the reformists as well as politicians were not only able to project the real image of India outside but also were in a position to falsify the belief that Britain represented a higher civilization and the English had a civilizing mission in India. "The awakening of India," in the words of Jawaharlal Nehru, "was of two folds: She looked to the West and at the same time, she looked at herself and her own past for inspiration."[47]

Raja Rammohun Roy, who is generally called pioneer of the Modern Age in India,[48] had contributed tremendously to the renaissance movement. He, during the later part of his life, worked mainly for the reorientation and revitalization by the corrupt priestly class interested in keeping the general masses ignorant by feeding them on superstitions and fears relating to something mystical beyond their life. Rammohun Roy openly decried the age-old faith and practices of the Hindu society from the standpoint of contemporary Western values, e.g., rationalism, humanism and humanitarianism. Strictly speaking, a direct challenge to the philosophy of renunciation and the fatal incubus of ancient abstraction came from Ramkrishna Paramahansa and still more from his great disciple– Swami Vivekananda. Vivekananda tried to awaken national consciousness through his preaching, deriving inspiration from the philosophy of Karma-yoga. His usual theme of speech was "above all, be strong, be manly" and exhorted, "anything that makes you weak physically, intellectually and spiritually, reject as poison, there is no life in it, it cannot be true."[49] He believed in a spirit that would inculcate national self-respect. He opposed Europeanization of the Indians and taught self-respect and inspired his countrymen to cherish their own traditional culture and values. By his speeches and activities he stimulated the pride of the Indians in their own cultural heritage and strengthened the spirit of political nationalism. Although Vivekananda was not in favour of political agitation, the building up of a strong, brave, dynamic nation was dear to his heart.

The Hindu society underwent considerable changes in social and religious spheres under the influence of various reformatory socio-cultural organisations like the Ram Krishna Mission and the Brahmo Samaj in Bengal; the Paramahansa Mandali and the Prarthana Samaj in Maharashtra; and the Arya Samaj in North India. They were led by great reformists namely, other than those mentioned above, Devendranath Tagore, Keshub Chandra Sen, Ishwar Chandra Vidyasagar, Gopal Hari Deshmukh, Mahadev Govind Ranade, Gopal Ganesh Agarkar, K. T. Telang, R. G. Bhandarkar, N. G. Chandvarkar, Swami Dayananda Saraswati, etc. These reformers collectively gave a new lease of life to the decaying Hindu society and heightened the sense of greatness among the masses through reformatory movements and demagogic preaching. They not only helped revitalize the Hindu society but also helped foster a strong sense of national spirit.[50]

Another movement which also contributed to the nationalist sentiment came into being in the early eighties of the nineteenth century, and that was the Theosophist Movement under the dynamic leadership of Mrs Annie Besant, an Irish Home Ruler, which was born out of the Christian mysticism and Hindu spiritualism. The theosophists proclaimed in a confident language the greatness and superiority of the ancient Indian wisdom and offered an open apology in defence of Hindus faith and practice. The message coming from the representatives of so-called advanced people of the world raised Indians in their own estimation and reposed self-confidence among the Indians. Significance which its services rendered to the cause of nationalist movement in India hardly needs any emphasis.

From the foregoing discussion it is not to be inferred that the leaders of the Indian renaissance were directly concerned with the movement. They were, in fact, primarily interested in doing away with contemporary evil practices and unfounded dogmas as well as in the revival of moribund Indian social and cultural order. They were, in a true sense, reformists rather politicians. But the twentieth century reformists certainly showed a deep sense of interest in the freedom struggle. It was Gandhi who first blended religion with mass politics and tactfully handled it as one of the powerful tools, awakening the dormant masses against the colonial misrule. In his view religion and politics were not two different entities. It was he who successfully transformed "the legacy of renaissance movements and regionalism into a truly mass supported and all-embracing Hindu nationalism."[51] By that he successfully confronted the despotic colonial master, and this made him a great charismatic leader of the twentieth century world.

The side-effect of the socio-cultural reform movements and rising militancy in Hindu society proved disastrous to the force of freedom struggle in the sense that it created mutual distrust between Hindus and Muslims and helped promote sectarianism in the country. Since Hindu religious and political leaders championed some ancient and medieval Hindu emperors and warriors as national heroes and derived inspiration from their life, the Muslim elites began to doubt the increasing dominance of Hindus in politics. And, thus, the state of uneasiness among Muslims intensified. Their growing fear of lagging far behind Hindus in the political game found expression in the Muslim League. Although some distinguished Muslims identified themselves with the Congress, the League was able to project itself with increasing success as a party dedicated "to protect and advance the political and other rights of the Mussalmans of India."[52] The British, taking advantage of this reality enforced the Morley-Minto Reforms of 1909 which embedded the principle of communal representation in the legislature and thus the cleavage was further widened between the two communities. "To begin with its (League's) programme was largely negative: what the Congress was for, the League was against."[53] The hostility between two communities became so implacable with the leading Congress leaders like Mahatma Gandhi, Jawaharlal Nehru, Maulana Abul Kalam and several others, too numerous to be mentioned here, became futile. This ultimately culminated in the historic division of the country into India and Pakistan.

Several Indian historians, more often than not, had accused the British rules and continue to do so for pursuing the Roman policy of "*divide et impera*" in India. But it, if viewed from the perspective of rule's interest, was certainly not an unfair and improper policy on their part. They did not create India as a colony to generate lasting love between Hindus and Muslims and promote all-round development activities. Politics is the art of possible. What they did was quite expected and fair. After all, they had been governing

India in the interest of their own country and kept her in their imperial yoke so long as it was possible for them.

To sum up, introduction of English education, spread of new learning, Hindu reformation movements, increasing pauperization of the people ensuing from economic exploitation, the despotic nature of bureaucracy, racial arrogance of the colonial masters, discrimination of natives in matters of high ranking jobs, business and commerce and above all people's united struggle for the common cause of *Swaraj* were the most important causes of the anti-imperialist movement in India. The able stewardship of Mahatma Gandhi and people's faith in his leadership played no less an important role in the success of movement.

Hodson, besides conceding the development of public opinion along liberal lines both in Britain and India and political consciousness and solidarity of the Indian people, considers the natural evolution of imperialism as an important factor which led the movement to liberation.[54] This cannot be taken as an historical reality, for no colonial regime has ever culminated in liberation of its own as the aftermath of natural evolution of imperialism. Had the natural evolution of imperialism been the reason, India would not have attained her freedom at midnight on the 14th of August 1947. For India was a very gainful enterprise, the British took all measures to preserve the moribund capitalist slavery. It was a Herculean task for the decadent reactionary imperialist to hold out against the virulent stroke of stormy revolutionary upsurge of the downtrodden and benighted people who had awakened completely from the mediaeval stagnancy to a new life. Suzerainty, no matter how mighty or tyrannical it is, can last as long as the ruled-race can tolerate it.

The movement took a considerably long time to spread throughout the country and percolate throughout all the strata of society. It so happened because India, then as today, was a country of considerable regional, cultural, lingual, racial and economic diversities with poor means of communication and transportation, besides being vast both in respect of size of population and the area of land. The nationalist leaders had to strive very hard to reach the life of common men, who lacked adequate formal education and political consciousness.

It is also to be noted that the nationalist movement of India, like that of several other ex-colonial countries, came in the wake of religious and cultural reform movements and had been imbued with traditionalism and ethnocentrism. The sentiment of unity of culture, religion and race encouraged the sentiment of patriotism and nationalism among the people, giving rise to a desire for political and economic liberation. And the sense of unity was infused and spirited up by the presence of a foreign sovereign of an entirely different race and culture.

In the beginning, the movement was largely an urban-based middle class movement which was later supported by the people of other classes all-over the country such as peasantry, feudal princes, semi-feudal landlords and workers for the common cause of decolonization of India, except for a negligible minority of people having vested interests in the perpetuation of colonial rule.[55] V. Kiernan's view that the working class was not drawn into the struggle has been rightly refuted by the several authors.[56] The leadership of the movement had been mainly in the hands of middle class people. They, with some exceptions, were drawn from the groups which traditionally enjoyed a high social and ritual position in the society, and had been most exposed to the Western culture in British commercial companies, administrative services, and educational institutions. A higher level of political participation of a particular section of our society is not to be taken as surprising fact. Right from the ancient times the so-called upper castes namely, Brahmin, Kshatriya (later Rajput), and Kayastha had been either rulers themselves or associated with rules in one way or the other. They had been so grossly involved with the political processes of this country for a great length of time that they were bound to have a higher level of political participation in the struggle for freedom. In the post-Independent era they have become successful enough to occupy state power and transform themselves into new dominant classes. In order to perpetuate their traditional supremacy and continue to be in a dominant power position they have taken recourse to nepotism, casteism, and the hollow sounding slogan of democracy. They have been hindering and flouting in every possible way the revolutionary initiative of mass action and the seizure of power by the people from below.

Notes

1. Annie Besant, *The Future of Indian Politics* (Madras, Theosophical Publishing House, 1922), p. 225. Also see V. C. P. Chaudhary, Imperial Policy of British in India (Calcutta: Punthi Pustak, 1968).
2. Since the revolt spread beyond the army, it was more than a mutiny. See S. Gopal, *British Policy in India, 1858-1905* (London: Cambridge University Press, 1965), pp. 1-2. Also see S.D. Singh's novel on the Indian Mutiny (New Delhi: Arnold Heinemann, 1980), p. 226.
3. The Congress was not the innovation of one man: it was not the creation of a few individuals. It is hard to say as to who actually first conceived the idea of the

Indian National Congress, but the credit for its establishment goes to Allen. O. Hume. See W. R. Smith, *Nationalism and Reform in India* (New Haven: Yale University Press, 1938), p. 43. Also see Rafiq Zakaria, *The Rise of Muslims in Indian Politics* (Bombay: Somaiya Publications Pty. Ltd., 1970), p. 47.

4. The President of the Indian National Congress either belonged to the Brahmin caste or to the Christian, Parsee, and Muslim communities. Very few of them, not more than four out of sixty-two Presidents, belonged to the lower castes during the period of sixty years, i.e., from the time of inception of the INC in 1885 to the Independence of India in 1947. Even among the Congress workers, the lower castes were in insignificant minority. The dominance of Brahmins in early Congress politics, besides some others, has been pointed out by Edwardes also. M. Edwardes, *The Last Years of British India* (London: Cassel & Co., Ltd., 1963), p. 15.
5. A.R. Desai, *Social Background of Indian Nationalism* (Bombay: Popular Prakashan, 1976), p. 319.
6. Daniel Thorner (ed.), *The Shaping of Modern India* (Delhi: Allied Publishers Pty. Ltd., 1980), P. 27.
7. The fact that the Congress party and its leaders supported the British rule in India whole heartedly is clear enough in the second presidential address of Dadabhai Naoroji at Calcutta in 1886. Dadabhai Naoroji, Speeches and writings of Dadabhai Naoroji (Madras: G.A. Nateson & Co., n.d.), pp.1-19.
8. Congress President Address, Second Series (Madras: Nateson & Co., 1934). Also see E.L. Farmer et al., Comparative History of Civilization in Asia, Vol. II, (Philippines: Addison-Wesley Publishing Co., Inc., 1977), p. 682.
9. K. R. Minogue, *Nationalism* (London: University Paperbacks, 1967), p. 69.
10. A.R. Desai, 1976, *op. cit.*, pp. 326-327.
11. Taya Zinkin, *India* (London: Thames and Hudson Ltd., 1965), p. 55.
12. Dadabhai Naoroji, *op. cit.*, pp. 1-19.
13. Congress President Address, Second Series, 1934, *op. cit.*, p. 11.
14. Karl Marx and F. Engels (eds.), *On Colonialism* (Moscow: Progress Publishers, 1965). Also see Bipan Chandra *et al., India's Struggle for Independence* (New Delhi: Penguin Books, 1989).
15. The nature of economic exploitation has been vividly described in the following works: R.C. Dutt, *Economic History of India* (Under Early British Rule, 1757-1857), Vol. I (Delhi: Publications Division, 1976); R. Palme Dutt, *India Today* (Bombay, People's Publishing House Ltd., 1949); and R.C. Majumdar, The History and Culture of the Indian People, Vol. X (*British Paramountacy and Indian Renaissance)* Part I (Bombay: Bhartiya Vidya Bhawan, 1963), pp. 1144-1162.
16. Speech of Padam Raj Jain, Report of the Thirty Three Indian National Congress, 1918 (Delhi: Reception Committee, 1919), pp. 128-129.
17. V.V. Balabushevich and A.M. Dyakov (eds.), *A Contemporary History of Ind*ia (New Delhi: Peoples Publishing House, 1964), p. 4.
18. Bipan Chandra *et al., Freedom Struggle* (New Delhi: National Book Trust, 1972), pp. 16-17.

19. Numerous are the example of peasant struggles throughout the country against the British rule in a recent work of Desai. A.R. Desai (ed.), *Peasant Struggles in India,* (Bombay: Oxford University Press, 1979). Also see Bipan Chandra *et al.,* India's Struggle for Independence (New Delhi: Penguin Books, 1989), pp.50-60.
20. Tara Chand, *History of the Freedom Movement in India*, Vol. I (New Delhi: Publications Division, 1961), p. 352.
21. A. R. Desai, 1976, *op. cit.*, p.174.
22. Niharranjan Ray, *Nationalism in India* (Aligarh: Aligarh Muslim University, 1973), p. 15.
23. Sardul S. Caveeschar, *India's Fight for Freedom* (Lahore: National Publications, 1936), p. 156.
24. Ripon papers, Hume to Ripon, March 14, 1884, Add. MSS-43616.
25. Lytton Papers, Lytton to Sir E. Perry, April 18, 1877, 518/2.
26. K. Marx, "The Revolt in India," "The Indian Revolt," and "Investigation of Tortures in India," in K. Marx and F. Engels (eds.), 1965, *op. cit.*, pp. 112-130.
27. Bernard Houghton, The Revolt of the East (Madras: S. Ganesan, 1921), pp. 1-2. The real character of the British Government is reflected in the observation of Edwards: "… the best form of government for India was despotism. The men who ruled India saw themselves in one sense as Indian rules, carrying on a traditional form of government which had operated in India before the British conquered it." M. Edwardes, 1963, op. cit., p. 14.
28. Larry Collins and D. Lapierre, *Freedom at Midnight* (Delhi: Vikas Publishing House Pty. Ltd., 1976), p. 17.
29. S. Gopal, 1965, *op. cit.*, p. 121.
30. B.N. Pandey, *The Break-up of British India* (London: Macmillan & Co., Ltd., 1969), p. 21.
31. Francis G. Hutchins, *The Illusion of Permanence: British Imperialism in India* (New Jersey: Princeton University Press, 1967), p. 118.
32. Henry J.S. Cotton, *New India or India in Transition* (London: Kegan Paul, Trench Trubner and Co., 1904), pp. 30-45.
33. B.B. Mishra, *The Indian Political Parties* (An Historical Analysis of Political Behaviour up to 1947) (Delhi: Oxford University Press, 1976), p. 635. Also see Curzon to Hamilton, June 10, 1901, I.O. MSS Eur. B 510/18, f. 316.
34. H.V. Hodson, *The Great Divide Britain, India and Pakistan* (London: Hutchinson & Co., Ltd., 1969), pp. 7-8.
35. A high sense of superiority of the Englishmen has been vividly described in the following books: William Digby, "Prosperous" British India (London: T. Fishers Unwin, 1901); J.R. Seeley, 1921, *op. cit.*, S.D. Singh, 1980, *op. cit.*, pp. 78-79.
36. Hans Kohn, *A History of Nationalism in the East* (London: George Routledge and Sons Ltd., 1929), pp. 94-95.
37. Mulak Raj Anand, "Pigeon-Indian: Some Notes on Indian English Writing," *The Karnatak University Journal: Humanities*, Vol. XVI, 1972, p. 69.
38. B.N. Pandey, 1969, *op. cit.*, p.14.

39. Anil Seal, *The Emergence of Indian Nationalism* (Competition and Collaboration in the Later Nineteenth Century) (London: Cambridge University Press, 1968), pp. 133-134.
40. Henry J.S. Cotton, 1904, *op. cit.*, p. 108.
41. M. Edwardes, *High Noon of Empire (*London: Eyre and Spottiswoode, 1965), p. 207.
42. R. Palme Dutt, 1949, *op. cit.*, p. 283.
43. S. K. Mitra, *Resurgent India* (Bombay: Allied Publishers Pty. Ltd., 1963), p. 154.
44. There has been serious controversy with regard to the propriety of the word "renaissance" in the case of India among the Indian historians. Since there is a great resemblance between the nature of great transformation that took place in India in the nineteenth century and the European renaissance and no new term has yet been coined to designate the great Indian transformation, the word "renaissance" is still in common use. R.C. Majumdar, *Renascent India* (First phase) (Calcutta: G. Bhardwaj & Co., 1976) , pp. 1-2.
45. Glorification of remote past and installation of some Hindus of Historic significance as national heroes played an important role in the rise of nationalist spirit. Though it was directed against the British, it generated communal feeling among the Muslims. They could not be expected to get enthusiastic about the Hindu heroes. Thus the process of national integration was greatly hampered. Bipan Chandra, "Historians of Modern India and Communalism," in Romila Thapar *et. al.* (ed.), *Communalism and the Writing of Indian History* (New Delhi: People's Publishing House, 1977), pp. 39-61.
46. M. Edwardes, 1963, *op. cit.*, p. 25.
47. Jawaharlal Nehru, *The Discovery of India* (London: Meridian Books, 1956), p. 392.
48. R.C. Majumdar does not consider Raja Rammohan Roy as the pioneer of Modern age so far as the Hindu religion is concerned. According to him, Ramkrishna and Vivekananda were the real persons to inaugurate the Modern Age in India. R.C. Majumdar, 1976, *op. cit.*, pp. 232-233.
49. Romain Rolland, *The Life of Vivekananda and the Universal Gospel* (Translated by Malcolm Smith from French to English) (Almora: Mayavati Publications, 1953), pp. 165-166.
50. C. H. Heimsath, *Indian Nationalism and Hindu social Reform* (New Jersey: Princeton University Press, 1964).
51. E. L. Farmer *et. al.*, 1977, *op. cit.*, pp. 684-685.
52. R.C. Majumdar, *History of the Freedom Movement in India*, Vol. II (Calcutta: Firma K.L. Mukhopadhyay, 1963), p. 167
53. Patwant Singh, *India and the Future of Asia* (London: Faber and Faber Ltd., 1966), pp. 33-34.
54. H.V. Hodson, 1969, *op. cit.*, pp. 1-8.

55. Bipan Chandra *et al., India's Struggle for Independence* (New Delhi: Penguin Books, 1989).
56. V. Kiernan, "Nationalist Movement and Social Classes," in Anthony D. Smith (ed.), 1976, *op. cit*., pp. 110-113; A.R. Desai, 1976, op. cit.; Bipan Chandra et al., 1972, *op. cit*. and Anthony D. Smith, 1971, *op. cit*.

Chapter- 9

Economic and Social Impact of Colonialism

Under this section an effort is made to assess and highlight the nature of changes that have occurred in the socio-economic conditions of India following British rule. It appears from the study of available literature on this subject that British imperialism was more pragmatic than that of other colonial powers. Its motivation was economic, not evangelical. British interests were of several kinds. At first, the main purpose was to achieve a monopolistic trading position. Later it was felt that a regime of free trade would make India a major market for British goods and a source of raw materials, but British capitalists who invested in India continued effectively to enjoy monopolistic privileges. India also provided interesting and lucrative employment opportunities for a sizeable portion of the British upper middle class, and the remittances they sent home made an appreciable contribution to Britain's balance of payments and capacity to save. Finally, control of India was a key element in the world power structure, in terms of geography, logistics and military manpower. The British were not averse to Indian economic development if it increased their markets but refused to help in areas where they felt there was conflict with their own economic interests or political security. Hence, they refused to give protection to the Indian textile industry until its main competitor became Japan rather than Manchester, and they did almost nothing to further technical education. They introduced some British concepts of property, but did not push them too far when they met vested interests.

The main changes which the British made in Indian society were at the top. They replaced the wasteful warlord aristocracy by a bureaucratic-military establishment, carefully designed by utilitarian technocrats, which was very efficient in maintaining law and order. The greater efficiency of government permitted a substantial reduction in the fiscal burden, and a bigger share of the national product was available for landlords, capitalists and the new professional classes. Some of this upper class income was siphoned off to the UK, but the bulk was spent in India. However, the pattern of consumption changed as the new upper class no longer kept harems and palaces, nor did they wear fine muslins or had swords. This caused some painful readjustments in the traditional handicraft sector. It seems likely that there was some increase in productive investment which must have been near zero in Moghul India. Government itself carried out productive investment in railways and irrigation and as a result there was a growth in both agricultural and industrial output. The new elite established a Western life-style using the English language and English schools. New towns and urban amenities were created with segregated suburbs and housing for them. Their habits were copied by the new professional elite of lawyers, doctors, teachers, journalists and businessmen. Within this group, old caste barriers were diminished and social mobility increased.

As far as the mass of the population was concerned, colonial rule brought few significant changes. The British educational effort was very limited. There were no major changes in village society, in the caste system, the position of untouchables, the joint family system, or in production techniques in agriculture. British impact on economic and social development was, therefore, limited. Total output and population increased substantially but the gain in per capita output was small or negligible.

It is interesting to speculate about India's potential economic fate if it had not had two centuries of British rule. There are three major alternatives which can be seriously considered. One would have been the maintenance of indigenous rule with a few foreign enclaves, as in China. Given the fissiparous forces in Indian society, it is likely that there would have been major civil wars in China in the second half of the nineteenth century and the first half of the twentieth century and the country would probably have split up. Without direct foreign interference with its educational system, it is less likely that India would have developed a modernizing intelligentsia than China because Indian society was less rational and hence more conservative, while the Chinese had a much more homogeneous civilization around which to build their nationalism. If this situation had prevailed, population would certainly have grown less, but the average standard of living might have been a little higher because of the bigger upper class, and the smaller drain of resources abroad. Another alternative to British rule would have been conquest and maintenance of power by some other West European country such as France or Holland. This probably would not have produced results very different in economic terms from British rule. The third hypothesis is perhaps the most intriguing, i.e. conquest by a European power, with earlier accession to independence. If India had had self-government from the 1880s, after a century and a quarter of British rule, it is likely that both income and population growth would have been accelerated. There would have been a smaller drain of investible funds abroad, greater tariff protection, more state enterprise and favours to local industry, more technical training- the sort of things which happened after 1947.

Establishment of New Westernized Elite

The biggest change the British made in the social structure was to replace the warlord aristocracy by an efficient bureaucracy and army. The traditional system of the East India Company had been to pay its servants fairly modest salaries, and to let them augment their income from private transactions. This arrangement worked reasonably well before the conquest of Bengal, but was inefficient as a way of remunerating the officials of a substantial territorial Empire because (a) too much of the profit went into private hands rather than the Company's coffers, and (b) an over-rapacious short-term policy was damaging to the productive capacity of the economy and likely to drive the local population to revolt, both of which were against the Company's longer-term interests.

Clive had operated a 'dual' system, i.e. Company power and a puppet Nawab. Warren Hastings displaced the Nawab and took over direct administration, but retained Indian officials. Finally, in 1785, Cornwallis created a professional cadre of Company servants who had generous salaries, had no private trading or production interests in India, enjoyed the prospect of regular promotion and were entitled to pensions. All high-level posts were reserved for the British, and Indians were excluded. Cornwallis appointed British judges, and established British officials as revenue collectors and magistrates in each district of Bengal.

From 1806 the Company trained its young recruits in Haileybury College near London. Appointments were still organized on a system of patronage, but after 1833 the Company selected amongst its nominated candidates by competitive examination. After 1853, selection was entirely on merit and the examination was thrown open to any British candidate. The examination system was influenced by the Chinese model, which had worked well for 2,000 years and had a similar emphasis on classical learning and literary competence. The Indian civil service was therefore able to secure high quality people because (a) it was very highly paid; (b) it enjoyed political power which no bureaucrat could have had in England.

In 1829 the system was strengthened by establishing districts throughout British India small enough to be effectively controlled by an individual British official who henceforth exercised a completely autocratic power, acting as revenue collector, judge and chief of police (functions which had been separate under the Moghul administration). This arrangement later became the cornerstone of Imperial administration throughout the British Empire. As the civil service was ultimately subject to the control of the British parliament, and the British community in India was subject to close mutual surveillance, the administration was virtually incorruptible.

The army of the Company was a local mercenary force with 20,000-30,000 British officers and troops. It was by far the most modern and efficient army in Asia. After the Mutiny in 1857, the size of the British contingent was raised to a third of the total strength and all officers were British until the 1920s when a very small number of Indians was recruited. Normally, the total strength of the army was about 200,000. This army was very much smaller than those of Moghul India, but had better training and equipment, and the railway network for greater mobility, better logistics and intelligence (Moreland, 1962: 72).

The higher ranks of the administration remained almost entirely British until the 1920s when the Indian civil service examinations began to be held in India as well as the UK (Woodruff, 1963: 363). In addition, there was a whole hierarchy of separate bureaucracies in which the higher ranks were British, i.e. the revenue, justice, police, education, medical, public works, engineering, postal and railway services as well as the provincial civil services. India thus offered highly-paid careers to an appreciable portion of the British middle and upper classes.

From the 1820s to the 1850s the British demonstrated a strong urge to change Indian social institutions, and to Westernize India (Sivasubramonian, 2000). They, as stated before, stamped out infanticide and ritual burning of widows (sati). They abolished slavery and eliminated dacoits (religious thugs) from the highways. They legalized the remarriage of widows and allowed Hindu converts to Christianity to lay claim to their share of joint family property. They took steps to introduce a penal code (the code was actually introduced in 1861) based on British law, which helped inculcate

some ideas of equality. Under the old Hindu law, a Brahmin murderer might not be put to death, while a Sudra who cohabited with a high-caste woman would automatically suffer execution. Under the new law, Brahmin and Sudra were liable to the same punishment for the same offence (Tinker, 1967: 172).

One of the most significant things the British did to westernize India was to introduce a modified version of English education. Macaulay's 1835 Minute on Education had a decisive impact on British educational policy and is a classic example of a Western rationalist approach to Indian civilization. Before the British took over, the Court language of the Moghuls was Persian and the Muslim population used Urdu, a mixture of Persian, Arabic and Sanskrit. Higher education was largely religious and stressed knowledge of Arabic and Sanskrit. The Company had given some financial support to a Calcutta Madrassa (1781), and a Sanskrit college at Benares (1792), Warren Hastings, as governor general from 1782 to 1795 had himself learned Sanskrit and Persian, and several other Company officials were oriental scholars. One of them, Sir William Jones, had translated a great mass of Sanskrit literature and had founded the Asiatic Society of Bengal in 1785. But Macaulay was strongly opposed to this orientalism: "I believe that the present system tends, not to accelerate the progress of truth, but to delay the natural death of expiring errors. We are a Board for wasting public money, for printing books which are less value than the paper on which they are printed was while it was blank; for giving artificial encouragement to absurd history, absurd metaphysics, absurd physics, absurd theology ... I have no knowledge of either Sanskrit or Arabic ... But I have done what I could to form a correct estimate of their value ... Who could deny that a single shelf of a good European library was worth the whole native literature of India and Arabia ... all the historical information which has been collected from all the books written in the Sanskrit language is less valuable than what may be found in the most paltry abridgements used at preparatory schools in England."

"For these reasons Macaulay had no hesitation in deciding in favour of English education, but it was not to be for the masses: "It is impossible for us, with our limited means to attempt to educate the body of the people. We must at present do our best to form a class who may be interpreters between us and the millions whom we govern; a class of persons, Indian in blood and colour, but English in taste, in opinions, in morals, and in intellect. To that class we may leave it to refine the vernacular dialects of the country, to enrich those dialects with terms of science borrowed from the Western

nomenclature, and to render them by degrees fit vehicles for conveying knowledge to the great mass of the population" (Edwardes, 1967).

Until 1857 it was possible to entertain the view (as Marx believed) that the British may eventually destroy traditional Indian society and westernize the country. But activist westernizing policies and the attempt to extend British rule by taking over native states whose rulers had left no heirs provoked sections of both the Hindu and Muslim communities into rebellion in the Mutiny of 1857. Although the Mutiny was successfully put down with substantial help from loyal Indian troops including the recently conquered Sikhs, British policy towards Indian institutions and society became much more conservative. The Crown took over direct responsibility and the East India Company was disbanded. The Indian civil service attracted fewer people with innovating ideas than had the East India Company and was more closely controlled from London. The British forged an alliance with the remaining native princes and stopped taking over new territory. Until the end of their rule about a quarter of the Indian population remained in quasi-autonomous native states. These had official British residents but were fairly free in internal policy, and the effort of Westernization came to a standstill.

The education system which developed in India was a very pale reflection of that in the UK. Three universities were set up in 1857 in Calcutta, Madras and Bombay, but they were merely examining bodies and did no teaching work. Higher education was carried out in affiliated colleges which gave a two-year B.A. degree with heavy emphasis on rote learning and examinations. Drop-out ratios were always very high. They did little to promote analytic capacity or independent thinking and produced a group of graduates with a half-baked knowledge of English, but sufficiently Westernized to be alienated from their own culture.[1] It was not until the 1920s that Indian universities provided teaching facilities and then only for M.A. students. Furthermore, Indian education was of a predominantly literacy character and the provision for technical training was much less than in any European country. Education for girls was almost totally ignored throughout the nineteenth century. Because higher education was in English, there was no official effort to translate Western literature into the vernacular, nor was there any standardization of Indian scripts whose variety is a major barrier to multi-lingualism amongst educated Indians.

Primary education was not taken very seriously as a government obligation and was financed largely by the weak local authorities. As a result, the great mass of the population had no access to education and, at

Independence in 1947, 88 percent were illiterate. Progress was accelerated from the 1930s onwards, but at independence only a fifth of children were receiving any primary schooling.

Education could have played a major role in encouraging social mobility, eliminating religious superstition, increasing productivity, and uplifting the status of women. Instead it was used to turn tiny elite into imitation Englishmen and a somewhat bigger group into government clerks.

Having failed to westernize India completely, the British established themselves as a separate ruling caste. Like other Indian castes, they did not intermarry or eat with the lower castes. Thanks to the British public-school system, their children were shipped off and did not mingle with the natives. At the end of their professional careers they returned home. The small special class of Anglo-Indians were outcastes and unable to integrate into Indian or local British society. The British kept to their clubs and bungalows in special suburbs known as cantonments and civil lines. They maintained the Moghul tradition of official pomp, sumptuary residences, and retinues of servants.[2] They did not adopt the Moghul custom of polygamy, but remained monogamous and brought in their own women. Society became prim and priggish (Edwardes, 1967: 33). The British ruled India in much the same way as the Roman consuls had ruled in Africa 2,000 years earlier, and were very conscious of the Roman paradigm. The elite with its classical education and contempt for business were quite happy establishing law and order, and keeping 'barbarians' at bay on the frontier of the raj. They developed their own brand of self-righteous arrogance, considering themselves purveyors not of popular but of good government. For them the word 'British' lost its geographic connotation and became an epithet signifying moral rectitude.

The striking thing about the British raj is that it was operated by so few people. There were only 31,000 British in India in 1805 (of which 22,000 were in the army and 2,000 in civil government).[3] The number increased substantially after the Mutiny, but thereafter remained steady. In 1911, there were 164,000 British (106,000 employed, of which 66,000 were in the army and police and 4,000 in civil government).[4] In 1931, there were 168,000 (90,000 employed, 60,000 in the army and police and 4,000 in civil government). They were a thinner layer than the Muslim rulers had been (never more than 0.05 percent of the total population).

Because of the small size of the administration and its philosophy of minimal government responsibility outside the field of law and order, India ended the colonial period with a very low level of taxation. The British had inherited the Moghul tax system which provided land revenue equal to 15 percent of national income, but by the end of the colonial period land tax was only one percent of national income and the total tax burden was only six percent. It is curious that this large reduction in the fiscal burden has passed almost without comment in the literature on Indian economic history. [5] On the contrary, emphasis is usually placed on the heaviness of the tax burden, e.g. by D. Naoroji and R.C. Dutt.

Most of the benefits of the lower fiscal burden were felt by landlords, and were not passed on to the common people. In urban areas new classes emerged under the British rule, i.e. industrial capitalists and a new bourgeoisie of bureaucrats, lawyers, doctors, teachers and journalists whose social position was due to education and training rather than heredity. In the princely states, the remnants of the Moghul aristocracy continued their extravagances- large palaces, harems, hordes of retainers, miniature armies, ceremonial elephants, tiger hunts, and stables full of Rolls Royces.

Agriculture

The colonial government made institutional changes in agriculture by transforming traditionally circumscribed property rights into something more closely resembling the unencumbered private property characteristic of Western capitalism. The beneficiaries of these new rights varied in different parts of India. The top layer of Moghul property, the jagir, was abolished (except in the autonomous princely states), and the bulk of the old warlord aristocracy was dispossessed. Their previous income from land revenue, and that of the Moghul state, was now appropriated by the British as land tax. However, in the Bengal Presidency (i.e. modern Bengal, Bihar, Orissa and part of Madras) the second layer of Moghul property rights belonging to Moghul tax collectors (zamindars) was reinforced. All zamindars in these areas now had hereditary status, so long as they paid their land taxes, and their judicial and administrative functions disappeared. In the Moghul period the zamindars had usually kept a tenth of the land revenue to themselves, but by the end of British rule their income from rents was a multiple of the tax they paid to the state. In Bihar, for instance, five-sixths of the total sum levied by 1950 was rent and only one-sixth revenue (Warriner, 1969: 158). However, zamindars were not really the equivalent of Western landowners. Dominant families in each village remained as their 'tenants-in-chief' and continued to enjoy many of the old customary rights, i.e. they could not be evicted, their rights were heritable and their rental payments could not be raised easily. Lower-caste families were usually sub-tenants of the tenants-in-chief, rather than direct tenants of the zamindars. Often there were several layers of tenancy between the actual cultivator and the zamindar. Sub-tenants had less security and less defence against rack-renting than tenants-in-chief. It is worth noting that when zamindari rights were abolished around 1952 and the old zamindar rental income was converted into state revenue, the amount involved was only about two percent of farm income in the relevant areas of India. This suggests that by the end of the colonial period, the zamindars were not able to squeeze as much surplus out of their chief tenants as is sometimes suggested.

The typical zamindari estate at the end of British rule seems to have been very different from that at the end of the eighteenth century. In Bengal the total number of landowners which did not exceed 100 in the beginning of Hasting's administration in 1772, rose in the course of a century to 154,200. B. B. Misra attributes this fall in the average size of zamindari properties to the fact that they could be inherited or sold freely, whereas the Moghul state wanted to keep the number small because zamindars had administrative functions under the Moghul Empire. Under the British, transfers became much more frequent, particularly into the hands of moneylenders. The moneylenders are frequently presented as squeezing out poor peasants and tenants and thus promoting the concentration of wealth, but the evidence of what happened to zamindar estates suggests that village moneylenders may also have helped to break up concentrations of wealth (Neale, 1962: 63).

In the Madras and Bombay Presidencies, which covered most of Southern India, the British dispossessed many of the old Moghul and Maratha nobility and big zamindars, and vested property rights and tax obligations in individual 'peasants'. This settlement was known as the ryotwari (peasant tenure) system. However, the term peasant is misleading, because most of those who acquired land titles belonged to the traditionally dominant castes in villages. Lower-caste cultivators became their tenants. Thus there was no change in social structure at the village level, except that the new ownership rights gave greater opportunities for sale and mortgage, and the security of the tenant was less than it had been under the previous system. The change in legal status was limited by several factors. First of all, illiterate peasant did not always understand the new situation, and there were strong social ties in the joint family and the caste panchayats to prevent major deviations from old habits. Secondly, the new administration was rather remote from individual villages (with a district officer responsible for over a thousand villages), and many British administrators had a personal bias in favour of customary tenant rights because by maintaining them they could avoid political trouble. At a later stage, the government itself introduced a good deal of legislation to protect customary rights in response to peasant disturbances.[6] Land policy was, therefore, another instance of British policy of half-Westernization. The British were more concerned with arrangements which would guarantee their revenue and not provoke too much political disturbance rather than in increasing productivity or introducing capitalist institutions. The Utilitarians who dominated the Company from 1820 to 1850 would have liked to push in this direction, but they were displaced at mid-century by the paternalist conservatives of the Imperial raj.

Nevertheless, there were some economic consequences of the new legal situation. Because of the emergence of clear titles, it was now possible to mortgage land. The status of moneylenders was also improved by the change from Muslim to British law. There had been moneylenders in the Moghul period, but their importance grew substantially under British rule, and over time a considerable amount of land changed hands through foreclosures (Darling, 1947: 178).

One might have expected the legal changes introduced by the British to have had a positive effect on efficiency. They removed the class of jagirdars who had no incentive to invest in agriculture, and gave land rights to rural capitalists who could buy and sell land fairly freely and enjoy an increasing portion of the product. Moneylenders helped to root out improvident or inefficient landowners. However, most farmers were illiterate and the government did not help through extension services, or encourage the use of fertilizers. Until recently, with the arrival of the tubewell, there were technical limits to the possibility of small-scale irrigation. There were also organisational difficulties in changing technique to improve productivity. The division of labour in the village and hereditary attitudes to work as a semi-religious ritual rather than a means to improve income were obstacles to change. Furthermore, a good many of the cultivating landowners whose income was increased were relatively poor and used their increased income for consumption rather than investment. Some of those who were better off probably improved their land or took over waste land, but as religion inculcated the idea that manual labour was polluting, some of them probably worked less (Thorner, 1956: 12). The big zamindars used some of their extra income to develop waste land, but many cultivated a life style rather like the old Moghul aristocracy and had a high propensity to consume. According to Raychaudhuri (1969), a zamindar's house with a hundred rooms was not exceptional. Some of the enterprising ones probably transferred their savings out of agriculture into trade and industry or bought their children a Western-type education. Thus the effect of the change was to increase productivity and savings, but not much.

During the period of British rule, agricultural production grew substantially in order to feed a population which grew from 165 million in 1757 to 420 million in 1947. The new system of land ownership offered some stimulus to increase output, and there was substantial waste land available for development.

The colonial government made some contribution towards increased output through irrigation. The irrigated area was increased about eightfold, and eventually more than a quarter of the land of British India was irrigated.[7] Irrigation was extended both as a source of revenue and as a measure against famine. A good deal of the irrigation work was in the Punjab and Sind. The motive here was to provide land for retired Indian army personnel, many of whom came from the Punjab, and to build up population in an area which bordered on the disputed frontier with Afghanistan. These areas, which had formerly been desert, became the biggest irrigated area in the world and a major producer of wheat and cotton, both for export and for sale in other parts of India. Apart from government investment in irrigation, there was a substantial private investment, and by the end of British rule private irrigation investment covered nearly 25 million acres of British India.

Improvements in transport facilities (particularly railways) helped agriculture by permitting some degree of specialization on cash crops. This increased yields somewhat, but the bulk of the country stuck to subsistence farming. Plantations were developed for indigo, sugar, jute and tea. These items made a significant contribution to exports, but in the context of Indian agriculture as a whole, they were not very important. In 1946, the two primary staples, tea and jute, were less than 3.5 percent of the gross value of crop output (Blyn, 1966). Thus the enlargement of markets through international trade was less of a stimulus in India than in other Asian countries such as Ceylon, Burma or Thailand.

Little was done to promote agricultural technology. There was some improvement in seeds, but no extension service, no improvement in livestock and no official encouragement to use fertilizer. Lord Mayo, the Governor General, said in 1870, "I do not know what is precisely meant by ammoniac manure. If it means guano, superphosphate or any other artificial product of that kind, we might as well ask the people of India to manure their ground with champagne" (Edwardes, 1967: 219).

Statistics are not available on agricultural output for the first century and a half of British rule, but all the indications suggest that there was substantial growth. We do not know whether output rose faster or more slowly than population, but it seems likely that the movements were roughly parallel.

For the last half century of British rule, the main calculations of output are those by George Blyn. His first study, which has been widely quoted, was published in 1954 by the National Income Unit of the Indian government and showed only a 3 percent increase in crop output in British India from 1893 to 1946, i.e. a period in which population increased 46 percent! His second study, published in 1966 showed a 16.6 percent increase, and this, too, has been widely quoted, but he also gives a 'modified' series which shows a 28.9 percent increase. This seems preferable, as the official figures on rice yields in Orissa, which are corrected in his "modified" estimate, seem obviously in error. However, even Blyn's upper estimate is probably an understatement because he shows a very small increase in acreage. It is difficult to believe that per capita food output could have gone down as much as he suggests, whilst waste land remained unused. There has been a very big increase in the cultivated area since independence and it seems likely that the increase in the preceding half century was bigger than Blyn (1966) suggests.

The basic reports on areas under cultivation are those provided by village accountants (patwaris) in areas where land revenue was periodically changed, and by village watchmen (chowkidars) in areas where the land revenue was permanently settled. There was some incentive for farmers to bribe patwaris to under-report land for tax purposes, and chowkidars are all too often illiterate and drowsy people, who would usually report that things were normal, i.e. the same as the year before. There is, therefore, a tendency for under-reporting of both levels and rates of growth in areas covered by statistics, and the areas not covered by statistics were generally on the margin of cultivation and may have had a more steeply rising trend than the average area covered. Thus Blyn shows no growth in output in Bengal where the chowkidars did the basic reporting. He did not cover the Sind desert area in which the British built the huge Sukkur barrage in 1932. Blyn was, of course, aware of these difficulties and tried to correct for them as far as possible, but the fundamental problems are not amenable to 'statistical' manipulation but require 'hunch' adjustment.

Evidence suggests that agricultural output per head was at least as high at the end of British rule as it was in the Moghul period, and that rural consumption levels were somewhat higher because of the lower tax burden on agriculture, and the smaller degree of wastage which allowed surplus areas to sell their grains. This slight improvement in standards may have contributed to the expansion in population. However, agricultural yields and nutritional levels at independence were amongst the lowest in the world.

Under the British rule, the Indian population, stated before, remained subject to recurrent famines and epidemic diseases. In 1876-8 and 1899-1900 famine killed millions of people. In the 1890s there was a widespread outbreak of bubonic plague and in 1919 a great influenza epidemic. It is sometimes asserted by Indian nationalist historians that British policy increased the incidence of famine in India, particularly in the nineteenth century (Digby, 1901). Unfortunately we do not have any figures on agricultural production for this period, and it is difficult to base a judgement merely on catalogues of famine years whose intensity we cannot measure. As agriculture was extended to more marginal land one would have expected output to become more volatile. But this was offset to a considerable extent by the major improvement in transport brought by railways, and the greater security of water supply brought by irrigation. It is noteworthy that the decades in which famines occurred were ones in which population was static rather than falling (Davis, 1951: 28). In the 1920s and 1930s there were no famines, and the 1944 famine in Bengal was due to war conditions and transport difficulties rather than crop failure. However, the greater stability after 1920 may have been partly due to a lucky break in the weather cycle rather than to a new stability of agriculture.

British rule reduced some of the old checks on Indian population growth. The main contribution was the ending of internal warfare and local banditry. There was some reduction in the incidence of famine. The death rate was also reduced to some degree by making ritual suicide and infanticide illegal. The British contributed to public health by introducing smallpox vaccination, establishing Western medicine and training modern doctors, by killing rats, and establishing quarantine procedures. As a result, the death rate fell and the population of India grew by 1947 to more than two-and-a-half times its size in 1757.

Industry

Several Indian authors have argued that British rule led to de-industrialization of India. R.C. Dutta (1901) argued, "India in the eighteenth century was a great manufacturing as well as a great agricultural country, and the products of the Indian loom supplied the markets of Asia and Europe. It is, unfortunately, true that the East India Company and the British Parliament, following the selfish commercial policy of a hundred years ago, discouraged Indian manufacturers in the early years of British rule in order to encourage the rising manufactures of England. Their fixed policy, pursued during the last decades of the eighteenth century and the first decades of the nineteenth, was to make India subservient to the industries of Great Britain, and to make the Indian people grow raw produce only, in order to supply material for the looms and manufactories of Great Britain".

R. Palme Dutt (1940: 165), writing forty years later, argued that the process had been continuous: "the real picture of modern India is a picture of what has been aptly called "de-industrialization"- that is, the decline of the old handicraft industry without the compensating advance of modern industry. The advance of factory industry has not overtaken the decay of handicraft. The process of decay characteristic of the nineteenth century has been carried forward in the twentieth century and in the post-war period".

Nehru, in his popular history is a conflation of the two Dutts, argued that the British deindustrialized India, and that this "is the real the fundamental cause of the appalling poverty of the Indian people, and it is of comparatively recent origin" (Nehru, 1946: 299).

There is a good deal of truth in the deindustrialization argument. Moghul India did have a bigger industry than any other country which became a European colony, and was unique in being an industrial exporter in pre-colonial times. A large part of the Moghul industry was destroyed in the course of British rule. However, it is important to understand precisely how this deindustrialization came about and to try to get some idea of its quantitative significance in different periods. Oversimplified explanations, which exaggerate the role of British commercial policy and ignore the role of changes in demand and technology, have been very common and have had some adverse impact on post-independence economic policy.

Between 1757 and 1857 the British wiped out the Moghul court, and eliminated three-quarters of the warlord aristocracy (all except those in princely states). They also eliminated more than half of the local chiefs (zamindars) and in their place established a bureaucracy with European tastes. The new rulers wore European clothes and shoes, drank imported beer, wines and spirits, and used European weapons. Their tastes were copied by the male members of the new Indian 'middle class' which arose to act as their clerks and intermediaries. As a result of these political and social changes, about three-quarters of the domestic demand for luxury handicrafts was destroyed. This was a shattering blow to manufacturers of fine muslins, jewellery, luxury clothing and footwear, decorative swords and weapons. It is not known how important these items were in national income, but that the home market for these goods was about 5 percent of Moghul national income. The export market was probably another 1.5 percent of national income, and most of this market was also lost. There was a reduction of European demand because of the change in sartorial tastes after the French revolution, and the greatly reduced price of more ordinary materials because of the revolution of textile technology in England.

The second blow to Indian industry came from massive imports of cheap textiles from England after the Napoleonic wars. In the period 1896-1913, imported piece goods supplied about 60 percent of Indian cloth consumption, and the proportion was probably higher for most of the nineteenth century (Levkovsky, 1966: 78). Home spinning, which was a spare-time activity of village women, was greatly reduced. A large proportion of village handloom weavers must have been displaced, though many switched to using factory instead of home-spun yarn. Even as late as 1940 a third of Indian piece goods were produced on handlooms (Desai, 1953: 95).

The new manufactured textile goods were considerably cheaper and of better quality than handloom products, so their advent increased textile consumption. At the end of British rule, there can be no doubt that cloth consumption per head was substantially larger than in the Moghul period. We do not know how big an increase in textile consumption occurred, but if per capita consumption of cotton cloth doubled, then the displacement effect on handloom weavers would have been smaller than at first appears. The handloom weavers who produced a third of output in 1940 would have been producing two-thirds if there had been no increase in per capita consumption. In time, India built up her own textile manufacturing industry which displaced British imports. But there was a gap of several decades before manufacturing started and a period of 130 years before British textile imports were eliminated. India could probably have copied Lancashire's technology more quickly if she had been allowed to impose a protective tariff in the way that was done in the USA and France in the first few decades of the nineteenth century, but the British imposed a policy of free trade. British imports entered India duty free, and when a small tariff was required for revenue purposes Lancashire pressure led to the imposition of a corresponding excise duty on Indian products to prevent them gaining a competitive advantage. This undoubtedly handicapped industrial development. If India had been politically independent, her tax structure would probably have been different. In the 1880s, Indian customs revenues were only 2.2 percent of the trade turnover, i.e. the lowest ratio in any country. If India had enjoyed protection there is no doubt that its textile industry would have started earlier and grown faster.

The first textile mills were started in the 1850s by Indian capitalists who had made their money trading with the British and had acquired some education in English. Cotton textiles were launched in Bombay with financial and managerial help from British trading companies. India was the first country in Asia to have a modern textile industry, preceding Japan by twenty years and China by forty years. Cotton mills were started in Bombay in 1851, and they concentrated on coarse yarns sold domestically and to China and Japan; yarn exports were about half of output.

Modern jute manufacturing started about the same time as cotton textiles. The first jute mill was built in 1854 and the industry expanded rapidly in the vicinity of Calcutta. The industry was largely in the hands of foreigners (mainly Scots). Between 1879 and 1913 the number of jute spindles rose tenfold- much faster than growth in the cotton textile industry. The jute industry was able to expand faster than cotton textiles because its sales did not depend so heavily on the poverty-stricken domestic markets. Most of jute output was for export.

Coal mining, mainly in Bengal, was another industry which achieved significance. Its output, which by 1914 had reached 15.7 million tons, largely met the demands of the Indian railways. In 1911 the first Indian steel mill was built by the Tata Company at Jamshedpur in Jharkhand. However, production did not take place on a significant scale before the First World War. The Indian steel industry started fifteen years later than in China, where the first steel mill was built at Hangyang in 1896. The first Japanese mill was built in 1898.

Indian firms in industry, insurance and banking were given a boost from 1905 onwards by the swadeshi movement, which was a nationalist boycott of British goods in favour of Indian enterprise. During World War I, lack of British imports strengthened the hold of Indian firms on the home market for textiles and steel. After the war, under nationalist pressure, the government started to favour Indian enterprise in its purchase of stores and it agreed to create a tariff commission in 1921 which started raising tariffs for protective reasons. By 1925, the average tariff level was 14 percent compared with 5 percent pre-war (Lewis, 1949: 48). The procedure for fixing tariffs was lengthy and tariff protection was granted more readily to foreign-owned than to Indian firms, but in the 1930s protection was sharply increased (Kidron, 1965: 13). The government was more willing to protect the Indian textile industry when the threat came from Japan and not the UK. Between 1930 and 1934 the tariff on cotton cloth was raised from 11 to 50 percent, although British imports were accorded a margin of preference. As a result of these measures, there was considerable substitution of local textiles for imports. In 1896, Indian mills supplied only 8 percent of total cloth consumption; in 1913, 20 percent; in 1936, 62 percent; and in 1945, 76 percent. By the latter date there were no imports of piece goods.

Until the end of the Napoleonic wars in Europe, cotton manufactures had been India's main export. They reached their peak in 1798, and in 1813 they still amounted to £2 million, but thereafter they fell rapidly (Dutt, 1901). Thirty years later, half of Indian imports were cotton textiles from Manchester. This collapse in India's main export caused a problem for the Company, which had to find ways to convert its rupee revenue into resources transferable to the UK. The Company therefore promoted exports of raw materials on a larger scale, including sugar, silk, saltpetre and indigo, and greatly increased exports of opium which were traded against Chinese tea. These dope-peddling efforts provoked the Anglo-Chinese war of 1842, after which access to the Chinese market was greatly widened. By the middle of the nineteenth century opium was by far the biggest export of India, and remained in this position until the 1880s when its relative and absolute importance began to decline. Another new export was raw cotton, which could not compete very well in European markets against higher quality American and Egyptian cottons, (except during the US Civil War), but found a market in Japan and China. Sugar exports were built up after 1833 when the abolition of slavery raised West Indian production costs, but India had no long-run comparative advantage in sugar exports. Indigo (used to dye textiles) was an important export until the 1890s when it was hit by competition from German synthetic dyes. The jute industry boomed from the time of the Crimean War onwards, when the UK stopped importing flax from Russia. In addition to raw jute (shipped for manufacture in Dundee) India exported jute manufactures. Grain exports were also built up on a sizeable scale, mainly from the newly irrigated area of the Punjab. The tea industry was introduced to India from China and built up on a plantation basis. Tea exports became important from the 1860s onwards. Hides and skins and oil cake (used as animal feed and fertilizer) were also important raw material exports.

Manufactured textile exports form India began to increase in the 1850s when the first modern mills were established. The bulk of exports were yarn and crude piece goods which were sold in China and Japan. As the Chinese and Japanese were prevented by colonial-type treaties from imposing tariffs for manufactured imports they were wide open to Indian goods, and particularly cotton textiles and yarn. Indian jute manufactures were exported mainly to Europe and the USA.

However, India began to suffer from Japanese competition in the 1890s. Indian yarn exports to Japan dropped sharply from 8,400 tons in 1890 to practically nothing in 1898, and India also suffered from Japanese competition in China. The Japanese set up factories in China after the Sino-Japanese War of 1894-5. Before this, India had supplied 96 percent of Chinese yarn imports, the UK 4 percent, and Japan none. By the end of the 1930s, Indian exports of yarn to China and Japan had disappeared, piece goods exports had fallen off, and India imported both yarn and piece goods from China and Japan.

Indian exports grew fairly rapidly in the period up to 1913, but their growth was slower than that of most other Asian countries which had a natural resource endowment offering greater opportunities for trade. As a consequence, in 1913, India had a smaller trade per head than most countries except China. Nevertheless, exports were 10.7 percent of national income, probably a higher ratio than has been reached before or since.

Indian exports fell from 1913 to 1937, a poorer performance than that of almost any other country. At Independence exports were less than 5 percent of national income. If we look at the Indian export performance from 1850 to 1950 it was worse than that of any other country in Asia. The World War II gave a fillip to Indian industrial output, but there was not much increase in capacity because of the difficulty of importing capital goods and the lack of domestic capital goods industry.

Many of the most lucrative commercial, financial, business and plantation jobs in the modern sector were occupied by foreigners. Although the East India Company's legally enforced monopoly privileges were ended in 1833, the British continued to exercise effective dominance through the system of 'managing agencies'. These agencies, originally set up by former employees of the East India Company, were used both to manage industrial enterprise and to handle most of India's international trade. They were closely linked with British banks, insurance and shipping companies. Managing agencies had a quasi-monopoly in access to capital, and they had interlocking directorships which gave them control over supplies and markets. They dominated the foreign markets in Asia. They had better access to government officials than did Indians. The agencies were in many ways able to take decisions favourable to their own interests rather than those of shareholders. They were paid commissions based on gross profits or total sales and were often agents for the raw materials used by the companies they managed. Thus the Indian capitalists who did emerge were highly dependent on British commercial capital and many sectors of industry were dominated by British firms, e.g. shipping, banking, insurance, coal, plantation crops and jute.

Indian industrial efficiency was hampered by the British administration's neglect of technical education, and the reluctance of British firms and managing agencies to provide training of managerial experience to Indians. Even in the Bombay textile industry, where most of the capital was Indian, 28 percent of the managerial and supervisory staff were British in 1925 (42 percent in 1895) and the British component was even bigger in more complex industries. This naturally raised Indian production costs (Buchanan, 1966: 211, 321). At lower levels there was widespread use of jobbers for hiring workers and maintaining discipline, and workers themselves were a completely unskilled group who had to bribe the jobbers to get and retain their jobs. There were also problems of race, language and caste distinctions between management, supervisors and workers (Morris, 1965). The small size and much diversified output of the enterprises hindered efficiency. It is partly for these reasons that Indian exports had difficulty in competing with Japan.

The basic limitations on the growth of industrial output were the extreme poverty of the rural population, and the fact that a large proportion of the elite had a taste for imported goods or exported their purchasing power. The government eventually provided tariff protection but did not itself create industrial plants, sponsor development banks, or give preference to local industry in allotting contracts. The banking system gave little help to industry and technical education was poor. Most of these things changed when India became independent except the first and most important, i.e. the extreme poverty of the rural population which limited the expansion of the market for industrial goods.

By the time of Independence, large-scale industries in India employed less than 3 million people as compared with 12 1/4 million in small-scale industries and handicrafts, and a labour force of 160 million (Sivasubramonian, 2000). This may appear meagre, but India's per capita industrial output at Independence was higher than elsewhere in Asia outside Japan, and more than half of India's exports were manufactures. British policy was less repressive to local industry than that of other colonial power, and had permitted the emergence of a small but powerful class of Indian entrepreneurs. It should be noted, however, that modern industry was heavily concentrated in Calcutta, Bombay and Ahmedabad. The area which was to become Pakistan had practically no industry at all.

In the last half century of British rule the output of industries rose about six-fold (about 4.2 percent a year) whereas the output of small-scale industries declined. Their joint output rose about two-thirds (1.2 percent a year), and per head of population, joint output was rising by 0.4 percent a year. We know that output in the modern factory sector was zero in 1850, and if we assume that small enterprise output grew parallel with population from 1850 to 1900, then total industrial output would have grown by 0.8 percent a year in this period, or about 0.3 percent a year per head of population. Some increase seems plausible in this period of railway development and expanding international trade. It, therefore, seems possible that in the last century of British rule, per capita output of industrial goods rose by a third. But in the first century of British rule, i.e. 1757-1857, it seems certain that industrial output fell per head of population because (a) the home and domestic market for luxury goods was cut so drastically; (b) the home market for yarn and cheap cloth was invaded by foreign competition. Over the whole period of British rule it therefore seems likely that industrial output per head of the population was not significantly changed.

Economic Burden of Foreign Rule

The major burden of foreign rule arose from the fact that the British raj was a regime of expatriates. Under an Indian administration, income from government service would have accrued to the local inhabitants and not to foreigners. The diversion of upper-class income into the hands of foreigners inhibited the development of local industry because it put purchasing power into the hands of people with a taste for foreign goods. This increased imports and was particularly damaging to the luxury handicraft industries.

Another important effect of foreign rule on the long-run growth potential of the economy was the fact that a large part of its potential savings was siphoned abroad. This 'drain' of funds from India to the UK has been a point of major controversy between Indian nationalist historians and defenders of the British raj. However, the only real grounds for controversy are statistical. There can be no denial that there was a substantial outflow which lasted for 190 years. If these funds had been invested in India, they could have made a significant contribution to raising income levels.

The first generation of British rulers was rapacious. Clive took quarter of a million pounds for himself as well as a jagir worth £27,000 a year, but the British did not pillage on the scale of Nadir Shah, who probably took as much from India in one year as the East India Company did in the twenty years following the battle of Plassey.[8] They were also shrewd enough to realize that it was not in their long-run interest to devastate the country.

However, British salaries were high. The Viceroy received £25,000 a year, and governors £10,000. The starting salary in the engineering service was £420 a year or about sixty times the average income of the Indian labour force. From 1757 to 1919, India also had to meet administrative expenses in London, first of the East India Company, and then of the India Office, as well as other minor but irritatingly extraneous charges. The cost of British staff was raised by long home leave in the UK, early retirement and lavish amenities in the form of subsidized housing, utilities, rest houses, etc.

Under the rule of the East India Company, official transfers to the UK rose gradually until they reached about £3.5 million in 1856, the year before the mutiny. In addition, there were private remittances. In the twenty years 1835-54, India's average annual balance on trade and bullion was favourable by about £4.5 million a year.

During the period of direct British rule from 1858 to 1947, official transfers of funds to the UK by the colonial government were called the "Home Charges". They mainly represented debt service, pensions, India Office expenses in the UK, purchases of military items and railway equipments. Government procurement of civilian goods, armaments and shipping was carried out almost exclusively in the UK. By the 1930s these home charges were in the range of £40 to £50 million a year. Some of these flows would have occurred in a non-colonial economy, e.g. debt service on loans used to finance railway development, but a large part of the debt was incurred as a result of colonial wars. Some government expenditure was on imports which an independent government would have bought from local manufacturers. Of these official payments, we can legitimately consider service charges on non-productive debt, pensions and furlough payments as a balance of payment drain due to colonialism.

There were also substantial private remittances by British officials in India either as savings or to meet educational and other family charges in the UK. In the inter-war period, these amounted to about £10 million a year, and Naoroji estimated that they were running at the same level in 1887 (Banerji, 1963:136; Naoroji, 1962: 223). These items were clearly the result of colonial rule. In addition, there were dividend and interest remittances by shipping and banking interests, plantations, and other British investors; to some extent, these were normal commercial transactions, but there was a large element of monopoly profit due to the privileged position of British business in India. In many cases, the original assets were not acquired by remitting funds to India but by savings from income earned locally, or by purchase of property on favourable terms, e.g. the land acquisitions of plantation companies. About a third of the private profit remittances should therefore be treated as the profits of colonialism.

The total 'drain' due to government pensions and leave payments, interest on non-railway official debt, private remittances for education and savings, and a third commercial profits amounted to about 1.5 percent of national income of undivided India from 1921 to 1938 and was probably a little larger before that. Net investment was about 5 percent of national income at the end of British rule, so about a quarter of Indian savings were transferred out of the economy, and foreign exchange was lost which could have paid for imports of capital goods. As a consequence of this foreign drain the Indian balance of trade and bullion was always positive. In spite of its constant favourable balance of trade, India acquired substantial debts. By 1939 foreign assets in India amounted to $2.8 billion, of which about $1.5 billion was government bonded debt and the rest represented direct investment (mainly tea, other plantations and the jute industry).

India did not reduce its foreign debt during World War I as many other developing countries did. Instead, there were two 'voluntary' war gifts to the UK amounting to £150 million ($730 million). India also contributed one-and-a-quarter million troops, which were financed from the Indian budget. The 'drain' of funds to England continued in the interwar years because of home charges and profit remittances. There was also a small outflow of British capital.

In the depression of 1929-33, many developing countries defaulted on foreign debt or froze dividend transfers, but this was not possible for India.

The currency was kept at par with sterling and devalued in 1931, but the decisions were based on British rather than Indian needs. Furthermore, the salaries of civil servants remained at high level, and the burden of official transfers increased in a period of falling prices. During World War II, India's international financial position was transformed. The UK had enormous military expenditures for its own troops in India and also financed local costs of allied troops. Indian war finance was much more inflationary than in the UK and prices rose threefold, so these local costs of troop support were extremely high in terms of sterling, as the exchange rate remained unchanged. As a result, India was able to liquidate $1.2 billion of pre-war debt and acquired reserve assets of $5.1 billion, ending the war a large net creditor. These new assets and the disappearance of the colonial drain gave a formidable boost to post-war development policy.

There has been a good deal of controversy amongst statisticians about the rate of growth of income in India in the colonial period. The argument is politically coloured and the statistics are poor. From the beginning of British conquest in 1757 to independence, it seems unlikely that per capita income could have increased by more than a third and it probably did not increase at all. In the UK itself there was a tenfold increase in per capita income over these two centuries. The most noticeable change in the economy was the rise in population from about 170 million to 420 million from 1757 to 1947.

Society

There were some significant changes in social structure and in the pattern of output. The social pyramid was truncated because the British lopped off most of the top three layers of the Moghul hierarchy, i.e. the Moghul court, the Moghul aristocracy and quasi-autonomous princes, and the local chieftainry (zamindars who survived in about 40 percent of India). In place of these people the British installed a modern bureaucracy which took a smaller share of national income. The newcomers had a more modest life-style than the Moghuls, but siphoned a large part of their savings out of the country and provided almost no market for India's luxury handicrafts. The modern factory sector which they created produced only 7.5 percent of national income at the end of British rule and thus did little more than replace the old luxury handicrafts and part of the village textile production.

The British reduced the tax squeeze on agriculture and turned warlords into landlords, but the new order had little dynamism. A good deal of the old fuzziness about property rights remained, and landlords were still largely parasitic. The bigger zamindars copied the Moghul lifestyle by maintaining hordes of retainers and huge mansions, the smaller landowner's ambition was to stop working and enhance his ritual purity by establishing a seedy gentility. Very little incentive was provided for investment and almost nothing was done to promote technical change in agriculture. At the bottom of society the position of sharecropping tenants and landless labourers remained wretched. In urban areas a new Westernized 'middle class' of Indians emerged and became the major challenge to the British Raj.

Over time, two forces raised the income of landowners. One of these was the increasing scarcity of land as population increased. This raised land values and rents. The second was the decline in the incidence of land tax. Indian literature usually stresses the heavy burden of land tax in the early days of British rule, but the fact that it fell substantially over time is seldom noted. The Moghul land tax was about 30 percent of the crop, but by 1947 land tax was only 2 percent of agricultural income. The fall was most marked in Bengal where the tax was fixed in perpetuity in 1793, but it was also true in other areas.

As a result of these changes, there was not only an increase in village income but a widening of income inequality within villages. The village received relatively higher incomes because of the reduced burden of land tax and the increase in rents; tenants and agricultural labourers may well have experienced a decline in income because their traditional rights were curtailed and their bargaining power was reduced by land scarcity. The class of landless agricultural labourers grew in size under British rule, but modern scholarship has shown that they were not a "creation" of the British (Kumar, 1965). They were about 15 percent of the rural population at the end of the eighteenth century, and about a quarter of the labour force now.

Although these were important modifications in the village structure, the traditional hierarchy of caste was not destroyed. Income differentials widened, but the social and ritual hierarchy in villages did not change its character. Village society was not egalitarian in Moghul times, and in most cases those whose income rose in the British period were already socially dominant, although there were exceptions. Recent sociological studies, although they indicate changes in the British period, also portray a village hierarchy in the 1940s and 1950s which cannot be very different from that in the Moghul period (Marriott, 1955; Srinivas, 1969). We still find a dominant caste of petty landlords, an intermediate group of tenants, village artisans tied by jajmani relationships, a group of low-status labourers, untouchable menials with the whole held together by the same elaborate system of caste.

It can be seen that the British were a very thin layer at the top of society but they took about 5 percent of national income. Their allies, the native princes and zamindars, took about 3 percent. Eight percent is a sizeable proportion for the ruling class but, under the Moghul regime, the equivalent group collected 15 percent of national income in taxes and spent most of it on their own consumption. Immediately under this group were two new indigenous classes- capitalists and professionals- who became the dominant elite in independent India. They were relatively larger in number and probably had a bigger share of national income than their counterparts under the Moghuls, i.e. the shroffs (indigenous urban bankers), merchants, qazis and pundits (lawyers), hakims (indigenous doctors), etc.

There were also changes in the lower class in the non-village economy. At the end of British rule there were 3 million factory workers making cheap textiles and jute sacking, whose Moghul predecessors had worked on muslins and silks, and a million railway workers who had no earlier counterpart. This lower-class urban group was probably bigger than in Moghul times, because they had displaced some of the village artisans.

Within village society the social structure was probably similar to that in Moghul India, with the two top economic groups corresponding to the old dominant castes, the next group to peasant castes, and the bottom group consisting largely of untouchables. The main difference form the Moghul economy is that village proprietors and tenants-in-chief were no longer heavily squeezed by taxation and their share of national income had probably increased.

Thus the main gainers from the British regime (apart from the British) were the so-called 'middle' class of Indian capitalists and professionals, and the village squirarchy. Most of these were high caste Hindus though the Parsis and Sikhs did fairly well. The main losers were the Muslims who had formed the major part of the Moghul aristocracy, officer corps, lawyers, and artisans in the luxury handicrafts.

References

Banerji, A. K. (1963), *India's Balance of Payments*. Bombay: Asia Publishing House.

Blyn, G. (1966), *Agricultural Trends in India, 1891-1947*. Pennsylvania: University of Pennsylvania.

Buchanan, D.H. (1966), *The Development of Capitalist Enterprise in India*. London: Cass.

Darling, M.L. (1947), *The Punjab Peasant in Prosperity and Debt*. London: Oxford University Press.

Davis, Kingsley (1951), *The Population of India and Pakistan*. New York: Princeton University, Press.

Desai, R.C. (1953), *Standard of Living in India and Pakistan 1931-32 to 1940-41*. Bombay: Popular Book Depot.

Digby, William (1901), *Prosperous British India*. London.

Dutt, R. C. (1901, 1976), *Economic History of India* (Under Early British Rule, 1757-1857), Vol. I. Delhi: Publications Division.

Dutt, R. Palme (1940, 1949), *India Today*. Bombay: People's Publishing House Ltd.

Edwardes, M. (1967), *British India 1772-1947*. London: Sidgwick and Jackson.

Heaton, H. (1965), *Economic History of Europe*. London: Harper and Row.

Kidron, M. (1965), *Foreign Investments in India*. London: Oxford University Press.

Kumar, Dharma (1965), *Land and Caste in South India*. Cambridge: Cambridge University Press.

Levkovsky, A. I. (1966), *Capitalism in India: Basic Trends in Development*. Bombay: People's Publishing House.

Lewis, W.A. (1949), *Economic Survey, 1919-39*. London: Allen and Unwin.

Marriott, M. (ed.), (1955), *Village India.* Chicago: Chicago University Press.

Moreland, W.H. (1962), *India at the Death of Akbar.* Delhi: Atma. Ram (Indian reprint)

Morris, M.D. (1965), *The Emergence of an Industrial Labour Force in India*. Cambridge: Cambridge University Press.

Naoroji, D. (1901, 1962), *Poverty and Un-British Rule in India*. London (Delhi: Governments of India Reprint).

Neale, W.C. (1962), *Economic Change in Rural India*. Yale: Yale University Press.

Nehru, Jawaharlal (1946), *The Discovery of India*. New York: Day.

Raychaudhuri, T. (1969), "Permanent Settlement in Operation: Bakarganj District, East Bengal" in R.E. Frykenberg (ed.), *Land Control and Social Structure in Indian History*, Madison,

Sivasubramonian, S. (2000), National Income of India 1900-1 to 1946-7, in *The National Income of India in the Twentieth Century.* New Delhi: Oxford University Press.

Srinivas, M. N. (ed.) (1969), *India's Villages*. Bombay: Asia Publishing House.

Thorner, Daniel (1956), *The Agrarian Prospect in India*. Delhi: Delhi School of Economics.

Tinker, H. (1967), *India and Pakistan*. London: Pall Mall.

Warriner, D. (1969), *Land Reform in Principle and Practice*. London: Oxford University Press.

Woodruff, P. (1963), *The Men who Ruled India*, The Guardians, Cape, London,

Notes

1. See Government of India, Report of the Education Commission 1964-66, Delhi, 1966.
2. See Lord Beveridge's life of his parents, India Called Them, Allen and Unwin, London, 1957. Beveridge's father did not have a very successful career, but had 21 servants to start married life, 39 when he had three children, and 18 when living on his own. The 18 servants cost him less than 6 percent of his salary.
3. See D.A.B. Bhattacharya (ed.), Report on the Population Estimates of India (1820-30), Census of India 1961, Government of India, Registrar General, Delhi, 1963, pp. 4-5.
4. See Census of India 1911, Vol. I, India, Part II, Tables, Calcutta, 1913, pp. 374-6. The total population of all India (including native states) was 313 million and the total labour force 149 million. It is interesting to note that the European population of India was of relatively much lower importance than in Indonesia, where there were 95,000 Europeans in a population of 38 million in 1905: see J.S. Furnivall, Colonial Policy and Practice, Cambridge, 1948, p. 255; or in French Indo-China with 42,000 Europeans and a total population of 23 million in 1937; see C. Robequain, The Economic Development of French Indo-China, Oxford University Press, London, 1944.
5. Tapan Raychaudhuri is the only Indian historian to have stressed this point. See his essay in R.E. Frykenberg (ed.), Land Control and Social Structure in Indian History, Madison, 1969, p. 168: 'the relatively low and unchanging rate of revenue demand which left a large surplus to be distributed among a numerous and parasitical class of rather poor intermediaries'.
6. e.g. the Bengal Act X of 1859, the Bengal Tenancy Act of 1885, the Oudh Sub-Settlement Act of 1866, the Deccan Agriculturalists Relief Act of 1879 and the Punjab Alienation of Land Act of 1900.
7. See The First Five Year Plan, Planning Commission, Delhi, December, 1952, pp. 338 and 344. In 1850, 2 to 3 million acres were irrigated by tank or canal and 5 million acres by wells. In 1941-5, 58.1 million out of 216.6 million acres of cultivated land in British India were irrigated of which 33.6 million acres by government works.
8. There is a tendency amongst Marxist and anti-British historians to exaggerate the size of the Indian plunder. R.P. Dutt argues that 'the spoliation of India was the hidden source of accumulation which played an all important role in helping to make possible the Industrial Revolution in England', see R.P. Dutt, op. cit. An even more extreme view is taken by P.A. Baran, The Political Economy of Growth, Prometheus, New York, 1957, p. 145. See also B. Adams, The Law of Civilization and Decay, New York, 1910 and W. Digby, Prosperous British India, 1901. In fact a good deal of the Indian revenue was used to finance local wars and did not reach the UK. The latest scholarly estimates suggest that the transfer to the UK was about one-tenth of the amounts estimated by Digby.

Chapter- 10

Summary and Conclusion

The British came to India at the start of the seventeenth century. This was the time when the British East India Company was established in India to break the Dutch monopoly over spice trade. Merchants of the East India Company never imagined that British presence in the subcontinent could mean anything more than peaceful trading. French arrived in the middle of the 17th century, signalling the beginning of militarization. Within 100 years the French were a spent force and the British possessed the most efficient military machine in the subcontinent. With time the East India Company increased its powers and started to administer the country. However, its policies were disliked by Indians and together they revolted against the company. This led to the downfall of the company and the administration of India went directly under the Queen in 1858.

The Crown's representative in India was now the Viceroy, who had almost absolute authority. On the political front, after the mutiny of 1857, most factions of Indian society expressed absolute loyalty to the Raj. And despite the fact that the British tried to blame the Muslims for the mutiny, support from the Muslim westernized elite did not diminish. Some Muslims saw that they had difficult times ahead, wondering how they should assimilate to developments under the British while still holding on to their traditions.

The British annexed many princely states and formed laws and policies of their own. Slowly but rapidly the entire Indian sub-continent came under the British rule. By mid nineteenth century, the British introduced the railways, telegraph and postal service in India. This was a move to establish their rule permanently in India. The first railway line was from Howrah in

Calcutta to Raniganj in Bihar. The introduction of telegraph and postal services simplified communication all over the country. The British rule over India changed the course of history in India.

The British passed many acts that were met with dissatisfaction and resentment by the Indians. As a result the Indians formed large groups and revolted against the British. Each movement was brutally crushed by the British forces. Leaders like Mahatma Gandhi, Jawaharlal Nehru, Lala Lajpat Rai, Subhash Chandra Bose, etc. arose and openly condemned the British. They were people's leaders who inspired the masses not to be afraid of the tyrannical forces. Finally after 200 years of the British rule, India gained independence from them on 15th August, 1947. Many innocent lives were sacrificed for this achievement and India was also separated from Pakistan.

Stages of Colonialism

British colonialism established its firm roots in India in three stages, each stage representing a different pattern of subordination of the colony and consequently different colonial policies, ideologies, impact and the colonial people's response. The change from one stage to another was partly due to the changes in the metropolis itself and partly to the changes in the colonies. The three stages are not strictly bound. But each stage has some main features, though the features of the earlier one may continue into the later one. Again some stages are atrophied in some colonies, as the third stage in India.

Period of mercantilism (1757-1813)— The objectives of the British during this time were monopoly of trade and direct appropriation of revenue. The main features were:

1. Very strong element of plunder and direct seizure of power.
2. Absence of large-scale import of British goods.
3. No basic changes in the colony's administration, judiciary, culture, economy, etc.

Period of *Laissez Faire* (1813-1860)— The main features of this period were:

1. Determination of the administrative policies and economic structure of the colony by the interests of the industrial bourgeoisie of the metropolis.
2. Making the colony a subordinate trading partner which would export raw materials and import manufactured goods.

3. Transformation of the colony's economy, polity, administration, society, culture and ideology under the guise of development and modernization in order to exploit for furthering British interests.

Economic imperialism (1860-1947)— This period was marked by:

1. Intense struggle for new, secure and exclusive markets and sources of raw materials among the industrialised countries.
2. The consequent export of capital by these countries to the colonies.
3. Replacement of liberal policies by reactionary ones in the administration of colonies.

The following are the important timelines, marking the beginning of establishment of East India Company of India:

1611 AD: East India Company is established in India by the British

1751 AD: Britain becomes the leading colonial power in India

1757 AD: British defeat Siraj-ud-daulah at the Battle of Plassey

1761 AD: Marathas rule over most of northern India

1764 AD: Britain expands to Bengal and Bihar

1769 AD: A famine kills ten million people in Bengal and the East India Company does nothing to help them

1773 AD: Warren Hastings, governor of Bengal establishes a monopoly on the sale of opium. Regulating Act passed by the British.

1793 AD: Permanent Settlement of Bengal

1799 AD: British defeat Tipu Sultan

1829 AD: Prohibition of Sati by law

1831 AD: Administration of Mysore is taken over by East India Company

1848 AD: Lord Dalhousie becomes the Governor-General of India

1853 AD: Railway, postal services & telegraph line introduced in India

1857 AD: First War of Indian Independence also known as Revolt of 1857 or Sepoy Mutiny

1858 AD: British Crown officially takes over the Indian Government

1877 AD: Queen of England is proclaimed as the Empress of India

1885 AD: First meeting of the Indian National Congress

1899 AD: Lord Curzon becomes Governor-General and Viceroy of India

1905 AD: The First Partition of Bengal takes place

1906 AD: Muslim League is formed

1912 AD: The Imperial capital shifted to Delhi from Calcutta

1919 AD: The cruel Jallianwalla Bagh massacre takes place due to protests against the Rowlatt Act

1920 AD: Non-cooperation Movement launched

1922 AD: Chauri-Chaura violence takes place due to Civil Disobedience Movement

1928 AD: Simon Commission comes to India and is boycotted by all parties

1930 AD: Salt Satyagraha is launched as an agitation against salt tax. First Round Table Conference takes place

1931 AD: Second Round Table Conference takes place and Irwin-Gandhi Pact is signed

1934 AD: Civil Disobedience Movement is called off 1942 AD: Cripps Mission is formed; Quit India Movement is launched; Indian National Army is formed.

3rd June 1947 AD: Lord Mountbatten's plan for partition of India comes into light

15th August 1947 AD: Partition of India and Independence from the British rule

Impact of British rule

Under the impact of the British rule in India, radical changes started taking place, rather slowly in the beginning, but fairly rapidly after 1850, in the spheres of administration, means of transport and communications, the structure of commerce, the organisation of agriculture and Industries, as also in social and political institutions in the country and more importantly, in the attitude and ideas of the people. During the 17th century and early part of the 18th century, the European trading companies used to purchase various finished goods from India, for sale in European markets. But markets in India for various European goods were then extremely limited. There used to be thus a net excess of India's exports over her annual imports.

British Empire in India and the struggle for every Indian to achieve its own identity through Independence has perhaps been the most talked-about subject in modern history. Indeed, staying lavishly in the modern cosmopolitan Indian society, it is always hard to comprehend the then pre-independent Indian society, with no such thing as to call one's own and no trace of modernity touching any household. The British rule in India had tenaciously tolerated for 200 prolonged years, with their everlasting impression been forever etched upon the succeeding Indian citizens. Impact of British rule in India, in this context, is one that had perhaps emerged forth right from the 16th century, when British missionaries had sailed to eastern soil to spread Christianity, much before the East India Company. Although, all is not bad and even worse for the British impact upon India. There always exists a bright side to every dark silhouette; hence, impact of the British rule upon India and Indians both constitutes superior and appalling elements, still in use in present times.

It is a well-known fact that British invasion on India was not the first of its kind; rather, India has prior to British arrival, had been host to pellets of ruthless foreign invasions. During its last 5000 years, the country was invaded by Aryans, Greeks, Huns, nomadics from central Asia, Muslims and European Christians. All the former invaders slowly but surely got assimilated within the Hindu and Muslim dominated Indian society. As can be conceivable, they just did not come single-handedly; these invaders also brought along with them their language, culture, architecture and food habits. They, in turn, became 'Indianised' in good time. The British, in this regard, were the last to arrive in the European 'take over sport'. However, when it came to speaking of the 'power game', it undoubtedly was the British and their East India Company, who completely captured Indian power and people. They surreptitiously and smoothly expanded their empire with the competent aid of Indian soldiers. Indians however had joined the East India company army solely for the reason that they received salary on the first day of every month, very much unlike the Indian emperors and their system of reign. As such, impact of British rule in India already had begun to do its work, with the very first Christian missionaries arriving to India, with the intention to turn a majority of population into Christians. They tried to cast Christianity in the light of a superior religion and with economic inducements convinced the poor Indians into Christianity.

The very foremost impact of British rule on India was the religious impact, as was established by the missionaries and their establishment of churches in every possible corner of the country. In this regard, the port cities like Calcutta, Bombay and Madras gained sufficient importance, due to their accessibility for navigational purposes. They were later turned into the three cardinal Presidency towns. The ardent attempt of British Christians to turn several bunches of Indians into a complete alien religion was successful, though only in parts. Some had gladly accepted it, in fear of inviting the wrath of the Company, while others had turned hostile, in turn giving rise to oft collisions and difference of opinion. The British rule lasted 200 years and their primary philosophy was to oppose 'Indianization', yet assimilate themselves into one out-and-out Indian society. Initially, during the 18th century, they walked the native way and branded themselves as nawabs. They dressed like Indians, consumed Indian food and married Indian women and lived in Indian-styled houses. As such, the socio-cultural impact of British rule upon India was also another profound impression that had lasted throughout their rule, never for once losing their significant status. From every field of living, be it in education, art, architecture, painting, literature, poetry, drama, novels or even Indian religion and philosophy, the whole Indian set-up had suffered a gradual metamorphosis, still making its mark in society.

After the abolition and termination of the East India Company rule, they chose to erect Europeanised cantonments far from the 'overcrowded' Indian cities or villages. Here they dwelled in spacious British bungalows in splendid segregation and the local 'whites only' gymkhana clubs became their cultural nerve-centres. Even braving this tropical humid climate, the colonialists struck to European mode of dressing during the early 20th century. They however went out of their way as much to learn the Hindi language, which was often satisfactorily presentable for their servants and cooks.

The conventional and ordinary Indian society however respected and dreaded the 'white' rulers. British aristocrats travelled throughout India in separate "Europeans only" first-class railway carriages. They had for themselves segregated waiting rooms in most of the major railway stations. They also came to establish elite schools for their children. In most of the theatre halls, the balcony was earmarked for the whites and the local maharaja. Their significant passionate pastime during late 19th and early 20th centuries appears to be hunting animals and birds in Indian jungles. As such, the population of tigers, lions and elephants slumped down because of indiscriminate hunting. Impact of British rule in India however, not only restricted to spheres like these being noted above, the economic impact was yet another domain, which practically had drained out the native populace, creating a forever draught in 1947. The chief aim of these settlers was to make India an agrarian country that would supply an industrialised England. As such, the Indian farmers suffered with their land revenue, most of which were ruthlessly being seized by the hyperbolic zamindar class. Each passing year further tightened the economy, making Indians go insane to the nerve; Indian local-manufactured products were sold in tremendously cheap rates in Britain, making the native money-making policy even harder, with the graph running penniless. The world-over societal degradation also had spilled in India, like World War I or the Great Depression of the 1930s. The situation had become so very dire that there could not be found any out of such an entangled mess.

Amidst all these alarming states and conditions, the imperial rule were compassionate enough to introduce European education in India. This ground-breaking impact of British rule in India truly has benefited India in the long run, carving out a prestigious position of India in the world map. Knowledge of English was essential to earn a job in the British bureaucracy, in the British trading firms and of course in the British Army in the officer's level. Many dignified concepts like 'parliamentary democracy', the 'European scientific ideas', 'industrialization' and 'liberal human philosophy' permeated into the Indian brain. They had even travelled a step further to introduce the system of railways in a chain method, with the whole of the country staying witness to placing of railways tracks, railway platforms and railway carriages. Indeed India's railways, postal services, legal and judicial systems and other government-based services have all been derived primarily from the British administration. British rule virtually had helped unify India, which till then was quite fragmentary.

The 'in-built' inferiority complex was the characteristic trademark of the mass of the native population, till Mahatma Gandhi arrived onto the scene. Most of the people in an almost reflexive manner started to revere a white man or a woman, looked upon them as a race in equalising terms. The bulk of Indian students who set sail to England for higher studies were at first profoundly shocked in seeing white men and women performing lowly jobs in England. Hence, in spite of such harsh impacts of British rule upon India, they did still try to maintain equilibrium.

Impact on Law and Administration

The most abiding impacts of the British rule in India are manifested in the fields of administration. The British Rulers introduced Rule of Law in their territories. Even the meanest subject enjoyed personal liberty according to the Rule of Law. The principle of habeas corpus provided that no person could be arrested or kept in prison without a written order from the local executive or the judicial authority, even if the viceroy when desired. Even the Government servant, if the acts done in their official capacity could be sued in the court of Law. The natural upshot of the Rule of Law was the Equality before the Law, which subsequently followed the Rule of Law. The Equality before the Law appeared as a novel feature in the caste-ridden society.

The British rulers further established a codification of law. The Code of Civil Procedure, the code of Criminal Procedure laid down in clear, precise and in exact terms, the law applicable to all citizens, high and low breed and irrespective of caste, creed and religion. The British rulers also set up a gradation of courts, civil and criminal for the trial of the petty and heinous crimes with the right to appeal at the high Courts ands even an appeal to a Committees of Privy Council in civil suits.

The legal system introduced by the British Government in India had several shortcomings. It was very expensive and the rich had the opportunity to wear out the poor and uneducated. The British legal system stimulated the growth of the falsehood, chicanery, and deceit. The inordinate delay in the decision of the case was one of the significant negative features of the Legal system of the British. The lawyer class in the British legal system was interested in delaying and prolonging cases and pleading for clients who could afford to pay them. The worst aspects of the legal system in the British time were the special procedures for the trial of the European in the criminal cases. The Ilbert Bill highlighted the injustice involved in the racial discrimination in judicial matters but no remedial measures were provided.

The organisation of an Indian Civil Service, which worked according to the codified rules and with efficiency and impartiality, was a striking feature of the administration. The administrative system established by the British was completely different from the personal rules and regulations of a dictator monarch. The ICS officers, under the British administrative system worked as collectors, Magistrates, Judges and maintained a high standard of impartiality and integrity.

However highly applauded system of Indian civil Services, had several drawbacks. In spite of the repeated resolutions of the British Parliament and announcements by the British crown about the recruitments to the ICS on the basis of Competitive Examination irrespective of racial discriminations. The British system of Indian civil Service was completely aimed to constitute as a close preserve of the Europeans. In this way the British Government wanted to strengthen their own position in the politics and administrative field of India. Various measures like holding of examination in London, reducing the average age limit of the examination, etc. were adopted to keep the Indians out of the Civil services or to participate in the administrative system directly. Therefore the British impact on the law and administration was immense and was directed to fortify the British administration in India.

Impact on Various Social Classes

The peasants, artisans, craftsmen and plantation workers all were victims of British imperialism. The workers in modern industries had a new social outlook. They were concentrated in factories and cities. They lived and worked under highly unsatisfactory conditions. The average worker lived below the margin of existence while conditions in the tea and coffee plantations were also worse. The planters kept the workers on the plantations as virtual slaves. The Government gave them full help to enable them to keep the plantation workers under oppressive subjugation. The planters also frequently tortured them physically.

In course of time the working class joined the peasants, the craftsmen and the artisans in the struggle against imperialist exploitation. The status of the middle and the lower middle-classes were also miserable. In the first half of the 19th century the British government recruited a large number of educated Indians as petty government servants. Later some more found employment in schools and law courts. The number of merchants increased along with the trade expansion. But by the end of the 19th century even those few who were educated could not find employment. All these who constituted the middle and lower-middle classes of society realized that only a country that was economically developing and culturally and socially modern could provide them economic and cultural opportunities to lead a worthwhile and meaningful life.

The Indian industrial capitalist class, which developed after 1858, had to face the competition of the British capitalists. It realized that the official trade, tariff, transport and financial policies of the Government checked its growth. After 1918 the giant British industrial corporations began to invest in Indian industries in order to take advantage of the tariff protection. This was granted during 1920's and 1930's. Thus the Indian capitalists realized that they needed a government favourable to them. This could be only a national government.

Impact on Society and Culture

The British era is considered one of the most eventful eras in the history of India. The era brought about a lot of changes in almost every aspect of the Indian society. The socio cultural impact under the British rule was probably the most prominent one amongst them. The rational and scientific outlook of the British way of life influenced the Indian society from the very beginning of the British imperialism. The art, architecture, painting, literature, poetry, drama, novels and even Indian religion and philosophy were greatly influenced by the western thoughts. However, most of the changes were not brought about by the British people. The English educated Indian people like the journalists, teachers, lawyers, doctors, etc. took the responsibility of leading movements for making the significant socio cultural changes.

The socio cultural impact under the British rule started with the establishment of various English schools in different cities of India. The British rulers first studied the Indian languages, literature, religion and social structure and then educated the Indians in English to establish a new administrative structure. The British Governor, Warren Hastings (1772-85) was a supporter of 'Orientalism' and during his tenure, the British rulers demonstrated linguistic proficiency, a deep understanding of India and a sense of benevolent responsibility in regard to the Indian people. He established the Calcutta Madrasah for the Muslim officials of the East Company and the students were taught in Persian in this institution. The Orientalist dream of Hastings was taken forward by Lord Wellesley, who established the Fort William College to train the civil servants.

The scholars at the Fort William College in Calcutta started to translate the ancient texts, write grammars, compile dictionaries and collect manuscripts to research further on India. On the other hand, the Baptist missionaries in Serampore became successful to print works in the Indian vernacular languages like Bengali, Urdu, Oriya, Tamil, Telugu, Kanarese and Marathi. Many individuals and organisations also started to study literature in both classical and vernacular languages during that period. As a result, the importance of the vernacular languages increased. The demand for the use of English as the language of administration and education was also increased during that time. The scenario was similar in Bombay, Gujarat, Tamil Nadu and other parts of India.

During the first half of the nineteenth century, the British rulers decided to make English as the primary medium of education in India. They also envisioned the creation of a class of people in India that would act as a link between the rulers and ruled. The class would also become a source of inexpensive manpower for the lower levels of the administration. With the efforts made by the British, knowledge in English soon became a key to get government services for the Indians. It also became a key to make successful careers in the fields like law, medicine, teaching, business, journalism, etc. The Indian people started to learn English to get advantage in professional and other fields. With the establishment of various educational institutions, the number of English educated Indians increased significantly.

Indian response to new opportunities created by the British was determined largely by their place in pre-British society. At the height of the Orientalist period, scholars of Sanskrit, Arabic, Persian, and of South Asian learning were hired by such Indian educational institutes. With the shift to English education those castes that were already literate became students to master this new language; in practice this meant primarily Bengali Hindus of the Brahman, Baidya, and Kayastha castes. Earlier individuals from these groups learnt Persian to gain employment under the Mughal and post-Empire Muslim rulers. With the influence of the British on the mode of education they switched to English.

By the late nineteenth century, new anglicized elite began to establish institutions to serve their own interests. For instance in 1816, the Hindu College in Kolkata was founded. On the other hand in 1825 the Elphinstone Institute was established in Bombay (Mumbai). These educational institutes were primarily responsible for producing the core of English educated elite. A trend toward English education and the acceptance of western knowledge appeared in Poona. In 1832, the government founded an English high school. To counter this socio-cultural impact of the British ways several associations were formed across India to revive the ancient Indian traditions.

Besides education western models and English pattern were followed in the social etiquette, dress, eating habits, dwelling units, awareness in the public and hygiene, new modes of entertainment etc were penetrated deep into the Indian way of life and society. Although the traditional Indian habits were dominating in the countryside, the western outlook influenced the inhabitants of the urban India. With the arrival of the British people in India, the rapid changes took place in the mainstream of Indian society. The international currents influenced the Indian pattern of social outlook, dress, food habits and even fashion with the British rule in India.

The British rulers built town hall after the Renaissance palazzi style, railway stations in the Gothic cathedral style, government building and secretariat offices in the western style blended with the traditional Mughal style. However, the socio-cultural impact under the British rule was more prominent in the urban areas rather than the rural areas, where the traditional Indian habits were in dominance. The socio-cultural influence was prominent in the field of painting as well. The eminent Indian painters like Ravi Verma, Abanindranath Thakur, Jamini Roy, etc were greatly influenced by the Western style. Apart from them, the great literary figures like Rabindranath Tagore, Aurobindo Ghosh, Sarojini Naidu, Mulk Raj Anand, R.K. Narayanan, etc. were also influenced by the English pattern and the spirit of Renaissance.

With the course of time, the way of learning in India was also influenced by the English style and the English words and idioms were penetrated into the vernacular languages. As a result, even the illiterate rural people in India were acquainted with the English terms and idioms. In this way, the socio cultural impact under the British rule completely spread through the Indian society and changed the course of Indian pattern of socio-cultural life.

Appendices

Appendix-1: History of South Asia

History of South Asia

Dwapara Yuga	before 3300 BC
• Mehrgarh Culture	• 7000–3300 BC
Indus Valley Civilization	3300–1700 BC
• Late Harappan Culture	• 1700–1300 BC
Vedic Civilization	2000–600 BC
Iron Age	1200–1 BC
• Maha Janapadas	• 700–300 BC
• Magadha Empire	684–424 BC
• Nanda Empire	• 424-321 BC
• Maurya Empire	• 321–184 BC
• Sunga Empire	• 185-73 BC
• Kanva Empire	• 75-26 BC
• Kharavela Empire	• 209–170 BC
• Kuninda Kingdom	•200s BC–300s CE
• Indo-Scythian Kingdom	• 200 BC–400 CE
• Chera Kingdom	• 300 BC–1200 CE
• Chola Empire	• 300 BC–1279 CE
• Pandyan Kingdom	• 250 BC–1345 CE

• Satavahana Empire	• 230 BC–220 CE
• Indo-Greek Kingdom	• 180 BC–10 CE
Middle Kingdoms	1CE–1279 CE
• Indo-Parthian Kingdom	• 21–130s CE
• Western Satrap Empire	• 35–405 CE
• Kushan Empire	• 60–240 CE
• Indo-Sassanid Kingdom	• 230–360 CE
• Vakataka Empire	• 250–500 CE
• Kalabhras Kingdom	• 250–600 CE
• Gupta Empire	• 280–550 CE
• Pallava Kingdom	• 275–800 CE
• Kadamba Empire	• 345–525 CE
• Western Ganga Kingdom	• 350–1000 CE
• Vishnukundina Empire	• 420-624 CE
• Huna Kingdom	• 475-576 CE
• Chalukya Empire	• 543–753 CE
• Harsha Empire	• 590-647 CE
• Shahi Kingdom	• 565-670 CE
• Eastern Chalukya Kingdom	• 624-1075 CE
• Pratihara Empire	• 650–1036 CE
• Pala Empire	• 750–1174 CE
• Rashtrakuta Empire	• 753–982 CE
• Paramara Kingdom	• 800–1327 CE
• Yadava Empire	• 850–1334 CE
• Solanki Kingdom	• 942–1244 CE
• Western Chalukya Empire	• 973–1189 CE
• Hoysala Empire	• 1040–1346 CE
• Sena Empire	• 1070–1230 CE

• Eastern Ganga Empire	• 1078–1434 CE
• Kakatiya Kingdom	• 1083–1323 CE
• Kalachuri Empire	• 1130–1184 CE
Islamic Sultanates	1206–1596 CE
• Delhi Sultanate	• 1206–1526 CE
• Deccan Sultanates	• 1490–1596 CE
Ahom Kingdom	1228–1826 CE
Vijayanagara Empire	1336–1646 CE
Mysore Kingdom	1399–1947 CE
Mughal Empire	1526–1858 CE
Madurai Nayak Kingdom	1559 –1736 CE
Thanjavur Nayak Kingdom	1572–1918 CE
Maratha Empire	1674–1818 CE
Sikh Confederacy	1716–1799 CE
Sikh Empire	1799–1849 CE
Company rule in India	1757–1858 CE
British India	1858–1947 CE
Partition of India	1947 CE

Appendix-2: List of Governors-General

I. Governors-General of Fort William in Bengal (Regulating Act of 1773)

1774 (October)	Warren Hastings
1785 (February)	Sir John Macpherson
1786 (September)	Earl (Marques) Cornwallis
793 (October)	Sir John Shore (Lord Teignmouth)
1798 (March)	Sir A. Clarke
1798 (May)	Earl of Mornington (Marquess Wellesley)

1805 (30th July)	Marquess Cornwallis (for the second time)
1805 (October)	Sir George Barlow
1807 (July)	Baron (1st Earl of) Minto (I)
1813 (4th October)	Earl of Moira (Marquess of Hastings)
1823 (January)	John Adam
1823 (1st August)	Baron (Earl) Amherst
1828 (March)	William Butterworth Bayley
1828 (4th July)	Lord William Cavendish-Bentinck

II. Governors-General of India (Charter Act of 1833)

1833	Lord William Cavendish-Bentinck
1835 (20th March)	Sir Charles (Lord) Metcalfe
1836 (March)	Baron (Earl of) Auckland
1842 (February)	Baron (Earl of) Ellenborough
1844 (June)	William Wilberforce Bird
1844 (July)	Sir Henry (Viscount) Hardinge
1848 (January)	Earl (Marquess) of Dalhousie
1856 (February)	Viscount (Earl) Canning

III. Governors-General and Viceroy

1858 (1st November)	Viscount (Earl) Canning
1862 (March)	8th Earl of Elgin (I)
1863	Sir Robert Napier (Baron pier of Magdala)
1863	Sir William T. Denison
1864 (January)	Sir John (Lord) Lawrence
1869 (January)	Earl of Mayo
1872	Sir John Strachey

1872	Lord Napier of Merchistoun
1872 (May)	Baron (Earl of) Northbrook
1876 (April)	Baron (1st Earl of) Lytton (I)
1880 (June)	Marquess of Ripon
1884 (december)	Earl of Dufferin (Marquess of Dufferin and Ava)
1888 (December)	Marquess of Landsdowne
1894 (January)	9th Earl of Elgin (II)
1899 (6th January)	Baron (Marquess) Curzon of Kedleston
1904 (April)	Lord Ampthill
1904 (December)	Baron (Marquess) Curzon of Kedleston (re-appointed)
1905 (November)	4th Earl of Minto (II)
1910 (November)	Baron Hardinge of Penshurst (II)
1916 (April)	Baron Chelmford
1921 (April)	Earl of Reading
1925	2nd Earl of Lytton (II)
1926 (April)	Lord Irwin\
1929	Lord Goschen (during the absence of Lord Irwin on leave)
1931 (April)	Earl of Willingdon
1934 (May-August)	Sir George Stanley (Offg.)
1934	Earl of Willingdon
1936 (18th April)	Marquess of Linlithgow

IV. Governors-General and Crown Representatives (Act of 1935)

1937 (31st March)	Marquess of Linlithgow
1938 (June-October)	Baron Brabourne (Offg.)
1938	Marquess of Linlithgow
1943	Viscount (Earl) Wavell

1945	Sir John Colville (Offg.)
1947 (March-August)	Viscount (Earl) Mountbatten (last Viceroy of United India, First Governor-General of the Indian Domiion, 1947-1948)

V. Governor-General (Indian Independence Act) Indian Union

Earl Mountbatten

1947 (November)	Sri Chakravarti Rajagopalachari (Offg.)
1948 (June)	Sri Chakravarti Rajagopalachari

Appendix-3: Princely States

Colonial India	
Portuguese India	1510–1961
Dutch India	1605–1825
Danish India	1696–1869
French India	1759–1954
British Empire in India	
East India Company	1612–1757
Company rule in India	1757–1857
British Raj	1858–1947
British rule in Burma	1826–1948
British India	1612–1947
Princely states	1765–1947
Partition of India	1947

There were as many as 568 states in India before independence. A Princely State (also called Native State or Indian State) was a *nominally sovereign* entity of British rule in India that was not directly administered by the British, but rather by an Indian ruler under a form of indirect rule such as suzerainty or paramountcy.

A Short List of Native States in 1909

The native states in 1909 included five large states that were in "direct political relations" with the Government of India. Of these, Nepal, differed from others, in that it was independent in its internal administration, but was represented internationally by the Government of India.

Under Suzerainty of the Central Government

Five large Princely States in direct political relations with the Central Government in India1[1]

Name of Princely State	Area in Square Miles	Population in 1901	Approximate Revenue of the State (in hundred thousand Rupees)	Title, ethnicity, and religion of ruler	Gun-Salute for Ruler	Designation of local political officer
Hyderabad	82,698	approx. 11.14 million (Hindus and Muslims)	359	Nizam, Turk, Sunni Muslim	21	Resident in Hyderabad
Mysore	29,444	5.53 million (mostly Hindu)	190	Maharaja, Rajput, Hindu	21	Resident in Mysore
Baroda	8,099	1.95 million (chiefly Hindu)	123	Maharaja, Maratha, Hindu	21	Resident at Baroda
Kashmir and Jammu	80,900	2.91 million including Gilgit, Skardu, Ladakh, and Punch (Chiefly Muslim)	87	Maharaja, Dogra Rajput, Hindu	19 (21 within Kashmir)	Resident in Kashmir
Total	**445,891**	**25.54 million**	**909**			

1. Imperial Gazetteer of India vol. IV 1907, p. 92.

Central India Agency, Rajputana Agency and the Baluchistan Agency

148 Princely States forming the Central India Agency[2]

Name of Princely State	Area in Square Miles	Population in 1901	Approximate Revenue of the State (in hundred thousand Rupees)	Title, ethnicity, and religion of ruler	Gun-Salute for Ruler	Designation of local political officer
Gwalior	25,041	2.93 million (Chiefly Hindus)	163	Maharaja, Maratha, Hindu	19 (21 within Gwalior)	Resident at Gwalior
Indore	9,500	0.85 million (Chiefly Hindu)	72	Maharaja, Maratha, Hindu	19 (21 within Indore)	Resident at Indore
Bhopal	6,859	0.66 million (mostly Hindu)	29	Nawab(m)/ Begum(f), Afghan, Muslim	19 (21 within Bhopal)	Political Agent in Bhopal
Rewah	13,000	1.33 million (chiefly Hindu)	29	Maharaja, Baghel Rajput, Hindu	17	Political agent in Baghel-khand
144 smaller and minor states	22,995	2.74 million (Chiefly Hindu)	129			
Total	**77,395**	**8.51 million**	**421**			

2. Imperial Gazetteer of India vol. IV 1907, p. 93.

20 Princely States forming the Rajputana Agency[3]

Name of Princely State	Area in Square Miles	Population in 1901	Approximate Revenue of the State (in hundred thousand Rupees)	Title, ethnicity, and religion of ruler	Gun-Salute for Ruler	Designation of local political officer
Udaipur (Mewar)	12,691	1.02 million (Chiefly Hindus and Bhils)	24	Maharana, Sisodia Rajput, Hindu	21 (including two guns personal to the then ruler)	Resident in Mewar
Jaipur	15,579	2.66 million (Chiefly Hindu)	62	Maharaja, Kachwaha Rajput, Hindu	21 (includ-ing two guns personal to the then ruler)	Resident at Jaipur
Jodhpur (Marwar)	34,963	1.94 million (mostly Hindu)	56	Maharaja, Rathor Rajput, Hindu	17	Resident in the Western States of Rajputana
Bikaner	23,311	0.58 million (chiefly Hindu)	23	Maharaja, Rathor Rajput, Hindu	17	Political agent in Bikaner
16 other states	42,374	3.64 million (Chiefly Hindu)	155			
Total	**128,918**	**9.84 million**	**320**			

3. Imperial Gazetteer of India vol. IV 1907, pp. 94-95

2 Princely States forming the Baluchistan Agency[4]

Name of Princely	Area in Square	Population in	Approximate Revenue of the State (in hundred thousand	Title, ethnicity, and religion	Gun-Salute for	Designation of local political
Kalat	71,593	0.37 million (Chiefly Sunni	8	Khan or Wali, Brahui, Sunni	19	Political Agent in
Las Bela	6,441	56 thousand (Chiefly Sunni	2	Jam, Kureshi Arab, Sunni		Political Agent in
Total	**78,034**	**0.43 million**	**10**			

4. Imperial Gazetteer of India vol. IV 1907, p. 96.

Under a Provincial Government

Burma (52 States)

52 States in Burma: all except the Karen States were included in British India[5]

Name of Princely State	Area in Square Miles	Population in 1901	Approximate Revenue of the State (in hundred thousand Rupees)	Title, ethnicity, and religion of ruler	Gun-Salute for Ruler	Designation of local political officer
Hsipaw (Thibaw)	5,086	105,000 (Buddhist)	3	Sawbwa, Shan, Buddhist	9	Superintendent, Northern Shan States
Kengtung	12,000	190,000 (Buddhist)	1	Sawbwa, Shan, Buddhist	9	Superintendent Southern Shan States
Mongnai	2,717	44,000 (Buddhist)	0.5	Sawbwa, Shan, Buddhist	9	Superintendent Southern Shan States
5 Karen States	4,830	45,795 (Buddhist and Animists)	0.5			Superintendent Southern Shan States
44 Other States	42,198	792,152 (Buddhist and Animist)	8.5			
Total	**67,011**	**1,177,987**	**13.5**			

5. Imperial Gazetteer of India vol. IV 1907, p. 101.

Other states under provincial governments

30 States under the suzerainty of the Provincial Government of Bengal[6]

Name of Princely State	Area in Square Miles	Population in 1901	Approximate Revenue of the State (in hundred thousand Rupees)	Title, ethnicity, and religion of ruler	Gun-Salute for Ruler	Designation of local political officer
Sikkim	2,818	59,014 (chiefly Buddhist and Hindu)	1	Maharaja, Tibetan, Buddhist	15	Political Officer, Sikkim
Cooch Behar	1,307	566,974 (chiefly Hindu and Muslim)	24	Maharaja, Kshattriya, Brahmo	13	Com-missioner of Rajshahi (ex officio Political Agent)
Hill Tippera	4,086	173,325 (chiefly Hindu)	7	Raja, Kshattriya, Hindu	13	Com-missioner of Rajshahi (ex officio Political Agent)
Bhutan	20,000	250,000 (Buddhist)	2	Deb Raja, Bhotia, Buddhist		Com-missioner of Rajshahi (ex officio Political Agent)
26 Other States	30,441	2,949,231	44			
Total	**58,652**	**3,998,544**	**78**			

6. Imperial Gazetteer of India vol. IV 1907, p. 98.

5 States under the suzerainty of the Provincial Government of Madras

Name of Princely State	Area in Square Miles	Population in 1901	Approximate Revenue of the State (in hundred thousand Rupees)	Title, ethnicity, and religion of ruler	Gun-Salute for Ruler	Designation of local political officer
Travancore	7,091	2,952,157 (chiefly Hindu and Christian)	100	Maharaja, Kshattriya, Hindu	21 (including two guns personal to the then ruler)	Resident in Travancore and Cochin
Cochin	1,362	812,025 (chiefly Hindu and Christian)	27	Raja, Kshattriya, Hindu	17	Resident in Travancore and Cochin
Paduk-kottai	1,100	380,440 (Hindu)	11	Raja, Kallar, Hindu	11	Com-missioner of Rajshahi (*ex*Collector of Trichinopoly (ex officio Political Agent)officio Political Agent)
2 minor states (Bangana-palle and Sandur)	416	13,464	3			
Total	**9,969**	**4,188,086**	**141**			

354 states under the suzerainty of the Provincial Government of Bombay[7]

Name of Princely State	Area in Square Miles	Population in 1901	Approximate Revenue of the State (in hundred thousand Rupees)	Title, ethnicity, and religion of ruler	Gun-Salute for Ruler	Designation of local political officer
Kolhapur	2,855	910,011 (chiefly Hindus)	48	Maharaja, Kshatriya, Hindu	19	Political Agent for Kolhapur
Cutch	7,616	488,022 (chiefly Hindus)	20	Maharao, Jadeja Rajput, Hindu	17	Political Agent in Cutch
Khairpur	6,050	199,313 (chiefly Muslims)	13	Mir, Talpur Baloch, Muslim	15	Political Agent for Khairpur
Junagarh	3,284	395,428 (chiefly Hindus)	27	Nawab, Pathan, Muslim	11	Agent to the Governor in Kathiawar
Navanagar	3,791	336,779 (chiefly Hindus)	31	Jam Sahib, Jadeja Rajput, Hindu	11	Agent to the Governor in Kathiawar
349 other states	42,165	4,579,095	281			
Total	**65,761**	**6,908,648**	**420**			

7. Imperial Gazetteer of India vol. IV 1907, p. 97.

Two states under the suzerainty of the Provincial Government of the United Provinces[8]

Name of Princely State	Area in Square Miles	Population in 1901	Approximate Revenue of the State (in hundred thousand Rupees)	Title, ethnicity, and religion of ruler	Gun-Salute for Ruler	Designation of local political officer
Rampur	899	533,212 (chiefly Hindus and Muslims)	33	Nawab, Pathan, Muslim	13	Commissioner for Bareilly (ex officio Political Agent)
Tehri (Garhwal)	4,180	268,885 (chiefly Hindus)	3	Raja, Rajput Hindu	11	Commissioner of Kumaun (ex officio Political Agent)
Total	**5,079**	**802,097**	**36**			

8. Imperial Gazetteer of India vol. IV 1907, p. 99.

15 States under the suzerainty of the Provincial Government of the Central Provinces[9]

Name of Princely State	Area in Square Miles	Population in 1901	Approximate Revenue of the State (in hundred thousand Rupees)	Title, ethnicity, and religion of ruler	Gun-Salute for Ruler	Designation of local political officer
Kalahandi	3,745	284,465 (chiefly Hindus)	4	Raja, Rajput, Hindu	9	Political Agent for the Chattisgarh Feudatories
Bastar	13,062	306,501 (chiefly Animists)	3	Raja, Kshatriya, Hindu	13	Political Agent for the Chattisgarh Feudatories
13 other states	12,628	1,339,353 (chiefly Hindus)	16		11	
Total	**29,435**	**1,996,383**	**21**			

9. Imperial Gazetteer of India vol. IV 1907, p. 102.

34 states under the suzerainty of the Provincial Government of the Punjab[10]

Name of Princely State	Area in Square Miles	Population in 1901	Approximate Revenue of the State (in hundred thousand Rupees)	Title, ethnicity, and religion of ruler	Gun-Salute for Ruler	Designation of local political officer
Bahawal-pur	15,000	720,877 (chiefly Muslims)	24	Nawab, Daudputra, Muslim	17	Political Agent for Phulkian States and Bahawalpur
Patiala	5,412	1,596,692 (chiefly Hindus and Sikhs)	57	Maharaja, Sidhu Jat, Sikh	17	Political Agent for Phulkian States and Bahawalpur
Nabha	928	297,949 (chiefly Hindus and Sikhs)	12	Raja, Sidhu Jat, Sikh	15 (includ-ing 4 guns personal to the then ruler	Political Agent for Phulkian States and Bahawalpur
Jind	1,259	282,003 (chiefly Hindus and Sikhs)	15	Raja, Sidhu Jat, Sikh	11	Political Agent for Phulkian States and Bahawalpur
Kapurthala	630	314,351 (chiefly Muslims and Hindus)	13	Raja, Ahluwalia Kolal, Sikh	11	Com missioner of the Jullundur Division (ex-officio Political Agent)
Faridkot	642	124,912 (Sikhs, Hindus, and Muslims)	4	Raja, Barar Jat, Sikh	11	
28 other states	12,661	1,087,614	30			
Total	**36,532**	**4,424,398**	**155**			

10. Imperial Gazetteer of India vol. IV 1907, p. 100.

26 States under the suzerainty of the Provincial Government of Assam[11]

Name of Princely State	Area in Square Miles	Population in 1901	Approximate Revenue of the State (in hundred thousand Rupees)	Title, ethnicity, and religion of ruler	Gun-Salute for Ruler	Designation of local political officer
Manipur	8,456	284,465 (chiefly Hindus and Animists)	4	Raja, Kshatriya, Hindu	11	Political Agent in Manipur
25 Khasi States	3,900	110,519 (Khasis and Christians)	0.5			Deputy Com-missioner, Khasi and Jaintia Hills
Total	**12,356**	**394,984**	**4.5**			

11. Imperial Gazetteer of India Vol. IV 1907, p. 103.

Appendix-3: Important Events

The following are the sequence of events that took place during the colonial era:

- European colonies in India
- British East India Company
- Company rule in India
- Indian rebellion of 1857
- British Raj
- Indian Independence Movement
- Indian National Congress
- Partition of India

Wars— The wars that took place involving the British East India Company or British India during the Colonial era:

- Anglo-Mysore Wars
- First Anglo-Maratha War

- Second Anglo-Maratha War
- Third Anglo-Maratha War
- Anglo-Sikh wars
- Gurkha War
- Burmese Wars
- Opium Wars
- First Anglo-Afghan War
- Second Anglo-Afghan War
- Third Anglo-Afghan War
- India in World War II

Sovereign Indian kingdoms and other states that ruled during the colonial era included:

- Kingdom of Mysore
- Maratha Empire
- Sikh Confederacy
- Rajputana
- Hyderabad State
- Travancore

Appendix-4: Timeline

Viceroy	Period of Tenure	Events/Accomplishments
Charles Canning	1 November 1858–21 March 1862	1858 reorganisation of British Indian Army (contemporaneously and hereafter Indian Army) Construction begins (1860): University of Bombay, University of Madras, and University of Calcutta Indian Penal Code passed into law in 1860. Upper Doab famine of 1860–61 Indian Councils Act 1861 Establishment of Archaeological Survey of India in 1861 James Wilson, financial member of Council of India reorganizes customs, imposes income tax, creates paper currency. Indian Police Act of 1861, creation of Indian Police Service.
Lord Elgin	21 March 1862–20 November 1863	Dies prematurely in Dharamsala
Sir John Lawrence	12 January 1864–12 January 1869	Anglo-Bhutan Duar War (1864–1865) Orissa famine of 1866 Rajputana famine of 1869 Creation of Department of Irrigation. Creation of Imperial Forestry Service in 1867 now Indian Forest Service).
Lord Mayo	12 January 1869–8 February 1872	Creation of Department of Agriculture (now Ministry of Agriculture) Major extension of railways, roads, and canals Indian Councils Act of 1870 Creation of Andaman and Nicobar Islands as a Chief Commissionership (1872). Assassination of Lord Mayo in the Andamans.
Lord Northbrook	3 May 1872–12 April 1876	Mortalities in Bihar famine of 1873–74 prevented by importation of rice from Burma. Gaikwad of Baroda dethroned for misgovernment; dominions continued to a child ruler. Indian Councils Act of 1874 Visit of the Prince of Wales, future Edward VII in 1875–76.

Viceroy	Period of Tenure	Events/Accomplishments
Lord Lytton	12 April 1876– 8 June 1880	Baluchistan established as a Chief Commissioner-ship Queen Victoria (in absentia) proclaimed Empress of India at Delhi Durbar of 1877. Great Famine of 1876–78: 5.25 million dead; reduced relief offered at expense of Rs. 8 crore. Creation of Famine Commission of 1878–80 under Sir Richard Strachey. Indian Forest Act of 1878 Second Anglo-Afghan War.
Lord Ripon	8 June 1880– 13 December 1884	End of Second Anglo-Afghan War. Repeal of Vernacular Press Act of 1878. Compro-mise on the Ilbert Bill. Local Government Acts extend self-government from towns to country. University of Punjab established in Lahore in 1882 Famine Code promulgated in 1883 by the Govern-ment of India. Creation of the Education Commission. Creation of indigenous schools, especially for Muslims. Repeal of import duties on cotton and of most tariffs. Railway extension.
Lord Dufferin	13 December 1884– 10 December 1888	Passage of Bengal Tenancy Bill Third Anglo-Burmese War. Joint Anglo-Russian Boundary Commission appointed for the Afghan frontier. Russian attack on Afghans at Panjdeh (1885). The Great Game in full play. Report of Public Services Commission of 1886-87, creation of Imperial Civil Service (later Indian Civil Service, and today Indian Administrative Service) University of Allahabad established in 1887 Queen Victoria's Jubilee, 1887.
Lord Lansdowne	10 December 1888– 11 October 1894	Strengthening of NW Frontier defense. Creation of Imperial Service Troops consisting of regiments contributed by the princely states. Gilgit Agency leased in 1899 British Parliament passes Indian Councils Act of 1892 opening the Imperial Legislative Council to Indians. Revolution in princely state of Manipur and subsequent reinstatement of ruler. High point of The Great Game. Establishment of the Durand Line between British India and Afghanistan, Railways, roads, and irrigation works begun in Burma. Border between Burma and Siam finalized in 1893. Fall of the Rupee, resulting from the steady depreciation of silver currency worldwide (1873-93). Indian Prisons Act of 1894

Viceroy	Period of Tenure	Events/Accomplishments
Lord Elgin	11 October 1894– 6 January 1899	Reorganisation of Indian Army (from Presidency System to the four Commands). Pamir agreement Russia, 1895 The Chitral Campaign (1895), the Tirah Campaign (1896-97) Indian famine of 1896–97 beginning in Bundelkhand. Bubonic plague in Bombay (1896), Bubonic plague in Calcutta (1898); riots in wake of plague prevention measures. Establishment of Provincial Legislative Councils in Burma and Punjab; the former a new Lieutenant Governorship.
Lord Curzon	6 January 1899– 18 November 1905	Creation of the North West Frontier Province under a Chief Commissioner (1901). Indian famine of 1899–1900. Return of the bubonic plague, 1 million deaths Financial Reform Act of 1899; Gold Reserve Fund created for India. Punjab Land Alienation Act Inauguration of Department (now Ministry) of Commerce and Industry. Death of Queen Victoria (1901); dedication of the Victoria Memorial Hall, Calcutta as a national gallery of Indian antiquities, art, and history. Coronation Durbar in Delhi (1903); Edward VII (in absentia) proclaimed Emperor of India. Francis Younghusband's British expedition to Tibet (1903-04) North-Western Provinces (previously Ceded and Conquered Provinces) and Oudh renamed United Provinces in 1904 Reorganisation of Indian Universities Act (1904). Systemization of preservation and restoration of ancient monuments by Archaeological Survey of India with Indian Ancient Monument Preservation Act. Inauguration of gricultural banking with Cooperative Credit Societies Act of 1904 Partition of Bengal (1905); new province of East Bengal and Assam under a Lieutenant-Governor.
Lord Minto	18 November 1905– 23 November 1910	Creation of the Railway Board Anglo-Russian Convention of 1907 Government of India Act of 1909 (also Minto-Morley Reforms) Appointment of Indian Factories Commission in 1909. Establishment of Department of Education in 1910 (now Ministry of Education)

Viceroy	Period of Tenure	Events/Accomplishments
Lord Hardinge	23 November 1910– 4 April 1916	Visit of King George V and Queen Mary in 1911: commemoration as Emperor and Empress of India at last Delhi Durbar King George V announces creation of new city of New Delhi to replace Calcutta as capital of India. Indian High Courts Act of 1911 Indian Factories Act of 1911 Construction of New Delhi, 1912-1929 World War I, Indian Army in: Western Front, Belgium, 1914; German East Africa (Battle of Tanga, 1914); Mesopotamian Campaign (Battle of Ctesiphon, 1915; Siege of Kut, 1915-16); Battle of Galliopoli, 1915-16 Passage of Defence of India Act 1915
Lord Chelmsford	4 April 1916 2 April 1921	Indian Army in: Mesopotamian Campaign (Fall of Baghdad, 1917); Sinai and Palestine Campaign (Battle of Megiddo, 1918) Passage of Rowlatt Act, 1919 Government of India Act of 1919 (also Montagu-Chelmsford Reforms) University of Rangoon established in 1920.
Lord Reading	2 April 1921– 3 April 1926	University of Delhi established in 1922. Indian Workers Compensation Act of 1923
Lord Irwin	3 April 1926– 18 April 1931	Indian Trade Unions Act of 1926, Indian Forest Act, 1927 Appointment of Royal Commission of Indian Labour, 1929 Indian Constitutional Round Table Conferences, London, 1930-32, Gandhi-Irwin Pact, 1931.
Lord Willingdon	18 April 1931– 18 April 1936	New Delhi inaugurated as capital of India, 1931. Indian Workmen's Compensation Act of 1933 Indian Factories Act of 1934 Royal Indian Air Force created in 1932. Indian Military Academy established in 1932. Government of India Act of 1935 Creation of Reserve Bank of India
Lord Linlithgow	18 April 1936– 1 October 1943	Indian Payment of Wages Act of 1936 Burma administered independently after 1937 with creation of new cabinet position Secretary of State for India and Burma Indian Provincial Elections of 1937 Cripps' mission to India, 1942. Indian Army in Middle East Theatre of World War II (East African campaign, 1940, Anglo-Iraqi War, 1941, Syria-Lebanon campaign, 1941, Anglo-Soviet invasion of Iran, 1941 Indian Army in North African campaign (Operation Compass, Operation Crusader, First Battle of El Alamein, Second Battle of El Alamein) Indian Army in Battle of Hong Kong, Battle of Malaya, Battle of Singapore Burma Campaign of World War II begins in 1942.

Viceroy	Period of Tenure	Events/Accomplishments
Lord Wavell	1 October 1943– 21 February 1947	Indian Army becomes, at 2.5 million men, the largest all-volunteer force in history. World War II: Burma Campaign, 1943-45 (Battle of Kohima, Battle of Imphal) Bengal famine of 1943 Indian Army in Italian campaign (Battle of Monte Cassino) British Labour Party wins UK General Election of 1945 with Clement Atlee as prime minister. 1946 Cabinet Mission to India Indian Elections of 1946.
Lord Mountbatten	21 February 1947– 15 August 1947	

Bibliography

Anand, Mulak Raj (1972), "Pigeon-Indian: Some Notes on Indian English Writing," *The Karnatak University Journal*: Humanities, Vol. XVI.

Anderson, Clare (2007), *Indian Uprising of 1857–8: Prisons, Prisoners and Rebellion*, New York: Anthem Press.

Ansari, Sarah (2005), *Life after Partition: Migration, Community and Strife in Sindh: 1947–1962*, Oxford and London: Oxford University Press.

Ashman, Sam (1997), "India: Imperialism, partition and resistance", *International Socialism* (77).

Bairoch, Paul (1995), *Economics and World History*, University of Chicago Press.

Baker, David, *Colonialism in an Indian Hinterland: The Central Provinces, 1820–1920*, Delhi and Oxford: Oxford University Press.

Balabushevich, V.V. and A.M. Dyakov (eds.) (1964), *A Contemporary History of India*, New Delhi: Peoples Publishing House.

Bandyopadhyay, Sekhar (2004), *From Plassey to Partition: A History of Modern India*, New Delhi and London: Orient Longmans.

Banthia, Jayant & Tim Dyson (1999), "Smallpox in Nineteenth Century India", *Population and Development Review* 25 (4): 649-689.

Bayly, C. A. (1990), *Indian Society and the Making of the British Empire* (The New Cambridge History of India), Cambridge and London: Cambridge University Press.

Bayly, C. A. (2000), *Empire and Information: Intelligence Gathering and Social Communication in India, 1780-1870* (Cambridge Studies in Indian History and Society), Cambridge and London: Cambridge University Press.

Besant, Annie (1922), *The Future of Indian Politics*, Madras, Theosophical Publishing House.

Bhatia, B. M. (1985), *Famines in India: A study in Some Aspects of the Economic History of India with Special Reference to Food Problem*, Delhi: Konark Publishers Pvt. Ltd.

Bose, Sugata & Ayesha Jalal (2003), *Modern South Asia: History, Culture, Political Economy*, London and New York: Routledge, 2nd edition.

Bowle, John (1974), *The Imperial Achievement*, Secker & Warburg, London.

Brown, Giles (1948), *The Hindu Conspiracy, 1914-1917.The Pacific Historical Review*, Vol. 17, No. 3. (Aug., 1948), Pp. 299-310.

Brown, Judith M. (1994), *Modern India: The Origins of an Asian Democracy*, Oxford and New York: Oxford University Press.

Brown, Judith M. (ed.) & Wm. Roger Louis (ed.) (2001), Oxford History of the British Empire: The Twentieth Century, Oxford and New York: Oxford University Press.

Brown, Judith M. (2001), "India", in Brown, Judith M. & Wm. Roger Louis, *Oxford History of the British Empire: The Twentieth Century*, Oxford and New York: Oxford University Press, Pp. 421-446.

Butalia, Urvashi (1998), *The Other Side of Silence: Voices from the Partition of India*, Durham, NC: Duke University Press.

Caveeschar, Sardul S. (1936), *India's Fight for Freedom*, Lahore*: National Publications.*

Chand, Tara (1961), History of the Freedom Movement in India, Vol. I, New Delhi: Publications Division.

Chandavarkar, Rajnarayan (1998), *Imperial Power and Popular Politics: Class, Resistance and the State in India, 1850-1950*, (Cambridge Studies in Indian History & Society). Cambridge and London: Cambridge University Press.

Chandler, Malcolm & John Wright (2001), *Modern World History*, Heinemann Educational Publishers. 2nd Review edition.

Chandra, Bipan et al. (1972), *Freedom Struggle*, New Delhi: National Book Trust.

Chandra, Bipan *et al*. (1989*), India's Struggle for Independence*, New Delhi: Penguin Books.

Chatterji, Joya (1993), *Bengal Divided: Hindu Communalism and Partition, 1932–1947*, Cambridge and New York: Cambridge University Press.

Chaudhary, V. C. P. (1968), *Imperial Policy of British in India*, Calcutta: Punthi Pustak.

Coates, Tim (2000), The Amritsar Massacre 1919- General Dyer in the Punjab (Official Reports, including Dyer's Testimonies), Her Majesty's Stationary Office (HMSO) 1925.

Collett, Nigel (2007), *The Butcher of Amritsar: General Reginald Dyer*, Hambledon & London.

Collins, Larry (1997), *Freedom at Midnight*. Dominique Lapierre.

Collins, Larry and D. Lapierre (1976), *Freedom at Midnight*, Delhi: Vikas Publishing House Pvt. Ltd.

Copland, Ian (2001), *India 1885-1947: The Unmaking of an Empire (Seminar Studies in History Series)*, Harlow and London: Pearson Longmans.

Copland, Ian (2002), *Princes of India in the Endgame of Empire, 1917-1947*, (Cambridge Studies in Indian History & Society). Cambridge and London: Cambridge University Press. .

Cotton, Henry J.S. (1904), *New India or India in Transition*, London: Kegan Paul, Trench Trubner and Co.

Davis, Mike (2001), Late Victorian Holocausts: El Niño Famines and the Making of the Third World.

Derbyshire, I. D. (1987), "Economic Change and the Railways in North India, 1860-1914", *Population Studies* 21 (3): 521-545.

Desai, A.R. (ed.) (1979), *Peasant Struggles in India*, Bombay: Oxford University Press.

Desai, A.R. (1976), *Social Background of Indian Nationalism*, Bombay: Popular Prakashan.

Digby, William (1901), "Prosperous" British India, London: T. Fishers Unwin.

Drayton, Richard (2001),"Science, Medicine, and the British Empire", in Winks, Robin, *Oxford History of the British Empire: Historiography*, Oxford and New York: Oxford University Press, 2001, 264-276.

Dutt, R. Palme (1949), *India Today*, Bombay, People's Publishing House Ltd.

Dutt, R.C. (1976), *Economic History of India* (Under Early British Rule, 1757-1857), Vol. I, Delhi: Publications Division, Govt. of India.

Dutt, Romesh C. (2005), *Open Letters to Lord Curzon on Famines and Land Assessments in India*, Adamant Media Corporation, Elibron Classics Series.

Dutt, Romesh C. (1902, 2001), *The Economic History of India under early British Rule*, London: Routledge and Kegan Paul.

Edwardes, M. (1963), *The Last Years of British India*, London: Cassel & Co., Ltd.

Edwardes, M. (1965), *High Noon of Empire, London*: Eyre and Spottiswoode.

Farmer, E.L. et al. (1977), *Comparative History of Civilization in Asia*, Vol. II, Philippines: Addison-Wesley Publishing Co., Inc.

Fay, Peter W. (1993), *The Forgotten Army: India's Armed Struggle for Independence, 1942-1945.*, Ann Arbor, University of Michigan Press

Fieldhouse, David K. (2000), "Colonialism", Encyclopedia Americana Online.

Forbes, Geraldine (1998), *Women in Modern India* (The New Cambridge History of India). Cambridge: Cambridge University Press.

Forbes, Rosita (1939), *India of the Princes, London.*

Forrest, G. W. (2000), *The Indian Mutiny 1857–1858.* Delhi: Low Price Publications.

Forrest, G. W., CIE, (edit.) (1910), *Selections from The State Papers of the Governors-General of India - Warren Hastings* (2 vols), Blackwell's, Oxford.

Fraser, Thomas G (1977), *Germany and Indian Revolution, 1914-18. Journal of Contemporary History, Vol. 12, No. 2 (Apr., 1977*), Pp. 255-272., Sage Publications.

Frykenberg, Robert E. (2001), "India to 1858", in Winks, Robin, *Oxford History of the British Empire: Historiography*, Oxford and New York: Oxford University Press.

G. Hutchins, Francis (1967), *The Illusion of Permanence: British Imperialism in* India, New Jersey: Princeton University Press.

Gandhi, Mohandas (1993), *An Autobiography: The Story of My Experiments With Truth*. Boston: Beacon Press.

Gilmartin, David (1988), *Empire and Islam: Punjab and the Making of Pakistan*. Berkeley: University of California Press.

Gilmartin, David (1994), "Scientific Empire and Imperial Science: Colonialism and Irrigation Technology in the Indus Basin", The Journal of Asian Studies 53 (4): 1127-1149.

Goodwin, William (2000), Modern Nations of the World: India, San Diego: Lucent Books.

Gopal, S. (1965), British Policy in India, 1858-1905, London: Cambridge University Press.

Goswami, Manu (1998), "From Swadeshi to Swaraj: Nation, Economy, Territory in Colonial South Asia, 1870 to 1907", Comparative Studies in Society and History 40 (4): 609-636.

Gould, William (2004), *Hindu Nationalism and the Language of Politics in Late Colonial India*, (Cambridge Studies in Indian History and Society). Cambridge and London: Cambridge University Press.

Gump, James O. (2000), "The West and the Third World: Trade, Colonialism, Dependence and Development", Journal of World History, Pp. 396-398.

Ghurye, G. S. (1961), Caste, Class and Occupation. Bombay: Popular Book Depot.

Harnetty, Peter (1991), "'Deindustrialization' Revisited: The Handloom Weavers of the Central Provinces of India, c. 1800-1947", Modern Asian Studies 25 (3): 455-510.

Heimsath, C. H. (1964), Indian Nationalism and Hindu social Reform, New Jersey: Princeton University Press.

Heuman, Gad (2001), "Slavery, the Slave Trade, and Abolition", in Winks, Robin, *Oxford History of the British Empire: Historiography*, Oxford and New York: Oxford University Press, 315-326

Hodson, H.V. (1969), *The Great Divide Britain, India and Pakistan*, London: Hutchinson & Co., Ltd.

Hoepli, Nancy L. (1973), *Aftermath of Colonialism*, New York: The H.W. Wilson Company.

Hoover, Karl (1985), *The Hindu Conspiracy in California, 1913-1918. German Studies Review, Vol. 8, No. 2. (May, 1985)*, Pp. 245-261, German Studies Association.

Hopkirk, Peter (1997), *Like Hidden Fire: The Plot to Bring Down the British Empire.*, Kodansha Globe.

Houghton, Bernard 1921), *The Revolt of the East*, Madras: S. Ganesan.

Hyam, Ronald (2007), *Britain's Declining Empire: The Road to Decolonization 1918-1968*, Cambridge University Press.

Imperial Gazetteer of India Vol. II (1908), The Indian Empire, Historical, Published under the authority of His Majesty's Secretary of State for India in Council, Oxford at the Clarendon Press.

Imperial Gazetteer of India Vol. III (1907), *The Indian Empire, Economic (Chapter X: Famine*, Pp. 475–502, Published under the authority of His Majesty's Secretary of State for India in Council, Oxford at the Clarendon Press.

Imperial Gazetteer of India Vol. IV (1907), *The Indian Empire, Administrative*, Published under the authority of His Majesty's Secretary of State for India in Council, Oxford at the Clarendon Press.

Jalal, Ayesha (1993), *The Sole Spokesman: Jinnah, the Muslim League and the Demand for Pakistan*, Cambridge, UK: Cambridge University Press.

James, Lawrence (1997), *Raj - The Making and Unmaking of British India*, London.

Judd, Dennis (2004), *The Lion and the Tiger: The Rise and Fall of the British Raj, 1600-1947*, Oxford and New York: Oxford University Press.

Keay, John (1991), *The Honourable Company - A History of the English East India Company*, Harper Collins, London.

Khan, Yasmin (2007), *The Great Partition: The Making of India and Pakistan*, New Haven and London: Yale University Press.

Khosla, G. D. (2001), "Stern Reckoning", in Page, David; Anita Inder Singh & Penderal Moon et al., *The Partition Omnibus: Prelude to Partition/ the Origins of the Partition of India 1936-1947/Divide and Quit/Stern Reckoning*, Delhi and Oxford: Oxford University Press.

Klein, Ira (1988), "Plague, Policy and Popular Unrest in British India", *Modern Asian Studies* 22 (4): 723-755.

Klein, Ira (2000), "Materialism, Mutiny and Modernization in British India", Modern Asian Studies 34 (3): 545-580.

Kohn, Hans (1929), *A History of Nationalism in the East*, London: George Routledge and Sons Ltd.

Krieger, Larry S., Kenneth Neill, Steven L Jantzen (1994), World History: Perspectives on the Past, Lexington: D.C. Heath and Company.

Kubicek, Robert (2001), "British Expansion, Empire, and Technological Change", in Porter, Andrew, *Oxford History of the British Empire: The Nineteenth Century*, Oxford and New York: Oxford University Press, Pp. 247-269.

Kulke, Hermann & Dietmar Rothermund (2004), A History of India, 4th edition. Routledge.

Lovett, Sir Verney (1920), *A History of the Indian Nationalist Movement*, New York, Frederick A. Stokes Company.

Low, D. A. (1993), *Eclipse of Empire*, Cambridge and London: Cambridge University Press.

Low, D. A. (2002), *Britain and Indian Nationalism: The Imprint of Amibiguity 1929-1942*, Cambridge and London: Cambridge University Press.

Low, D. A. (ed.) (1977, 2004), Congress & the Raj: Facets of the Indian Struggle 1917-47, New Delhi and Oxford: Oxford University Press.

Ludden, David (2002), India and South Asia: A Short History, Oxford: Oneworld Publications.

Majumdar, R. C. (1963), History of the Freedom Movement in India, Vol. II, Calcutta: Firma K.L. Mukhopadhyay.

Majumdar, R. C.; H. C. Raychaudhuri & Kalikinkar Dutta (1950), *An Advanced History of India*, London: Macmillan and Company Limited.

Majumdar, R.C. (1963), The History and Culture of the Indian People, Vol. X (British Paramountacy and Indian Renaissance) Part I, Bombay: Bhartiya Vidya Bhawan, Pp. 1144-1162.

Majumdar, R.C. (1976), Renascent India (First phase), Calcutta: G. Bhardwaj & Co.

Markovits, Claude (ed.) (2005), A History of Modern India 1480-1950 (Anthem South Asian Studies), Anthem Press.

Marx, K. (1965), "The Revolt in India," "The Indian Revolt," and "Investigation of Tortures in India," in K. Marx and F. Engels (eds.).

Marx, Karl and F. Engels (eds.) (1965), On Colonialism, Moscow: Progress Publishers.

Mastanduno, Michael (1998), "Colonies and Colonialism", Microsoft Encarta 98 Encyclopedia.

Mastanduno, Michael (1998), "Imperialism", Microsoft Encarta 98 Encyclopedia.

Metcalf, Barbara & Thomas R. Metcalf (2006), *A Concise History of Modern India (Cambridge Concise Histories)*, Cambridge and New York: Cambridge University Press.

Metcalf, Thomas R. (1991), *The Aftermath of Revolt: India, 1857-1870*, Riverdale Co. Pub.

Metcalf, Thomas R. (1997), *Ideologies of the Raj*, Cambridge and London: Cambridge University Press.

Minogue, K. R. (1967), *Nationalism,* London: University Paperbacks.

Mishra, B.B. (1976), *The Indian Political Parties* (An Historical Analysis of Political Behaviour up to 1947), Delhi: Oxford University Press.

Mitra, S. K. (1963), *Resurgent India,* Bombay: Allied Publishers Pty. Ltd.

Moore, Robin J. (2001) "Imperial India, 1858-1914", in Porter, Andrew, *Oxford History of the British Empire: The Nineteenth Century*, Oxford and New York: Oxford University Press, Pp.422-446.

Moore, Robin J. (2001) "India in the 1940s", in Winks, Robin, *Oxford History of the British Empire: Historiography*, Oxford and New York: Oxford University Press, Pp. 231-242.

Moorhouse, Geoffrey (1983) *India Britannica*, Book Club Associates, UK.

Morris, Jan, with Simon Winchester (1986), *Stones of Empire - The Buildings of the Raj,* Oxford University Press.

Naoroji, Dadabhai, *Speeches and Writings of Dadabhai Naoroji*, Madras: G. A. Nateson & Co., n.d.

Nehru, Jawaharlal (1989), *Discovery of India*, Delhi: Oxford University Press.

Oldenburg, Philip (2007), "India: Movement for Freedom", *Encarta Encyclopedia.*

Pandey, B.N. (1969), *The Break-up of British India*, London: Macmillan & Co., Ltd.

Pandey, Gyanendra (2002), *Remembering Partition: Violence, Nationalism and History in India.*

Peers, Douglas M. (2006), *India under Colonial Rule 1700-1885*, Harlow and London: Pearson Longmans.

Popplewell, Richard J. (1995), *Intelligence and Imperial Defence: British Intelligence and the Defence of the Indian Empire 1904-1924*, Routledge.

Porter, Andrew (ed.) (2001), *Oxford History of the British Empire: Nineteenth Century*, Oxford and New York: Oxford University Press.

Raj, Kapil (2000), "Colonial Encounters and the Forging of New Knowledge and National Identities: Great Britain and India, 1760-1850", Osiris, 2nd Series 15 (Nature and Empire: Science and the Colonial Enterprise): Pp.119-134.

Ramusack, Barbara (2004), *The Indian Princes and their States* (The New Cambridge History of India), Cambridge and London: Cambridge University Press.

Ray, Niharranjan (1973), *Nationalism in India*, Aligarh: Aligarh Muslim University.

Ray, Rajat Kanta (1995), "Asian Capital in the Age of European Domination: The Rise of the Bazaar, 1800-1914", Modern Asian Studies 29 (3): 449-554.

Raychaudhuri, Tapan (2001), "India, 1858 to the 1930s", in Winks, Robin, *Oxford History of the British Empire: Historiography*, Oxford and New York: Oxford University Press, Pp. 214-230.

Robb, Peter (1997), "The Colonial State and Constructions of Indian Identity: An Example on the Northeast Frontier in the 1880s", *Modern Asian Studies* 31 (2): 245-283.

Robb, Peter (2004), *A History of India* (Palgrave Essential Histories), Houndmills, Hampshire: Palgrave Macmillan.

Rolland, Romain (1953), The Life of Vivekananda and the Universal Gospel

(Translated by Malcolm Smith from French to English), Almora: Mayavati Publications.

Roy, Tirthankar (2002), "Economic History and Modern India: Redefining the Link", *The Journal of Economic Perspectives* 16 (3): 109-130.

Sarkar, B.K. (1921), *Political Science Quarterly, Vol. 36, No. 1. (Mar., 1921)*, Pp. 136-138.

Sarkar, Sumit (1983), *Modern India: 1885-1947*, Delhi: Macmillan India Ltd.

Schmiechen, James (1999), "The Age of Imperialism", in A History of Western Society.

Seal, Anil (1968), *The Emergence of Indian Nationalism, Competition and Collaboration in the Later Nineteenth Century*. London: Cambridge University Press.

Sen, Amartya (1982), Poverty and Famines: An Essay on Entitlements and Deprivation, Oxford, Clarendon Press.

Shaikh, Farzana (1989), *Community and Consensus in Islam: Muslim Representation in Colonial India, 1860—1947*. Cambridge, UK: Cambridge University Press.

Simmons, Colin (1985), "'De-Industrialization', Industrialization and the Indian Economy, c. 1850-1947", *Modern Asian Studies* 19 (3): 593-622.

Singh, Patwant (1966), *India and the Future of Asia, London*: Faber and Faber Ltd.

Smith, Vincent A. (1921), *India in the British Period: Being Part III of the Oxford History of India*, Oxford: At the Clarendon Press, Pp.469-784.

Smith, W. R. (1938), *Nationalism and Reform in India*, New Haven: Yale University Press.

Sofri, Gianni (1995–1999), *Gandhi and India: A Century in Focus*. Janet Sethre Paxia (translator) (English edition translated from the Italian ed.). Gloucestershire: The Windrush Press.

Spear, Percival (1990), A History of India, Volume 2, New Delhi and London: Penguin Books.

Srinivas, M. N. (1977), *Social Change in Modern India*, New Delhi: Orient Longman.

Srivastava, H.C. (1968), *The History of Indian Famines from 1858-1918*, Sri Ram Mehra and Co., Agra.

Stein, Burton (2001), A History of India, New Delhi and Oxford: Oxford University Press.

Strachan, Hew (2001), *The First World War. Volume I: To Arms*, Oxford University Press, USA.

Talbot, Ian (2001), "Pakistan's Emergence", in Winks, Robin, *Oxford History of the British Empire: Historiography*, Oxford and New York: Oxford University Press, Pp. 253-263.

Talbot, Ian and Gurharpal Singh (eds) (1999), *Region and Partition: Bengal, Punjab and the Partition of the Subcontinent.* Oxford and New York: Oxford University Press.

Talbot, Ian (2002), *Khizr Tiwana: The Punjab Unionist Party and the Partition of India.* Oxford and New York: Oxford University Press.

Thapar, Romila *et al.* (ed.) (1977), *Communalism and the Writing of Indian History*, New Delhi: People's Publishing House, Pp. 39-61.

Thorner, Daniel (ed.) (1980), *The Shaping of Modern India*, Delhi: Allied Publishers Pvt. Ltd.

Tinker, Hugh (1968), *India in the First World War and after.Journal of Contemporary History, Vol. 3, No. 4, 1918-19: From War to Peace. (Oct., 1968)*, Pp. 89-107, Sage Publications.

Tomlinson, B. R. (2001), "Economics and Empire: The Periphery and the Imperial Economy", in Porter, Andrew, *Oxford History of the British Empire: The Nineteenth Century*, Oxford and New York: Oxford University Press, Pp.53-74.

Verlinden, Charles (2000), "Articles on Imperialism, Colonialism, Islam Below."

Voelcker, John Augustus (1897), *Report on the Improvement of Indian Agriculture,* Indian Government publication, Calcutta, 2nd edition.

Wainwright, A. Martin (1993), *Inheritance of Empire: Britain, India, and the Balance of Power in Asia, 1938-55*, Praeger Publishers.

Ward, Geoffrey C. (1997), "India: Fifty Years of Independence", *National Geographic.*

Washbrook, D. A. (2001), "India, 1818-1860: The Two Faces of

Colonialism", in Porter, Andrew, *Oxford History of the British Empire: The Nineteenth Century*, Oxford and New York: Oxford University Press, Pp. 395-421.

Watts, Sheldon (1999), "British Development Policies and Malaria in India 1897-c. 1929", *Past and Present* (no. 165): 141-181.

Wolpert, Stanley (2003), *A New History of India*, Oxford and New York: Oxford University Press.

Wolpert, Stanley (2006), *Shameful Flight: The Last Years of the British Empire in India,* Oxford and New York: Oxford University Press.

Wolpert, Stanley (2007), "India: British Imperial Power 1858-1947 (Indian nationalism and the British response, 1885-1920; Prelude to Independence, 1920-1947)", *Encyclopædia Britannica.*

Wylie, Diana (2001) "Disease, Diet, and Gender: Late Twentieth Century Perspectives on Empire", in Winks, Robin, *Oxford History of the British Empire: Historiography*, Oxford and New York: Oxford University Press, Pp. 277-289.

Zakaria, Rafiq (1970), *The Rise of Muslims in Indian Politics*, Bombay: Somaiya Publications Pvt. Ltd.

Zinkin, Taya (1965), *India*, London: Thames and Hudson Ltd.

Index

C

D

Q

R